'THE PUBLIC INTEREST' IN REGULATION

'The Public Interest' in Regulation

by

MIKE FEINTUCK

OXFORD
UNIVERSITY PRESS

*This book has been printed digitally and produced in a standard specification
in order to ensure its continuing availability*

OXFORD
UNIVERSITY PRESS

Great Clarendon Street, Oxford OX2 6DP

Oxford University Press is a department of the University of Oxford.
It furthers the University's objective of excellence in research, scholarship,
and education by publishing worldwide in

Oxford New York

Auckland Cape Town Dar es Salaam Hong Kong Karachi
Kuala Lumpur Madrid Melbourne Mexico City Nairobi
New Delhi Shanghai Taipei Toronto
With offices in
Argentina Austria Brazil Chile Czech Republic France Greece
Guatemala Hungary Italy Japan South Korea Poland Portugal
Singapore Switzerland Thailand Turkey Ukraine Vietnam

Oxford is a registered trade mark of Oxford University Press
in the UK and in certain other countries

Published in the United States
by Oxford University Press Inc., New York

© Mike Feintuck, 2004

The moral rights of the author have been asserted

Database right Oxford University Press (maker)

Reprinted 2007

ISBN 978-0-19-926902-0

To Lisa
Ten years, eh?
Thank you!

Preface

Though written mostly in the past two years, the origins of this book go back much further. I first gave a paper on what was rapidly becoming my main academic preoccupation in the context of a staff seminar here at the University of Hull back in the mid-1990s. Even before that, however, from the time I first started teaching at the University of Sheffield in 1990, I shared, and indeed encouraged, my students' dissatisfaction when the answer to many questions raised in classes seemed to point towards the intangible 'public interest'.

I thought, briefly, that I had cleared the issue from my system in 1999 when I wrote a monograph on media regulation and the public interest. However, on subsequent reflection, I shared the view of a good friend, and then colleague, that while it had a lot to say about media regulation, it didn't say nearly enough about the public interest. Hopefully, this volume does rather more in respect of the latter.

Of course, this volume makes no attempt to be the last word on the subject. It is narrowly focused on the concept's use in regulation, and offers a particular (I hope, persuasive) perspective on it. Even if readers are not wholly convinced by my argument, I trust that I have at least achieved a secondary objective of ensuring that, in future, they do not allow use of the term 'the public interest' to go unchallenged. I hope that it might also provide a framework for future research.

Inevitably, a work of this kind results in enormous debts of gratitude to many different sources of assistance. First, I must thank those colleagues here at the Law School who covered my teaching during my study leave in the second half of 2002, allowing me the vital space in which to develop the book's structure. I must also thank the University of Hull for providing funding to support my trip to Washington DC in the summer of 2001, to undertake research on the US context.

Beyond such institutional support, I have also received generous assistance from many individuals in their personal capacities. I have received invaluable, and consistently willing and cheerful, assistance throughout, from trawling for obscure material to ploughing through lengthy and patchy lists of references, from 'Ido' Zhongdong Niu, University Research Scholarship Student here at Hull. Douglas Lewis and Alan Parkin both spent considerable time reading and providing scholarly comment on early drafts of the first part of the book, as did Mike Varney, who also provided me with much useful material. As well as offering particular insights into the literature of corporate social responsibility, Lisa Whitehouse has read and commented on the whole work at various stages – greater love hath no one! I must also

thank Colin Tyler for giving me access to his ongoing work on civic republicanism. I extend special thanks to Gary Edles, not only for his detailed
comments on Chapter Four, but also for opening so many doors for me in
Washington DC.

I am also happy to have the opportunity to thank a number of extremely
busy people who agreed to be interviewed, and provided invaluable back-
ground material for this book. At Ofcom, I met with Stephen Carter
(Chief Executive) and David Currie (Chairman), and at the Food Standards
Agency, David Dunleavy (Head of Legal Services) and Barbara Richard-
son (Head of Corporate Secretariat, Consumers and International Division).
In Washington DC I met with Stephen Klitzman (Federal Communications
Commission), Erwin Krasnow (Verner, Liipfert, Bernhard, McPherson and
Hand), Randolph May (Progress and Freedom Foundation), and Andrew
Schwartzman (Media Access Project). I extend my sincere thanks to all
of them.

I would also like to thank the publisher's anonymous and extremely positive readers, and of course those many individuals who have made comments
on the work-in-progress in various forms and contexts.

Finally I must thank my friends and family, especially my parents, and
Anna and Lisa, none of whom have had as much of my attention as they
deserve, or as I would have liked, while I have been working on this project.

The weaknesses which remain in the finished work, despite the best efforts
of all those listed above, are my sole responsibility.

MF
April 2004

Contents

List of Abbreviations

APA	Administrative Procedure Act 1946 (US)
BBC	British Broadcasting Corporation
BSE	bovine spongiform encephalopathy
CJD	Creutzfeldt-Jakob Disease
CSR	corporate social responsibility
DEFRA	Department for the Environment, Food and Rural Affairs
DoH	Department of Health
DTI	Department of Trade and Industry
DTT	digital terrestrial television
ECHR	European Convention on Human Rights
EFSA	European Food Safety Authority
EPA	Environmental Protection Agency (US)
FCC	Federal Communications Commission (US)
FDA	Food and Drug Administration (US)
FMD	foot and mouth disease
FRC	Federal Radio Commission (US)
FSA	Food Standards Agency
FTA	Fair Trading Act 1973
FTC	Federal Trade Commission (US)
FVO	Food and Veterinary Office (EU)
GM	genetically modified
GMO	genetically modified organism
HRA	Human Rights Act 1998
IBA	Independent Broadcasting Authority
IPPR	Institute for Public Policy Research
ITC	Independent Television Commission
MAFF	Ministry for Agriculture, Fisheries and Food
MMC	Monopolies and Mergers Commission
OFT	Office of Fair Trading
PSB	public service broadcasting
USDA	US Department of Agriculture
USO	universal service obligation
WTO	World Trade Organization

PART I
THE ANALYTICAL FRAMEWORK

1

How is the Public Interest Determined?

THE NATURE AND PARAMETERS OF THE INQUIRY

'A convenient cover for ignorance' which 'saves us from asking difficult
questions',[1] is how Maitland described the concept of 'the crown' in British
constitutional discourse: it may be that the concept of 'the public interest' can
be viewed in much the same way. Certainly, the public interest will often appear
to be an empty vessel, to be filled at different times with different content. Given
that different people will seek to fill it with differing values, if we 'drink' from the
vessel, we cannot be sure about the extent to which it might meet our particular
expectations of its content. However, such problems do not prevent the concept
being used in debate; in the context of regulation and elsewhere, it remains an
important part of the daily language of politics, law and economics. As will
become apparent, it can be used as a means of justifying or legitimating actions
or proposals; it can serve as a contested arena for debate, and, it will be argued, it
might have some considerable, if as yet largely untapped, potential in the service
of democratic values. Despite its frequent invocation in this range of important
actual and potential applications, and despite an absence of agreed content, its
use and meaning is questioned surprisingly rarely.

However, anything more than the most superficial examination of the term
'the public interest' reveals enormous difficulties in defining this deceptively
familiar concept. The wide range of perspectives and usages which are revealed
by such an examination, together with the concept's very persistence, will make
it no surprise to find that the concept is sometimes discussed in terms such
as 'goal, process or myth?',[2] or 'that vague, impalpable but all-controlling
consideration'.[3]

When even preliminary exploration of the concept does take place, however,
the immediately apparent lack of agreement as to the concept's content, and
resulting doubt as to whether its use can add anything meaningful to debate, has
led to some commentators quite reasonably viewing 'public interest theory' as

---

[1] Maitland, F. W., *The Constitutional History of England* (Cambridge: Cambridge University Press,
1908), 418.

[2] Sorauf, F. J., 'The Conceptual Muddle', in Friedrich, C. J. (ed.), *Nomos V: The Public Interest*
(New York, N.Y.: Atherton Press, 1962), 183.

[3] Justice F. Frankfurter, quoted in Colm, G., 'The Public Interest: Essential Key to Public Policy',
in Friedrich (ed.), *Nomos V*, 115.

so ill as to be beyond resuscitation.[4] The agenda of this book is to understand both how the concept is and might be used, and to consider whether it is possible and/or advisable to establish a meaningful construct of the public interest. At the very least, the objective is to ensure that the concept's use does not go unchallenged.

The first part of this book (this chapter and the next) will seek to explore some of the competing claims put forward in the name of the public interest, and identify the strengths and weaknesses of various approaches to it. On the whole, this chapter will point towards problems with using the concept, which might suggest its abandonment, while the next will consider whether it is possible to identify a potentially robust and worthwhile, reinvigorated, version of the public interest.

This will be followed in Part Two by case studies of how the concept of public interest is currently used in the regulation of certain industries, both in Britain and the United States, which appear to be central to individual and collective expectations of modern life. Particular attention will be paid to regulation of the food supply industry, still highly topical in the UK in the aftermath of the BSE and foot and mouth disease sagas, and recent controversies over genetic modification of foodstuffs, and where concerns of public health and safety have the clear potential to be in direct competition with the profit-making objectives of food producers and retailers. A study will also be made of how the media industries, especially broadcasting, are regulated, in pursuit of public interest standards that are found either implicitly, or in the case of the US Federal Communication Commission (FCC), explicitly, at the heart of the regulator's brief. Much briefer comment will also be made on the more commonly discussed area of utilities (water, power, telecommunications and transport), where, in the UK, public interest values were once pursued via public ownership, but are now embodied in the regulation of these privatized industries. The final chapters of the book will synthesize the comparative findings of Part Two with the more abstract discussion of this first part, in order to reach some conclusions as to the future of the concept of public interest, and in particular how the values contained within it might be best furthered via existing or novel legal institutions.

The nature of the concept of public interest, its location at the intersection of economics, politics and law, and its widespread usage already suggested, all indicate the necessity for any serious exploration of it to be undertaken in an inter-disciplinary context. While economists of different schools may have their own takes on the concept, lawyers may approach the concept from different angles, while politicians, and political scientists may offer yet more different perspectives. The result is that it is often impossible to make meaningful comparisons between claims made on the basis of the public interest.[5]

---

[4] See, for example, Schubert, G., 'Is there a Public Interest Theory?', in Friedrich (ed.), *Nomos V*.

[5] See Mitnick, B. M., *The Political Economy of Regulation: Creating, Designing and Removing Regulatory Forms* (New York, N.Y.: Columbia University Press, 1980), 108.

Thus, although this work is written by a lawyer, the nature of the work is far removed from what is generally found in traditional 'black letter' law texts, where the chronicling of cases and statutes, and doctrinal exposition may be viewed as the ultimate goals. Instead, the very essence of the inquiry undertaken here is to bring together relevant arguments from law, economics and political science, in an attempt to establish a better triangulated view of the context and manner in which the concept operates. Thus, there will be no attempt to offer an encyclopedic account of every example of the term being used in statute or courtroom, but rather to examine how the concept of public interest, whether explicitly or implicitly stated, informs and influences regulatory activity in particular contexts. The view of what law is, to be adopted in pursuit of this agenda, will be expounded in Chapter Two, and at this stage it is probably sufficient to note that the model of law adopted here is broad, and seeks to avoid the inward looking, self-referential approach adopted in much traditional British legal scholarship. The forms of law in which the public interest might be manifested are an important element in Part Three, and Chapter Seven in particular.

In addition to taking this inter-disciplinary approach to its subject, the book will also employ a comparative method, again requiring the lawyer to look beyond the cases and statutes to be found in their traditional, domestic literature, and instead demanding 'knowledge not only of the foreign law, but also of its social, and above all its political context'.[6] It may appear, to both lawyer and non-lawyer alike, that the peculiarities of the British constitutional arrangements, and the dominant British tradition of common law (despite the distinctiveness of Scots law) would mean that there is little to learn from the experiences of other jurisdictions. However, the increasing influence of predominantly codified, civil law, European legal perspectives and concepts, both via the EU and the ECHR, mean that British law no longer operates in isolation. This is increasingly true, and especially so in the context of regulation[7] where the centrality of the nation-state, and national boundaries has been replaced in the modern context by trans-national and even global corporations, alongside international governmental organizations, implying the existence of very different relationships, or in Hancher and Moran's terms, 'regulatory spaces'.[8] Looking beyond Europe, though constitutional differences and markedly different administrative structures between the UK and US may appear to make meaningful comparison difficult,[9] similarities in terms of both regulatory objectives and

---

[6] Kahn-Freund, O., 'On Uses and Misuses of Comparative Law', *Modern Law Review*, 37/1 (1974), 1, at 27.

[7] Baldwin, R. and Cave, M., *Understanding Regulation: Theory, Strategy and Practice*, (Oxford: Oxford University Press, 1999), Ch. 12; also Majone, G. (ed.), *Regulating Europe* (London: Routledge, 1996), generally.

[8] Hancher, L. and Moran, M., 'Organizing Regulatory Space', in Hancher, L. and Moran, M. (eds.), *Capitalism, Culture and Economic Regulation* (Oxford: Clarendon, 1989).

[9] Probably the best available work, providing both technical and theoretical comparisons, is Craig, P. P., *Public Law and Democracy in the United Kingdom and the United States of America* (Oxford: Clarendon, 1990).

common law method require serious consideration to be given to comparative trans-Atlantic findings. In addition, insights may also be drawn from the experiences of Commonwealth jurisdictions, where the legal systems and constitutional and administrative structures often closely parallel Britain's. Thus, while recognizing the caveats as regards comparative method offered by Kahn-Freund, it should be understood that the book is premised upon an inter-disciplinary and comparative approach.

It is also important to be clear from the outset that only certain aspects of the use of the term 'the public interest' will be focused upon in this study. As the book's title should suggest, it is the way the concept is used in the field of 'regulation' that is the central theme. While Selznick's definition of regulation in terms of 'sustained and focused control exercised by a public agency over activities that are valued by a community'[10] captures much of the range of activities that will be considered under the head of 'regulation' here, one point of clarification, and another of emphasis, might helpfully be added. First, by way of clarification, that 'public agency' in this sense should, in many modern contexts in Britain, be read to include 'private' bodies carrying out 'public' regulatory functions.[11] Classic examples would be the Advertising Standards Authority, or the Press Complaints Commission, which have private form, but clearly undertake the activities of a 'public agency'. The second, really only a matter of emphasis, is that it might be helpful to insert an explicit reference to the target of regulation being to limit the exercise of private power; thus, '. . . control exercised over private power . . .' would seem preferable for present purposes. Thus, the focus of this book will be on the use of the concept of public interest as a justification for regulatory intervention into private activity, limiting the exercise of private power, in pursuit of objectives valued by the community.

Of course, this book makes no more attempt to offer an account of all aspects of regulatory activity than it does to chronicle all the relevant law. Although the activities of many 'public' organizations, such as government departments, statutory regulators and certain self-regulatory bodies will be of central concern, these bodies will be examined here primarily in relation to the impact of their activities on the private bodies which they regulate, and the citizens and consumers who have an interest in these industries or services, rather than how the power of such public bodies is itself regulated via the limiting mechanisms of public law. Though the place of such bodies in the constitutional order is of

---

[10] Selznick, P., 'Focusing Organizational Research on Regulation', in Noll, R. (ed.), *Regulatory Policy and the Social Sciences* (Berkeley, CA.: University of California Press, 1985), quoted in Ogus, A. I., *Regulation: Legal Form and Economic Theory*, (Oxford: Clarendon, 1994), 1.

[11] Historically, the case of *R. v. Panel on Take-overs and Mergers ex parte Datafin* [1987] QB 815, and the line of cases following it, has been significant in establishing a kind of definition of 'public body', via establishing a test for determining whether a body is susceptible to judicial review. This does not, however, go anywhere like as far as the concept of *service public* found in France, which is considered in Ch. 7, below. In addition to being viewed in relation to the concept of 'emanations of the state' in EU law, the definition of 'public body' must now also be seen in relation to the HRA, where the provisions will be binding only against 'public authorities'.

great importance,[12] and their accountability fundamental to the fulfilment of democratic expectations, their relationship with other organs of state will only be discussed where public interest arguments are raised either explicitly or implicitly. Thus, neither the law nor regulation are studied as ends in themselves, but rather instrumentally, as crucial aspects of the attempt better to understand the concept of public interest.

Though this is likely to become obvious shortly, it is important to be clear from the outset that this book is written without any attempt to claim a value-neutral standpoint as regards its subject matter. It will be argued that in so far as constructs of the public interest currently in play can be viewed as insubstantial, this is a result of their reflecting almost exclusively *economic* considerations, and therefore containing inadequate recognition of important *democratic* expectations. In particular, therefore, this book will take issue with the economic approach to public interest regulation which has formed the dominant strand of recent analysis. At different points, reference will be made to various schools of thought which challenge this economic analysis.[13] We find Dworkin, from a liberal perspective, arguing that such an economic approach tends to understate individual rights and freedoms.[14] We should note also the 'Critical Legal Studies' argument, summarized by Kelman,[15] 'that there is absolutely no politically neutral, coherent way to talk about whether a decision is potentially Pareto efficient, wealth maximizing, or whether its benefits outweigh its cost'.[16] To this we can add Leff's dazzling 'legal realist' critique of Posner, as regards the reliance of such an approach on head-counting, simplistic majoritarianism, and its failure to take account of power inequalities.[17] Though each of these perspectives raises their own problems, their collective effect is sufficient to throw substantial doubt upon the validity of claims for justifying regulation in the public interest by reference exclusively, or even primarily, to economic argument.

Thus, informed in part by such critiques of economic analysis, and in places building positively upon the approach of 'civic republicanist' constitutionalists such as Sunstein,[18] this book will adopt a committed viewpoint as regards law and regulation, which emphasizes a series of expectations immanent within the

[12] See, generally, Prosser, T., *Law and the Regulators* (Oxford: Clarendon, 1997); also Graham, C., *Regulating Public Utilities: a Constitutional Approach* (Oxford: Hart Publishing, 2000).

[13] See the excellent collection of materials in Katz, A. V. (ed.), *Foundations of the Economic Approach to Law* (Oxford: Oxford University Press, 1998).

[14] Dworkin, R., 'Is Wealth a Value', *Journal of Legal Studies*, 9 (1980), 191, reproduced in Katz (ed.), *Foundations of the Economic Approach to Law*, 314.

[15] Kelman, M., 'Legal Economists and Normative Social Theory', from *A Guide to Critical Legal Studies* (Cambridge, Mass.: Harvard University Press, 1987), reprinted in Katz, *Foundations of the Economic Approach to Law*, 326.   [16] Ibid., 329.

[17] Leff, A. A., 'Economic Analysis of Law: Some Realism About Nominalism', *Virginia Law Review*, 60 (1974), 451, reprinted in Katz, *Foundations of the Economic Approach to Law*, 353.

[18] See generally, Sunstein, C. R., *After the Rights Revolution: Reconceiving the Regulatory State* (Cambridge, Mass.: Harvard University Press, 1990), and *Designing Democracy: What Constitutions Do* (Oxford: Oxford University Press, 2001). Issues relating to potential problems in 'translating' civic republicanism into the UK context will be addressed in Ch. 6.

liberal–democratic polity. Particular emphasis is placed upon expectations of citizenship, discussed further in Chapter Two, and especially equality of citizenship, in arguing that an adequately defined or focused concept of public interest, which emphasizes such matters, may indeed have something significant to offer the regulatory endeavour in liberal democracies.

Public Interest Theory and Public Choice Theory

Before moving the discussion forward any further, it is worth pausing briefly in order to seek to avoid any confusion which might otherwise arise from the use of some terminology which is widely used in the literature: 'public interest theory' and 'public choice theory'.

Public choice theory is based upon what Ogus summarizes as an assumption that 'behaviour in the political arena is, in its essence, no different from behaviour in the market, the individual acting in both contexts rationally to maximize his or her utility'.[19] As Ogus puts it, 'The exchange relationship which lies at the heart of, and fuels, the market system of production, is thus perceived to play an equally crucial role in the political system',[20] or in Craig's terms, '*Homo economicus* who inhabits the ordinary market-place also inhabits the political arena and behaves in much the same way, operating so as to maximize his own individual preferences.'[21] Thus, public choice theorists assume that general welfare will be maximized by the exercise of individual choices, with regulatory intervention demanded for the most part only where examples of 'market failure' require to be corrected in order to ensure the 'proper' operation of the market.

In much the same way as visitors to Britain might be puzzled by references to 'public schools', which they may take to refer to schools funded 'publicly' (by the state, out of taxation), but which in fact implies quite the opposite (privately established schools in which education must be paid for directly by the pupil), with the historically nuanced foundations of the term now long lost, so the term 'public choice' also has the potential to be misleading. Though its label might suggest choices made for, or in pursuit of, the interests of the general public, in essence, 'public choice' theory amounts to an approach to analyzing and seeking to legitimate decisions, which emphasizes and embraces the pursuit and exercise of *private* interests. In fact, public choice theories can, quite properly be alternatively categorized as a sub-species of 'private interest theories' of regulation,[22] within which regulatory systems are seen to be dominated by powerful private interests which subvert 'public' regulatory systems to their 'private' ends; an aspect of what would be seen, from a Marxist, class struggle perspective as the pursuit of an objective of representing class interests as the general interest.

---

[19] Ogus, *Regulation*, 59.   [20] Ibid.   [21] Craig, *Public Law and Democracy*, 80.
[22] See Baldwin and Cave, *Understanding Regulation*, 21.

It can be argued forcefully that this alternative categorization actually captures more accurately the essence of 'public choice' theories.

There is therefore, a significant difference in emphasis or focus between public interest and public choice approaches; the former, as will be seen, referring to one or more of a number of different approaches which seek to ascertain and represent directly collective interests, while the latter is premised entirely upon the outcomes of the pursuit of private interests, which, it is claimed, will ultimately reflect the best interests of general welfare. Thus, the distinction may not be what non-economists might first think, and the term 'public choice' should properly be understood as no more than a shorthand, and potentially misleading tag, for 'the operation of market economics in decision-making', which in turn can be subjected to the range of criticisms of economic analysis of regulation referred to above. Given the fundamental differences in perspective, and the consequent lack of points of contact between public interest and public choice theories, it should be concluded that Prosser is quite right to dismiss debate between these schools of thought as being 'remarkably sterile'.[23]

It is awfully tempting, on some kind of perhaps perverse principle, to offer oneself up as a fully paid-up member of what Posner terms 'The Marxists and the muckrakers',[24] by which seems to be intended 'those who refuse whole-heartedly to embrace uncritically the merits of capitalism'. Tempting though 'capture' theories and class analysis are, however, the critique of the public choice approach adopted in this book will be premised more upon the fundamentals of liberal democracy, which remain central to the rhetoric of the modern western polity, rather than the politics of the 'hard left' which have become so marginalized in recent years. By engaging in analysis from *within* the liberal–democratic mainstream, focusing upon the immanent democratic promises which are so often ignored in economic analysis, it is hoped that a more telling critique should emerge.

CALCULATING THE PUBLIC INTEREST

As has just been discussed, public choice theory is premised upon the belief that general welfare is best served by the exercise of private choices. This, might, in shorthand, be reduced to private choices serving a version of the public interest, as conceptions of general welfare are often to be found to underlie use of the concept. However, there are a range of arguments and models, some more influential than others, which seek to pursue more explicitly, and more directly, public interest objectives. In truth, lawyers can be seen as having contributed

---

[23] Prosser, *Law and the Regulators*, 10.

[24] Posner, R. A., 'Theories of Economic Regulation', *Bell Journal of Economics*, 5 (1974) 335, reproduced with omissions in Ogus, A. I. and Veljanovski, C. (eds.), *Readings in the Economics of Law and Regulation* (Oxford: Clarendon, 1984), 243.

surprisingly little to the development of such models, despite the concept being used routinely in legal argument.[25] This is especially true in Britain, but even in the US, where debate on the concept has been more developed, it has been political scientists, and, as we have seen, economists, who have made the major contributions.

Teubner notes that 'When certain sectors of society such as economy, politics, law, culture and science become so autonomous that they not only program themselves, but exclusively react to themselves, they are no longer directly accessible to one another.'[26] It is therefore not only lawyers who fall foul of the risk of becoming self-referential, and problems are therefore especially likely to arise in the context of regulation, where the interplay of legal, political, and economic processes will be critical in achieving regulatory objectives. It has been properly observed that there is a significant risk that 'The legal system is only likely to respond to instructions from the political system on its own terms, and these may or may not coincide with those of the political system.'[27] Examples of what might be considered poor or defective translation of political object-ives into legal modes, or of legal principles into regulatory practice, will arise in later chapters,[28] and it is sufficient for the moment to note that in relation to a concept such as the public interest, substantial difficulties may result from a lack of common language, and lack of a genuine inter-disciplinary dialogue.

However, a major landmark work in this field which avoids many of these pit-falls, and which positively seeks to bring together thinking across law, politics, philosophy and economics, is Virginia Held's 'The Public Interest and Individual Interests'.[29] Building especially upon work carried out by political and legal philosophers,[30] Held establishes a critical typology of public interest theories, surveys the existing literature, and tests hypotheses in legal/regulatory contexts. Though Mitnick prefers the more complex typology of conceptions of the pub-lic interest established by Banfield,[31] the accessibility and relative simplicity of Held's approach have much to commend them.

Held establishes a tripartite categorization of public interest theories: 'prepon-derance theories', 'common interest theories', and 'unitary conceptions'. Much of the argument set out in the remainder of this book falls into the last category, which refers to the kind of value-laden, contestable claim as to the objectives of

---

[25] See, for example, judgment of Lord Hoffman, in *R. (on the application of Alconbury Develop-ments Ltd.) v. Secretary of State for the Environment, Transport and the Regions*, [2001] 2 All ER, 929, at Paras. 72 and 74.

[26] Teubner, G., *Juridification of Social Spheres* (Berlin: Walter de Gruyter, 1987), extracts in Baldwin, R., Scott, C., and Hood, C. (eds.), *A Reader on Regulation* (Oxford: Oxford University Press, 1998), 407.   [27] Baldwin, Scott and Hood (eds.), *A Reader on Regulation*, 29.

[28] See especially Chs. 3 and 4, below.

[29] Held, V., *The Public Interest and Individual Interests* (New York, N.Y.: Basic Books, 1970).

[30] See, for example, the collection of essays in Friedrich (ed.), *Nomos V*.

[31] See Mitnick, *The Political Economy of Regulation*, 263–4 and Ch. 4 therein, generally, referring to Banfield, E. C., 'Note on Conceptual Schema' in Meyerson, M. and Banfield, E. C., *Politics, Planning and the Public Interest* (New York: Free Press, 1955).

the regulatory endeavour which will in this book be based upon basic tenets of democratic theory. It is necessary, however, to be clear as to why this approach is to be preferred to either of the first two approaches which Held identifies.

It is important to note at this stage that public interest theories may be advanced either on a general level, advocating direction for society as a whole, or on a more specific level, focusing on a particular issue, as for example in a number of recent studies of media regulation.[32] In relation to either level of approach, however, it can be observed that the public interest 'may variously be an ethical imperative (such as the natural law), some superior standard of rational and "right" political wisdom, or the goals or consensus of a large portion of the electorate'.[33] While 'unitary theories' will derive from a single, unifying ethical value, both common interest and preponderance theories of the public interest clearly relate to the latter category, being based upon some sort of utilitarian calculus, and can be viewed essentially as quantitative methods[34] for ascertaining where the public interest lies by reference to the sum of individual interests present in society. Thus, common interest accounts assume the existence of interests common to *all* members of society, while preponderance accounts look to a *majority*. However, an underlying concern relating to both preponderance and common interest accounts of the public interest, which give the appearance of determining mathematically the locus of the public interest, is that they are essentially devices used to determine where the public interest resides, rather than methods which tell us anything about what values should be protected in its name; they represent what Held identifies as an approach which 'defines the public interest in terms of the processes used to arrive at it'.[35]

It may also be true that, as Barry[36] observes, interests genuinely common to all members of society will occur only rarely, and are likely to be confined to the realm of 'public goods', where all depend on the provision of a service which does not lend itself readily to the application of market forces. In such a situation, although the empirical discovery of a common interest may well offer a signpost, indicating consensus, it will in itself do little to advance informed debate over public policy options.[37] Preponderance theories share the common interest approach of identifying where the public interest lies by reference to a sum of individual interests, but on this occasion take on a strongly majoritarian

---

[32] See, for example, Feintuck, M., *Media Regulation, Public Interest and the Law* (Edinburgh: Edinburgh University Press, 1999); McQuail, D., *Media Performance, Mass Communication and the Public Interest* (London: Sage, 1992); Sauter, W., 'Regulation for Convergence: Arguments for a Constitutional Approach', in Marsden, C. and Verhulst, S. (eds.), *Convergence in European Digital Television Regulation* (London: Blackstone, 1999).

[33] Sorauf, 'The Conceptual Muddle', 184, in Friedrich (ed.), *Nomos V*.

[34] See Bodenheimer, E., 'Prolegomena to a Theory of the Public Interest', in Friedrich (ed.), *Nomos V*.　　　　　　　　　　　　　[35] Held, *Public Interest and Individual Interests*, 205.

[36] Barry, B. M., 'The Use and Abuse of the Public Interest', in Friedrich (ed.), *Nomos V*.

[37] The treatment of 'common goods' within the civic republicanist, deliberative, approach to democracy is considered in Ch. 6.

flavour, potentially serving to exclude minority interests from the public interest so defined. For preponderance accounts, given their potential for rendering individual and minority rights extremely vulnerable, the need for a 'counter majoritarian'[38] response becomes pressing. More generally still, simple head-counting is unlikely to do much to assist in bringing about a polity in which citizens can engage, as they should be able to, in a considered and deliberative process of dialogue. In Sunstein's terms, the 'liberal republicanism' which he finds underlying the American constitutional settlement, contains 'a set of ideas treating the political process not as an aggregation of purely private interests, but as a deliberative effort to promote the common good'.[39] This may well require what Sunstein calls 'political empathy', and an ability to look beyond one's own perspective, in pursuit of meaningful consensus. The point is, in effect that 'if the members of a community think and act merely as private individuals, its interest will largely go by default and it will degenerate into a collectivity',[40] and it is quite clear, as Christodoulidis notes, that this school of thought seeks to establish that 'private interest cannot be a sufficient basis for deliberation'.[41]

All this suggests, at the general level, that there are matters within the polity which require more multi-faceted responses than the simple strategy of head-counting. Just as economic approaches to the public interest may neglect the vital democratic element of the liberal–democratic settlement, so aggregative methods for arriving at preponderance and common interest accounts of the public interest, which in effect amount to no more than the sum of individual interests, may fail to acknowledge the existence of any deliberative or collective elements in the polity: truly the victory of Thatcher's vision of there being 'no such thing as society'. It will be suggested in later chapters that by linking a concept of the public interest to 'citizenship', which can only properly be said to exist within the context of an identifiable political community, some resistance may be offered to this atomistic vision.

While calculating the public interest from the sum of existing individual interests, whether by common interest or preponderance theories, might offer some potential as the basis for validating policy options, it assumes both that preferences and interests can be ascertained with adequate clarity (which in turn seems to depend on near-perfectly informed choices and interests being identi-fiable), and denies the complications presented by individuals acting in different capacities. The approach also seem likely to be of utility only in relation to fairly specific policy options, rather than more complex, general considerations regarding the direction to be taken by society as a whole. It is also proper to

---

[38] The term is adopted from Alexander Bickel. See Christodoulidis, E. A., *Law and Reflexive Politics* (Dordrecht: Kluwer, 1998), 14; also Ely, J. H., *Democracy and Distrust: a Theory of Judicial Review* (Cambridge, Mass.: Harvard University Press, 1980), especially Ch. 6.

[39] Sunstein, *After the Rights Revolution*, 12.

[40] Milne, A. J. M., 'The Public Interest, Political Controversy, and the Judges' in Brownsword, R. (ed.), *Law and the Public Interest* (Proceedings of the 1992 ALSP Conference) (Stuttgart: Franz Steiner, 1993), 43.   [41] Christodoulidis, *Law and Reflexive Politics*, 41.

reiterate that genuinely common interests will arise only in a very limited range of areas.

Finally, two particular issues relating to common interest and preponderance theories should be highlighted. First, that they may fail to take account of one of the key features identified by many authors as being closely associated with the public interest, namely the interests of future generations: in Held's terms, 'Clearly the polity may be more than an existing aggregate of individuals since it may include, at the very least, yet unborn members of it.'[42] Thus, quantitative methods for identifying the public interest seem fundamentally problematic, unless we are confident that existing individuals can be trusted to act not only in their own interests, but also to act diligently as altruistic agents for future generations. Second, though common interest and preponderance theories of the public interest may appear to have no flavour of the moral or ethical qualities that appear to be central to many definitions of the public interest, it can be argued that in reality this is not true. Rather, like public choice theories discussed above, though they may appear value-neutral, in reality they will incorporate the values of the *status quo*, serving to reflect and reinforce the values and inequalities inherent in existing power relationships.

THE PUBLIC INTEREST, PRIVATE PROPERTY, AND LAW WITHIN A CAPITALIST SYSTEM

What has been suggested so far is that within 'public choice' theories, and also preponderance and common interest accounts of the public interest, debate is dominated by economic and/or mathematical modelling. The wisdom or desirability of thus separating the economic from the politico-legal within a modern western democracy seems highly questionable, given the long, historical intertwining of capitalism, liberal-individualism, and notions of community and democracy, within the polity.

In presenting his vision of the public interest, Ogus[43] identifies a range of economic goals that are typically presented as examples of public interest goals within the regulatory system in a liberal democracy. Broadly speaking, these goals are premised upon an economic model of the public interest which derives from an identification of allocative efficiency, in Ogus's terms 'a situation in which resources are put to their most valuable use',[44] which is said to contribute to the economic welfare of society as a whole. In western democracies, great faith is placed in the ability of market forces to deliver such efficiency, and thus attempts are made via competition (or 'anti-trust') law to regulate (in what might be called 'the perceived public economic interest') and limit the exercise of monopolistic and oligopolistic power which may otherwise subvert

---

[42] Held, *Public Interest and Individual Interests*, 173.   [43] Ogus, *Regulation*, 29–46.
[44] Ibid., 29.

market forces. Special regulatory measures may also be focused on instances of 'market failure', such as 'public goods', where the conventional rigours of market forces may not readily be applied, and 'externalities' where the market fails to attribute costs properly, allowing producer costs to fall upon third parties.[45]

At the heart of such economic modelling of the public interest, is the recognition of private property rights as the basis for market activity. However, it is clear that the untrammelled exercise of private property rights has the potential to cut across the legitimate democratic expectations of others in terms of parity of esteem and the ability to participate fully in society. Simply put, in Lasswell's terms,[46] though 'private' and 'public' matters may often be readily distinguished, apparently private matters may nonetheless raise matters of public interest. Though most commentators today would recognize the phenomenon of compenetration of public and private realms, and the absence of any bright-line distinction between the two, accepting the existence of a distinction is of some heuristic utility in the present context.

Regulation of private property rights is often justified by reference to the public interest, and, as Niemayer[47] asserts, such 'public' intervention may be legitimate despite being focused on 'private' activity. Consideration of how this version of the public interest is defined, and its relationship with 'private' interests, is informative both in terms of the role it envisages for the state, and the democratically grounded justification for intervention which it reveals.

Given that private property rights are deemed central to the liberties enshrined in liberal–democratic theory, it is proper that incursion into the realm of private property should only be undertaken with the utmost care, and with strong democratic justification. There is a *prima facie* assumption in capitalist economic theory, reflected in the work of the likes of Ogus, that profit maximization by private enterprises maximizes welfare for society as a whole. However, it can be argued that in a capitalist *democracy*, if the exercise of private property power, even if in pursuit of profit maximization, results in fundamentally undemocratic outcomes, in terms of limiting the ability of others to enjoy their entitlements of citizenship, then the assumption is rebutted and intervention may be justified and necessitated.[48]

From this perspective, the assignment of private property rights must be viewed, at least in part, as legitimated by the associated benefits supposed to derive for society as a whole. Bodenheimer[49] talks in terms of a proper

---

[45] See Crampton, P. S. and Facey, B. A., 'Revisiting Regulation and Deregulation Through the Lens of Competition Policy', *World Competition*, 25/1 (2002), 25.

[46] Lasswell, H. D., 'The Public Interest: Proposing Principles of Content and Procedure' in Friedrich (ed.), *Nomos V*.

[47] Niemayer, G., 'Public Interest and Private Utility', in Friedrich (ed.), *Nomos V*.

[48] Consider Robertson, M., 'Liberal, Democratic, and Socialist Approaches to the Public Dimensions of Private Property', in McLean, J. (ed.), *Property and the Constitution* (Oxford: Hart Publishing, 1999), discussed in Ch. 7, below.   [49] Bodenheimer, 'Prolegomena'.

accommodation between individual freedom and the public interest, while Montgomery views the public interest as 'a means for advancing individualism as a creative force calling for efforts beyond those required for immediate personal goals'.[50] In considering the underlying logic of a capitalist system of economic organization, Bjork[51] observes that the assignment of property rights is made on an assumption that it will provide 'incentives to individual members of society to increase the economic output available to society'. He argues,

That the assignment of property claims should increase only the income of the individual who utilizes them is not enough. The members of a society have an interest in granting property rights to an individual member of society only when they enjoy an increase in their own welfare from the recognition of the guarantees given to one of their members.[52]

In Krause's terms, those controlling a private property-based enterprise are in essence interested only in maximizing their capital interest, but, 'at the same time they promote *nolens volens* the common interest'.[53] It is this latter aspect that is crucial for present purposes, as it emphasizes, like Bjork, that the claim of acting in pursuit of profit maximization, is not, *by itself*, sufficient to defend against the imposition of restrictions on private property power. Rather, private property holders must show that their activities also serve the broader goals and needs of society, fulfilling a requirement of what might be characterized as 'trickle-down social utility'. If the activities of private entities in practice result in damage to the democratic fabric of society, by restricting the ability of others to act as citizens, they should expect such activities to be challenged or indeed curtailed, and economic forces should not remain unconstrained.

As Craig demonstrates,[54] the legal issues raised here are thrown into sharper relief in the somewhat clearer constitutional context of the USA than in Britain. Though Kahn-Freund's caveats regarding the uses (and abuses) of comparative law must again be acknowledged,[55] it seems that despite differences in constitutional, legal, political, and social traditions, there is sufficient shared common law heritage for these US cases usefully to shed light on the issue, and indeed serve to highlight the relative paucity of development in this sphere in Britain. In fact, as Craig and also Mitnick point out,[56] much of the seminal, nineteenth

[50] Montgomery, J. D., 'Public Interest in the Ideologies of National Development', in Friedrich (ed.), *Nomos V*, 223.

[51] Bjork, G. C., *Private Enterprise and Public Interest: the Development of American Capitalism* (Eaglewood Cliffs, NJ: Prentice-Hall, 1969).   [52] Ibid., 65.

[53] Krause, D., 'Corporate Social Responsibility: Interests and Goals', in Hopt, K. J. and Teubner, G. (eds.), *Corporate Governance and Directors' Liabilities: Legal, Economic and Sociological Analyses on Corporate Social Responsibility* (Berlin: Walter de Gruyter, 1985), 101.

[54] Craig, P. P., 'Constitutions, Property and Regulation', *Public Law*, 1991, Winter, 538.

[55] Kahn-Freund, 'On Uses and Abuses'.

[56] See Mitnick, *The Political Economy of Regulation*, 243–7.

century, US case law in this area is actually based upon consideration of British precedents.

In considering the relationship between the US state and private property, and in particular commenting on the regulation of corporate power, Bjork[57] points towards a string of instances where American courts confirmed the constitutionality of state regulation of private property interests where the results of non-intervention would run counter to perceived public interests. In essence, the examples used by Bjork derive from positions of monopoly or control of 'essential facilities', classically the subject of competition law; however, he successfully brings out the democratic underpinnings of these decisions which appear to be of wider application.

Bjork charts the change from the earlier concept of 'corporate charters', as a grant of privilege assigned by the state, to its replacement in the nineteenth century by general laws of incorporation and of limited liability; a conceptual change 'in viewing the grant of incorporation as a contract between individuals rather than as a contract between individuals and the state which granted certain individuals special privileges'.[58]

In considering the 1839 Supreme Court case of *Charles River Bridge v. Warren Bridge*,[59] in rejecting a claim that a private corporation could have been granted a permanent monopoly over the crossing of the Charles River in Boston, Bjork considers the ruling of Chief Justice Taney to demonstrate the approach taken towards corporations:

They were to be regarded as creations to provide for private performance of valuable commercial functions for the public, but grants of private monopoly not subject to public control could not be tolerated. The creation of valuable property by the grant of privileged monopoly was intolerable for a government pledged to promote the happiness and prosperity of the community by which it was established.[60]

Subsequently, in 1877, in *Munn v. Illinois*,[61] when state legislation sought to set maximum charges for services rendered to farmers by the controllers of grain elevators, the majority of the court found the legislation to be constitutional. Bearing in mind the terms of the Fourteenth Amendment, the Illinois legislation was found not to have deprived the elevator owners of their property, but merely regulated the use of that property. Bjork[62] notes how Chief Justice Waite, quoting from the English seventeenth-century Lord Chief Justice Hale, stated that 'An important principle of the common law was that when private property "was affected with a public interest, it ceases to be *juris privati* only".'

---

[57] Bjork, *Private Enterprise and Public Interest*, Chapter 8.   [58] Ibid., 110.
[59] *Charles River Bridge v. Warren Bridge*, 11 Peters 420 (1839).
[60] Bjork, *Private Enterprise and Public Interest*, 111.
[61] *Munn v. Illinois*, 94 US 139 (1877).
[62] Bjork, *Private Enterprise and Public Interest*, 116.

These cases, of course, pre-date both the Sherman Anti-Trust Act of 1890 and the *Terminal Railroad*[63] case of 1912 which gave concrete form to an 'essential facility' doctrine. Despite the fact that it is possible to be critical of the failure of the courts to define adequately the concept of 'affected with a public interest' and indeed to observe a degree of subsequent judicial retreat from the idea,[64] they remain of interest not only because they draw on a common law inheritance shared by the US and UK, but also because they demonstrate how, in justifying the regulation of commercial use of private property, it may be necessary, or helpful, to call in aid fundamental constitutional and democratic assumptions. As some lawyers will inevitably be quick to argue, their applicability might be limited to their factual situations, relating to monopoly and the application of 'essential facilities' doctrine. Perhaps this is why Mitnick concludes that the legal history offers 'little in the form of basic criteria' and turns for enlightenment instead to the literature of political philosophy.[65] However, it can be argued that even if they do not provide satisfactorily conclusive or comprehensive answers, in linking private property power with broad constitutional concerns, the principles and issues raised in the case law do seem worthy of further consideration.

It appears, therefore, that a construct of the public interest based upon democratic imperatives can help to legitimate the regulation of private property-related power. In so far as corporate activity and other exercises of private property rights cut across the fundamental democratic expectation of equality of citizenship, the legitimacy of the exercise of such power becomes highly questionable, and the need for regulatory intervention justified. While corporate actors and proponents of market forces may argue that profit maximization is their purpose or even, in the public economic interest, their duty,[66] the above discussions have indicated the contestability of these claims. There is no pressing reason why these claims should be privileged over democratic claims to equality of citizenship, why private property claims should automatically trump competing democratic claims, or, why private economic interests should be allowed to override automatically a democratically grounded concept of public interest. Indeed, there are very clear counter arguments indicated above, but, unfortunately, the citizenship-oriented account of the public interest has been far less well articulated than the economic version.

There is work, such as that of Breyer, which notes properly how the concept of 'spillovers' or 'externalities' will only be genuinely useful where monetary

---

[63] *US v. Terminal Railroad*, 224 US 383 (1912).

[64] See Mitnick, *The Political Economy of Regulation*, 256–9.   [65] Ibid., 259.

[66] Friedman, M., 'The Social Responsibility of Business is to Increase its Profits', *New York Times Magazine*, 13 September 1970, reproduced in Hoffman, W. M. and Frederick, R. E. (eds.), *Business Ethics: Readings and Cases in Corporate Morality*, 3rd edn. (New York, N.Y.: McGraw-Hill, 1995).

value can be attached, and how public interest intervention is in fact based on a broader set of principles which extends beyond economic efficiency.[67] However, the democratic aspects of public interest intervention, which go beyond issues that can be defined in economic terms such as externalities, have largely been lost behind the clamorous rhetoric of proponents of market forces. Any broader, democratic vision of public interest, once contained within a historical 'mixed economy of the public interest', has remained so ill-defined as to render it readily ignored, or highly vulnerable to 'take-over' by market economics. The challenge now, as suggested by the likes of Reifner[68] is to move beyond a model of 'socially ignorant markets' to a situation where social responsibility finds a position in the marketplace as a non-commodity value with a standing equal to other more readily quantifiable economic or monetary values. While the economist, accountant and mathematician may be drawn into coolly valuing what is measurable, a democratic audit should instead focus on measuring what is considered valuable: what Schelling refers to as 'valuing the priceless'.[69] This latter course of action must imply the existence of a set of moral values and principles underpinning the polity, which look beyond the calculation of private interests, and assumes the existence of a legitimate public sphere of activity.

Milne identifies the 'social responsibility' of government as being specifically that of representing community interests above and beyond sectional or individual interests.[70] While this does not necessarily prescribe a predetermined set of outcomes to the consideration of particular issues, it does establish the institutions of the state, as opposed to the institutions of the market, as the legitimate forum in which conflicting claims and interests are to be resolved in the interest of the community. As will be discussed in Chapter Seven, in relation to Charles Reich's thesis on 'The New Property',[71] this may not always be viewed as a positive development from within liberalism.

Changes in the relationship between 'public' and 'private' sectors, in the role of the state in society, and specifically any apparent withdrawal of the state from certain roles, does not reduce the need for the development and maintenance of an institutionally grounded democratic vision which serves the interests of the community. In the mid-1980s, McAuslan and McEldowney identified 'a progressive acquisition and centralisation of governmental power, a progressive arrogance and carelessness about its use and a progressive weakening of

---

[67] Breyer, S., *Regulation and Its Reform* (Cambridge, Mass.: Harvard University Press, 1982), Ch. 1.

[68] Reifner, U., 'The Lost Penny – Social Contract Law and Market Economy', in Wilhelmsson, T. and Hurri, S. (eds.), *From Dissonance to Sense: Welfare Expectations, Privatisation and Private Law*, (Aldershot: Dartmouth 1999).

[69] Schelling, T., 'Economic Reasoning and the Ethics of Policy', *The Public Interest*, 63 (1981), 37, reproduced in Katz (ed.), *Foundations of the Economic Approach to Law*, 21.

[70] Milne 'The Public Interest, Political Controversy and the Judges', 45.

[71] Reich, C., 'The New Property', *Yale Law Journal*, 73 (1964), 733.

any effective opposition to or check, political, legal or societal, on that use'.[72] Though there may have been many changes to the rhetoric of the leading political parties in Britain since they wrote this, and significant revisions to the apparent relationship between the public and private sectors, the phenomena and issues they identified can be said to have continued. Where 'privatization' has taken place, regulation in the public interest of those who exercise power remains just as necessary as under a nationalized structure;[73] unrestricted power, the absence of accountability, whether in the hands of public or private actors, carries an equal threat to any meaningful construct of democracy. As will be discussed in Chapter Seven, however, the dominant strain of liberal thought tends to emphasize the risks to freedom posed by the state rather than by private power.

A concept of public interest which encompasses not only economic perspectives but also democratic imperatives has wide-ranging implications for public lawyers, and, perhaps more surprisingly, also for private lawyers. In the context of privatization, Craig asks 'how far the common law may have a role to play in controlling ... concentrations of power',[74] while Wightman inquires into two complementary questions: first, '[W]hat claim do public interests have on the content of private legal obligation?' and second, 'Can private law be used in the pursuit of public interests?'[75]

The hybrid public/private nature of the legal issues involved is evident. Wightman considers case law from the fields of both contract and torts, noting especially in relation to the latter, a tendency in recent times for litigation to be used as 'an attempt to use private law, rather than public law or the democratic process, to hold public bodies to account for their actions'.[76] In the US and underlying British case law on monopoly, common calling and the like, Craig identifies 'the foundation for a constitutional discourse within which it is open to us, both to protect property rights within a constitution, and at the same time to accept that specific regulatory schemes need not be constitutionally damned as an infringement of such rights'.[77]

However, even if arguments for regulation of private property rights in the public interest are accepted, difficult problems remain in relation to devising techniques or mechanisms that can themselves be viewed as legitimate in intervening to restrict such power. We have already considered US examples of specific judicial and legislative interventions which appear to mesh with constitutional expectations, yet at a more general level, devices must be constructed

[72] McAuslan, P. and McEldowney, J. F., 'Legitimacy and the Constitution: the Dissonance Between Theory and Practice', in McAuslan, P. and McEldowney, J. F. (eds.), *Law, Legitimacy and the Constitution: Essays Marking the Centenary of Dicey's 'Law of the Constitution'* (London: Sweet and Maxwell, 1985).

[73] See generally, Prosser, *Law and the Regulators*; also Graham, *Regulating Public Utilities*.

[74] Craig, 'Constitutions, Property and Regulation', 538.

[75] Wightman, J., 'Private Law and Public Interests' in Wilhelmsson and Hurri (eds.), *From Dissonance to Sense*, 253.   [76] Ibid., 262.

[77] Craig, 'Constitutions, Property and Regulation', 542.

which effectively prohibit the anti-democratic exercise of private property-related power while (the unlikely possibility of revolution excepted) still meshing with the underlying logic of capitalism. So-called 'Third Way' approaches, and 'market socialist' approaches will be considered in Chapter Seven.

As Pennock notes,[78] American case law from *Munn v. Illinois*[79] onwards has demonstrated an awareness of a concept of businesses affected with the public interest, even if it is left somewhat undefined, while the FCC, which will be discussed in Chapter Four, has a version of the concept at the heart of its terms of reference, albeit one oft criticized on the basis of its vagueness.[80] Meanwhile in Britain, at the general level of regulating corporate activity, company law provides an example of the law recognizing little beyond the paramount private interests of shareholders, regardless of whether it can be argued that the degree of corporate power exercised by businesses may render them properly to be said to be 'affected with a public interest'.

It can be argued that many companies, especially but not exclusively those in dominant or oligopolistic situations, have the potential for producing externalities that impact on the social order – entrenching and exaggerating existing social inequalities, and potentially affecting the ability of individuals and groups to claim their (after Marshall[81]) 'civil, political and social' expectations of citizenship. Parkinson notes that:

The possession of social decision-making power by companies is legitimate (that is, there are good reasons for regarding its possession as justified) only if this state of affairs is in the public interest. Since the public interest is the foundation of the legitimacy of companies, it follows that society is entitled to ensure that corporate power is exercised in a way that is consistent with that interest.[82]

Despite such powerful arguments, these interests of the wider community remain largely beyond the scope of general company law, which continues to privilege almost absolutely the interests of shareholders.[83] As will be noted in later chapters, this can be seen as part of a broader phenomenon which implies substantial limitations on the extent to which the common law recognizes collective, as opposed to individual interests.

However, in certain sectors, and in relation to certain specific aspects of corporate activity, regulation of business and therefore private property power in

---

[78] Pennock, 'The One and the Many'.   [79] 94 US 139 (1877).   [80] See Ch. 4, below.

[81] Marshall, T. H., *Citizenship and Social Class* (Cambridge: Cambridge University Press, 1950), and *Sociology at the Crossroads and Other Essays* (London: Heinemann, 1963). See Ch. 2, below.

[82] Parkinson, J., *Corporate Power and Responsibility: Issues in the Theory of Company Law* (Oxford: Clarendon, 1996), 23.

[83] Current government proposals to reform, or at least codify, directors' duties do not seem to change this position significantly. Wider 'public interests' are not emphasized, and the primary duty of directors will be 'to promote the success of the company for the benefit of its members as a whole'. See Department of Trade and Industry, White Paper, *Modernising Company Law* (London: HMSO, 2002), Cm. 5553.

the UK does go beyond the basic framework of company and/or consumer protection law, with provisions recognizing and demanding the protection of wider public interests via regulatory intervention. Primarily, this kind of intervention is most visible in contexts such as competition law and environmental law, though the deregulatory trend perpetuated by recent and current British governments[84] has scarcely furthered any such agendas.

SOCIAL REGULATION IN THE PUBLIC INTEREST

Apparently deregulatory trends notwithstanding, in relation to utilities, formerly nationalized industries, regulatory frameworks have been established that seek to guarantee protection for certain citizenship interests (for example the imposition of Universal Service Obligations in relation to telecommunications), consequently limiting the commercial activities and ultimately the profitability of companies operating in these areas.[85] These areas will be returned to in Chapter Three, and in connection with the development of 'public service law', in Chapter Seven.

As will be seen in Chapter Three, study of the regulation of standards and safety in the food supply-chain in Britain throws questions of the public interest into vivid relief, in the context of the most fundamental prerequisite of human existence, let alone citizenship. Likewise, in relation to media corporations, the activity of which clearly touches intimately upon democratic concerns, a range of measures is employed to exert a degree of regulation on both a national and international basis.[86] The most obvious example, historically, is the control of commercial public service broadcasting in Britain, which, via the licensing and oversight powers of the Independent Television Commission (ITC) and under the Communications Act 2003, now Ofcom, consists in both structural regulation (in terms of how many channels can be controlled by one corporate group) and content regulation including positive programming requirements (in terms of minimum hours of coverage for, say news, current affairs and children's programmes, plus restrictions on advertising and, requirements of political impartiality). In the context of the development of digital terrestrial television, both the ITC and the telecommunications regulator, Oftel, were given roles in ensuring that the interests of both viewers and competitors are not damaged by the companies controlling crucial gateways in the form of the conditional access systems and electronic programme guides required to access programmes.[87] Though, as Sauter notes, 'the meaning and scope of universal

---

[84] See, for example, the Enterprise Act 2002, and Communications Act 2003.

[85] See generally, Prosser, *Law and the Regulators*; also Graham, *Regulating Public Utilities*.

[86] See generally, Feintuck, *Media Regulation*; also Gibbons, T., *Regulating the Media*, 2nd edn., (London: Sweet and Maxwell, 1998).   [87] Feintuck, *Media Regulation*, 107–16.

service access, and the future role of public broadcasting in the sense of guarantees of media pluralism, remain highly contested',[88] there has been nonetheless a fair degree of consensus and commitment regarding pursuit of such policies and objectives. That said, as will be discussed in Chapter Three, the Communications Act 2003 can be seen to constitute a significant lightening of regulatory touch in this field.[89]

Comparisons with the US will be developed in Chapters Four and Five, but it is clear that in Britain, especially in the regulation of the privatized utilities and the media, where the industries concerned have the clearest potential to impact upon democratic and citizenship expectations, regulatory regimes do exist which use more or less explicit notions of public interest. Though more far-reaching than the general company law framework, the regulatory regimes for utilities and the media can be viewed as weakened considerably by the absence of any clear conception of the public interest which consistently emphasizes democratic imperatives alongside potentially conflicting and competing economic interests and private property claims.[90]

As will be discussed in Chapter Two, it is clearly within the scope of the 'Law Jobs' to protect underlying democratic expectations, to support the continuation of society *as* society within the democratic framework upon which it has been built. As Held observes, a 'policy . . . cannot be in the public interest if it conflicts with the elements of the minimal value structures that define the society'.[91] Given 'the legal system's expertise in the practical and intellectual art of setting standards',[92] lawyers are therefore charged with the task of identifying institutions and devices which best serve such ends. Of course, the nature of the questions posed in constitutional adjudication will frequently take lawyers to the limits of, or even beyond, conventional practices of statutory interpretation or reasoning from precedent, a situation which seems only to highlight the need for the identification of fundamental principles and values upon which decisions can be based.[93] In Sandalow's terms, '[C]onstitutional law must . . . be understood as the means by which effect is given to those ideas that from time to time are held to be fundamental';[94] whether the concept of public interest may assist in this respect is a large part of what is being considered here.

However, it is generally the case that the concepts of public interest most commonly used tend to derive primarily from an economic model, with a heavy emphasis on the issues raised by competing private (property) rights and interests.

---

[88] Sauter, 'Regulation for Convergence', 83.

[89] Feintuck, M., 'Walking the High-Wire: the UK's Draft Communications Bill', *European Public Law*, 9/1 (2003), 105.

[90] Reference to the concepts of *service public* and *servizio pubblico*, in France and Italy respectively, is at Ch. 7, below.   [91] Held, *Public Interest and Individual Interests*, 222.

[92] Harden, I. and Lewis, N., *The Noble Lie: The British Constitution and the Rule of Law* (London: Hutchinson, 1986), 237.   [93] See generally, Sunstein, *Designing Democracy*.

[94] Sandalow, T., 'Judicial Protection of Minorities', *Michigan Law Review*, 75 (1977), 1162, quoted in Ely, *Democracy and Distrust*, 43.

Despite Sunstein's powerful observation that 'A democratic constitution has a lot to say about equality' and that democracy's 'internal morality ensures against second-class citizenship for anyone',[95] though citizenship-related visions of the public interest are on occasion referred to, tensions between them and economic rationales and private interests may fundamentally undermine the potential utility of the concept in this respect.[96]

The potential range of regulatory rationales is so wide as to render conflict between them inevitable. Even economic justifications for regulation relating to 'market failure' can themselves form a long and diverse list. Breyer[97] includes control of monopoly power, rent control, correction for spillovers, correction for inadequate information, for excessive competition, for moral hazard, rationalization, inequalities in bargaining power, and, scarcity,[98] to which Ogus and Veljanovski[99] add the problems of public goods. To such a list of factors can also be added a potentially wide range of non-economic or social goals which might be found to underpin regulation. Ogus[100] summarizes these in terms of distributional justice (from various perspectives), paternalism, and what he briefly, and somewhat dismissively, addresses as 'Community Values'.[101]

The extent to which some of these factors are prioritized over others will determine the objectives for regulation, though it is possible that the original justification, or more likely combination of justifications for regulatory intervention, may be only a hazy memory by the time regulatory objectives and strategies are determined and implemented. In the absence of some prominent overarching value system, there is a significant risk that regulatory intervention will become subjective and unpredictable. In particular, and this is illustrated vividly in the context of changing approaches to regulating the broadcast media in Britain and elsewhere,[102] given the dominance of economic modelling and market values in the politics of the post-Thatcher/Reagan era, any social values which may have formed a significant part of the original justification for intervention can easily become lost or badly distorted.

Where regulation of private enterprise does take place, it will be the role of the regulator to identify (if this has not already been done), interpret, and attain socially desirable objectives; a task which is likely to demand the resolution of competing interests/claims by reference to regulatory goals. As will be discussed in later chapters, the precise extent of a regulator's discretionary (as opposed to

---

[95] Sunstein, *Designing Democracy*, 242.

[96] For example, consider the wide and competing range of 'public interest' criteria which statutes require UK regulators of the media to take into account; Ch. 3, below.

[97] Breyer, *Regulation and its Reform*, 235–9. Breyer also includes 'Paternalism' as an economic rationale, yet this seems to fit much more comfortably into social rationales for intervention.

[98] A differently structured list, though covering essentially the same ground can be found at Ogus, *Regulation*, 29–46.   [99] Ogus and Veljanovski, *Readings*, 239.

[100] Ogus, *Regulation*, 46–54.   [101] Ibid., two short paragraphs at 54.

[102] See generally Feintuck, *Media Regulation*.

rule-bound) jurisdiction[103] will be context specific, and potentially an important issue where regulatory intervention takes place. However, in many areas of commerce and manufacturing, in the absence of monopoly, even though corporate social power remains, such public interest regulation does not exist at all, and the social costs of profit-driven decision-making are neither monitored nor limited. One response to this is suggested by the application of principles of corporate social responsibility, discussed in Chapter Seven, though the impact of such essentially voluntary measures seems likely to remain strictly limited.

FUNCTIONS AND LIMITATIONS OF THE CONCEPT OF PUBLIC INTEREST

The foregoing should have established the limitations of constructs of the public interest based upon common interest and preponderance accounts, and those premised upon economic rationales. While different combinations of these approaches can produce variations, all the end products suffer the same perceived defect: a near exclusive emphasis on economic values, reflecting the core liberal emphasis on the individual, which results in a failure to serve the 'public interest' that exists in the fundamental democratic expectation of equality of citizenship. That said, even if a model could be established premised firmly upon democratic principles, two related caveats must be acknowledged and indeed emphasized.

First, that this model of the public interest should not be considered a panacea; like antibiotics, the use of the concept may become counter-productive if over-prescribed. Held's approach[104] seems healthy, in arguing that where an alternative, clearer and less contentious concept is available then the public interest should not be utilized. In common usage the term 'public interest' generally carries no clear or shared meaning and can lead to confusion. However, she suggests that where the terms of debate are themselves ill-defined, for example citizenship, or human rights, then introducing a model of the public interest which emphasizes democratic imperatives may be of assistance in focusing debate.

Second, it is important that over-inflated versions of the public interest be avoided. Again, the point is that the public interest must not be presented as a cure-all, but rather, it must be applied only where it is appropriate and where it can have some impact. In pursuit of this agenda, Braybrooke[105] offers a 'deflated' version of the public interest, identifying three prerequisites that determine when it might appropriately be applied. The first of these is where a special interest group is arrayed against the general public (by which he intends all of those

---

[103] See Daintith, T., 'Law as Policy Instrument: a Comparative Perspective' in Daintith, T. (ed.), *Law as an Instrument of Economic Policy: Comparative and Critical Approaches* (Berlin: Walter de Gruyter, 1988).   [104] Held, *Public Interest and Individual Interests*, 163.

[105] Braybrooke, D., 'The Public Interest: the Present and Future of the Concept', in Friedrich (ed.), *Nomos V*.

outside the special group); second, that the issue arises in an area where genuine potential exists for the exercise of power by government; and, third, that the issue is one of domestic and internal concern for the society (even if foreign policy implications attach).

In some ways, this agenda for limiting the concept of the public interest is reminiscent of part of Davis's agenda in relation to discretion.[106] Davis seeks to 'confine' the use of discretionary powers in public administration to those areas where its application is appropriate and advantageous, cutting back discretion in those areas where clearer alternatives are available and suitable, and much the same can be seen in Braybrooke's deflated concept of the public interest. Despite the potential contentiousness of aspects of Braybrooke's specific construct, his approach is helpful in confining the scope of application of the public interest. Especially in conjunction with Held's approach, of not advocating its use when alternative, more precise, terms are available, it offers some potential for increasing the concept's utility.

Therefore, the argument should be not for the abandonment of the concept of public interest, but rather for confining its use to where it is appropriate, and for being clear as to a value system which underpins it, and should be constantly re-emphasized. That said, it remains the case that in the absence of such restricted usage and redefinition, abandoning the concept may be the most sensible option.

However, despite all the problems of lack of agreement over its meaning, the use of the concept remains remarkably persistent. Indeed, at times it seems that the public interest has an almost mythical or folkloric quality. Though folk-tales and proverbs change over time, they continue to embody, in allegorical form, vices and virtues, truths and fears, that remain of general application. Likewise, the public interest, if endowed with some democratic content, can illustrate, often in abstract form, very real democratic principles and dangers. In relation to both folk-tales and the public interest, the essential message is generally more important than their precise form.

Thus, though it may seem difficult to establish a once-and-for-all-time definition of the public interest, this does not deny the possibility of it serving a useful purpose; flexibility may be a sign of strength rather than weakness. Certainly, a concept of public interest must mesh with the dominant values of the society, yet to be of any utility it must not simply reflect such values. It is clear, for example, that 'public democratic interests' may clash with the economic imperatives of capitalism, yet, to obtain a sense of legitimacy in a capitalist society, must remain consonant with the system's underlying philosophy. Essentially, the task relates to that identified by Gamble and Kelly as 'reconciling the principles of social justice with those of market allocation'.[107]

---

[106] Davis, K. C., *Discretionary Justice: a Preliminary Inquiry* (Urbana, IL.: University of Illinois Press, 1971).

[107] Gamble, A. and Kelly, G., 'The New Politics of Ownership', *New Left Review*, 220 (1996), 62, at 77.

While much of the earlier material in this chapter might therefore have suggested a heavily redistributive agenda, in the absence of revolution such change will not occur, and will not be argued for here other than in the sense of redressing certain imbalances within the democratic system. It will therefore be argued that a greater degree of fulfilment of the promises of capitalist liberal democracy, especially in terms of a deliberative polity and equality of citizenship, will occur if greater attention is paid to the *democratic*, as opposed to the presently dominant *liberal* aspects of liberal democracy. Using economics to *explain* inequalities in citizenship is not the same as using economics to *justify* it. As Gamble and Kelly succinctly put it in making the case for an 'egalitarian market economy', '[I]f there is marked inequality in a society, it is a result of political choice, not of a deterministic and irresistible economic logic.'[108]

It seems clear that the key task in establishing a meaningful model of public interest in such societies is to be able to justify, in pursuit of collective and democratic interests, interference with private property rights. In considering what he identifies as the absence of a 'Capitalist Ethic', Bjork states that:

The possession of [property] rights imposed no obligations on their possessors other than the prudential obligation to support the society which guaranteed them ... What did not emerge with modern capitalism was a public philosophy which reconciled the interests of the individual with the interests of society.[109]

While it is, of course, possible to point towards great works endowed by capitalist property owners, including charitable foundations and so many of our great civic edifices, such as libraries and even universities, these can be viewed as examples of individual philanthropic exceptions to, rather than necessary aspects of, the capitalist system.

Reflecting the centrality of private property rights in a capitalist system, Montgomery writes that 'Both the economic and the juristic views in the Western national context represent the public interest as possessing an element of restraint upon the exercise of private rights, but capable of emerging only because such rights already exist.'[110] Thus, it is suggested that it is necessary to define public interests in relation to, or in opposition to property rights, and such opposition will be strengthened if rooted in the same democratic soil from which property rights have grown. Any construct of the public interest which reflects only, and in effect simply re-states, the economic rationale of wealth maximization, to the exclusion of democratic imperatives, leaves broader societal values totally vulnerable, and is of little, if any, utility in furthering the liberal–*democratic* settlement.

The question of legal forms in which the public interest as defined might be embodied is an open one; however, worthy of note in certain circumstances are

---

[108] Gamble, A. and Kelly, G., 'The New Politics of Ownership', *New Left Review*, 220 (1996), 96.   [109] Bjork, *Private Enterprise and Public Interest*, 235.
[110] Montgomery, 'Ideologies of National Development', 223.

models of stewardship. In replacing the 'incidents of ownership'[111] of property with a more limited set of powers of stewardship,[112] requiring consideration to be given not only to the interests of the property-holder but also to other interested parties, the profit-maximizing potential for property holding is restricted but not removed, thus meshing with the underlying capitalist ethic. At the same time, the interests of present and future members of society in the property are given a degree of protection. While absolute private property rights might allow 'the family silver to be sold', duties of stewardship would require the preservation of irreplaceable community assets, including democratic principles, for future generations. The recognition of such a broad-based legal principle undoubtedly raises problems for many lawyers, yet it may be that only by using principles that explicitly embody fundamental values can we move beyond the kind of piecemeal 'restrictive and fragmentary'[113] approach currently seen in much regulation of private property power. Stewardship, and other legal constructs which might reflect the public interest, will be given further consideration in Chapter Seven.

The question remains as to the extent to which it is possible to define a normative model of the public interest. It will be, to a degree, historically contingent, relating to the contemporary view of the state, and meshing with dominant values. It must, however, by reference to fundamental democratic principles, represent the validity of arguments against any such dominant values where they threaten the underlying basis of the polity. Where public or private policy conflicts with fundamental democratic interests, then it may meaningfully be said to run counter to the public interest.

Written in the 1980s, though of equal relevance today, is McAuslan and McEldowney's observation of a failure to fulfil the democratic promise extended to citizens of liberal democracy. They refer to

[T]he increasing gap between the ideology and public posturing of governments in Western Europe and their performance in practice; between on the one hand the rhetoric of democracy, of even-handed administration, and of equal opportunities for all, and on the other the increasing centralisation and insensitivity of public administration, [and] the unevenness of the distribution of the costs and benefits of economic growth and, increasingly, contraction ...[114]

Central to the thesis explored in this book is a suggestion that contemporary constructs of the public interest should at any time serve as a counterbalance to the power of the dominant interest group(s) in society, yet must also mesh with the prevailing view of the state and the economic apparatus. If this contention is established, then the presently unfashionable status of the concept

---

[111] See Honoré, A., *Making Law Bind* (Oxford: Clarendon, 1987), Ch. 8.

[112] Lucy, W. N. R. and Mitchell, C., 'Replacing Private Property: the Case for Stewardship', *Cambridge Law Journal*, 55 (1996), 566; discussed at Ch. 7, below.

[113] Gamble and Kelly, 'The New Politics of Ownership', 89.

[114] McAuslan and McEldowney, 'Legitimacy and the Constitution', 7.

may be explained by reference to the near-total hegemony of market forces and recently changed views of the state, and the absence of strong and organized forces of opposition able to develop and voice public interest claims contrary to the dominant interest groups and values. Such a situation may also explain why the concept is presently so hopelessly ill-defined and vulnerable to capture. The absence of both a clearly stated normative content (or its limitation in economic terms to simple wealth-maximization objectives), and an appropriate institutional framework with which to pursue it,[115] may be found on occasion to have 'relegated the "public interest" to represent the interest of the state',[116] but has also, inevitably, allowed for its potential capture by those powerful groups that dominate the economy and hence the state.

Noted at the outset, and running through this chapter have been essentially three different functions of the concept of public interest. These might be termed the 'legitimation function', the 'function as contested arena', and the 'democracy-serving function'.

It has been suggested strongly that the first of these, the concept's function as a means of legitimating intervention into private activity, in the absence of a strong value base which includes democratic expectations such as equality of citizenship, can be all too easily subverted to the cause of, or undermined by, dominant economic interest groups. This results in it serving simply as a force for conservatism, maintaining the existing power inequalities. Mathematical, preponderance and common interest, aggregative methods for calculating the public interest and thereby justifying or legitimating intervention, by reasserting crudely the claims of the dominant group over individuals or minority groups, will fail to offer any protection for minority interests and can be viewed as failing to incorporate the deliberative aspects identified within democracy by the likes of Sunstein. Simply put, neither an economic approach to the public interest, nor mathematical formulae for determining its content, provide adequate recognition of democratic values.

The second potential function of the concept of public interest, as a contested arena, to form part of the deliberative context which we are entitled to expect to find at the heart of a liberal–democratic system, seems to fit with a vision of the concept, as it is often presented, as an empty vessel free from inherent values. However, this function will also be undermined if assessing the public interest amounts to no more than an exercise in head-counting. Simply adding-up the sum of individual interests in the absence of consideration of the guiding liberal–democratic principles upon which the polity is built, does not further meaningful deliberation or debate. The 'arena' is also, arguably, not neutral, being too heavily tilted in favour of already dominant economic and political

---

[115] Jacob, J., 'Safeguarding the Public Interest: New Institutions and Procedures', in Cooper, J. and Dhavan, R. (eds.), *Public Interest Law* (Oxford: Basil Blackwell, 1986).

[116] Dhavan, R., 'Whose Law? Whose Interest?' in Cooper, J. and Dhavan, R. (eds.), *Public Interest Law* (Oxford: Basil Blackwell, 1986).

forces; it is distorted by pre-existing economic and political inequalities and the weight of market forces, which, though forming a legitimate *part* of the liberal–democratic settlement, should not be seen as the whole. In this context, there is a degree of inevitability in the arena of the public interest seeing the already powerful emerging triumphant at the expense of the weaker 'contestant'.

The third line of thought relating to the public interest, its 'democracy serving function' is in essence what seems to be lacking in terms of the 'legitimation' and 'contested arena' approaches. As will be seen in the next chapter, much of the literature of political science implies a close linkage between 'the public interest' and certain collective values and notions of general welfare within society, deriving from fundamental democratic tenets. However, lack of attention to these underlying ideas, especially in the face of the dominance of economic modelling in the modern era, has resulted in any potential for the public interest to serve such ends remaining largely untapped. A particular problem, to which we will return in Chapter Two and later, relates to the difficulty in accommodating collective notions within the heavily individualized common law systems.

As with so many folk-tales and proverbs, the significance of the 'The Tale of the Public Interest' is likely to lie in its consciousness-raising potential. The moral of this particular 'story' is that if democratic imperatives are not constantly borne in mind, and actively protected and promoted, they quickly become endangered. Democratic traditions and values matter, and, to borrow a phrase used by Breger and Edles in their survey of US federal agencies, and to apply it in the broader democratic context: 'Lore can be as important as law.'[117]

Just as citizenship might be viewed as 'the right to have rights', the public interest might be viewed not as an objective in itself, but rather as having a potentially important contribution to make in protecting and furthering democratic ideals and goals. At its best, it can facilitate the focusing and re-focusing of the legal and regulatory endeavour on these broader societal goals, connecting closely to the essential roles of law identified in 'Law Jobs' theory.[118] Scrutinizing policies, practices and proposals against a public interest standard in this sense, has the potential to serve as a kind of 'democratic impact assessment'.

That said, given the lack of agreed meaning for the concept, and the potential misunderstanding and vulnerability to capture thus implied, and the fact that public interest debate has become almost entirely dominated by economic modelling (reflected in law), readers might still believe that the concept remains too insubstantial to proceed with; that it does not have sufficiently solid foundations on which to build. It is true that, even at its most refined, a unitary model of the public interest should properly be viewed only as establishing contestable

---

[117] Breger, M. J. and Edles, G. J., 'Established by Practice: the Theory and Operation of Independent Federal Agencies', *Administrative Law Review*, 52/4 (2000), 1111, at 1115.

[118] See below, Ch. 2, for an account of the 'Law Jobs'.

claims, though if these claims have strong roots in democratic and constitutional legitimacy, these are claims that should rarely be defeated. The potential of a developed, normative concept of the public interest to serve as a form of resistance, imposing limits on the power of society's dominant groups by reference to democratic expectations, provides a pressing argument for the concept's retention and re-development; a normatively defined concept of the public interest linked to citizenship may be the only trump card in an otherwise weak hand held by those outside the dominant social group. It has been argued in this chapter that while proponents of an economic vision of the public interest might claim that it is value neutral, offering a nice simple hand played at 'No Trumps', the way the cards are distributed, the existing power co-ordinates, mean that the hand will inevitably be won by the team that enjoys economic power. Accepting the 'No Trumps' bid leaves those with economic power in total control, with no force of resistance available to those with the weaker hands.

We have seen how common interest accounts of the public interest are likely to be limited to those circumstances where all members of a community have identical individual interests. Meanwhile, preponderance accounts raise the spectre of the tyranny of the majority, again, premised upon an assessment of individual interests. These, essentially quantitative methods may be described more as methods for calculating the public interest, rather than saying what the public interest is in terms of values. An economic version of the public interest, within a capitalist democracy, however, emphasizes the values of the market, while claiming political neutrality for market forces. Yet it is clear that the exercise of such forces serve to reproduce and exaggerate hierarchy, entrenching inequality in the ability to act as citizens. It has rarely been put more eloquently than by Ranson:

Within the marketplace all are free and equal, only differentiated by their capacity to calculate their self-interest. Yet, of course, the market masks its social bias. It elides, but reproduces, the inequalities which consumers bring to the marketplace. Under the guise of neutrality, the institution of the market actively confirms and reinforces the pre-existing social order of wealth and privilege.[119]

Given the dominance of common interest, preponderance, and market-based approaches to the public interest, much of this chapter may well have been viewed as a counsel of despair in relation to the practical utility of the concept. However, despite such problems and limitations already noted, the remainder of this book constitutes an attempt to establish the case for using the concept in support of attempts to 'make democratic values trumps', in an attempt to avoid the otherwise inevitable dominance of the economically powerful, which may readily override presently vulnerable democratic promises and expectations of equality of citizenship. It will be argued that a re-framed and reinvigorated concept of

---

[119] S. Ranson, 'From 1944 to 1988; Education, Citizenship and Democracy', 1988, (14) *Local Government Studies*, 1.

the public interest could be developed which helpfully encapsulates such concerns, meshing with the liberal–democratic settlement, yet running counter to the presently dominant market forces. The next chapter seeks to develop further the case for moving away from an economic model of the public interest, towards a democratically oriented version.

2

Towards a Democratic Vision of the Public Interest

INTRODUCTION

The previous chapter suggested the lack of adequate investigation into the concept of public interest in regulation, and, where preliminary inquiries had been made, a failure to identify or develop any core meaning or clear function for the concept beyond the economic. Though the very phrase 'the public interest' has an air of democratic propriety, the absence of any identifiable normative content renders the concept insubstantial, and hopelessly vulnerable to annexation or colonization by those who exercise power in society. Given the potentially spurious air of legitimacy which claims of acting in the public interest might bring, the reader may have been tempted to conclude that meaningful discussion might, in general, be furthered more by abandoning, or avoiding the concept.

This chapter attempts to move beyond this position, and to consider whether the concept might in fact be capable of resuscitation and reinvigoration via closer examination and deeper understanding of its functions and conceptual connections. Though there will be no attempt in this chapter to reach final conclusions, which will be based in Part Three upon both the theoretical work here, and the empirical studies in Part Two, this chapter does seek to establish an analytical framework upon which a more robust construct of the public interest might be developed. The direction it will suggest for the investigations which follow, is that of exploring the concept's actual and potential structural significance within the liberal–democratic polity, and its potential capacity to serve in the defence of fundamental values.

In pursuit of this agenda, and by way of establishing the context for modern constructs of the concept, this chapter will consider the historically changing nature of the concept of public interest and its manifestation in law and regulation. The concept will be considered in the context of democratic values, and in particular its relationship with expectations of citizenship, with which, it will be argued, the public interest is intimately connected. Finally, there will be a preliminary consideration of what issues might be posed for the legal system by the incorporation of this particular value-laden concept.

The Absence of Definition

Noted in the previous chapter was the fact that though what is meant and understood by the term 'the public interest' is extremely fluid, the term itself remains persistently part of political, legal and regulatory discourse. Though Ogus may seek to avoid formulating a comprehensive list of public interest goals by observing that 'what constitutes the "public interest" will vary according to time, place, and the specific values held by a particular society',[1] this tends to hide rather more than it reveals. It does nothing to identify why the concept exists, why it changes, and especially, why it remains so persistent.

It would be unfair, however, to single out Ogus for criticism in respect of a failure to engage meaningfully with 'the public interest' in discussion of regulation. Though Hancher and Moran talk of '... an intense search for the "essential" nature of regulation – involving for instance, the issue of how it is shaped by the public interest',[2] their analysis, based on the concept of 'regulatory space', is focused elsewhere. Other esteemed recent studies of regulation have side-stepped the concept, or made more or less implicit assumptions about its meaning. Majone, talks of 'industries deemed to affect the public interest'[3] without interrogating or unpacking the concept. Baldwin and Cave reduce their discussion of public interest theories of regulation to less than two pages,[4] listing a series of weaknesses within the impoverished version of the concept which they consider, and nodding towards, but failing to unpack, the work of Sunstein[5] which actively seeks to develop a vision more closely identifiable with the concept. Even Prosser's thoroughly rigorous work does not really help us in terms of defining the public interest in the context of regulation. He does, however identify a range of meanings for 'social regulation' which go beyond the economic,[6] and discusses concepts of *service public* in France and *servizio pubblico* in Italy (to which we will return in Chapter Seven),[7] which, like his social regulation objectives, include meanings often to be found within the concept of public interest. Ultimately, Prosser concludes that what is necessary is a 'clearer articulation and development of the social principles'.[8] Though he makes connections from here to some of the literature on citizenship, he chooses to avoid using the term 'public interest'. In reality, none of these learned authors do much to enhance our understanding of the concept.

---

[1] Ogus, A., *Regulation: Legal Form and Economic Theory* (Oxford: Clarendon, 1994), 29.

[2] Hancher, L. and Moran, M. (eds.), *Capitalism, Culture and Economic Regulation* (Oxford: Clarendon, 1989), 2.   [3] Majone, G. (ed.), *Regulating Europe* (London: Routledge, 1996), 15.

[4] Baldwin, R. and Cave, M., *Understanding Regulation: Theory, Strategy and Practice* (Oxford: Oxford University Press, 1999), 19–21.

[5] Sunstein, C. R., *After the Rights Revolution: Reconceiving the Regulatory State* (Cambridge, Mass.: Harvard University Press, 1990), and *Designing Democracy: What Constitutions Do* (Oxford: Oxford University Press, 2001); discussed below in Chs. 4 and 6.

[6] Prosser, T., *Law and the Regulators* (Oxford: Clarendon, 1997), 10–15.

[7] See also Prosser, T., 'Public Service Law: Privatization's Unexpected Offspring', 63/4 *Law and Contemporary Problems*, (2000), 63.   [8] Prosser, *Law and the Regulators*, 305.

Perhaps predictably, governments are no more helpful in facilitating a developed understanding of the concept. Following the tragedy or farce that was Railtrack's management of the railway infrastructure, it was replaced late in 2002 by Network Rail, described by the government as 'a public interest company'. In practice, what this meant was defined only in terms of how profits will be reinvested in the railway system rather than ending up in shareholders' pockets: a phenomenon which has been described as 'Nationalisation Under the Third Way'. [9] As Prosser observed in relation to an earlier generation of nationalized industries in Britain, a major defect in the arrangements for the management of such industries via appointed boards was that 'the idea of a self-defining "public interest" which could be discovered unproblematically by expert boards proved to be a will-o'-the-wisp'.[10] In this sense, there has clearly been little progress in the last forty or fifty years!

There are a number of possible reasons for the failure of so many highly respected authors, and for that matter, legislators, to engage meaningfully with the concept of public interest. The first, simply put, is that they might consider the concept irrelevant. This seems unlikely, given that it is a term to which writers have recourse regularly. Indeed, some, such as Ogus, to whom we shall return, do set out their thoughts, though in a way which, it will be argued, does little to expand our understanding. A second possibility is that the concept is so uncontroversial that no explanation is necessary. This seems rather fanciful, given the range of meanings that can and have been attached to it. That said, there is clearly a core economic meaning, discussed in the previous chapter, that comes through accounts such as Ogus's, and which most closely approximates to an accepted meaning in the modern context. However, a third explanation seems more likely, namely, that the term is so commonly used, and so historically persistent, that we use it without thinking about what it means. To return to the source referred to at the very start of Chapter One, Maitland comments, when discussing the concept of 'the crown' in English constitutional history, 'I do not deny that it is a convenient term, and you may have to use it; but I do say that you should never be content with it.'[11] While the legal concept of 'the crown' has gradually been defined in many contexts in Britain, via statute and judicial decision,[12] and can now properly be viewed as a term of art for both public and private lawyers, the same cannot meaningfully be said of the public interest, despite its lengthy currency.

[9] Whitehouse, L., 'Railtrack is Dead; Long Live Network Rail. Nationalisation Under the Third Way', 30/2, *Journal of Law and Society*, (2003), 217.

[10] Prosser, T., 'Regulation of Privatized Enterprises: Institutions and Procedures', in Hancher and Moran (eds.), *Capitalism, Culture and Economic Regulation*, 136.

[11] Maitland, F. W., *The Constitutional History of England* (Cambridge: Cambridge University Press, 1908), 418.

[12] See, for example, Turpin, C., *British Government and the Constitution: Text, Cases and Material*, 4th edn. (London: Butterworths, 1999), 165–72 and 569–77.

A CHANGING CONCEPT

In the course of discussing the explanatory potential of competing 'public interest' and 'public choice' models in relation to regulatory law,[13] Ogus looks back as far as the Tudor and Stuart periods to examine the extent of, and rationales for, state intervention in private activity.[14] Ogus's conclusion that 'At no time in English legal history has the law governing industry and commerce been so extensively and intensively penetrated by regulation as in the Tudor and Stuart periods',[15] will seem controversial to many who might offer as alternative highpoints the latter part of the nineteenth century, or even the mid-late twentieth century, when nationalization of key industrial and economic sectors was brought about via statute. In another sense, however, his account is far more conventional, given that he identifies a clear trend of domination of the legislative and regulatory processes by interest groups, both private and public, throughout the period he covers.

It is clear, however, that a concept of public interest was developing in Britain by the seventeenth century. As noted in Chapter One, the late nineteenth-century US case of *Munn v. Illinois*[16] which laid the foundations for the development of the 'essential facilities doctrine', was influenced by English dicta from two centuries earlier which suggested an idea of private property being 'affected with a public interest'. However, the very fluid nature of the meaning of concepts such as the public interest, as a result of their capture and recapture by different interest groups, is also illustrated by Gunn,[17] who considers concepts of the public interest before and after the English Civil War. In examining this formative period for the modern British state, Gunn draws on contemporary sources to observe how, prior to the Civil War, 'the common good' (which can be identified as the nearest existing equivalent to a concept of 'the public interest') was considered to be essentially congruent with 'the welfare of the state', and was embodied exclusively in the monarch. During the course of the century, however, and especially during and following the Commonwealth (the period of establishment of parliamentary authority), Gunn identifies a change whereby the public interest, as defined by the propertied class which had come to dominate the institutions of the political system, becomes closely associated with the protection of private property rights against potential incursions by Parliament.

This early history of the modern British state is illustrative of how any prevailing vision of the public interest may change in tandem with, or possibly in reaction to, changes in state structure and perceptions of the extent and nature of the legitimacy of state activity. Gunn's account also demonstrates how the

---

[13] See above, Ch. 1.

[14] Ogus, A. I., 'Regulatory Law: Some Lessons from the Past', 12/1 *Legal Studies*, (1999), 1.

[15] Ibid., 17.   [16] 94 US 139 (1877).

[17] Gunn, J. A. W., *Politics and the Public Interest in the Seventeenth Century* (London: Routledge and Kegan Paul, 1969).

public interest can be readily captured by a powerful interest group, in this case the landed class.

What must be emphasized here is that both regulation, and any concept of public interest which informs it, are more than just economic concepts given legal form. Ogus notes that regulation is 'fundamentally a *politico*-economic concept',[18] and this should serve as a prompt, reminding us to examine the concept in its political, as well as economic or legal contexts. Viewed in this way, it should come as no surprise either to find the kind of change of meaning identified by Gunn following the political upheavals of the seventeenth century, or if it is discovered that the public interest, as an aspect of regulation, has changed in accordance with fluctuating fashions in political philosophy in the course of the twentieth century.

What is clear, however, is that the concept of public interest now becomes closely identified with changing visions of the proper relationship between state and the individual. Changes in this relationship, from the high-water mark of interventionism in the mid-twentieth century, to the end of that century and the start of our own in the post-Thatcher/Reagan years, with the wholesale reformation of the state, its apparent withdrawal from certain areas, and a reconceptualization of the relationship along laissez-faire individualist lines, should be expected to result in changes in what is understood by the public interest. In this modern era, as Ogus properly observes, 'Since social welfare is understood in terms only of individual utility the law is constructed on the basis of private interests',[19] leaving collective values in an enfeebled condition. Though the modern rhetoric of human rights may intend to protect fundamental values, it might be seen ultimately as re-emphasizing individual rights at the expense of the collective. As will be discussed shortly, it may be that our legal system offers little resistance to such a trend.

The marginalization of collective values in mainstream political discourse may, of course, be viewed simply as a continuation of the historical tendency suggested by accounts such as Gunn's, for politically dominant groups to use their power to fill an empty vessel of the public interest with their values. As such, this might serve to reconfirm a view of the concept of public interest as lacking definition, and offering little of substance in terms of political and/or legal debate. Thus, rather than being viewed as a contested arena, a more plausible account, as suggested in Chapter One, is to suggest that the concept of public interest is not robust enough to sustain struggle within it, but rather serves as an aspect of spoils, to be claimed and enjoyed by the winner of a larger political struggle, and to be filled with their values.

To summarize then, at this stage it would seem that although a model of public interest might be expected to have some potential for promoting a democratic agenda, perhaps acting as a bulwark against the dominance of private or individual interests, any such potential is generally undermined as a result of

---

[18] Ogus, *Regulation*, 1 (emphasis added).   [19] Ibid., 25.

the absence of any clear value base for the concept, or at least the absence of any clearly specified democratic value base autonomous of currently hegemonic politico-economic values. The content of the concept, though clearly relating to and reflecting longer-term trends in the development of the relationship between state and the individual, seems to be routinely changed in the shorter term to reflect the values of the temporarily dominant political group.

Are There any Underlying Values?

Though as was seen in Chapter One, constructs of the public interest based upon preponderance and common interest accounts will inevitably lack inherent and independent values, being in essence the result of head-counting exercises, this was shown not to be the case in what Held terms 'unitary' versions of the public interest.[20] Of course, it can argued with some force that an economic version of the public interest which merely reflects and supports market forces is not meaningfully value neutral; it privileges systems of market relations, and therefore tends to confirm and perpetuate existing social divisions and hierarchy. However, it is not really necessary to pursue this line further, as, both in political rhetoric and (as will be discussed further in Part Two) in law, the use of the term public interest does, on closer inspection, invariably imply a heavily value-laden base. The persistent problem, however, is that the value base is rarely *explicitly* articulated.

It can be argued, however, that close study of the language of public interest does reveal a number of recurrent themes, which go beyond the economic. Despite the public interest apparently remaining a hostage to usage, it is also clear that writers from a range of perspectives concur in identifying some under-lying, if sometimes vague, common elements in their analysis of the concept's contents.

A number of commentators (largely from within political philosophy rather than law) identify the public interest closely with a concept of 'community', and indeed some[21] will cite the writing of Plato and Aristotle in support of this proposition. It is clear, however, as Held illustrates,[22] that there is a potential conflation in these classical writings of the concepts of 'community', and that of 'state'. We should note the difficulties created by this position, given the potential for the interests of 'the state' to become synonymous with the interests of a group that dominates the organs of state, or perhaps in the modern era for the exercise of corporate power to take on functions which have the force

[20] Held, V., *The Public Interest and Individual Interests* (New York, N.Y.: Basic Books, 1970). See above, Ch. 1.
[21] See, for example, Niemayer, G., 'Public Interest and Private Utility', in Friedrich, C. J. (ed.), *Nomos V: The Public Interest* (New York, N.Y.: Atherton Press, 1962).
[22] Held, *Public Interests and Individual Interests*, 154–5.

and effect traditionally associated with state power without carrying with it the associated democratic expectations of accountability.[23]

However, we should acknowledge also Bodenheimer's observation that, for the concept to carry meaning, we should understand the public interest as more than 'the camouflaged interest of an elite or minority actuated by totally self-serving goals'.[24] In Bell's terms, 'The public interest is used to describe where the net interests of particular individuals may not be advanced, but where something necessary to the cohesion or development of the community is secured.'[25] Bell discusses 'the public interest' in terms of 'fundamental values [which] character-ize the basic structure of society',[26] while Milne also identifies the concept's close connections with an idea of a 'community' which represents more than a col-lection of individual interests.[27] A number of commentators also explicitly link the concept of public interest to an ideal of 'general welfare'.[28] Though Lewin notes a persuasive argument that 'it makes good sense to suppose that there are interests common to all the members of a community',[29] an awareness should be retained of the risk that such lines of argument can tend to lead towards the pursuit of common interest models of the public interest, the problems of which have already been identified in Chapter One.

Other commentators note how the public interest serves as a complement to concepts of human rights,[30] or view it as offering a degree of linkage or balance between the rights and duties associated with citizenship.[31] The citizenship con-nection, to which we will return shortly, appears to be furthered by Lasswell's discussion of 'dignity' in the context of the public interest, which he finds implies widespread and active participation in society.[32] Links are also made between a concept of 'common good' (often closely associated with public interest claims) and 'the establishment of social conditions under which individual persons are able to build ... a life which is in consonance with the dignity of the human being',[33] and it is claimed that 'the public interest approach looks primarily to

[23] See below, Ch. 6.

[24] Bodenheimer, E., 'Prolegomena to a Theory of the Public Interest', in Friedrich (ed.), *Nomos V*, 211.

[25] Bell, J., 'Public Interest: Policy or Principle?', in Brownsword, R. (ed.), *Law and the Public Interest* (Proceedings of the 1992 ALSP Conference) (Stuttgart: Franz Steiner, 1993), 30.

[26] Ibid., 34.

[27] Milne, A. J. M., 'The Public Interest, Political Controversy, and the Judges', in Brownsword, R. (ed.), *Law and the Public Interest* (Proceedings of the 1992 ALSP Conference) (Stuttgart: Franz Steiner, 1993).

[28] See, for example, Griffith, E. S., 'The Ethical Foundations of the Public Interest'; Cassinelli, C. W., 'The Public Interest in Political Ethics'; and, Pennock, J. R., 'The One and the Many: a Note on the Concept'; all in Friedrich (ed.), *Nomos V*.

[29] Lewin, L., *Self-Interest and Public Interest in Western Politics* (Oxford: Oxford University Press, 1991), 23.

[30] Cohen, J., 'A Lawman's View of the Public Interest', in Friedrich (ed.), *Nomos V*.

[31] Cassinelli, 'The Public Interest in Political Ethics'.

[32] Lasswell, H. D., 'The Public Interest: Proposing Principles of Content and Procedure', in Friedrich (ed.), *Nomos V*.   [33] Bodenheimer, 'Prolegomena', 213.

the social constituent in human beings'.[34] What appears at this stage, therefore, is a conjunction of opinion viewing the public interest as being intimately connected with some vision of community, human dignity, and an ongoing social order, and having a strong connection with citizenship.

Barry[35] is surely right, however, to suggest that in a pluralistic context a 'common interest' will rarely extend across all individuals or interest groups, and indeed he appears to conclude that, in different social capacities, even one individual may have a range of different perspectives on what constitutes the public interest, thus rendering definition of the public interest in this sense, difficult or impossible. However, the public interest can also be viewed as an important part of the structures in which expressions of pluralism take place. In talking of the public interest in terms of 'the complex procedures of political adjustment and compromise which the democratic polity employs to represent and accommodate the demands made upon its policy-making instruments',[36] Sorauf seems to capture a potential relationship with pluralism, though his focus is more on a procedural aspect of the concept than any substantive content, and he risks failing to take the concept's function beyond that of a contested arena within which the pluralist fray may take place, the limitations of which have already been noted. In any event, it remains doubtful whether any model of the concept identified thus far is sufficiently robust to bear the weight that it would be expected to carry in this context. However, a wide range of commentators[37] concur in what must be viewed as an implicit attack on common interest and preponderance theories, which attempt to define the public interest by reference to individual interests of, respectively, all or a majority of the existing population, instead suggesting that the public interest is linked not only to the interests of the current population, but also specifically, as noted in Chapter One, to the interests of future generations.

The net effect of such approaches seems to be to imply that far from being simply ascertainable on an empirical basis, as the sum of existing individual interests, the public interest has a degree of conceptual independence. This may be derived from the definite ethical content that so many commentators identify. Reference is sometimes made to the public interest as 'a spur to conscience and to deliberation',[38] or to the 'moral intrusion'[39] of the public interest into political discourse, though such observations are of limited assistance if the values they direct thoughts towards remain unspecified. However, a major criticism sometimes levelled at certain explications of the public interest is that they are

---

[34] Bodenheimer 'Prolegomena' 217.

[35] Barry, B. M., 'The Use and Abuse of the Public Interest', in Friedrich (ed.), *Nomos V*.

[36] Sorauf, F. J., 'The Conceptual Muddle', in Friedrich (ed.), *Nomos V*, 185.

[37] For example, Ogus, *Regulation*; Griffith, 'The Ethical Foundations'; Colm, G., 'The Public Interest: Essential Key to Public Policy', and, Pennock, 'The One and the Many', both in Friedrich (ed.), *Nomos V*.   [38] Pennock, 'The One and the Many', 182.

[39] Bailey, S. K., 'The Public Interest: Some Operational Dilemmas', in Friedrich (ed.), *Nomos V*, 106.

premised on what is identified, pejoratively, as a 'natural law' model.[40] If a 'natural law' basis is indeed proposed as a legitimate foundation for the public interest, a question is likely to be posed as to what is the normative or moral content upon which it is premised. Downs may be of some assistance here, in linking the public interest with 'elements of the minimal value structure that define the society'[41] and we will return to this theme later in this chapter, in the context of Llewellyn's 'Law Jobs'.[42]

Some Interim Conclusions

The elements common to many constructs of 'the public interest' which have been identified so far are therefore connections with community, general welfare, human dignity, and the maintenance of conditions that permit an ongoing social order. Further, the public interest is viewed as having the potential to play a facilitative role in accommodating the range of different individual and group interests that might exist in a pluralist society, but in particular, to turn attention away from concerns exclusively for the interests of the existing population, or of dominant groups within it, to consider also the interests of future members of society. The main lines of division that have so far become apparent concern the method for assessing what the public interest is; whether it should be determined empirically, by observing where the interests of all, or a majority of individuals lie, or whether it may be identified by reference to overarching moral principles.

It may be possible to identify a degree of consensus amongst commentators on viewing the public interest as one of the means for ensuring the circumstances under which achievement of social goals can be attempted. In this sense, the public interest might, though need not necessarily be, reduced to a portmanteau term referring to the prerequisites of the social/democratic enterprise. Though such an approach may identify the potential for a model of the public interest to play a facilitative role in defending the institutions and activities which serve social and democratic objectives, the breadth of definition seems to provide too vague a notion to contribute to meaningful debate, and far too uncertain a concept to be attractive to many lawyers.

That said, the very important themes identified above as underlying so many accounts of the public interest suggest that although the presently nebulous version of the concept may be unsatisfactory, a remodelled construct may yet have a significant role to play in defending and furthering important aspects of the democratic system. It is therefore necessary to consider whether the concept can

---

[40] See, for example, Friedman, W., 'The Changing Content of the Public Interest', in Friedrich (ed.), *Nomos V*, taking issue with Lasswell's approach.

[41] Quoted in Held, *Public Interest and Individual Interests*, 222.

[42] Llewellyn, K., 'The Normative, the Legal and the Law-Jobs', 49, *Yale Law Journal* (1940), 1355.

be further refined, or whether linkages with other core democratic concepts can be more clearly established.

So far it has been possible to infer that supposedly 'value free' models of the public interest, based on preponderance or common interest calculi, may amount to no more than a reflection of crude majoritarianism and a legitimation of existing power relationships. Equally, it is clear that economic concepts of the public interest serve primarily to confirm existing market relationships. Either approach may offer a degree of justification for regulatory intervention premised upon, respectively, identified majority interests, or, a faith in the efficacy of market forces to deliver society's needs. Neither, however, incorporate into their view of the public interest anything beyond the values of the interests of currently dominant social groups, whether determined by head-counting, or the identification of those best able to utilize and benefit from market forces.

In essence, what is being observed here confirms the view that what is referred to as the public interest may in reality be reduced to an aspect of a 'spoils' system of democracy; an aspect of hegemony whereby those in political and economic power enjoy the freedom to define the public interest according to their vision and group interests. Models of the public interest based upon the value of market forces, or calculated by reference to political majorities, fail to recognize or incorporate a wider set of values, and a broader set of interests. Such models do not reflect a broader democratic value-set, ignoring perhaps a range of philosophical and constitutional principles and expectations identified earlier as implicit in so much of the rhetorical usage of the term public interest. They certainly run totally counter to the kind of model envisaged by some of the commentators referred to above, who give emphasis to the need to understand the concept of public interest as referring to the interests of the community as a whole, including future generations.

The question therefore becomes, at this stage, to consider whether it is possible to construct a vision of the public interest which incorporates these broader values and interests, is inclusive of a range of social group interests, and which does more than merely confirm existing power relationships. If it is possible to identify normative foundations for the public interest, within the mainstream of liberal–democratic theory and independent of temporarily dominant value subsets, it may be possible to establish a concept which is much less vulnerable to capture by the hegemony, and one which might take on a much more dynamic role in supporting democratic objectives. On what foundations might such a construct be built?

THE CITIZEN, THE STATE AND THE PUBLIC INTEREST

Perhaps it is worth considering first the fact that the key common element identified earlier, when considering commentaries on the public interest, was its intimate connection with community, general welfare, human dignity, and the maintenance of conditions which support an ongoing social order. Here we have a broad range of concerns, which could in general terms be described as focusing on the relationships both between the state (in whatever historical form) and individual human beings, and, between people and groups *inter se*. It is important to re-emphasize the historically changing nature of such relationships, both in their practical manifestations and in dominant philosophical and political thought. An awareness of the historical development of what we now call 'human rights', or of 'citizenship', both concepts central to our modern model of the relationship between the individual, the state and society, is essential if they are to be understood in their modern guise. The establishment of links between such core democratic values and the concept of public interest, may substantially strengthen the concept, and perhaps allay some fears as to its application.

As with 'the public interest' or 'the crown', British law has been slow to adopt tight definitions of 'human rights' or 'citizenship'. Despite Britain having been a signatory of the ECHR in 1950, it was only with the arrival of the Human Rights Act 1998 (HRA) that legal force was given to many of its principles in the UK courts, at least in an organized and principled, as opposed to piecemeal manner. As regards citizenship, though some legal definition of this term has existed historically in the context of immigration and welfare benefits, it has remained a limited notion, perhaps reflecting the historical view of Britons as 'subjects of the Crown'. Of course, the European influence is not confined to the ECHR, and debate over citizenship has also developed in recent years within the context of the European Union's growing influence in this area.[43] This lack of definition for an apparently central concept such as citizenship may well relate to what Prosser[44] has identified as the absence of a developed concept of 'state' in Britain, at least when compared to its continental neighbours. It may prove difficult to define 'citizen', in the absence of a developed concept of 'state'.

The early history of the modern British state, as discussed by Gunn (see above), is illustrative of how the prevailing vision of the public interest is likely to change in tandem with, or possibly in reaction to, changes in state structure and in the focus and extent of legitimate state activity. It is clear, however, that though such changes are very likely to occur after such highly charged constitutional events as civil war, interregnum and restoration, changes in the vision of the state and of its structures are virtually continuous, and generally more evolutionary and gradual. The absence of dramatic landmark events in long periods of constitutional history, especially in the case of Britain, should not be taken to be indicative of a lack of change in the meaning attached to the public interest.

---

[43] See literature on EU citizenship generally, including, Birkinshaw, P., *European Public Law* (London: Butterworths, 2003), Ch. 9; also Pinder, J., 'European Citizenship: a Project in Need of Completion', in Crouch, C. and Marquand, D. (eds.), *Reinventing Collective Action: From the Global to the Local* (Oxford: Blackwell, 1995), 112; and, Hervey, T., *European Social Law and Policy* (Harlow: Addison Wesley Longman, 1998), 202–5.

[44] Prosser, T., 'Towards a Critical Public Law', *Journal of Law and Society*, 1982, 1.

The changes in the concept of the public interest which Gunn notes in seventeenth-century England, appear to relate to a change in the prevalent concept of state, away from a near total focus on securing the boundaries of the realm and international military and diplomatic concerns, to the beginnings of a more active state concern with domestic matters and greater intervention in 'private' activity: the growth of 'public policy'. It is possible to place such developments within a grand pattern such as that established by Kamenka and Tay,[45] who talk in terms of shifts from organization by community principles (*Gemeinschaft*) to one of social organization by association (*Gesellschaft*) to a position where state bodies actively set agendas and execute policy (*bureaucratic-administrative* model). In Hill's terms,[46] which run parallel, historically, to Kamenka and Tay's account, it is possible to note, from the seventeenth century onwards, developments in the role of the state from a concern primarily with defence and security, to one in which it serves to facilitate private activity in trade and commerce, to one which develops strongly in the latter part of the nineteenth century where the state begins to play a more active role as regulator of private activity. Beyond this phase, Hill identifies a further accretion of roles to the state as the twentieth century unfolded, beginning with the extension of the state's role to include acting as provider of services, via the welfare state, and later including entrepreneurial roles as controller of certain key economic sectors in the form of nationalized industries. In the last years of the twentieth century we can observe a different phase, in which the state no longer expands its activities following the pattern established by Hill, but rather appears to withdraw from certain roles, via the privatization of nationalized industries and a lack of investment in welfare provision, and an increased faith in market forces to deliver society's needs. Such changes might well imply consequent, parallel, changes to any prevalent notion of public interest. However, later in this chapter it will be suggested that there is a potential for a more fully developed concept of public interest to serve as a potential force of resistance: a counterweight, preventing excessive swings that might upset the delicate equilibrium of liberal democracy. In this sense, the public interest could be viewed as a force for conservatism.

Noted earlier[47] was a degree of overlap between the concepts of public interest and citizenship, and over the same historical period just outlined, an expansionist trend in citizenship expectations should also be observed, both in terms of greater inclusivity (expanding franchise rights etc.) and content (the range of values and expectations incorporated). Whilst, as is the case for 'the public interest',

---

[45] Kamenka, E. and Tay, A. E. S., 'Beyond Bourgeois Individualism – the Contemporary Crisis in Law and Legal Ideology', in Kamenka, E. and Neale, R. S., *Feudalism, Capitalism and Beyond* (London: Arnold, 1975).

[46] Hill, M., *The State, Administration and the Individual* (London: Fontana/Collins, 1976).

[47] See Lasswell, 'Principles of Content and Procedure', and Cassinelli, 'The Public Interest in Political Ethics'.

there exists no single definition of the term 'citizenship', the task of establishing
the basic characteristics of the latter concept is assisted by Marshall's attempt to
define elements of citizenship, which he divides into three; the civil, the political
and the social.[48] Of course, many well-charted tensions and difficulties within
and between these elements must be acknowledged.[49] In particular we might
note the failure to offer any causal, as opposed to descriptive account of the
evolution of rights,[50] and a failure to give adequate prominence to the place
of social struggle, or perhaps to acknowledge the role played in the maintenance of a capitalist economy by the granting of citizenship rights as a means of
handling social pressures.[51] Nonetheless, and in the absence of anything 'which
could be described as a *theory* of citizenship',[52] Marshall's work continues to
serve as a useful sketch of the historically changing nature of the concept of
citizenship.

Marshall traces the historical development of the three elements, and claims
that the formative period in the life of civil rights can be assigned to the eighteenth
century. Freedom from servile labour enabled people to obtain the civil element
of citizenship which Marshall describes as '. . . the rights necessary for individual
freedom – liberty of the person, freedom of speech, thought and faith, the right
to own property and to conclude valid contracts, and the right to justice'.[53]
Built upon this foundation, during the nineteenth and early twentieth centuries,
was the development of the political element. This element encompasses the
entitlements most immediately associated with citizenship, namely the '. . . right
to participate in the exercise of political power, as a member of a body invested
with political authority or as an elector of the members of such a body'.[54] The
final element essential to the status of citizenship is the least clearly defined and
forms the focus of much recent debate on citizenship; indeed, in Loughlin's terms,
'some would argue that the issue of socio-economic citizenship rights has become
the political question'.[55] The social element, according to Marshall, provides
the foundation upon which the individual can undertake the effective exercise
of their civil entitlements and obligations. This can be seen in his definition of the
social element as, '. . . the whole range from the right to a modicum of economic
welfare and security to the right to share to the full in the social heritage and
to live the life of a civilised being according to the standards prevailing in the
society'.[56]

---

[48] Marshall, T. H., *Citizenship and Social Class* (Cambridge: Cambridge University Press, 1950),
and *Sociology at the Crossroads and Other Essays* (London: Heinemann, 1963).

[49] See, for example, the various essays in Turner, B. S. (ed.), *Citizenship and Social Theory*,
(London: Sage, 1993); also Van Steenbergen, B. (ed.), *The Condition of Citizenship* (London: Sage,
1993).   [50] Turner (ed.), *Citizenship and Social Theory*, 8.

[51] Miliband, R., *Capitalist Democracy in Britain* (Oxford: Oxford University Press, 1982).

[52] Barbalet, J. M., *Citizenship* (Milton Keynes: Open University Press, 1988), original emphasis.

[53] Marshall, *Citizenship and Social Class*, 10–11.   [54] Ibid.

[55] Loughlin, M., *Public Law and Political Theory* (Oxford: Clarendon, 1992), 222, original
emphasis.   [56] Marshall, *Citizenship and Social Class*, 11.

Inevitably, as the roles of the state change, until recently consistently along expansionist lines, and as expectations of citizenship also expand over the same period, the relationship between the two must continually evolve. If society is to continue, the relationship between the changing concepts of citizen and state must be redefined in order to absorb pressures and accommodate potentially conflicting claims. Social and constitutional change will also result in shifting patterns of conflicting interests between different groups, and democratically legitimate mechanisms must be devised which reconcile or resolve such underlying tensions, recognizing the inherent links between citizens, groups and the community. Though referring to the US context, where, as will be discussed in Chapter Six, civic republicanism appears to offer a different perspective on citizenship, it is important, in this changing environment, to maintain a focus on the goal, as Sunstein puts it, of 'adhering to the original belief in the governmental process as one of deliberation oriented to the public good rather than a series of interest-group tradeoffs',[57] again reasserting the relevance of collective or community values.

In the context of changing or newly developed democratic expectations, a concept such as 'the public interest' may be of significant value if it reflects overarching societal values yet remains sufficiently flexible to adapt to changing visions of the relationship between groups, and between the state and the individual. Indeed, it may be thought that the concept could play a facilitative role in the development of new rights and expectations such as those of citizenship or, say, human rights, which may, in their infancy, be highly vulnerable to reactionary forces. Thus, in addition to the potential 'conservative' force of a developed concept of the public interest suggested earlier, what is suggested here now is a further potential function as a developmental, or 'progressive' tool.

I have discussed at some length elsewhere the central nature of citizenship to one particular regulatory context, that of media regulation.[58] Here, expectations of citizenship, and especially perhaps equality of citizenship, have historically informed and justified, and continue to underlie much intervention in media, and especially the Western European public service broadcasting tradition. To be considered in Part Two of this book are further examples of how 'public interest' regulation may be seen as serving primarily citizenship agendas. In contexts such as this, there seems to be a clear connection between concepts of citizenship and the public interest. While the public interest reflects the fundamental concerns and objectives of citizenship, it may also helpfully serve to add a collective element to what has often and increasingly been viewed as an individualistic version of citizenship.

However, what is being referred to here is much more the *potential*, both 'conservative' and 'progressive' that the public interest has to offer rather than

---

[57] Sunstein, *After the Rights Revolution*, 12.

[58] Feintuck, M., *Media Regulation, Public Interest and the Law* (Edinburgh: 1999), especially 77–87.

the reality of its current roles. In present reality, its ability to fulfil such democratic functions is significantly reduced, indeed the whole concept effectively
rendered impotent, by virtue of the narrow construct which, so far as one can
be identified, is the current model used in regulation. Stripped of much of its
wider meaning, and merely reflecting the perceived public *economic* interest,
such a model lacks any normative power in terms of defending or advancing
fundamental *democratic* values. While an economic model of public interest
might be the best established, and the model most clearly reflected in law, it
fails to engage with the democratic context. It is telling that Baldwin, Scott, and
Hood note that while economists have taken a particular interest in the regulation of utilities, their concern has been 'protecting consumers and promoting
competition';[59] note the absence of *citizenship* concerns, which clearly extend
beyond the interests of consumers. In its failure to import a vision of values such
as equality of citizenship, or any other values within the democratic settlement
beyond market economics, the currently dominant economic concept of public
interest, as manifested in law and regulation, seems to bring little to the debate.

THE PUBLIC INTEREST AS A LEGAL CONCEPT

While I have just referred to 'the public interest, as manifested in law', it is worth
noting at this stage also that in fact, the public interest in British law has, by and
large, a somewhat mirage-like quality, appearing to take various concrete forms
but then receding or evaporating as one approaches. This is perhaps unsurprising
given some fundamental problems that can be identified in relation to what has
been described as the tendency of common law systems to individualize what are
essentially collective issues.[60] In relation to 'the nature of law within the context
of the market system', in Ogus's terms, 'Since social welfare is understood in
terms only of individual utility, the law is constructed on the basis of private
interests.'[61]

Of course, given the ability of the large corporate entity, or those who control
them, to acquire an 'individual' legal personality, there is an underlying irony,
noted by Crouch and Marquand, that 'individual' may be used, both in the
context of 'New Right individualism' and in law, in 'the fundamentally deceptive sense of "person able to mobilise the resources of a large, privately-owned
collective unit" '.[62] In this sense, proponents of individualism are furthering a
collective notion, though in the form of a collectivity which only serves those
with significant capital.

[59] Baldwin, R., Scott, C., and Hood, C. (eds.), *A Reader on Regulation* (Oxford: Oxford University
Press, 1998), 8.
[60] Dhavan, R., 'Whose Law? Whose Interest?' in Cooper, J. and Dhavan, R. (eds.), *Public Interest
Law* (Oxford: Basil Blackwell, 1986), 33.   [61] Ogus, *Regulation*, 25.
[62] Crouch, C. and Marquand, D., 'Reinventing Collective Action', in Crouch, C. and Marquand, D.
(eds.), *Reinventing Collective Action: From the Global to the Local* (Oxford: Blackwell, 1995), 7.

There are various examples of the law being used to promote group interests in specific fields, especially, for example, welfare rights. Britain has seen an increase in the use of litigation to promote interests of vulnerable and marginalized or excluded groups,[63] though such actions do remain a limited exception to the norm: 'The welfare state has cautiously redefined the entitlements of disadvantaged groups but individuated these entitlements in a way that cannot always be collectively pursued through the claiming process.'[64] Though Dhavan identifies such difficulties as stemming substantially from the 'black-letter' tradition in English law, especially the emphasis placed upon individual transactions and rights in contract and torts law, Wightman[65] is clear that it is worth exploring the extent to which there may be scope within the existing private law system for greater recognition of public interest factors, particularly as regards the development of the concept in the context of privatized utilities. Wightman argues that present limits on the recognition of public interests in private law are not necessarily inherent in the private law system. In a similar vein, Craig identifies, in the context of monopoly and common calling, examples of restrictions on private property power being on occasion justified by reference to broader public interest concerns.[66] This perhaps confirms Parkinson's view of company law, noted in Chapter One, that 'Since the public interest is the foundation of the legitimacy of companies, it follows that society is entitled to ensure that corporate power is exercised in a way that is consistent with that interest.'[67] Daintith goes so far as to promote the idea of a body of law with 'collective and democratic origins', 'collective interest law', which he suggests should provide an informing spirit for those legal interventions which change existing private rights to reflect 'collective interests', and would further the objective of a more participatory democracy.[68]

The potential for developing a model of public interest from such examples will be returned to in later chapters, but for the moment it is perhaps sensible to note that in the very nature of these areas and cases, and as a result of the individualized, precedential, system in which they originate, lies a problem. It is rather easy within a common law environment for cases to be confined to their own facts, and for nascent principles of more general application to be strangled

---

[63] See Cooper and Dhavan, *Public Interest Law*, and by way of an interesting comparison, from a jurisdiction influenced by both British and US approaches, Whyte, G., *Social Inclusion and the Legal System: Public Interest Law in Ireland* (Dublin: Institute of Public Administration, 2002).

[64] Dhavan, 'Whose Law?', 33.

[65] Wightman, J., 'Private Law and Public Interests', in Wilhelmsson, T. and Hurri, S. (eds.), *From Dissonance to Sense: Welfare Expectations, Privatisation and Private Law* (Aldershot: Dartmouth, 1999).

[66] Craig, P. P., 'Constitutions, Property and Regulation', *Public Law*, 1991, Winter, 538.

[67] Parkinson, J., *Corporate Power and Responsibility: Issues in the Theory of Company Law* (Oxford: Clarendon, 1996), 23.

[68] Daintith, T., 'Law as Policy Instrument: a Comparative Perspective', in Daintith, T. (ed.), *Law as an Instrument of Economic Policy: Comparative and Critical Approaches* (Berlin: Walter de Gruyter, 1988), 18–19.

at birth or very shortly thereafter, or simply left to die through lack of nurture, reflecting another perspective on the individualized system of case law.

This was considered as long ago as the mid-1980s by Griffith, who wrote of judicial decisions 'that transcend the parties and deeply involve political issues and the public interest', and which, when dealt with through regular, adversarial court procedure, 'as if they were similar to the common run of litigation, . . . result in decision-making by the courts which is or may be inappropriate and sometimes grossly inefficient'.[69] Whether Griffith's recommendation of the development of an Advocate-General type role, with a brief to pursue the public interest and a consequent shift towards a more inquisitorial system, would assist is an open question. It might be expected to sit uncomfortably within the mainstream tradition of British common law, but in any event, it would seem reasonable to conclude that a major prior task to the successful development of such a role would be the explication of a concept of public interest, or something quite like it.

It is, however, important at this juncture to identify something of a trans-Atlantic bifurcation. The historically nebulous nature of fundamental rights and freedoms in Britain, and the enduring concept of parliamentary supremacy, are strikingly different to that in the United States, where the country's founders identified a series of such rights and empowered the judiciary, as unchallenged guardians of the constitution, to enforce, interpret and develop them. That is not to say that the concept of public interest is necessarily uncontroversial in the US; far from it! For example, as will be seen in Chapter Four, though the term 'the public interest, necessity and convenience' is at the heart of the Federal Communication Commission's statutory brief, it has proven difficult to define, even for its supporters,[70] and has led to calls for its removal, as unconstitutional, by its opponents.[71] That said, however, we will also see in later chapters how the likes of Sunstein have, in reviewing the US regulatory system, pursued what can be recognized as public interest objectives, even if that tag has not always been applied.

Within the confine of the courtroom, the concept of 'class actions', very familiar in the US, has only recently begun to creep into British legal consciousness. There has been no British equivalent to the American 'Common Cause' movement of the 1960s and 1970s,[72] which may be viewed as an embodiment of an approach to the public interest which demonstrates its potential to protect via law nascent and infant claims relating to citizenship and human rights which may be either vulnerable or not yet fully embedded.

[69] Griffith, J. A. G., 'Judicial Decision Making in Public Law', *Public Law*, 1985, Winter, 564, at 565.

[70] Krasnow, E. and Goodman, J., 'The Public Interest Standard: the Search for the Holy Grail', *Federal Communications Law Journal*, 50 (1998), 605.

[71] May, R., 'The Public Interest Standard: Is it too Indeterminate to be Constitutional?', *Federal Communications Law Journal*, 53 (2001), 427.

[72] Barbrook, A., *Protest and Pressure: the Public Interest and Pressure Groups in the USA* (Hull: University of Hull, 1979), Hull Papers in Politics No. 11.

In the public law context, the concept of public interest is most concretely manifested in questions of standing in the context of judicial review. Interesting developments have been seen in Australia, where in the context of environmental law in particular, there has been a relaxation of standing rules over the last twenty years, and the introduction of increased use of *amicus curiae* briefs, plus findings as to costs in favour of 'public interest litigants',[73] despite ongoing judicial disagreement over the possibility of defining the concept of public interest.[74] Clearly, environmental law can be considered a *locus classicus* of the kind of interests of future generations associated with the public interest, noted earlier. Though UK courts have also in recent years taken a somewhat more liberal view of those bodies that will be permitted to bring actions for judicial review in this kind of area, it should not be supposed that progress in terms of standing to sue, with permission for bodies such as Greenpeace[75] or the World Development Movement[76] to bring public law actions, is the last word on this matter. A normative concept of the public interest may have both procedural and substantive impact in such a field, and may help, in Davis's terms,[77] to 'structure' discretion in public administration. Thus, though public interest criteria are presently applied primarily in relation to determining standing, they also have potential to serve as an interpretative aid in the scrutiny of the exercise of substantive powers. Though we must note Harlow's concerns over interest group litigation, which she has come to view as 'a partial colonisation of the legal by the political process',[78] such developments can also properly be considered to be no more than the ongoing development of law as what Stewart calls 'a surrogate political process',[79] which perhaps better captures the inter-relationship of the political and legal spheres.

A further area which appears to raise significant 'public interest concerns' is that of release of information into the public domain,[80] arguably an aspect of a broader issue of freedom of communication (or expression). Within the open-textured constitutional context of Britain, as Boyle[81] noted over twenty years ago, judges have had to weigh claims of freedom of expression against

---

[73] See Chakrabarti, S., Stephens, J., and Gallagher, C., 'Whose Cost the Public Interest?', *Public Law*, 2003, Winter, 697.

[74] Goodie, J. and Wickham, G., 'Calculating "Public Interest": Common Law and the Legal Governance of the Environment', *Social and Legal Studies*, 11/1, (2002), 37.

[75] *R v. Inspector of Pollution, ex parte Greenpeace (No. 2)* [1994] 4 All ER 329.

[76] *R v. Secretary of State for Foreign and Commonwealth Affairs ex parte World Development Movement* [1996] 1 WLR 386.

[77] Davis, K. C., *Discretionary Justice: a Preliminary Inquiry* (Urbana, IL.: University of Illinois Press, 1971).

[78] Harlow, C., 'Public Law and Popular Justice', *Modern Law Review*, 65 (2002), 1, at 2.

[79] Stewart, R. B., 'The Reformation of American Administrative Law', *Harvard Law Review*, 88 (1975), 1670.

[80] See generally, Birkinshaw, P. J., *Freedom of Information: the Law, the Practice and the Ideal*, 4th edn. (London: Butterworths, 2001).

[81] Boyle, A., 'Freedom of Expression as a Public Interest in English Law', *Public Law*, 1982, Winter, 574.

competing claims such as the administration of justice or the protection of confidentiality and privacy.[82] The absence of clear constitutional guidance on such matters rendered this task unenviable, and the effective incorporation of the ECHR into domestic law via the HRA may prove to be of limited assistance here, given the potential conflict between the demands of privacy and freedom of expression inherent in Articles 8 and 10. As Boyle concludes, in practice the judgment has, historically, often gone against the claims of freedom of expression, and it may be that a clearer explication of the democratic nature of these public interest claims may go some way to redress this imbalance. The difficulty here, as Scraton et al. have noted, more recently, may be not so much in recognizing the validity of the public interest involved, 'but in establishing it as a workable concept'.[83]

The different trans-Atlantic approaches and experiences will be explored more fully in Parts Two and Three, but the key point to establish at this stage is that, as perhaps demonstrated by the US experience, there seems to be no fundamental obstacle within common law systems to the establishment of legal principles which embody collective concepts such as the public interest. Though Harlow[84] is right to note differences between US and British judicial attitudes, and though constitutional matrices of power may serve to limit the concept's application in Britain, in a developed concept of the public interest lies a potential response to the tendency just noted for common law systems to individualize essentially collective issues.[85] Arguably, this has particular significance in a jurisdiction such as the UK, where the constitutional and democratic fundamentals can often remain nebulous.

The nervousness and/or scepticism of lawyers over utilizing the public interest is perfectly understandable given its generally undefined and vague content. However, though some might also raise concern about the use of a concept with an explicit normative content, their concerns should, logically, be somewhat allayed if the model proposed derives directly from the democratic imperatives on which the polity is premised; citizenship values being central amongst such imperatives. Indeed, it can be argued that the government, through legal mechanisms, 'is entitled to control and direct the activities of community-members . . . to the extent that this is required by the community's interest'.[86]

What is being undertaken here can be viewed as an attempt to go some way towards remedying the problem identified by Minor,[87] of what he terms the 'bifurcation' of 'technological' concerns (with institutions and rule-play, the

[82] See, for example, *A v. B plc* [2002] 2 All ER 545, and *Campbell v. Mirror Group Newspapers* [2002] HRLR 28.
[83] Scraton, P., Berrington, E., and Jemphrey, A., 'Intimate Intrusions? Press Freedom, Private Lives and Public Interest', *Communications Law*, 3/5 (1998), 174, at 179.
[84] Harlow, C., 'Public Interest Litigation in England: the State of the Art', in Cooper, J. and Dhavan, R. (eds.), *Public Interest Law* (Oxford: Basil Blackwell, 1986).
[85] Dhavan, R., 'Whose Law?'.   [86] Milne, 'Political Controversy and the Judges', 46.
[87] Minor, W. S., 'Public Interest and Ultimate Commitment', in Friedrich (ed.), *Nomos V*, 30.

traditional focus of many lawyers) from philosophy. In importing the moral essence of democracy into the legal and regulatory endeavour, a normative version of the public interest may serve as a useful adjunct to 'black-letter' law, again, potentially especially significant in the UK, where constitutional principles are often unclear. Of course, the aspirational qualities inherent in the concept may, by certain lawyers, be viewed as too vague to be readily applicable, as posing a threat to 'legal certainty', or as being improper by virtue of its value-laden nature. However, it can be argued that far from posing such a threat, the concept may usefully complement hard legal rules. Dworkin identifies 'propositions having the form and force of principles'[88] as being properly within the legal realm, and indeed the concept can be viewed as a valuable escape route from unduly constricting doctrine, or 'a means of justifying judicial activism'[89] within the bounds of legitimacy established by the constitutional schema. It can be argued that there is significant latent potential in this kind of less-specific norm, provided always that its value-laden content is understood, acknowledged, justified (in democratic terms) and widely accepted. The perceived risk associated with this value-laden concept of the public interest is, in reality, strictly limited by virtue of its close association with fundamental democratic values which, presumably, can be agreed to inform the legal and constitutional endeavour as a whole.

The precise legal form in which a concept such as the public interest might be manifested clearly presents problems, especially in the context of a legal system which is generally much more responsive to individual, as opposed to collective, interests. This subject will be addressed more directly in Part Three of this book; however, it is necessary at this stage to unpack what is intended by 'law' and 'legal system': like 'the public interest', terms too often used with inexplicit assumptions.

A MODEL OF LAW IN THE FIELD OF PUBLIC INTEREST REGULATION

Considered earlier were the historically changing relationships between state and the individual, and in particular the changing concept of citizenship. The evolving relationships between state and citizen, and shifting patterns of conflict between interest groups must be authoritatively and legitimately resolved if society is not to be torn apart. The form that legal intervention takes will also, inevitably, change, reflecting the shift from *Gemeinschaft* to *Gesellschaft* and to *bureaucratic-administrative* models,[90] yet throughout, the fulfilment of those tasks which permit society to continue to exist *qua* society remains the very essence of the 'Law Jobs' identified by Llewellyn[91] in the 1940s and adopted

---

[88] Dworkin, R., *Taking Rights Seriously* (London: Duckworth, 1977), 76.
[89] Goodie and Wickham, 'Calculating Public Interest', 50.
[90] Kamenka and Tay, 'Beyond Bourgeois Individualism'.
[91] Llewellyn, 'The Normative, the Legal and the Law Jobs'.

by Harden and Lewis[92] in their critique of the British constitution. Llewellyn's claim, simply put, is that there are certain tasks that must be performed within any group, large or small, to allow it to continue to operate as a group rather than disintegrate. Harden and Lewis go on to draw from Llewellyn's work, a fourfold classification of these Law Jobs, which must now be considered in the context of regulatory activity.

We need not, in the present context, be detained unduly by the first of these, 'disposition of the trouble case' or dispute resolution, crucial to the maintenance of an ongoing community, which is reasonably self-explanatory and is perhaps generally identified as the archetypal law job by lawyers and lay person alike. The other three, however, require a little explanation.

The second Law Job, Harden and Lewis term 'preventive channeling', or what Llewellyn refers to as 'producing and maintaining a going order instead of a disordered series of collisions'.[93] Harden and Lewis view this as involving 'the channeling of people's conduct preventively and arranging for participating in the scarce and the desirable'. Though this is clearly not the exclusive domain of the lawyer, it is equally clear that central to lawyers' activity is the establishment of norms and institutional structures for the ordering of social activity. The third Law Job, which Harden and Lewis term 'the constitution of groups' refers to the task of establishing the location of legitimate institutional power. As the authors note, 'it is not limited to parliaments or courts', and is 'a central issue in administration and organized social life at large'. In essence, this Law Job concerns the allocation of legitimate authority to take decisions which impact upon others. The fourth and final Law Job, 'goal orientation', involves processes for determining the desired direction to be taken, either by society generally or in specific policy areas.

Harden and Lewis note that, in a constitutional context, consideration of the Law Jobs emphasizes questions of 'legitimacy' in the exercise of powers, to be measured against the immanent expectations of liberal democracy. The problem to be faced here, however, is in establishing with any precision exactly what such expectations are. Especially in Britain, where a modern written constitution is absent, and, as Prosser has noted,[94] a developed concept of 'the state' is lacking, the ascertainment of constitutional and democratic rights and expectations can be fraught with difficulties. Students and scholars in search of British constitutional principles must scour a wide range of written fragments both ancient and modern, constitutional conventions and judicial decisions both domestic and European, in an attempt to understand the fundamental basis of their democratic arrangements, while in other modern democracies, such basics, though subject to contemporary reinterpretation, will be set out, at least

---

[92] Harden, I. and Lewis, N., *The Noble Lie: The British Constitution and the Rule of Law* (London: Hutchinson, 1986), 66–70.

[93] Llewellyn, 'The Normative, the Legal and the Law Jobs', 1376.

[94] Prosser, 'Towards a Critical Public Law'.

superficially, in a single written document. Of course, the traditional situation has now changed somewhat, as a result of the incorporation into UK law of the ECHR via the HRA. Though the protection thus provided for certain fundamental rights and freedoms might be thought to have increased significantly as a result, and certainly early indications suggest that the British judiciary have taken to the task of implementation with a fair degree of alacrity,[95] the HRA is of course much less far-reaching than a written constitution, the compass of which would extend beyond a Bill of Rights.

Any statement of constitutional principle is likely to be at least indicative of the foundations on which the polity is premised, and, in the absence of such clear statement, the task of ascertaining the democratic fundamentals becomes that much more difficult. That said, while there remains no single authoritative account of what the values are which underpin the liberal–democratic settlement, just as is the case with citizenship, it is possible to sketch, from history, a reasonable outline.

For present purposes, it might be helpful to consider the modern liberal democracy as involving three core values, which emerged at different historical moments, which should, for a more complete picture, be mapped against the development of the state and citizenship, discussed earlier in this chapter. These three values can be thought of as capital (manifested in private property), liberal-individualism (in the form of fundamental freedoms of the person), and collective or community-oriented values (typified by the welfare state social provisions and other interventions related perhaps to the social expectations of citizenship and social solidarity). It is clear that, just as the civil and political elements of Marshall's construct of citizenship pre-date the social element, both capitalism and individualism were historically established well before the kind of reform that ultimately led to the inclusive model of democracy widely advocated in the modern era. Although the benefits of property ownership and personal freedom must inevitably be seen as existing within an essentially collective entity – society – they both emphasize individualism, an emphasis reflected, as was discussed earlier, in the common law, which also has roots well established prior to the modern democratic era in which collective interests came to be reflected. Though this version of history may go some way towards explaining why the political system and legal system may ultimately be more responsive to claims of individual freedom and capital than they are to collective claims, it does not legitimate what must amount to failure in a 'liberal–democratic' system that, by definition, promises both liberalism *and* democracy. Institutions such as the law, and regulators, fail to fulfil the promises of the liberal–democratic settlement if they fail to give adequate consideration to the full range of interests, yet it seems highly questionable whether, in an era where the interests of capital and individualism

---

[95] For an account of some of the early judicial developments arising out of the HRA see Bonner, D. and Graham, C., 'The Human Rights Act 1998: the Story so Far', *European Public Law*, 8/2 (2002), 177.

have been prioritized, while collective interests have been heavily marginalized, the institutions have been able to meet this demand. It is suggested that the public interest, in this context in its 'conservative' guise, could have a role to play as an institution protecting these marginalized interests, but is generally too poorly defined to be able to make an impact.

By now it should come as little surprise to find that 'the public interest', though potentially central to democratic expectations and the achievement of the Law Job tasks, and sharing their common objective of facilitating the social endeavour, is adequately defined neither in itself nor in relation to the constitutional and democratic background against which it operates. However, it is clear that the common elements of the public interest identified earlier locate it close to, and indeed within the gravitational pull of, the constantly evolving spheres of state activity and citizenship expectations. The public interest appears to speak to fundamental democratic concerns, and although a developed version of the concept is elusive, it has been, and continues to be, continually invoked in argument concerning matters of public policy. It may, if more fully understood, serve usefully to re-focus the legal and regulatory endeavour upon the societal objectives and themes identified in Llewellyn's 'Law Jobs'.

In considering how a concept of public interest might be applied in fields of public policy, Virginia Held[96] observes in both political and legal systems the existence of notions of validity of rules, familiar to lawyers from Hart's idea of 'rules of recognition'.[97] Her interim conclusion is that, in the absence of a normative concept of the public interest, disputes within the political system will inevitably be determined in favour of the party with superior authority: a straightforward example of what was earlier described as a 'spoils' system. If, however, she argues, interposed in such a dispute is 'an assertion of the public interest as *normative*, as a claim regarding *justifiability*'[98] then this outcome will not be inevitable. She continues that 'Acceptance of the existence of a political system may depend upon widespread acceptance of the ethical judgment that it is justifiable for the political system to use coercion to enforce its decisions. In this way the political system may be grounded upon an ethical assumption that its existence is justified.'[99]

Held has in effect returned us to the concept identified by Harden and Lewis as being central to their constitutional study, legitimacy, and has furthered her argument that recourse to ethical underpinnings may provide the basis for resolution of conflicts between interests, and specifically between private and collective interests. Her conclusion, that 'A dispute between a valid claim of public interest and a valid claim of individual interest can only be resolved at a level outside the political system',[100] identifies the underlying ethical nature of such issues, and

---

[96] Held, *Public Interest and Individual Interests*, 176–84.
[97] Hart, H. L. A., *The Concept of Law* (Oxford: Clarendon, 1961).
[98] Held, *Public Interest and Individual Interests*, 187, original emphasis.   [99] Ibid., 189.
[100] Ibid., 197.

at the same time, in tennis terms, appears to send the ball into the lawyer's court for resolution. Unfortunately, many lawyers feel either incapable of playing, or unwilling to deal with a ball with this particular spin on it. This is in part accounted for by the strongly positivist approach prevalent in much conventional legal thinking. As Dworkin observes, 'some of the standards to which judges and lawyers appeal pose special problems for positivism, because these standards cannot readily be captured under a fundamental test for law like Hart's rule of recognition'.[101]

For the moment it is sufficient to note that lack of ability or will to deal with such matters is regrettable, because although in Dworkin's terms differing constructs of the public interest may be viewed as either 'policies' or 'principles', he states that:

[A]n accurate summary of the considerations lawyers must take into account, in deciding a particular issue of legal rights and duties, would include propositions having the form and force of principles, and ... judges and lawyers themselves, when justifying their conclusions, often use propositions which must be understood in that way.[102]

Bell draws from Dworkin's work an underlying acknowledgment that 'Principle sets the framework, but policy helps us to decide what shall be done.'[103] Inevitably, a part of any normative content for the concept of public interest which can be ascertained is likely to be only transient and contingent, as much of its precise content will be heavily influenced by the constitutional, social and political context in which it exists. Milne confirms also that 'the principled character of public interest arguments does not prevent their being controversial' and that 'many judgments of the requirements of the public interest have to be based on reasons which are not decisive and evidence which is not conclusive'.[104] At a fundamental level, however, the primary public interest must be to prefer the continuation of society over its disintegration. In this sense, the aspirational quality of the concept links it closely to the overarching objective of the Law Jobs, though it will, to be perceived as legitimate, need to mesh with contemporary visions of the state and with dominant values and interests. However, it can be argued that it must also embody a degree of resistance to changing contemporary values, and must ensure that temporary hegemonies are not allowed to alter the underlying democratic basis or 'minimal value structure'[105] of society. The public interest must therefore, rather like the sometimes equally nebulous 'Rule of Law', to be considered further in Chapter Six, reflect the more constant, and ultimately ethical, democratic underpinnings of the polity. In so far as these might be generally accepted in the modern era, examples might include a degree of equality of standing and participation in society. Though such examples may be termed modern, in the sense of arising relatively late in the development of

---

[101] Dworkin, *Taking Rights Seriously*, 71.   [102] Ibid., 76.
[103] Bell, 'Policy or Principle?', 29.   [104] Milne, 'Political Controversy and the Judges', 49.
[105] Held, *Public Interest and Individual Interests*, 187.

state and citizenship outlined above, the rights and duties of citizens have always included an element of equality; the modern aspect is merely the universal extension of such expectations to all of a nation's people rather than only the ruling class of ancient city states or the landed classes of the European Middle Ages. If this is the case, then a concept of 'public interest' may usefully serve as a force of resistance against dominant, or potentially dominant, group interests that would otherwise diminish the equality of standing and participatory capabilities of others outside the group.

In this sense, the concept of public interest becomes defined by reference to the fundamental, value-laden, democratic imperatives that underlie our society: human dignity, parity of esteem and an ability to participate actively in society. As will become apparent, this is likely to have implications for private, as much as public lawyers.[106] This approach will be returned to in later chapters; however, as was observed in Chapter One, the most clearly established current models of public interest observable in law and regulation are premised not on democratic imperatives, but rather by reference to economic criteria or via contrast with private interests. Though the adoption of either of these perspectives may, contingently, service democratic and social objectives, neither *necessarily* offers support for the democratic public interests identified above.

SUMMARIZING THE AGENDA: TOWARDS A MEANINGFUL CONCEPT OF THE PUBLIC INTEREST

The next two chapters will consider the empirical realities of the use of the concept of public interest in regulatory activities in Britain and the USA. It is therefore crucial to re-state clearly in summary form, even at the risk of repetition, the conceptual framework within which this analysis will take place.

Chapter One will have suggested to many readers that the general absence of definition for the concept of public interest might make it seem unwise to attempt to build upon it. The present chapter, however, should have indicated that it is possible to further the pursuit of worthwhile and democratically legitimate objectives via a theory of public interest *if* it can be given sufficiently clear normative content. In order to achieve this, it is necessary to avoid crude majoritarian approaches such as the preponderance or common interest versions, and to move beyond exclusively economic understandings of the concept, which focus solely on quantifiable measures of output.[107] Such approaches will have an inevitable tendency to value and defend what is measurable, as opposed to measuring and defending things of democratic value.

---

[106] See below, Ch. 6; also Wightman, 'Private Law and Public Interests'.

[107] Daintith, T., 'Legal Measures and their Analysis', in Daintith, T. (ed.), *Law as an Instrument of Economic Policy: Comparative and Critical Approaches* (Berlin: Walter de Gruyter, 1988), 350–1; also Breyer, S., *Regulation and Its Reform* (Cambridge, Mass.: Harvard University Press, 1982), especially Chapter 1.

The Analytical Framework

Of course, Chapter One raised the typical arguments as to the weaknesses of the public interest approach, and in particular what Baldwin et al. describe as its tendency to 'understate the extent to which regulation is the product of clashes between different interest groups', 'the degree to which regulatory regimes are established by, and run in, the interests of the economically powerful', 'that regulation often seems to fail to deliver public interest outcomes',[108] and/or experience failures in relation to expertise, efficiency or competence of the regulators.[109] It has been suggested in this chapter that a concept of the public interest which looks beyond economic modelling, but which is instead based explicitly upon the fundamental democratic expectation of equality of citizenship, may avoid many of these problems.

Harden and Lewis identify a need for 'a theory of the public interest that can enhance the rationality of political discourse'.[110] It is to be hoped that if the connections are made and emphasized between the core of the concept of public interest and the concept of citizenship, as a central feature of democratic theory, the public interest will be more clearly defined and better oriented to help with this agenda. It may be that, via this route, enhanced protection for increasingly marginalized collective or community values may also be achieved, thereby better fulfilling the immanent promises of the liberal–democratic settlement. If progress towards a theory of public interest is to be made, attention must be paid to Teubner's observations in the context of his study of the phenomenon of juridification. Teubner observes the tendency within the fields of economy, politics, law, culture and science to be inward-looking, self-referential,[111] and in particular notes an 'inadequate structural coupling of politics, law, and the area of social life'.[112] The model of public interest proposed here attempts to address this issue, making explicit some of these connections.

It should be clear from Chapter One that much so-called public interest regulatory intervention into private activity is justified by reference to an economic belief in the efficacy of competitive market forces. Without either supporting or opposing this premise, it is possible to argue, as can perhaps be inferred from Breyer, that such an economics-based model tends to emphasize 'output' rather than social 'outcomes'.[113] In order to add anything to this economic formula, a meaningful concept of public interest must incorporate a broader set of values; if not, it will add nothing to the economics/competition-based approach and the market relations thus fostered, other than a (possibly spurious) air of legitimacy.

[108] Baldwin, Scott, and Hood, *Reader on Regulation*, 9.
[109] Baldwin and Cave, *Understanding Regulation*, 19–21.
[110] Harden and Lewis, *The Noble Lie*, 44.
[111] Teubner, G., *Juridification of Social Spheres* (Berlin: Walter de Gruyter, 1987), extracts in Baldwin, R., Scott, C., and Hood, C. (eds.), *A Reader on Regulation* (Oxford: Oxford University Press, 1998), 407.   [112] Ibid., 408.
[113] Breyer, *Regulation and its Reform*.

In effect, what all this leads towards is an argument for a vision of public interest which builds upon and reflects other aspects of the liberal–democratic settlement. While the operation of markets, in the service of private property holding, do form part of this settlement, there is a wider set of expectations, relating to democracy, that also form part of the basis for the political and constitutional systems' claims to legitimacy. Though it is clear that market forces are valued exceptionally highly in the modern era, central to the core democratic values are expectations of citizenship, and in particular expectations of equality of citizenship.

One problem here, however, is that the emphasis on market forces, in an era in which individualism is given strong emphasis and the public sphere much diminished, may lead to a heavily individualized notion of citizenship. This same emphasis on market forces which allows the affluent to dominate society while others are 'socially excluded', is likely to, in the absence of countervailing forces, diminish any meaningful sense of equality of citizenship which must surely form a central element of 'the minimal value structures that define the society'.[114]

Thus, there is a significant potential for a concept of the public interest which harnesses these broader democratic values to act as a force which reaffirms the overall liberal–democratic settlement, acting as a counterbalance to the current dominance of individualism and property over collective values. There are limited examples of how legal intervention may effectively promote certain claims of public interest,[115] and of representative bodies obtaining standing to pursue actions in pursuit of public interest objectives. However, such examples should ultimately be categorized as perpetuating, rather than challenging, an individualized notion of law, and fail to go even a small way towards developing the kind of public interest agenda, referred to earlier, identified by Griffith back in 1985.[116]

If a concept of the public interest is to add anything to political or legal discourse in the context of regulation, it must therefore incorporate a broader range of interests and values. It has the potential to redress the balance of the liberal–democratic settlement away from its current emphasis on individual rights and especially the power of private property in the marketplace (into which it will often be translated), towards a range of collective and community concerns, which, though properly part of the settlement, are presently heavily marginalized. Of course, in a different era, perhaps one where the collective values were being given undue precedence over individual liberties or the interests of capital, the public interest might properly be invoked to represent those marginalized interests. This falls within what Sunstein identifies as a 'countercultural' constitutional function.[117] Clearly, therefore, the historically changing nature of such

---

[114] Held, *Public Interest and Individual Interests*, 187.
[115] See Cooper and Dhavan, *Public Interest Law*; Whyte, *Social Inclusion*; and, Goodie; and Wickham, 'Calculating Public Interest'. [116] Griffith, 'Judicial Decision Making'.
[117] Sunstein, C. R., *Free Markets and Social Justice* (Oxford: Oxford University Press, 1997), 8.

a concept of public interest must be seen as inevitable. However, rather than appearing problematic, this ability to morph so as to fit changed circumstances, while retaining core values, might be seen as a strength.

If we now reflect on the difficulties explored in Chapter One, of the dominance of preponderance and common interest accounts of the public interest which tend to serve crude majoritarianism, it becomes clear that such a limited vision of the public interest fails to serve as any sort of counterbalance to temporarily dominant groups. Worse than that, the claim to act in the public interest may be relegated to being one of the spoils going to the victor of political struggle, with dominant political groups being permitted to claim legitimacy for their actions and policies in its name. As such, it may serve only to facilitate the representation of their group interests as the general interest. If, however, it has foundations established within the core values of liberal democracy, for example citizenship expectations, it will have normative foundations independent of temporarily dominant value sub-sets. As such, it would be less vulnerable to capture by those temporarily in power, and might, in effect, become a powerful force of opposition, seeking to maintain the equilibrium of the liberal–democratic settlement, and avoiding its distortion or manipulation too far in favour of one particular set of values.

Macpherson observes that 'the problem which the first liberal-*democratic* thinkers faced, in the nineteenth century, was to find a way of accommodating the pre-democratic liberal tradition of the previous two centuries to the new moral climate of democracy'.[118] It is a version of this problem which in effect underlies present day debates over public interest regulation. What we witness are a series of tensions between the private interests of liberal-individualism, often represented by the power of capital within market systems (strongly protected by the legal system), and the younger but nonetheless democratically central, expectations of equality of citizenship (much less well recognized in law), which may indicate a need to mitigate the inegalitarian outcomes of markets which would otherwise render some less able to act as citizens than others. We will return to what Robertson calls 'the public dimensions of private power'[119] in Part Three.

In the 1980s, McAuslan was quite clear that what he understood as the public interest related to the world view of 'the political and intellectual consensus which produced the welfare state, the mixed economy, and fashioned the political and administrative tools that ran it'.[120] He is quite clear that to 'advance the public interest' is 'to adopt policies and practices which advance the good of all citizens directly or indirectly'.[121] Since the time that McAuslan voiced these

[118] Macpherson, C. B., *Democratic Theory: Essays in Retrieval* (Oxford: Oxford University Press, 1973), 5, original emphasis.
[119] Robertson, M., 'Liberal, Democratic, and Socialist Approaches to the Public Dimensions of Private Property', in McLean, J. (ed.), *Property and the Constitution* (Oxford: Hart Publishing, 1999), 256.
[120] McAuslan, P., 'Public Law and Public Choice', *Modern Law Review*, 51/6 (1988), 681, at 687.
[121] Ibid., 688.

views, there is no doubt that trends towards political emphasis on individualism have continued apace, serving to challenge further the collective elements he identified. Within the modern liberal–democratic settlement, which includes the remainders of what McAuslan identified as the welfare state and the current version of what can be called 'the regulatory state', the proper objective must be to design public interest institutions, such as regulation, that represent the whole broad set of values which underlie that settlement, rather than only currently fashionable, liberal-individualist, aspects of liberal–democratic philosophy.

The form of such institutions, and its relationship to their function, should not be overlooked as an issue, and will be explored in the next two chapters, and again, in a wider context, in Chapter Seven. Majone points us towards the contrasting trans-Atlantic historical traditions in terms of forms of regulatory intervention. While the American tradition has been one of regulation via independent agencies, in Britain and Europe, public ownership, in the form of nationalization or municipalization, once served as what he sees as the 'functional equivalent', sharing the objective of protecting 'the public interest against powerful private interests'.[122] As Majone observes,[123] there is a world of difference between replacing market criteria because an alternative, such as nationalization, is considered preferable, and regulating a market, which implicitly recognizes the value of the market and that it is appropriate as a means of delivering that service. In the present era, it is a virtually unquestioned belief that market forces are the best way to deliver goods and services. That said, as stated earlier, the manner in which markets operate will, by their nature, tend to produce results more favourable to those who are able to exert most power in the marketplace.[124] Thus, in an era in which market principles are increasingly adopted in the supply of services which relate intimately to the ability to act as a citizen (for example health care, or education, or access to communications and media) it will be necessary to ensure that the operation of such markets, or quasi-markets, does not tend to reproduce or exaggerate inequalities in the ability to enjoy expectations of citizenship.[125] As Lewis notes,[126] regulatory intervention is often in effect targeted at 'containing the externalities produced by imperfect

---

[122] Majone, G., 'The Rise of the Regulatory State in Europe', *West European Politics*, 17 (1994), 77, reproduced in Baldwin, Scott, and Hood, *Reader on Regulation*, 193. Asimow, M., 'Delegated Legislation: United States and United Kingdom', *Oxford Journal of Legal Studies*, 3/2 (1983), 253, at 270, also identifies the greater emphasis on regulatory structure in the US as a consequence of the political aversion to nationalization.   [123] Majone, 'Rise of the Regulatory State', 196.

[124] Consider Galanter, M., 'Why the "Haves" Come Out Ahead: Speculations on the Limits of Legal Change', *Law and Society Review*, 9/1 (Fall) (1974), 95.

[125] See generally Le Grand, J., 'Quasi Markets and Social Policy', *Economic Journal*, 101 (1991), 1256, and for a more detailed account, Le Grand, J., *Quasi-Markets and Social Policy* (Basingstoke: Macmillan, 1993). For a study of the introduction of market forces into state education, see Feintuck, M., *Accountability and Choice in Schooling* (Buckingham: Open University Press, 1994), especially 46–51.

[126] Lewis, N., 'Markets, Regulation and Citizenship: a Constitutional Analysis', in Brownsword, R. (ed.), *Law and the Public Interest* (Proceedings of the 1992 ALSP Conference) (Stuttgart: Franz Steiner, 1993), 126–7.

markets', or 'justified by the need to create surrogates for the working of competitive markets where conditions do not permit the real thing'. However, Breyer[127] notes that the concept of externalities or spillovers only becomes useful where a monetary value can be attached to the commodity in question, which will not necessarily be the case with some of the citizenship-impacting markets identified above. In practice, of course, as Lewis properly observes, 'Much regulation is quite unrelated to the economist's need to provide surrogates for competitive markets, and in fact is based on the theme that certain rights are so important that they should prevail over the working of even "perfect" markets.'[128] The model of 'social regulation' identified by Baldwin et al.,[129] and referred to by Prosser,[130] would fall into this category. The myth told by proponents of exclusively economic regulation, that economic goals are objective, and therefore suitable for pursuit by regulators, while social objectives are subjective, and can properly be pursued only by elected governments, is convincingly disposed of by Graham, who points towards the very obvious differences in the range of schools of thought and values subsumed within the term 'economics', and questions the real extent to which electoral and other mechanisms are necessarily substantively stronger in relation to government than to a properly accountable regulator.[131]

Brownsword observes that 'governance in the public interest must be conceived of as a quest and a claim for legitimate governance',[132] and implied by this approach is both the democratic expectation of the absence of unlimited power, and also the necessity to legitimate such regulatory intervention which does take place in relation to, in the terms established in Chapter One, 'objectives valued by the community'. In Milne's terms, 'The principle of "social responsibility" ... puts community-members under an obligation to give precedence to its interest over their personal and sectional interests', with the implication being that the community is therefore entitled 'through agents acting on its behalf to control and direct the activities of its members to the extent that this is required by the community's interests'.[133] Thus, the quest must be for institutions which mesh with the underlying democratic foundations (the value-set inherent in the liberal democratic settlement), but which protect community interests by running counter to narrower, temporarily dominant or hegemonic interest group values.

In the terms of American scholar Richard Stewart, 'In a liberal society, institutional design must protect liberal principles against subversion by the

[127] Breyer, *Regulation and its Reform.*
[128] Lewis, 'Markets, Regulation and Citizenship', 127.
[129] Baldwin, Scott and Hood, *Reader on Regulation*, 41. See also Ch. 1, above.
[130] Prosser, *Law and the Regulators.*
[131] See Graham, *Regulating Public Utilities*, 23–7.
[132] Brownsword, R., 'Law and the Public Interest', in Brownsword, R. (ed.), *Law and the Public Interest* (Proceedings of the 1992 ALSP Conference) (Stuttgart: Franz Steiner, 1993), 11.
[133] Milne, 'Political Controversy and the Judges', 45.

private economic and ideological forces that shape regulatory policy.'[134] The
risk identified is commonly known as 'capture' of the regulatory agenda by
particular interest groups. It is only proper here to acknowledge Hancher and
Moran's thesis on regulatory space, and in particular their subtle understanding
of the interplay between public and private interests,[135] which may be thought to
represent reality more accurately than apparently straightforward 'capture' theories. Similarly, Harden and Lewis's emphasis on the compenetration of state and
society seems to offer a more telling view than do traditional accounts describ-
ing deceptively clear-cut sounding public/private divides.[136] However, one does
not need to subscribe to any particular one of these approaches in order to
agree that private interests will be able to exert some degree of influence within
the regulatory sphere. Thus, with market forces threatening what Stewart calls
'non-commodity values', and with the regulatory agenda potentially shaped by
private interests, it falls to lawyers, as guardians of the constitution, and within
their particular local constitutional tradition,[137] to be charged with the difficult
task of designing institutions that protect the wider liberal–democratic value-set.
In effect, it has been argued in this chapter that, though controversies will remain
as regards the precise nature and extent of community interests, a normatively
based concept of public interest could act, after Sunstein, as an 'interpretive
principle',[138] one such 'institution' with the potential to act as a doctrine of
restraint, limiting potential excesses of both public and private power by reference to fundamental values, in the protection of basic democratic expectations
such as equality of citizenship.

In this connection, by way of summary, what might a developed concept of the
public interest bring, which is not already adequately covered by human rights,
or citizenship, or existing concepts of social regulation? Essentially, three claims
can be made.

First, that in making explicit the connections between law and the values
inherent in the political philosophy of liberal democracy, it serves to facilitate Teubner's objective[139] of strengthening the structural coupling of these
fields of endeavour, repairing some of the 'bifurcation' between technical and
philosophical concerns.[140] Second, that it gives due prominence to the marginalized values of community, restraining the ongoing political trend to give
absolute prominence to the values of individualism and capital, and helping
to address the tendency of common law systems to individualize issues. Third,
that it provides a coherent justification for social regulation that is clearly and

---

[134] Stewart, R. B., 'Regulation in a Liberal State: the Role of Non-Commodity Values', *Yale Law
Journal*, 92 (1983), 1537, at 1587.
[135] Hancher, L. and Moran, M., 'Organizing Regulatory Space', in Hancher and Moran,
Capitalism, Culture and Economic Regulation, 274.
[136] Harden and Lewis, *The Noble Lie*, 56–62.
[137] See Hancher and Moran, 'Organizing Regulatory Space', 282.
[138] Sunstein, *After the Rights Revolution*, 158–9 and Ch. 5.
[139] Teubner, *Juridification of Social Spheres*.
[140] Minor, 'Public Interest and Ultimate Commitment'.

unashamedly independent of reliance on justifications for intervention based on market economics.

Given the functional centrality of formal law in implementing and enforcing such norms in *Gesellschaft* and bureaucratic-administrative systems, it will inevitably be necessary to give the concept a legal form. Though this poses certain challenges for lawyers, as was indicated above, it should not offer insuperable difficulties. As Bell suggests,[141] if legislators and judges are able to state and interpret fundamental principles of human rights, it might be expected that they should also be able to develop an enforceable and meaningful concept of the public interest which is independent of, and serves as a restraint on, the powerful. Evidence as to the extent to which those who regulate, and the legal systems they operate under, have effectively done this will be considered in the next three chapters, before some conclusions are reached in the final part of this book as to how a meaningful concept of the public interest may be further nurtured in the context of law and regulation, and may in turn serve to sustain democratic values.

[141] Bell, 'Policy or Principle', 34.

PART II
CASE STUDIES OF PUBLIC INTEREST REGULATION

3

The Public Interest in Regulatory Practice: the UK

The previous two chapters have sought to unpack at a theoretical level, what might be meant by the term 'the public interest', and to consider in outline and generally abstract terms how objectives related to the concept might be protected and furthered. It is hoped that they served to establish a mode of thinking about the public interest which avoids many of the pitfalls of common interest and preponderance approaches to the subject, and seeks to move beyond a predominantly economic and individualistic focus in order to reflect and serve the wider set of citizenship-related and community-oriented values promised within the liberal–democratic settlement. In this and the next chapter, an attempt will be made to consider at a practical level, the extent to which substantive public interest values are present and identified in current regulatory activity, and how regulatory procedures serve, or fail to serve, these values.

There will be no attempt to be comprehensive or even expansive in the survey of current regulatory activity. Rather, a primary focus will be maintained upon a small number of examples which most clearly illustrate the public interest issues identified earlier. While some readers may therefore be disappointed by the absence of detailed consideration of their particular area of interest, it is hoped that the analytical approach adopted in the case studies may be adopted and applied in other areas where public interest issues arise.

The particular fields chosen for study, in this chapter in the context of the UK and in the next in the USA, are regulation of the food industries and of the mass media. Though briefer discussion will also be had, and comparisons made with, other areas of regulation, these two areas raise with particular clarity the kind of issues identified previously as lying at the heart of discussions of the public interest. They incorporate matters of concern from the perspective of citizenship, and collective as well as individual interests, and, especially important in the present deregulatory climate, questions regarding the extent of legitimate regulatory intervention in relation to commercial activity in areas of rapid change and development. This simple structure will allow for comparisons to be drawn between regulators and their practices within each jurisdiction, and also, in Chapter Five, for Anglo-American comparisons to be made in order to consider whether and how, despite their shared democratic and common law heritage, the substantial difference in constitutional tradition of the two countries is of significance in this context.

After brief introductory sections in this chapter, which establish the context in terms of the constitutional and legal background and of 'social regulation' of the utility industries in the UK, each of the case studies will follow a very similar pattern. Following an identification of the kinds of public interest issues raised in the particular regulatory context, a brief history will be given of the development of the recent and present regulatory structure, before an analysis is undertaken of how, in practice, the regulatory mechanisms address public interest concerns, and the extent to which they effectively further such values. In conjunction with the material in Part One, the case studies will provide the basis for an attempt in the final Part of the book to draw conclusions as to how public interest values might most effectively be embedded in regulatory practice.

The Constitutional and Administrative Law Context

Of course, the constitutional and administrative traditions of the UK and USA differ dramatically. To a substantial extent, such differences can be accounted for by the existence of the explicit terms of the Constitution and Bill of Rights in the US, compared with the uncodified amalgam of statute, common law, treaty, custom and convention which structures British constitutional arrangements. Certainly, the position in the US, with the Supreme Court as the unchallenged guardian of the Constitution, may seem to have contributed significantly to the much more apparent role of administrative law in debate over regulation when compared with the UK. Though there are honourable exceptions, which are drawn upon in this book, British public lawyers have in general not focused on regulation as a theme in its own right to the same extent as their American counterparts. Whether such factors have resulted in one system offering better protection for public interest values than the other is a matter to be explored in Chapter Five, following discussion of the individual case studies.

It should be made clear from the outset that the concept of supremacy or sovereignty of Parliament, along with the Rule of Law traditionally presented as the twin pillars of the British constitution, may well serve to inhibit the ability of the courts to intervene in relation to regulatory activity. In particular, the perceived constitutional impropriety of the British judiciary reviewing the substance of primary legislation seems to have led to a broader position, whereby the judiciary will seek at almost any cost to confine its decisions to the procedure of administrative decision-making rather than risking giving the slightest appearance of reviewing the substance of decisions. Though it might be argued that certain recent developments in British public law indicate something of a shift away from this traditional position,[1] it remains the dominant approach, and current government proposals to establish a 'Supreme Court' look likely to be structural reforms rather than any fundamental change to the constitutional powers of the highest courts.

A further feature of the British administrative law framework which must be borne in mind throughout, is the traditional lack of specialism within the British judicial structure. Reflecting Dicey's account of the constitution being the result of, and properly protected by, the decisions of 'ordinary' courts of law, in individual cases, and his distrust of the separate system of *droit administratif* found in France, only recently have there even been limited moves towards a true administrative division of the courts. In the context of regulation, Prosser observes that, in relation to the role of the courts as the central institutional feature of early regulation of transport in Britain, 'It is difficult to imagine an approach more likely to make regulation ineffective than to entrust it to the unreformed courts of common law.'[2] Of course, in the modern context the courts would not be expected to take the central role in regulation, but would still have a significant part to play in overseeing and holding to account specialist statutory regulators or self-regulatory bodies. Any problems arising from the courts' lack of expertise in the specific areas being subjected to regulation would thus be somewhat alleviated, given that their primary concern would therefore be with legal principle rather than the technicalities of the subject matter being regulated. However, the courts may still make less impact than might be anticipated, even in relation to the establishment of procedural requirements if, as a result of adherence to the concept of parliamentary supremacy, they were to be overly deferential to the extremely broad grants of discretion made to some regulators, and failed to establish a framework of principle within which judges could properly exercise their powers, or arguably their duties, to hold regulators to account. While there may also be a range of issues arising from the difficulties of the polycentric nature of many disputes over regulation being sent for resolution in the traditional, adversarial, bipartite dispute resolution of the British courts,[3] it remains true that 'At the heart of the British conception of administrative law lies the power of the ordinary courts to review the activities of public authorities.'[4] It is therefore perhaps disappointing, though unsurprising, to find that in Britain, 'Historically, judicial review has nevertheless had a relatively small impact on regulation, a consequence no doubt of the Diceyan tradition of administrative law which concentrates on the protection of individual

---

[1] See Craig, P. P., *Administrative Law* (5th edn.) (London: Sweet and Maxwell, 2003), 632–8. Consider also Jowell, J. and Lester, A., 'Beyond *Wednesbury*: Substantive Principles of Administrative Law', *Public Law*, 1987, Autumn, 368, and, Elliott, M. C., 'The Human Rights Act 1998 and the Standard of Substantive Review', *Cambridge Law Journal*, 60/2 (2001), 301.

[2] Prosser, T., *Law and the Regulators* (Oxford: Clarendon, 1997), 183.

[3] See, for example, Griffith, J. A. G., 'Judicial Decision Making in Public Law', *Public Law*, 1985, Winter 565.

[4] Ogus, A., *Regulation: Legal Form and Economic Theory* (Oxford: Clarendon, 1994), 115.

rights against illegitimate government interference and thereby largely shuns a functionalist concern with public purposes.'[5]

If, as Prosser suggests, regulators are in fact 'governments in miniature', it is democratically necessary for some body to establish the constitutional and administrative law framework, to set the internal structures and external parameters, within which such 'governments' act.[6] It may therefore be surprising, and of some concern in relation to the accountability of those exercising broad discretionary powers, to find that 'British regulators in general have been remarkably free from judicial interventions'.[7] Certainly, as will be seen in relation to expert bodies such as the Independent Television Commission (ITC), the track record of the British courts in relation to expert regulators indicates a tendency towards a deferential, rather than dynamic, judicial role which is unpromising in this respect. This will be returned to in Chapter Five, but the reader is asked to bear this context in mind as the UK case studies unfold.

REGULATION IN PURSUIT OF SOCIAL OBJECTIVES

As was noted in Chapter One, corporate bodies are frequently found to exercise powers which, by their nature or degree, are able to impact upon the ability of individuals or groups to enjoy their expectations of citizenship. We will now consider some areas of commercial and regulatory activity where values closely related to the public interest might appear to underlie intervention in the UK, even though the concept is not necessarily referred to as such. Only brief treatment is necessary, as the areas are reasonably well trodden.

In general, beyond areas subject to special regulatory regimes, such as the media, corporate power is relatively unconstrained by the context of company law within which it operates, it being considered that incursions into the economic liberty of corporations, an intrusion into the exercise of private property rights, must be justified in the strongest possible terms.[8] The likes of employment, health and safety, and consumer law provisions, and for that matter the law of contract and torts, may serve to impose outer limits on the lawful activities of companies in respect of specific evils, and tend to offer remedies to particular individuals affected directly by a company's actions. Insofar as such interventions may be seen as having the intention of rectifying some of the consequences of inequality of bargaining power,[9] this constitutes a very direct form of social regulation. In addition, regulation of issues such as monopoly power and market

---

[5] Ogus, A., *Regulation: Legal Form and Economic Theory* (Oxford: Clarendon, 1994), 115.

[6] Prosser, *Law and the Regulators*, 305.

[7] Baldwin, R. and Cave, M., *Understanding Regulation: Theory, Strategy and Practice* (Oxford: Oxford University Press, 1999), 298.

[8] See, generally Parkinson, J., *Corporate Power and Responsibility* (Oxford: Clarendon, 1996) and Parkinson, J., Gamble, A., and Kelly, G. (eds.), *The Political Economy of the Company* (Oxford: Hart, 2000). [9] Ogus, *Regulation*, 4–5.

failure generally, the central thrust of competition law seeks to protect the perceived economic interests of society within a capitalist system. Though voluntary initiatives under the headings of 'Corporate Social Responsibility' or 'Corporate Citizenship' will be considered in Chapter Seven, it can be argued that, in general, such interventions do little by way of protecting society's collective interest from any potentially citizenship-harming, and therefore anti-democratic, exercise of economic power by companies.[10]

That said, there is in Britain a very definite tradition of social regulation, addressing issues beyond market failure and the like, which extends beyond the examples of food supply and media industries which are the focus of this chapter. Generally speaking, it is in the area of utilities, where regulation is the successor (and in Majone's terms, noted in Chapter Two, perhaps the 'functional equivalent')[11] to public ownership as the preferred mode of intervention in such fields, and where social objectives may clearly be found to inform the regulatory agenda.

In relation to the utility industries such as power, water, and basic telecommunications at least, Graham notes that, 'In one sense they are just providing services for consumers, which those consumers pay for, like any other product or service in the marketplace. However, access to these services is a taken for granted aspect of modern society... These are basic needs that any person has if they want to participate in modern society.'[12] Thus, even here, there may be some confusion as to whether regulatory intervention is primarily market/economics-oriented or premised on some broader social objective. Graham summarizes the underlying difficulty as regards the relationship between an individual and a utility service, asking 'is it a matter of commodity or citizenship?'[13] Prosser,[14] however, notes how, though there appears to be a high degree of overlap between mainstream economic rationales for regulation and some of the consumer-oriented provisions contained in the regulation of utility industries, there are also distinctively *social* rationales, given particular legal form, which clearly take the regulatory endeavour beyond economics and into social regulation. Thus, the kind of Universal Service Obligations which may be imposed upon utility industries derive from fundamentally egalitarian principles, being 'justified by the need to provide access to public services for all groups regardless of their place in the distribution of incomes',[15] or to 'permit as wide a range of social groups to participate in the services provided in a given society'.[16] Discussing

---

[10] See Leys, C., *Market-Driven Politics: Neoliberal Democracy and the Public Interest* (London: Verso, 2001). For impressive, but somewhat polemical accounts, see Hertz, N., *The Silent Takeover: Global Capitalism and the Death of Democracy* (London: Arrow Books, 2002), and Monbiot, G., *Captive State: the Corporate Takeover of Britain* (London: Macmillan, 2000).

[11] Majone, G., 'The Rise of the Regulatory State in Europe', *West European Politics*, 17 (1994), 77, in Baldwin et al., *A Reader on Regulation*, 193.

[12] Graham, C., *Regulating Public Utilities: a Constitutional Approach* (Oxford: Hart, 2000), 192.

[13] Ibid., at 63.   [14] Prosser, *Law and the Regulators*, 13.   [15] Ibid., at 14.

[16] Ibid., at 15, drawing on Stewart, R. 'Regulation in a Liberal State: the Role of Non-Commodity Values', *Yale Law Journal*, 92 (1983), 1537.

the question of poverty, in the context of regulating utilities, Graham notes that 'Although the legislative duties do not single out low-income consumers explicitly, there are duties to represent the interests of consumers generally and of certain groups, such as the elderly and disabled, who will have a higher proportion of low-income consumers amongst them and this legitimates a certain level of regulatory intervention.'[17] Such distributive rationales for regulation, whether explicit or implicit within the legal framework, may appear to distinguish social regulation properly-so-called from measures such as those found in competition law, justified primarily by reference to market efficiency, which may incidentally or contingently serve 'social' purposes. These distributive rationales appear to relate closely to the kind of public service obligation traditionally associated with broadcasting in the UK, to be discussed shortly, and should properly be identified as having very close, if not always clearly articulated, connections with a citizenship agenda.

However, in Britain,[18] the citizenship-related interests incorporated into the regulatory agenda for utilities is often less apparent than it might be as a result of the social objectives being pursued being expressed or framed primarily in terms of *individual* rights or interests. Given the historical lack of recognition in Britain for group claims, noted in Part One, such an approach should be unsurprising, but does form something of a conceptual obstacle to the development of a legally enforceable vision of public interest, given the strong collective element generally found in public interest discourse.

The area of environmental regulation, as noted in Chapter Two, can be considered perhaps the *locus classicus* of the collective nature of public interest claims, relating very obviously to both present and future generations of citizens, and taking on many of the characteristics of a 'public good' where the interests of one individual cannot readily be separated from the interests of the group. In an area such as land-use planning there will indeed be 'various stakeholders in the process – developers, local authorities and third parties who wish to object to specific proposals',[19] but beyond this there will also be wider and longer-term interests for society as a whole. One response of the UK government, in its 2001 Green Paper,[20] was to emphasize the necessity for widespread participation in an apparent attempt to address or ameliorate conflicts between the ideologies of 'private property, public interest and public participation'.[21] While such participatory measures may certainly enhance procedural legitimacy, they may not necessarily speak to the substantive issues.

[17] Graham, *Regulating Public Utilities*, 58.
[18] See Prosser, *Law and the Regulators*, 287–92, for comparisons with France and Italy, where clear concepts of 'public service law' can be identified. See also below, Ch. 7.
[19] Parry, N. D., 'Delivering Fundamental Change in Planning: A Threat to the Environment?', *European Public Law*, 8/3 (2002), 349, at 350.
[20] *Planning: Delivering Fundamental Change* (London: HMSO, 2001).
[21] See McAuslan, P., *The Ideologies of Planning Law* (Oxford: Pergamon, 1980).

In seeking to fulfil potentially competing, 'environmental, social and economic purposes',[22] the legislative framework for planning will inevitably incorporate inherent tensions, and, at different historic moments, different choices will be made as to priorities. For example, Parry observes[23] how the Select Committee Report[24] into the 2001 Green Paper concluded that the proposals had largely ignored environmental issues while supporting business development. In the process of resolving such competing claims, collective values will remain extremely vulnerable to better-established individual, property-related claims, in the absence of some principle which requires such factors to be given a degree of priority;[25] a problem observable again later in this chapter in the discussion of citizenship values in relation to the media. Though we will discuss the 'precautionary principle', of increasingly wide application as a mechanism of risk management,[26] in the context of food policy and regulation, it is more established, and central, in the realm of environmental debate than any other area.[27] However, it is necessary to consider whether the precautionary principle may seem ultimately to fail to establish any system of substantive, as opposed to procedural, values which might assist in this respect.

In summary, it is clear that though the forms it takes will vary, regulation in pursuit of social objectives associated with the public interest is reasonably commonplace and recognized in areas such as the utilities and the environment. However, it is equally clear that the values represented by such interventions are generally poorly specified and are therefore likely to remain vulnerable to the play of interest group pressures.

THE PUBLIC INTEREST IN REGULATING THE FOOD INDUSTRIES – THE FOOD STANDARDS AGENCY

The Range of Interests

It might be thought that what constitutes the public interest in the food supply industries would be immediately apparent. At the level of the lowest common denominator, a reliable and safe food supply would appear to fit comfortably within the kind of model of public interest associated with 'common interest' theories discussed in Chapter One. However, even the briefest second glance

[22] Parry, 'Delivering Fundamental Change', 355.   [23] Ibid., at footnote 16.
[24] *Report of the Select Committee on Transport, Local Government and the Regions*, July 2002, HC 476-I.
[25] See Goodie, J. and Wickham, G., 'Calculating "Public Interest": Common Law and the Legal Governance of the Environment', *Social and Legal Studies*, 11/1 (2002), 37.
[26] See Morris, J. (ed.), *Rethinking Risk and the Precautionary Principle* (Oxford: Butterworth-Heinemann, 2000), for a wide range of examples of the principle's application.
[27] See, generally, Harremoës, P., Gee, D., MacGarvin, M., Stirling, A., Keys, J., Wynne, B., and, Guedes Vaz, S. (eds.), *The Precautionary Principle in the 20th Century: Late Lessons from Early Warnings* (London: Earthscan, 2002).

will reveal a range of competing group interests, not all of which can be accommodated comfortably within such a construct.

The UK food industries consist of a wide range of food producers and retailers, large and small, and generalist or specialist (for example organic producers and retailers, or retailers serving a particular ethnic group), which, though generally sharing a clear primary motive in profitability, will have sufficiently differing priorities and objectives to render it unwise to represent these sectors as a monolithic whole. Beyond the retail sector, importers and exporters of foodstuffs will have their own, often competing or conflicting interests. The food industries supply a vast range of diverse products, from staple, basic foodstuffs at one end of the spectrum, to novelty products, snack-foods and luxury goods at the other, some of which might properly be compared more with aspects of the leisure industry than food properly-so-called. As regards food production, the use of novel scientific techniques and new farming and production methods, most obviously perhaps the utilization of genetically modified organisms (GMOs), may appear to raise the spectre of science's 'growing innovative powers increasingly outweighing its capacity to anticipate the consequences',[28] posing a potentially significant threat which we might reasonably expect regulation to address.

The UK government, via Parliament, the source of regulatory authority, has a proper interest in the basics of a reliable food supply, together with public health and nutrition, but also, inevitably, has an eye to the food industries as part of the broader economic and industrial policy scene. The underlying challenge for the government is 'how to integrate environmental and human health with a vibrant food economy'.[29] A critical factor in government policy over recent years has been the attempt to maintain public confidence in food, in the face of a wide range of crises, from bovine spongiform encephalopathy (BSE), to salmonella and E-coli, and most recently the foot and mouth disease (FMD) epidemic, plus concerns over novel products, and in particular genetically modified (GM) foodstuffs. Competition and overlap between government departments such as the Department for the Environment, Food and Rural Affairs (DEFRA), the Department of Trade and Industry (DTI) and the Department of Health (DoH), and clashes between their priorities and even perhaps their cultures, may parallel and illustrate the wider tensions between competing claims as to 'the public interest' in the food industries.

To a greater or lesser extent, identifiably separate from the political interests of the government of the day are the bureaucratic, administrative and institutional interests of the national and sub-national agencies that exercise statutory powers in relation to food safety legislation, and which also supply information and advice to central government. Central to this process, and the focus here, is

---

[28] Davies, S., 'The Precautionary Principle and Food Policy', *Consumer Policy Review*, 12/2 (2002), 65, at 66.

[29] Lang, T. and Rayner, G., 'Food and Health Strategy in the UK: a Policy Impact Analysis', *Political Quarterly*, 74/1 (2003), 66.

the Food Standards Agency (FSA), a national body which prides itself on its independence from government. However, note must also be made of the Advisory Committees,[30] operating under the FSA's umbrella, that have a particular brief for the constituent parts of the UK, and also the crucial role of local agencies, the Environmental Health Departments of local authorities, to which much of the day-to-day responsibility for enforcement is entrusted.

The final interest group to be considered is those at the end of the food supply-chain, who buy and use the products. Their interests will include not being misled in relation to the food they buy, and not being directly harmed by it, plus, inevitably, the central consumerist expectations of choice as to what they buy and 'value for money', and the taste, appearance and other qualities of foodstuffs, including their convenience in purchase and preparation. Though individuals and groups might emphasize different aspects of the consumerist agenda, everyone in the country (excluding perhaps any truly self-sufficient individuals) will share them. However, beyond these consumerist expectations lies a further range of interests in which all also share, but which are highlighted only when the language of consumerism is substituted by that of citizenship.

Citizenship, as discussed in the previous chapter, implying as it does the ability of all to play an active part in the liberal–democratic social enterprise, raises a range of potential claims as regards the food industries. Citizens are likely to share the demand of consumers for choice, but will tend to emphasize beyond this the need for fully educated and informed choice, and for meaningful choice, as opposed to the superficial choice offered by a range of products largely undifferentiated by anything other than their label, packaging, and perhaps price. Citizens will be concerned not only with the consumer's interest in food safety, avoiding immediate harm caused by the consumption of an individual product, but will also have longer-term concerns as regards the nutritional quality of food products, and also, beyond the consumer's concern with 'value for money', will stress the ready availability of a range of nutritionally sound foodstuffs at a price affordable by all. Thus, rather than the immediate self-interest which typifies the consumerist perspective, citizens will have a wider range of concerns, often longer-term, which may emphasize matters such as education regarding diet and nutrition, and the ability of all to benefit from the bountiful food supply which the UK enjoys. Still further beyond consumerist interests, citizens may have legitimate concerns regarding the production methods employed in the food industries, including environmental issues and sustainability, animal welfare, and social costs arising from production and distribution methods and employment practices, none of which would necessarily be included in, or would at best be marginal to, a consumerist perspective. Thus, while the agenda of consumers will be primarily or exclusively focused on self-interest, that of citizens will encompass a much wider range of concerns.

---

[30] Established under the Food Standards Act 1999, S.5.

At the very heart of this complex web of interests lies the FSA, 'led by a Board, which has been appointed to act in the public interest'.[31] What precisely, if anything, is meant by the use of the term 'public interest' in this context will be discussed below, but for the moment it is worth noting the title of the FSA publication from which the quotation is taken: 'Protecting the Interests of *Consumers*' (emphasis added). Clearly, if the title is indicative of the true focus of the FSA's activities, there is a significant risk that many of the citizenship interests in the food industries identified above, which might properly be thought to form part of a meaningful construct of 'the public interest', will, if not protected by other agencies, fail to be supported at all, or will at best be subjugated to the consumerist agenda.

Origins of the FSA

The genesis of the FSA began prior to the election of the New Labour government in 1997 when, while still in opposition, and in the context of ongoing concerns over the safety of beef, and E-coli food poisoning, Tony Blair commissioned a report from Professor Philip James of the Rowett Research Institute, Aberdeen. The key recommendation of the James Report was to transfer the main responsibility for food policy from the Ministry for Agriculture, Fisheries and Food (MAFF)[32] to the DoH, in order to 'remove the apparent conflict between public health and business interests'.[33] Historically, MAFF had been charged with the primary responsibility for safety in food production, yet had also been seen as having a significant role in 'sponsoring', or supporting the interests of the UK food production industry on the domestic and world-trade stage. MAFF was seen as having been 'responsible for working with farmers to promote British agricultural produce [while] at the same time being responsible for its safety'.[34] Thus, the James Report advocated the separation of these roles, and in relation to food safety, proposed the establishment of a 'statutory body governed by a commission and with executive powers analogous to those of the existing Health and Safety Executive'.[35] In response to concerns regarding lack of information relating to the operation of the existing administrative machinery, transparency of the new agency was a major concern. Although the new agency would act formally only in an advisory capacity, its position would be strengthened by the publication of its advice, from which government ministers would have to dissent publicly if they chose not to follow it. Public consultation on the James Report proceeded through 1997, revealing widespread support for the

---

[31] Quoted here from the FSA's leaflet FSA/0001/2001, but also prominent in accounts of the Board's role on the FSA website, www.foodstandards.gov.uk.

[32] MAFF, in the reforms associated with the establishment of the FSA, was subsumed within DEFRA.

[33] Warden, J., 'UK Food Standards Agency Aims to Rebuild Trust in Food', *British Medical Journal*, 17 May 1997, 1433.

[34] Wong, M., 'Playing Piggy in the Middle', *Financial Times*, 31 March 2000.   [35] Ibid.

proposed reforms from the outset, though some concerns were voiced as to how the range of interests within the food industries would be reconciled in practice. For example, the Soil Association, the major UK body for the certification of organic produce and in many ways the most high profile voice of the organic farming movement, actually opposed the proposal, failing to see 'how the new agency could reconcile the wide range of farming standards'.[36]

In essence, there were three major issues underlying the James Report's, and New Labour's, attack on the existing regime: an increase in the occurrence of food poisoning; loss of public confidence in food; and a strong suspicion that MAFF had in practice been favouring producer interests.[37] The last of these issues was highlighted when former Conservative Health Minister Edwina Currie was quoted as saying, in the course of the BSE Inquiry, that 'MAFF seemed to care more about the finances of the farming industry than about human health'.[38] However, inevitably perhaps, the strong rhetoric when in opposition took some time to take practical shape when New Labour came to power. Without doubt, some hesitancy derived from substantial opposition by powerful industry interest groups to the government's intention to fund the new agency via a levy on food outlets. In addition, active intervention in the food industries did not fit easily with the government's essentially non-interventionist philosophy, leading to the suggestion that 'Instead of robustly defending the right of governments to regulate industry, ministers have sought to demonstrate that New Labour is much more friendly to big business than old Labour.'[39] It is interesting to observe how even the more liberal end of the British press, though to an extent critical of New Labour's non-interventionist approach, failed to avoid the trope from the broad interest of citizens to the narrower concerns of consumers: 'Governments must worry less about being accused of fostering a nanny state and more about engaging with increasingly informed consumers.'[40]

Powers and Objectives; Policies and Practices

Consultation on the draft Food Bill ended in March 1999, with the structure of the proposed FSA established in terms of a non-ministerial department, reporting to Parliament via health ministers. The Food Standards Act 1999 passed into law, with the Agency's brief, established in Section 1(2) of the Act in the following terms:

The main objective of the Agency in carrying out its functions is to protect public health from risks which may arise in connection with the consumption of food (including risks caused by the way in which it is produced or supplied) and otherwise to protect the interests of consumers in relation to food.

[36] Green, E., 'Blair Should Listen to the Screamers', *New Statesman*, 11 December 1998, 27.
[37] Dean, M., 'Plans for UK Food Safety Agency go into Reverse', *The Lancet*, 28 November 1998, 1763.   [38] 'The BSE Inquiry: Cull MAFF', *The Economist*, 28 November 1998, 37.
[39] Ibid.   [40] *The Guardian*, 1 June 2001.

Beyond this 'main objective', the Act also specifies 'general functions' for the FSA. Under Sections 6–8 of the Act, in relation to 'matters connected with food safety or other interests of consumers in relation to food', the Agency is charged with developing policies and providing advice, information or assistance in respect of such matters to any public authority,[41] providing advice and information to the general public or any section of the public,[42] and 'obtaining, compiling and keeping under review information'.[43] Parallel functions relating to animal feedingstuffs (*sic*) are introduced under Section 9. In pursuit of these objectives and functions, the Agency is granted powers under Sections 12–16 to monitor the relevant enforcement activities of other authorities. Various powers under other statutes and statutory instruments are granted to the FSA via Section 18 and Schedule 3.

The Act's language, referring on occasion to 'the general public' but generally emphasizing 'consumers', does not bode well if viewed from the perspective of citizenship. Despite the very clear presence of citizenship interests amongst the expectations immanent within the liberal–democratic system, the Act's language might be thought to reflect clearly the lack of prominence for the concept of citizenship in the UK. In addition, though the term 'public interest' is prominent in the Agency's publicity material, noted above, the Act's only direct reference to the concept comes in the very specific context of Section 19(4), where, in determining whether to publish advice or information, 'the Agency must consider whether the public interest in the publication of the advice or information in question is outweighed by any consideration of confidentiality attaching to it'.

In addition to establishing the FSA's 'main objective' and 'general functions', the Act also requires the Agency to 'prepare and publish a statement of general objectives it intends to pursue, and general practices it intends to adopt, in carrying out its functions'.[44] This statement must include the objectives of securing consultation with those affected and where appropriate, members of the public, promoting links with food safety-related authorities, and maintaining and making available records of its decisions and the information on which they are based.[45] In summary form, the FSA has identified its role as being to:

- protect consumers by effective enforcement and monitoring of food safety and standards, in partnership with local authorities and through the work of the Meat Hygiene Service;
- support consumer choice through accurate and meaningful labelling; and,
- provide advice to the public and to government on food safety, food standards and nutrition.[46]

---

[41] Food Standards Act 1999, S.6(1).   [42] Food Standards Act 1999, S.7(1).
[43] Food Standards Act 1999, S.8(1).   [44] Food Standards Act 1999, S.22(1).
[45] Food Standards Act 1999, S.22(2).   [46] FSA/0001/2001.

Heading a twelve-member Board which, as noted earlier, the Agency states has been 'appointed to act in the public interest',[47] the FSA's Chair[48] from the Agency's inception has been Sir John Krebs, a zoologist previously in charge of the National Environmental Research Council. From the very start, the FSA sought to emphasize its transparency in operation, and its efforts to involve a broad spectrum of 'stakeholders' via active consultation processes, the principal stakeholders in this context being identified as 'consumers and consumer organizations, enforcement bodies, the food industry, public bodies, and research organizations'.[49]

The FSA remains essentially London-based,[50] and of an initial London headquarters staff of 500, some 300 were drawn from MAFF (subsequently subsumed within DEFRA), the majority of the remainder coming from the DoH, raising obvious questions as regards the extent to which the FSA could be expected to work within a culture distinct from that of traditional government departments. Despite this apparent degree of continuity, by the time of the FSA taking up its responsibilities in April 2000, there was still substantial opposition to the reforms being voiced by interests within the food manufacturing industry. In particular, the food industry had concerns regarding the apparently wide extent of the FSA's brief in relation to nutrition (as opposed to safety), arguing that the major concerns that had impacted on public confidence in food, such as BSE, salmonella, listeria, and dioxin contamination, were rooted in microbiological rather than nutritional concerns, with the former but not the latter being the proper focus of FSA activity. A representative of the Food and Drink Federation was quoted as identifying nutrition as being linked to 'lifestyle choices', while safety was the concern of everyone.[51] At the same time, the Chartered Institute of Environmental Health identified an ongoing 'tension between the food industry and consumer groups over what the FSA should be'.[52]

Examination of what the FSA actually does may suggest that the food industry had relatively little to fear in respect of a nutritional focus from the Agency. The practical reality is that the majority of the FSA's time and resources seems to be spent dealing with a wide range of safety and consumer information projects, with nutrition appearing relatively low down or marginal to the agenda.[53]

In part, the FSA's apparent emphasis on safety, as opposed to nutrition, is perfectly understandable, given the immediacy of food safety issues compared with nutritional issues. However, Anthony quotes from the James Report, stating that 'Public health analyses show that the nutritional aspects of food quality and safety have a far greater economic and health impact than [microbiological, chemical and genetic modification issues]. The issue of poor nutrition

---

[47] Ibid.   [48] Appointed under S.2(1).   [49] FSA/0001/2001.
[50] The Meat Hygiene Service, established as an executive agency of the FSA, is outposted in York.
[51] *Financial Times*, 31 March 2000.   [52] Ibid.
[53] For example, the Open Board Meetings of 13 February 2003 and 13 March 2003 reveal only one item explicitly focused on nutrition, and that in the specific context of a National Nutrition Strategy for Wales (Minute 17, 13 February 2003).

usually emerges over a longer period and in less dramatic form than the still rare E-coli-induced kidney failure or possible cases of the new variant of CJD.'[54] There is, however, inevitably, more political and popular pressure to produce readily measurable and short-term results rather than longer-term outcomes, potentially reinforcing any tendency to focus on safety rather than nutrition.

In addition to such tensions as that between prioritizing safety or nutrition, there have also been serious concerns voiced regarding the failure of the FSA to fulfill the expectation of cultural change from the MAFF era. Though the FSA sets great store on its openness and accessibility, some have still voiced concerns that there has not been quite the sea-change from previous practices that the Agency's rhetoric might imply. Anthony is highly sceptical as to the extent to which the FSA marks a break with the past, given that the Agency is utilizing the same civil servants and medical and scientific advisers as previously used by MAFF and the Department of Health, 'all of whom had grown used to co-operating closely with the food industry'.[55] Though not necessarily a typical response to the FSA, Anthony's concerns must at least be noted:

[B]ad habits are difficult to eradicate and the FSA does not seem to have shaken free of the previous policies of telling the general public as little as possible so as not to alarm them, of asserting that a food product or component is safe until that is conclusively disproved, and of applying standard reductionist scientific methods to all topics.[56]

Such criticisms, if established, would identify fundamental problems with the FSA. An underlying question is suggested of whether the Agency is sufficiently clear in terms of its priorities: in particular, whether its primary function is to advise government or the general public. Though it might be argued that, within a system of representative democracy, advising government in effect constitutes the same thing as advising the public, this would seem to deny the realities of party politics. In addition, the FSA retains a tricky problem of managing the extent to which it is capable of maintaining co-operation with, but also distance from, the food industries. However, despite such general concerns, and Anthony's more specific complaints, it would not be right to ignore some substantial advances that the FSA seems to have demonstrated in terms of its operational practices.

Two key features appear to distinguish the FSA from the regime which preceded it. First, and probably most significantly, the 1999 Act requires the FSA to act openly: in practice interpreted as acting as openly as possible, subject only to confidentiality.[57] Offering both a degree of protection against capture by interest groups, and potentially improving the quality of decision-making, transparency of operation has long been high on the agendas of public lawyers concerned with ensuring the accountability of public bodies exercising discretionary powers. The FSA, with its largely open Board Meetings, widespread

---

[54] Anthony, H., 'Food Standards Agency – Three Years On', *Journal of Nutritional and Environmental Medicine*, 11 (2001), 101.   [55] Ibid.
[56] Ibid.   [57] Food Standards Act 1999, S.19.

public consultation practices,[58] and willingness to publish advice in a format reasonably readily accessible to the general public (including internet publication), offers many progressive features which would be astonishing to students of British public bodies until very recently. Though retaining a degree of scepticism regarding the actual difference made by the FSA, Millstone and van Zwanenberg note the *potential* for these practices of openness to stop the previously all too common practice of policy-makers hiding behind 'experts',[59] with decisions and statements having been based not so much on 'sound science' as on 'sedation' and 'reassurance';[60] a practice which they suggest may have served primarily the interests of the historical relationship of mutual trust between MAFF and the farming industries.[61]

The second aspect of the FSA's operation which most distinguishes it from the prior arrangements is the Agency's distance from government. Though, as has already been noted, the FSA reports to Parliament via ministers from the DoH, the Agency is not part of any government department as such. This raises questions both as regards whether this 'arm's length' position enhances or reduces the Agency's effectiveness, and also whether in reality the Agency would be more or less accountable to Parliament were it to be directly within the brief of a particular minister. While undoubtedly important in maintaining a perception of independence from the government of the day, Millstone and van Zwanenberg question whether the FSA's constitutional position will ultimately serve either its, or consumers' long-term best interests.[62]

There seem to be significant risks inherent in leaving the nutrition brief shared or split between the FSA and the DoH. It may be either that it will fail to be central to the agenda of either, each having an expectation that the other is doing more than it actually is, or, it may be that nutrition will become the subject of potentially destructive inter-departmental struggles for dominance, distracting from nutritional objectives. The absence of a Minister clearly 'batting for' the FSA in Cabinet may also prove a weakness, especially perhaps in periods where there are no immediate crises keeping food standards at the top of government agendas. What is clear, however, is that the FSA's brief overlaps both DEFRA's ongoing interest in food production, and the DoH's concern with human health and nutrition. When certain types of issues arise, such as pesticide residues in fruit and vegetables, or veterinary medicine residues in meat, there are clearly significant areas in which more than one department or agency may have an interest. A high premium is therefore placed upon the effectiveness of mechanisms of liaison between the FSA and government departments, including formal concordats requiring cross-membership for meetings, and informal mechanisms via daily contact between FSA and DEFRA and other government departments.

---

[58] See, for example, FSA's report on consultation on GMOs: FSA, *Consumer Views of GM Food* (FSA/0841/0703), July 2003.

[59] Millstone, E. and van Zwanenberg, P., 'The Evolution of Food Safety Policy-Making Institutions in the UK, EU and Codex Alimentarius', *Social Policy and Administration*, (2002), 593, at 607.

[60] Ibid., at 599.   [61] Ibid., at 596.   [62] Ibid., at 606.

It is possible, however, that its extra-departmental position and overlapping brief may ultimately prove to be the Agency's real strength, in facilitating 'joined-up government' in relation to food- and health-related issues, permitting a rounded view of the relative costs and benefits of policy options.[63] It is also proper to say that the FSA's practice of publishing its advice to ministers may play a significant role in supporting the democratic interest in the transparency of, and accountability in, ministerial decision-making, given the need for ministers to dissent publicly from advice which they do not intend to follow. It is therefore probably right to say, by way of interim conclusion, that, in combination, the FSA's transparency of operation and distance from government ministers seem to offer some advances on what went before and some guarantee of independence, both from political and food industry interests.

European Food Safety Authority

It is important to note, however, that the FSA does not act entirely in isolation.[64] It is clear that, as Lobstein observes,[65] the EU, especially though not exclusively through the Common Agriculture Policy, has an enormous *potential* to encourage and require food production practices that prioritize safe and healthy food rather than simply production *per se*. Established following a series of food scares across Europe, and in particular the BSE crisis, the European Food Safety Authority (EFSA) may represent a significant development, though the Authority occupies a somewhat curious position in relation to the various food authorities of the Member States.

Appearing to serve primarily as a focal point and clearing house for food-related information from the EU's scientific committees, the effectiveness of the EFSA has been doubted on the grounds of its lack of regulatory and enforcement powers.[66] Given widely differing standards and practices across Member States in relation to the role and powers of food authorities, it might be thought that the EFSA will have some problems in exercising real authority in the absence of it being clearly established as the superior authority. While it might be true to say that 'in the context of the Internal Market, food safety issues need to be dealt with at a higher level than national government agencies',[67] the reality is that the principle of subsidiarity is defended strongly by the governments of Member States, especially where an industrial and commercial sector as important as food is concerned. Thus, the *realpolitik* has demanded that the EFSA has been

---

[63] See Lang and Rayner, 'Food and Health Strategy'.

[64] Note that the Act establishes reserve powers, under S.24(4), allowing the Secretary of State to give directions to the FSA, as appropriate, in pursuit of the implementation of EU treaties or other international agreements.

[65] Lobstein, T., 'Crisis in Agriculture: are we Learning from the Disasters?', *Consumer Policy Review*, 11/3 (2001), 78.

[66] O'Rourke, R., 'Europe Adopts New Approach to Food Safety', *New Law Journal*, (2000), 230.

[67] O'Rourke, R., 'Food Safety', *New Law Journal*, (1998), 1332, at 1333.

established essentially as an advisory body, without the kind of law-making or enforcement powers that might have necessitated potentially controversial amendments to the EU treaties.[68]

Underlying the review of European arrangements were essentially the same issues as those which led to the creation of the UK's FSA, including a series of food scares and crises, and concerns as to the extent to which food safety concerns appeared to risk being subjugated to the interests of the food industries. Wall notes how, again paralleling UK developments, in addition to the EU establishing the EFSA, responsibility for food safety within the European Commission was transferred from the agricultural directorate (DGVI) to consumer protection (DGXXIV), in order to 'shift the emphasis from protecting farmers and the food industry to protecting consumers'.[69] However, Wall also rightly comments on the practical difficulties inherent in separating trade issues from food safety, observing that safety can readily become a marketing issue, with question marks such as those over British beef, or foodstuffs containing GMOs, having the potential to be used as barriers to international trade.[70] There is no doubt, however, that the response of both the UK and EU governments, and for that matter Ireland also,[71] in seeking to establish food safety authorities clearly separated from the food industries and the government departments responsible for them, seems intuitively attractive.

It is early days in terms of reaching conclusions as to the real impact of the EFSA, yet it is obvious that its limited, advisory function may prove ineffective in resolving differences in the practices or standards of national regulatory regimes. On critical issues, it may well be the Commission's Food and Veterinary Office or other agencies or organs, rather than the EFSA, which will exercise real power in this field within the EU. It is unclear, as yet, whether O'Rourke is right to suggest that the ability of Member States to ignore or override EFSA's opinions and recommendations leads properly to 'a fear that the authority could too easily fall into the role of managing food emergencies rather than anticipating them'.[72] What is quite obvious, though, is that in its early years at least, the EFSA had relatively little impact on the activities of the UK FSA.[73] This may seem less

[68] Note, however, that this does not undermine the ability of the European Commission to act in relation to food standards issues, as it did in 1996 when banning the export of UK beef both to other Member States and third countries, as confirmed by the ECJ in *UK v. Commission*, Case C-180/96. Neither does it impact upon more general consumer and product safety legislation emanating from the EU, but rather it is specifically EFSA whose powers are limited in this context.

[69] Wall, P., 'The Food Safety Authority of Ireland', *Consumer Policy Review*, 9/5 (1999), 188, at 189.

[70] See Salmon, N., 'A European Perspective on the Precautionary Principle, Food Safety and the Free Trade Imperative of the WTO', *European Law Review*, 27 (2002), 138.

[71] Ireland was, in 1998 'the first country to adopt the EU principle of separating control of food safety from agriculture and trade at a national level'. Wall, 'The Food Safety Authority of Ireland', 189. [72] O'Rourke, 'Europe Adopts New Approach', 231.

[73] In the course of the Board's meeting on 13th March 2003, and the minutes of the previous meeting on 13th February 2003, there was, perhaps surprisingly, not a single mention of the EFSA, though the European Commission's Food and Veterinary Office (FVO) was referred to.

surprising if it is observed that the EFSA is primarily focused on risk assessment and communication as opposed to risk management, and is intended to consider new matters and issues, while much of the FSA's and its Board's activities relate to risk management and taking action on established and settled issues. Whether the EFSA will come to play a more active role remains to be seen, though it may well remain of less significance than high level inter-governmental decisions on food matters, taken within the mainstream EU fora. What the EFSA will not be, however, at least without major treaty reform, is a federal public health agency in the mould of the US Food and Drugs Administration, to be considered in Chapter Four, and there is a real risk that its role will remain 'ambiguous and indeterminate'.[74]

FSA – Discretion and Risk

But what of early conclusions as to the UK's FSA? Has it proved to be a marked improvement on the previous institutional arrangements, and to what extent can it meaningfully be said to embody or further a concept of public interest?

In considering the regulation of risk in the context of BSE, and the Phillips Report into it published in October 2000, prior to the FSA's establishment, Little[75] identifies some key problem areas with the previous regulatory regime, and suggests that the new arrangements might have gone some way towards remedying these defects. Little challenges a wide range of forms of risk analysis but is particularly sceptical regarding MAFF's presentation of scientific evidence in the context of the apparent conflict of interest between its roles as guardian of food safety and sponsor of the food industry. He identifies MAFF's effectiveness in limiting the risks presented to the public by BSE as having been further hampered by delay and confusion about how to proceed via secondary legislation,[76] and in particular concern, leading to a defensive attitude, arising from the potential for food industry interest groups to seek judicial review of such actions.[77]

Correctly, Little sees the BSE crisis as illustrative of the kind of problem created when complex risks combine with wide discretion and vested, conflicting interests.[78] He discusses the 'absence of effective rules to establish organisational objectives ... and ... the lack of established principles and rules as to how to proceed with risk analysis'.[79] Little suggests that primary legislation is the most appropriate mechanism for establishing 'organisational and general principles',[80] echoing perhaps the Phillips Inquiry conclusion that 'legislation should clearly empower Ministers to take precautionary measures in a situation where the existence of a hazard is uncertain'.[81]

---

[74] Millstone and van Zwanenberg, 'The Evolution of Food Safety', 605.
[75] Little, G., 'BSE and the Regulation of Risk', *Modern Law Review*, 64/5 (2001), 730.
[76] Ibid., 750.   [77] Ibid., 751.   [78] Ibid., 755.   [79] Ibid., 749.   [80] Ibid., 731.
[81] Ibid., quoted at 753.

At one level it is difficult to disagree with Little's conclusions. It should be well-known to even the first-year public law student that open-textured discretion, operating in the absence of outer boundaries or internal structures of principle, is likely to morph into arbitrariness, permitting any action or inaction, and is therefore unlikely to enhance the quality or legitimacy of decisions reached. Of course, the FSA, as noted above, does now have parameters established by the statute which created it. However, at another level, it may seem that both the Phillips Inquiry and Little may be placing too much reliance on primary legislation to provide key principles. The Animal Health Act 2002, a response to the FMD epidemic, to which we will shortly refer, perhaps confirms this view.

Section 23 of the Food Standards Act 1999 requires the FSA to have regard to its general functions and objectives identified earlier, but also goes on to establish guidance as to how risks, costs and benefits should be analysed in pursuit of these ends. It requires the Agency to take into account, *inter alia*, the nature and magnitude of any risks to public health, or other risks which are relevant to the decision (including any uncertainty as to the adequacy or reliability of the available information), the likely costs and benefits of the exercise, non-exercise or manner of exercise of its powers, and any relevant advice or information given to it by an advisory committee.[82] Though such general principles may be sound, they may be thought to amount to little more than common sense, and certainly do not provide an unduly constricting framework within which the FSA must take decisions. They do not necessarily provide an adequate sense of priority or hierarchy between the various factors. It may be worth returning to Davis's tripartite agenda for maximizing the benefits and minimizing the risks of discretion, referred to in Chapter One,[83] which talks of 'confining, structuring and checking' discretion. Though the kind of general principle found in primary legislation may go some way towards offering a degree of structure, and may set the lawful boundaries of its application, providing a legal standard against which discretionary action can be reviewed or checked, it can be argued that the kind of extensive discretion which the Phillips Report envisages and the Act vests in regulators (and ultimately Ministers in their reserve powers to give directions) is potentially so broad as to stand in need of substantial additional internal structuring.

There is, of course, a familiar difficulty here, of obtaining the optimum combination of rules and discretion, which permits the certainty of the former while enjoying the benefits of flexibility brought by the latter.[84] In an area as sensitive and important as safety in food supply, it is imperative both that the quality of

---

[82] S.23(2). Note also the reserve power given to the Secretary of State under S.24(1) for directions to be given to the FSA if it appears to have failed seriously in relation to its duties under S.23.

[83] Davis, K. C., *Discretionary Justice, a Preliminary Inquiry* (Urbana, IL.: University of Illinois Press, 1971).

[84] Consider, generally, Baldwin, R., *Rules and Government* (Oxford: Clarendon, 1995); Galligan, D.J., *Discretionary Power: a Legal Study of Official Discretion* (Oxford: Clarendon, 1986); Hawkins, K. (ed.), *The Uses of Discretion* (Oxford: Clarendon, 1992).

decision-making is high, and that the level of public trust in the decision-making processes, and the legitimacy of those processes, are also high.

In practice, distrust in the decision-making system for regulation of the food industries has tended to lead to reliance on some combination of government and the parliamentary system, together with 'science', to produce the 'right' answer.[85] However, as Fisher notes, scientific findings are rarely unambiguous or monolithic, and, as she quotes from an HM Treasury Report, 'government will often be acting in different guises whether it be as the "guardian of people's rights" or as "an agent of the consumer" '.[86] Consideration of such situations leads her to observe that 'Risk regulation standards have not emerged in a systematic or rationalist manner but are the product of historical and political happenstance.'[87] Given this congeries of factors, and their consequences, there is clearly the ongoing potential, within the wide expanse of open-textured discretion allowed even by the Section 23 provisions, for debatable 'scientific findings' to be presented as authoritative answers which serve whatever political or administrative interest is presently at the top of the agenda. The potential failings of such an approach have been catalogued by a number of authors. In addition to the concerns raised by the likes of Little, and Fisher, noted above, there is, for example, the real risk identified by Millstone and van Zwanenberg, that regulatory decisions, though represented as 'scientific' decisions, may in reality be based upon, or heavily distorted by, the regulator's perception as to the 'need' for a product.[88] In addition, Lobstein notes the risks of findings of committees being simplified and then repeated over lengthy periods, of advice given in cautious terms being interpreted as robust and definitive, of committee members having conflicts of interests, of rejection and hostility towards scientists who veer from the mainstream, of the quality of information given to advisory committees and the tendency of committees to give the advice they are asked for, as opposed to giving unsolicited advice or advice which they know or believe would not be acted upon. More generally, Lobstein reminds us again of the understandable, if ultimately undesirable, oft-noted risk, apparent in the crisis deriving from BSE, of 'a distinct bias away from precaution in favour of excessively reassuring the public'.[89]

Here, a brief excursus is warranted into one of the most shocking issues to have arisen in British food production in recent years: the foot and mouth disease (FMD) epidemic of 2001. Though, as Campbell and Lee observe, the FSA state that FMD has 'no implications for the human food chain',[90] the social, psychological, ecological and economic implications for the food and farming

---

[85] See Fisher, E., 'Drowning by Numbers: Standard Setting in Regulation and the Pursuit of Accountable Public Administration', *Oxford Journal of Legal Studies*, 20/1 (2000), 109.

[86] Ibid., 114.   [87] Ibid., 113.

[88] Millstone and van Zwanenberg, 'The Evolution of Food Safety', 598.

[89] Lobstein, 'Crisis in Agriculture', 82.

[90] Campbell, D. and Lee, R., 'Carnage by Computer: The Blackboard Economics of the 2001 Foot and Mouth Epidemic', *Social and Legal Studies*, 12/4 (2003), 426, at 429.

industries which they list,[91] and its impact on a British public already unnerved by previous scares regarding food safety, should not be underestimated. Though their account may feel too emotive for some tastes, Campbell and Lee catalogue clearly what they identify as failures throughout the entire regulatory process relevant to FMD. From the attitude of EU authorities, which sought to rely entirely on stamping out outbreaks of the disease, rejecting prophylactic vaccination, to MAFF's 'complete failure to identify the disease or to isolate it in anything like a timely fashion',[92] either complacency or ignorance on the part of the Secretary of State for Agriculture in believing the outbreak was under control,[93] through to 'confusion about the scope of the contiguous cull',[94] identified as 'a panic response to a crisis which MAFF had allowed to assume unknown dimensions which, of its nature, has made proper epidemiological analysis of the epidemic impossible',[95] there appears nothing positive to be said. Campbell and Lee comment that it is not even known with any certainty what role the costly, and as they observe, horrific, contiguous cull actually had on stopping the disease.[96]

Campbell and Lee[97] argue that the lack of regulatory effectiveness in relation to FMD arose from the adoption by the authorities of an approach based essentially on, after Coase,[98] 'purely abstract "blackboard economics" '. They set out what this means very succinctly:

An intervention may be shown on the blackboard to offer a theoretical solution, but the reason it appears to do so is that its own costs are very inadequately estimated because there is an underlying assumption that the intervention will be carried out by more or less efficient public bodies. The apparent plausibility of the interventionist solution rests on the inaccurate underestimate of the cost of intervention. Solutions which work well on a blackboard but are developed without sufficient sensitivity to the problems of their being implemented are very likely to be useless or pernicious when they actually come to be implemented.[99]

If it was the case, as Campbell and Lee seek to argue, that the FMD disaster had as an underlying cause the absence of 'rational appreciation of the cost of disease control',[100] fundamental problems must exist in relation to the policy-making and regulatory process generally, symptomatized most clearly by the absence of clear and rational criteria on which action can be based. Elsewhere,[101] the same authors argue forcefully that the Animal Health Act 2002, the government's response to the FMD epidemic of the previous year, is merely a continuation of the same discredited policy which was found to have led to the disastrous consequences they have chronicled. In effect, Campbell and Lee see the 2002

---

[91] Ibid., at 426, including a DEFRA estimate of £9 billion economic loss.   [92] Ibid., 430.
[93] Ibid., 432.   [94] Ibid., 434.   [95] Ibid., 437.   [96] Ibid., 437.
[97] Ibid., 444 *et seq.*
[98] Coase, R. H., 'The Regulated Industries: Discussion', *American Economic Review* (Papers and Proceedings), 54 (1964) 192.   [99] Campbell and Lee, 'Carnage by Computer', 445.
[100] Ibid., 452.
[101] Campbell, D. and Lee, R., 'The Power to Panic: the Animal Health Act 2002', *Public Law*, 2003, Autumn, 382.

Act as no more than an attempt to extend government powers under pre-existing legislation so as to legalize actions such as the contiguous cull, which were of questionable legality in 2001. The inevitable conclusion to be drawn is that legalizing such a panic response does nothing to address the circumstances and problems which lead to the development of such crises. This is hardly what Little[102] and others might hope would be achieved by placing greater reliance on primary legislation to establish a regulatory framework.

Campbell and Lee suggest that the logistical nightmare of addressing the outbreak once control had been lost was compounded by, or perhaps still worse, may have originated from, misunderstandings of the consequences of vaccination of livestock in terms of EU and WTO policies – misunderstandings apparently perpetuated by special interest groups such as the UK's National Farmers' Union who they, like most commentators, state exerted great influence over the regulatory agencies.[103] From this point of view, the need for better informed decision-making and greater transparency in governance and regulation, are strongly indicated. To borrow a phrase, 'Government by Moonlight' must be replaced by the sunshine of openness.[104]

However, while it is clearly the case that the post-BSE-crisis reforms to the regulatory structure, and especially the increased transparency, as represented by the working practices of the FSA in relation to human food supply, will in many ways serve to enhance accountability, this will not, in Fisher's terms, speak to 'the nature of what is being held to account'.[105] Nor will it entirely ensure that regulation is based upon rational principles, the absence of which is the fundamental problem which Campbell and Lee identify in the handling of FMD in 2001.

Whether in relation to proactive regulatory intervention, or response to crises, the existence of wide-ranging discretion, inadequately confined, structured or checked, albeit legal by virtue of wide grants of statutory powers, fails to satisfy legitimate democratic expectations of avoiding arbitrariness in the exercise of public power. It fails to ensure that discretion is structured against a series of principles that further the stated policy objective, while simultaneously also failing to ensure adequate standards against which the exercise of discretionary power can be scrutinized and challenged. It fails to meet expectations of both rationality and accountability.

In the absence of structuring provided externally, in the instrument which vests power in an agency or via some other superior authority, it is of course possible for agencies to develop their own, internal structuring via codes of practice, guidance etc., which can serve the same purpose. Though the Food Standards Act provides demarcation of the outer limits of the Agency's powers, there is little

---

[102] Little, 'BSE and the Regulation of Risk'.

[103] Campbell and Lee, 'Carnage by Computer', 442.

[104] Birkinshaw, P., Harden, I., and, Lewis, N., *Government by Moonlight: the Hybrid Parts of the State* (London: Unwin Hyman, 1990).   [105] Fisher, 'Drowning by Numbers', 129.

to suggest that the FSA has sought to undertake detailed internal structuring, preferring, perhaps understandably, to operate within the very broad degree of latitude provided in the primary legislation which established it. The pressing question, in the context of this book, thus becomes whether a concept of 'public interest', or something which equates to it, may be of assistance by way of serving as, after Sunstein,[106] an 'interpretative principle'.

When pressed as to the extent, if at all, to which a defined concept of 'public interest' plays a significant role in informing the Agency's activities, FSA officials unsurprisingly present the primary public interest to be that of safety,[107] and point towards attempts to protect this via a policy of proceeding according to a 'precautionary principle', or as the FSA's Chair prefers, a 'precautionary approach'.[108] Though this concept will be considered more fully in later chapters, it is worth pausing at this point in order to consider the extent to which the application of this principle serves as an advance on the pre-existing decision-making methods in the context of food supply.

The Precautionary Principle

The general thrust of the precautionary principle is summarized neatly by Davies: 'Put simply, the principle means that you should not wait for conclusive evidence of a risk before putting control measures in place designed to protect consumers or the environment.'[109] Throughout the three 'distinct but overlapping stages'[110] involved in the decision-making process relating to food safety (risk assessment, risk management and risk communication), cost/benefit analyses have traditionally been applied which, while claiming and offering the appearance of scientific objectivity, will in fact have incorporated 'many other considerations ... including social, economic and political factors'.[111] Davies observes that this task boils down to a process of identifying 'a socially acceptable level of risk', but inherent in any such judgment is the difficulty that 'short-term economic costs will always be easier to quantify than the long-term costs to public health or the environment'.[112] The long-term consequences of failing to take preventative measures at an early stage are, however, of course illustrated vividly in the BSE and FMD sagas.

Davies notes that the origins of the precautionary principle lie not specifically in relation to food supply or public health, but in environmental policy. Now found in international agreements such as the Biosafety Protocol of 2000,

---

[106] Sunstein, C. R., *After the Rights Revolution: Reconceiving the Regulatory State* (Cambridge, Mass.: Harvard University Press, 1990).

[107] Barbara Richards, Head of Corporate Secretariat, Consumers and International Division, Food Standards Agency; David Dunleavy, Head of Legal Services. Both interviewed 20 March, 2003.

[108] Sir John Krebs, FSA Chair, speech to National Farmers' Union, 19 February, 2003, at http://www.foodstandards.gov.uk/multimedia/webpage/nfuspeech, accessed 9 April, 2004.

[109] Davies, 'The Precautionary Principle and Food Policy', 65. For further discussion of the principle, and additional sources, see Chs. 4 and 7. [110] Ibid., 66.

[111] Ibid. [112] Ibid., 67.

the principle was perhaps first adopted clearly in the Rio Declaration of 1992, which states that, 'Where there are threats of serious or irreversible damage, lack of full scientific certainty should not be used as a reason for postponing cost-effective measures to prevent environmental degradation.'[113] Adopted by the EU in its Maastricht treaty amendment, and re-stated by the Commission in 2000 in its general communication on the application of the principle,[114] it has also been given recognition in the EU's regulation establishing general principles of food law: 'In those specific circumstances where a risk to life or health exists, but scientific uncertainty persists, the precautionary principle provides a mechanism for determining risk management measures or other actions in order to ensure the high level of health protection chosen in the Community.'[115]

However, the precautionary principle does not necessarily sweep away all pre-existing decision-making practices. Davies is clear that 'rather than being at odds with risk analysis and a scientific approach, the precautionary principle complements and reinforces this approach'.[116] In many ways, it might seem to offer particular attractions in terms of requiring the consideration of a more comprehensive set of factors, and certainly seems to mesh well with moves towards greater transparency in decision-making. In 'shifting the balance from an excessive focus on what we do know to a better perspective on what we do and don't know, and determining the most appropriate way to deal with uncertainties in order to protect public health',[117] it might be considered in this sense a more 'honest' approach to decision-making. It seems to reflect, and run reasonably comfortably alongside certain versions of a legal principle of 'proportionality', which might seem particularly relevant in relation to regulatory actions such as the use of contiguous cull in response to FMD, and to which we will return in Chapter Seven.

While the application of the precautionary principle might appear to imply a properly protective starting point for the consideration of regulatory intervention in contentious or difficult issues, Lobstein notes that it is perhaps rather less concrete than it might at first appear, and confirms that it is in some ways remarkably similar to the processes of cost/benefit analysis, given 'the need to modify precautionary activity in the context of the costs and difficulties of exercising that precaution'.[118] It may well be that the term 'precautionary approach' may well portray the reality more accurately than the potentially deceptive clarity suggested by 'precautionary principle'.

Potential for retreat from or variation of the precautionary principle, in light of very real costs and difficulties, especially perhaps in relation to a slow-acting and virtually invisible agent such as BSE, may limit the effectiveness of the principle's

---

[113] Davies, 'The Precautionary Principle and Food Policy', 65.

[114] See McNelis, N., 'EU Communication on the Precautionary Principle', *Journal of International Economic Law*, 3/3 (2000), 545.

[115] Davies, 'The Precautionary Principle and Food Policy', 68.   [116] Ibid.   [117] Ibid.

[118] Lobstein, 'Crisis in Agriculture', 81.

application in practice, and explain why, in Lobstein's words, it is 'struggling to be recognised'[119] in the context of food safety. In reality it does not in itself necessarily offer an answer as to how decisions will be made, or advice framed, where competing interests and opinions, especially as to degree of risk, differ widely. Such a situation will most obviously arise in the context of high profile issues such as GM food production, but will also occur in controversies such as those relating to the wisdom of approving or requiring the addition of supplements such as folic acid to staple foodstuffs like bread. This type of issue, like others such as the fluoridization of water supply, which may fall, perhaps inconveniently, on the divide or overlap of responsibilities between the DoH, DEFRA and the FSA, is such that not only might medical, scientific and public opinion differ, but there will also be differences of political philosophy as regards the proper extent of state intervention. In such a practical situation, the policy of the FSA is that any serious disagreement with its Board as to the proper course of action would not be hidden beneath a single official line, but would be revealed in the Agency's advice to government ministers and made available to the public. In practice, therefore, the central importance of openness and transparency is re-emphasized, while the precautionary principle as a manifestation of the public interest, though worthy of further consideration,[120] might seem to be of limited practical significance.

The Absence of Principles?

The previous two chapters have highlighted some of the theoretical difficulties inherent in the use of the concept of 'public interest', and the context in which the FSA operates appears to demonstrate some of the problems associated with its application in practice. Despite this, as was noted at the outset of this discussion, the term is placed at the heart of the FSA's own description of its brief. Part of the problem is that it remains undefined in this context, seeming to express a vague aspiration rather than a hard standard against which activity can be measured. The 'precautionary principle', which might be presented as approximating to public interest aspirations in a practical manifestation, appears in reality to offer little more in concrete terms than 'the public interest' often does, and any advances which the FSA has made on what went before stem from its more open and transparent procedures, rather than from the development of any substantive principles which structure its discretion. Neither in the rhetoric of 'public interest' or the 'precautionary principle' is it possible to discern sharply defined principles which interpret, structure or orientate the FSA's activities. Though the FSA's clear statement of three organizational commitments (putting consumers first, being open and accessible, and being independent) is welcome, it does little if anything to structure the discretion vested in the Agency, or establish hard

[119] Ibid.   [120] See Chs. 4 and 7.

standards against which it can be readily held accountable via either political or legal mechanisms.

The nature of the FSA's functions, and its manner of operation, can be usefully compared with those of other agencies operating in the different, though not unrelated, context of environmental regulation. Decision-making as regards, for example, restrictions on land-use premised on environmental factors, noted earlier in this chapter, seems to raise many of the same type of conflicts between individual and collective interests that are apparent in relation to regulation of the food industry, and some very similar concerns as to establishing the values to be applied. In the environmental context, Steele has sought to establish a case for participation and deliberation contributing to the quality and legitimacy of decision-making or 'problem solving'.[121] Steele is primarily pursuing a difficult concern, the *quality* of problem solving, ultimately perhaps amounting to the legitimate reconciliation of competing interests, and seeks to argue that increased and well-informed public participation leads ultimately to 'better' decisions in this sense. Underlying this argument, however, is a theme familiar to public lawyers: the potential for transparent processes enhancing the legitimacy and therefore acceptance of such decision-making, and the 'quality' of decisions.

Addressing the nature of competing private and collective interests in the field of environmental regulation, Steele draws on Sagoff's work to emphasize how 'immediate human interests rarely fully encapsulate the environmental impacts of development',[122] and how, in the context of 'deliberative democracy', 'individuals should be regarded as able to divest themselves of their self-interested consumer preferences for the limited purposes of coming together as citizens and of defining public values through a process of deliberation'.[123] In a phrase that can be equally usefully applied to the regulation of the food industries as to environmental regulation, she notes with apparent approval Sagoff's approach to deliberative democracy, which reasserts the difference noted earlier between consumer and citizen perspectives on such issues, and emphasizes how, in that context, 'Citizens are not mere maximisers of self-interest; and the public realm is not empty of values.'[124] She goes on to note how approaching problem-solving in this kind of spirit may lead to decisions and legislation regarding the environment being based not simply on 'preference-aggregation or interest-group negotiation',[125] but also on informed input from citizens, who, despite differing personal interests, can, if enabled in a deliberative context, 'contribute to a shared public culture'.[126] It must properly be observed that the idiom used here appears more closely related to a civic republicanist tradition found in the US than the pluralist, liberal–democratic basis of the UK polity. However, it will be argued in Chapter Six that some elements of this approach may be less alien to the UK context than they may seem.

---

[121] Steele, J., 'Participation and Deliberation in Environmental Law: Exploring a Problem-Solving Approach', *Oxford Journal of Legal Studies*, 21/3 (2001), 415.   [122] Ibid., 423.
[123] Ibid., 424.   [124] Ibid.   [125] Ibid.   [126] Ibid.

Of crucial significance here is the ability of all to act as citizens, not as mere consumers. This is as true in the context of regulation of the food industries as it is in relation to the environment, and it serves helpfully to highlight differences between consumers and citizens which may otherwise be elided. Though the short-term self-interest of consumers has a legitimate place to play in liberal democracy, it must not be allowed to dominate at the expense of other values, in particular, of course, longer-term and collective values. It is abundantly clear that though consumers of food have a legitimate, if limited, range of interests, this falls far short of the extent of the interests of citizens. To return to a simple example referred to earlier, though it may serve the purposes of some producer interest groups to argue that regulation of the food industries should be limited to safety, to the exclusion of nutritional issues, it is obvious that such consumer interests, however well-protected, do not fully encompass the wider range of concerns which citizens would legitimately expect to be reflected in the regulatory regime.

On balance, it seems fair to conclude that *consumer* interests are probably reasonably well-protected by the regulatory regime, as manifested in the FSA, which even appears to engage in processes which embody substantial consultative elements, such as those relating to GMOs,[127] and represents a welcome step forward from the previous arrangements. Indeed, it is important not to underrate the democratic 'value-added' by the FSA in terms of attempts to engage individuals and groups in debate – a very significant aspect of citizenship. The argument must remain, however, that though such procedural aspects of citizenship might be well served, the substantive values associated with it are vulnerable given the Agency's apparently predominantly consumerist perspective.

Meanwhile, though the use of the 'precautionary principle' may appear to serve as an organizing principle, offering some structure for the discretion enjoyed by regulators, the principle appears neither adequately clear, nor fully embedded in the area of food regulation, and in any event may tend to reflect and confirm rather than challenge the rather narrow, consumer/safety as opposed to citizen/nutrition oriented approach apparently adopted by the FSA. In reality, as has been suggested above, the precautionary principle may be both less concrete, and less distant from more traditional cost/benefit analysis methods, than it might at first seem. Though further consideration will be given to it in later chapters, a preliminary conclusion must be that the precautionary principle does not serve the same range of objectives as the kind of public interest principle suggested in the previous chapter, and in the absence of clearly identified, *substantive* principles there is a significant risk that even the most transparent and accountable system of regulation of the food industries may fail to protect the important but vulnerable values which extend beyond consumerism.

---

[127] See, for example, the FSA's report 'Consumer Views of GM Food', published July 2003 (FSA/0841/0703), summarizing the FSA's consultation on the subject.

Though not strictly related to food safety, but located centrally within the food industry, if the account offered by Campbell and Lee of the economics-driven approach underlying the 'management' of FMD is even remotely near the mark, it is apparent that there is a need for some stated and clear value base to be imported into regulatory discourse in such areas which ensure rationality. If Barling and Lang were right to say that, five years after New Labour came to power, 'the government's food policy is still shaped primarily by its macroeconomic priorities of generating national wealth and fostering economic growth through competitiveness in international trade',[128] the vulnerability of citizenship-related values and interests in food regulation is highlighted. It seems reasonable to conclude that the introduction into the FSA's brief of a citizenship-oriented concept of 'the public interest' may be of some assistance.

REGULATING THE MASS MEDIA IN THE PUBLIC INTEREST

Context and Rationales

In the process of scrutinizing the Draft Communications Bill 2002, the Puttnam Committee stated that 'there are public interests relating to the regulatory framework that are not encompassed in a consumer-driven objective',[129] and noted evidence given to the Committee expressing concern that 'the democratic, social and cultural interests of citizens' had not been given due weight in the formulation of the regulator's duties.[130] The Committee's Report went on to recommend the establishment of a 'principal duty' for Ofcom, the newly formed regulator of mass media, which should embody explicitly the concept of 'the long term interests of all citizens'.[131]

Such a high-profile endorsement of the need for the incorporation of a concept of public interest is to be welcomed, but is by no means representative of the practical realities of media regulation in the modern era. Indeed, it can be forcefully argued that the regulatory emphasis, since 1990 at least, and reflected in the Communications Act 2003, has been consistently away from intervention in pursuit of broader public interest objectives such as those suggested by the Puttnam Committee, and towards much narrower goals associated with market forces. In the context of ongoing trends of technological development and convergence, and corporate conglomeration in the media industries, the previously dominant 'public service' tradition in British broadcasting has been replaced by a model in which regulators must justify their interventions in relation primarily

---

[128] Barling, D. and Lang, T., 'A Reluctant Food Policy? The First Five Years of Food Policy Under Labour', *Political Quarterly*, 74/1 (2003), 8, at 8.

[129] Report of the Joint Committee on the Draft Communications Bill, HL Paper 169-I; HC 876-I, 25 July, 2002 (henceforth 'Puttnam Report'), Para. 24. See Feintuck, M., 'Walking the High-Wire: the UK's Draft Communications Bill', *European Public Law*, 9/1 (2003), 105.

[130] Puttnam Report, Para. 24.   [131] Ibid., Para. 26.

to the economics of the market. From a citizen-oriented vision embodied in the public service tradition, regulation has turned its focus to an agenda derived from perceptions of consumer interests, contributing to and reconfirming the commodification of the media within an increasingly producer-led, free-market media economy.

The essentially deregulatory agenda seen here is, of course, by no means unique to the media context; indeed it is symptomatic of the continuing hegemony of the economic vision originating from the Thatcher/Reagan era.[132] However, unlike many products and services, the media can be seen to play a unique and important role as part of the 'public sphere':[133] in Keane's terms, 'Communications media . . . should aim to empower a plurality of citizens who are governed neither by undemocratic states nor by undemocratic market forces.'[134] Thus, the liberalization of this particular market has the potential to bring about peculiarly deep social consequences which may, while perhaps remaining consistent with consumer ends, substantially cut across citizenship interests.

While it is easy to state a preference for public service values, and to criticize market-driven regulation, it is a different and more important matter to justify such a preference, especially in a deregulatory climate. In order to do this, it is necessary to establish the foundations upon which public interest values have been historically integrated into the process of media regulation. Only when these foundational rationales for intervention have been identified is it meaningful to consider the structures and techniques of regulation, as, ultimately, the success and legitimacy of regulation must be measured in relation to the justificatory rationales which underpin it, and the objectives which derive from them; the outcomes of regulation can only properly be assessed by reference to the degree to which they mesh successfully with the objectives of the regulatory regime. By way of establishing the context for considering actual and potential 'public interest' interventions in regulating the media, it is therefore necessary to consider, if briefly, the fundamental justifications for regulation of the media. I have written at length elsewhere on these themes,[135] and it is convenient here to do little more than summarize the fourfold classification into which rationales for regulating the media can be placed; namely, effective communication, diversity, economic justifications, and public service.

The first of these sets of rationales for regulation, *effective communication*, has clear roots in the freedom of expression ideal which is inherent in the liberal–democratic system.[136] Judicial rhetoric, even prior to the Human Rights Act 1998, has emphasized the centrality of freedom of expression. In considering the

---

[132] See Hertz, *The Silent Takeover*, 24–30, for a brief and lucid account.

[133] See Dahlgren, P., *Television and the Public Sphere: Citizenship, Democracy and the Media* (London: Sage, 1995).

[134] Keane, J., *The Media and Democracy* (Cambridge: Polity Press, 1991), p. xi.

[135] See Feintuck, M., *Media Regulation, Public Interest and the Law* (Edinburgh: Edinburgh University Press, 1999), especially 39–49.

[136] See, generally, Barendt, E., *Freedom of Speech* (Oxford: Clarendon, 1985).

ban imposed under Section 10 of the Broadcasting Act 1990 on broadcasting the spoken words of members of proscribed organizations, notably Sinn Fein, Lord Bridge inferred that the court was 'perfectly entitled to start from the premise that any restriction of the right to freedom of expression requires to be justified and that nothing less than an important competing public interest will be sufficient to justify it'.[137] That said, the statutory powers granted to the Secretary of State were sufficiently broad, and the intensity of review engaged in under the *Wednesbury* principle[138] so light, that the challenge was doomed to failure unless the Minister could be shown to have acted utterly outrageously; inevitably, he was found not to have. The burden of establishing the reasonableness of his actions was not as great as the reference to 'an important competing public interest' might suggest. Important though fundamental freedoms such as expression clearly are in terms of regulation of media content, the freedom of expression rationale for regulation of the structure of the broadcasting industries has, historically, been in general based largely upon more pragmatic, technology-related, reasoning arising from spectrum scarcity (within the limited available analogue radio spectrum), which has demanded regulatory intervention via allocation of frequencies in order to ensure effective separation between broadcast channels, avoiding interference between transmissions.

The second rationale relates closely to the 'freedom of expression' aspects of the first. Ensuring *diversity* in the material communicated via the media serves a number of objectives. These range from ensuring the availability of programming to suit a range of tastes and interests, through to serving the needs and interests of culturally and linguistically diverse groups within society, and, via ensuring diversity in the range of political opinion communicated through the mass media, serving the needs of supplying the 'marketplace of ideas' upon which democracy is said to thrive. Again, the function of a diverse media output as part of the 'public sphere' is emphasized: 'Democracy requires informed citizens. Their capacity to produce intelligent agreements by democratic means can be nurtured only when they enjoy equal and open access to diverse sources of opinion.'[139]

The third rationale, summarized as *economic* justifications for regulation, is equally multi-faceted. At one level, this heading can be thought of in terms of national economic policy. The national government will have a particular interest in ensuring a thriving and vibrant media, given the large and growing significance of the media industries to the national economy. Thus, regulators will be under pressure to establish conditions in which inward investment into the country is encouraged, and in which a dynamic media industry can contribute to exports. However, the heading 'economic justifications' also incorporates

---

[137] *R. v. Secretary of State for the Home Department, ex parte Brind* [1991] 1 All ER 720, at 723. Judicial reference to the concept of 'public interest', again without any exploration or explanation of the term's meaning, can also be seen in a different context in the judgment of Lord Hoffmann in *R (on the application of Alconbury Developments Ltd.) v. Secretary of State for the Environment, Transport and the Regions* [2001] 2 All ER 929, at Paras. 72 and 74.   [138] See below, Ch. 7.

[139] Keane, *The Media and Democracy*, 176.

the premise of facilitating the smooth operation of markets, widely claimed to be the most efficient mechanism for delivering goods and services, and which in relation to the media, as elsewhere, require a degree of regulation if they are to function effectively. Thus, the classical foci of competition law, as touched upon in Chapter One, in terms of avoidance of monopoly and oligopoly, cartels, predatory pricing and market failure, are all as relevant in the context of media markets as elsewhere. While individual media sectors, typified perhaps by the British press in recent years, have exhibited strong tendencies towards concentration of ownership, key differences arise in the modern era from trends towards horizontal integration, cross-media ownership cutting across conventional sectoral divides, and also vertical integration, up the broadcasting chain, so as to include all stages from production and obtaining broadcasting rights, to delivery mechanisms and transmission. At the same time, technological advances in the form of digital transmission, which permits the exclusion of non-paying viewers from decoding and therefore receiving transmissions, has the potential to remove substantially the 'public good' characteristic associated with conventional analogue broadcasting. New technology in digital broadcasting also establishes bottlenecks and gateways within the delivery structure, which may require behavioural regulation, via constructs functionally similar to the essential facilities doctrine, if market forces are to operate effectively. Arguably, given the power of the media in forming public opinion and our view of the world, and the ability of media owners to control the flow of information available to us,[140] the competition or anti-trust issues arising from concentration and conglomeration become still more pressing in this context,[141] though by emphasizing and focusing on market imperfections they may ultimately divert attention away from a wider range of democratic interests.

The fourth and final classification or regulatory rationale relating to the media, that of *public service*, has, historically, formed the basis for the dominant regulatory tradition in Britain and many of its Western European neighbours. Though it can be seen to incorporate elements of each of the other three lines of justification, the public service tradition in broadcasting represents a unique and important justification for regulation in its own right, in many places relating closely to various lines of 'public interest' discourse, therefore the meaning of this rationale, and threats to it, requires a little more discussion at this stage.

Though the precise form and content of public service expectations have included significant variations across Europe,[142] there are sufficient

---

[140] See Schiller, H., *Information Inequality* (New York, N.Y.: Routledge, 1996).

[141] The classic account is provided in Bagdikian, B., The Media Monopoly (6th edn.) (Boston, Mass.: Beacon Press, 2000).

[142] See Humphreys, P., *Mass Media and Media Policy in Western Europe* (Manchester: Manchester University Press, 1996). For comparative legal perspectives, see Barendt, E., *Broadcasting Law: a Comparative Study* (Oxford: Clarendon, 1993); also Hoffman-Riem, W., *Regulating Media: the Licensing and Supervision of Broadcasting in Six Countries* (New York, N.Y.: Guilford Press, 1996).

commonalities to be able to refer meaningfully to 'a public service model' in this context. The essential features of public service broadcasting (PSB) can be summarized in terms of a universally (or near-universally) available, party-political neutral service, offering a range of informative, educative and entertaining programming, free, or readily affordable by all, at the point of use. Though Humphreys also includes non-commercialism as an essential feature of any lowest common denominator concept of PSB,[143] the British experience of ITV and Channel 4 seems to suggest that a degree of commercialism has been, via active regulation, successfully incorporated into the PSB system without necessarily damaging, and arguably even enhancing, the ecology of PSB. Many of us grew up in Britain in a cosy world of terrestrial television in which 'commercial' television, heavily and unashamedly regulated according to PSB precepts, comfortably co-existed alongside the archetypal PSB service provided by the publicly funded BBC. However, this position has come under increasing pressure from two directions: technological development, and globalization, both of which may seem to accelerate the drive towards a stronger version of commercialism, and commodification.[144]

Technological advances, especially arising from digital compression and satellite and cable delivery systems, have increased exponentially the number of channels available for broadcasting, blowing away the 'spectrum scarcity' argument which provided a convenient justification for state regulation, and, via the introduction of many new channels apparently allowing enhanced consumer choice, has fragmented the audience and in turn challenged the legitimacy of public funding for the BBC. Of course, technological developments have not stopped there. Growth and advances in information technology and telecommunications have resulted in the potential for the ready transfer of digitalized data between these and more traditional mass media, producing a steady erosion of previous divides both between conventional media sectors (print and broadcast) and between conventional media and other forms of communication (information technology and telecommunications).[145] This increasing technological convergence has posed huge challenges to media regulators, both in terms of what and how to regulate, and how to legitimate their activities in this new, spectrum-rich, and much more complex, context.

Technological developments also form part of the second key trend which may pose a threat to PSB values: internationalization and globalization. Globalization has a particular impact in this field given the ready potential for new media technologies to deliver their products in ways which cross international and even continental borders, rendering regulation at the national level difficult or futile. The potential for international organizations and agreements, and regional bodies such as the EU, to play a leading role in regulatory activities

[143] Humphreys, *Mass Media*, 117.
[144] On commodification of the media, see Leys, *Market Driven Politics*, 149–62.
[145] See Negroponte, N., *Being Digital* (London: Hodder and Stoughton, 1995).

is thus emphasized. At the same time, a further and very significant aspect of globalization should be noted in this context which seems to point in the same direction. Internationalization and even globalization of ownership patterns within the media, part of a general trend in many commercial and industrial sectors, has also begun to make the nation-state at times seem an inappropriate and inadequate basis for regulatory decision-making in this field. Conglomeration, and concentration of ownership within the media, whether at the national or international level, raises familiar competition law issues, but also, given the significant democracy-related aspects of the media touched on above, raises issues of still broader concern in this particular context.[146] Given the centrality of mass media to the establishment of cultural identity, the distinct cultural and linguistic traditions of individual nations, and of groups within them, are threatened by any trends towards a monolithic, global media culture

The issues and factors just outlined indicate the context in which media regulation takes place, and should suggest some clear issues from the perspective of the public interest. Regulators concerned to preserve aspects of the PSB tradition must face up to the modern market context, both in terms of corporate conglomeration and technological development, when justifying their interventions, and may find their task made more difficult by a political climate in which the validity of markets is taken as virtually unquestioned, while the legitimacy of intervention in pursuit of non-commodity values must be established before any such move is made. While technological change has rendered availability of spectrum largely irrelevant, and market structure has made the British BBC/ITV duopoly seem little more than a historical curiosity, the democratically linked justifications for regulation of the media, in terms of diversity and the values which underpinned the PSB model, remain undiminished. The democratic significance of the media is unquestioned, and permits the assertion of substantial 'public interest' claims, in terms of collective values which, paralleling the interests in regulation of the food industries discussed in the previous section, go far beyond the consumerist expectation of choice. However, the reactive nature of regulatory responses to changes in the media, over a lengthy period,[147] has left the impression of a system which is driven much more by forces from within the media market than by democratic imperatives or regulatory initiatives.

Reactive Regulation

As long ago as 1981, Elliott[148] used the image of 'chasing the receding bus' to characterize the nature of British regulatory responses to changes in media markets. It is quite clear that this metaphor not only captured the trend of its

---

[146] See generally, Herman, E. and McChesney, R., *The Global Media* (London: Cassell, 1997).

[147] Hitchens, L., 'Get Ready, Fire, Take Aim. The Regulation of Cross Media Ownership – an Exercise in Policy-Making', *Public Law*, 1995, Winter, 620.

[148] Elliott, M., 'Chasing the Receding Bus: the Broadcasting Act 1980', *Modern Law Review*, 44 (1981), 683.

time, but also showed a good degree of foresight, given that it appears to reflect equally the trend over the twenty years since he wrote. Elliot's point was that the Broadcasting Act of 1980, produced in the wake of the Annan Committee Report[149] on the future of broadcasting, had simply *assumed* the desirability of ongoing detailed state regulation of broadcasting, without establishing justifications for continuing intervention in relation to media markets which were even then changing at an increasingly rapid pace. The consequent risk he pointed towards is that of reactive regulation, with statutes and regulatory practice struggling to respond to market and technological change, rather than setting in advance an agenda which pursued clearly identified values and objectives.

The failure to establish an adequate regulatory framework is illustrated by the need to pass substantial reforms to the legislative basis for media regulation in 1981, 1990, 1996, and most recently 2003, suggesting a lack of effectiveness, and certainly illustrating an absence of stability in the regulatory structures. Though to some extent the reforms focus on different aspects of regulatory activity, and though the 1990 and 2003 Acts can be viewed as attempts by the Thatcher and then Blair governments to re-shape broadcasting according to their particular vision, the common element across the various Acts can be said to be a reactive element.

Britain is not unique in this sense, as it can be argued that some of its Western European neighbours, with a shared, historical PSB tradition have followed similar paths. Humphreys describes reforms of the broadcasting regulation regime in Germany in terms of 'formal – but largely symbolic – re-regulation', [150] and talks of the reforms in Italy in the 1980s and 1990s as 'a case of market *fait accomplis*',[151] eventually formalized in legislative form. Though the existence of such parallels in different constitutional settings does suggest, and indeed goes some way to *explaining*, an underlying difficulty for the nation-state in terms of addressing rapid market and technological change in an increasingly globalized media context, it does not necessarily *excuse* failures to regulate proactively in relation to such trends, given the threat they pose to the democratic values inherent in media systems.

The power of such trends should not be underestimated, either at the national or global level.[152] In Britain, over a fifty-year period from 1945, ownership patterns in the newspaper market shifted from a position where twenty national daily and Sunday titles were owned by twelve different owners to one where only seven ownership groups shared the market. More significantly, by 1995,

---

[149] Annan Report, *Report of the Committee on the Future of Broadcasting* (London: HMSO, 1977), Cm. 6753.

[150] Humphreys, 'Power and Control in the New Media', paper presented at the ECPR Workshop, *New Media and Political Communication*, Berne, 27 February–4 March 1997, 6.   [151] Ibid.

[152] On Britain, see generally, Curran, J. and Seaton, J., *Power Without Responsibility: The Press, Broadcasting and New Media in Britain*, 6th edn. (London: Routledge, 2003); and Seymour-Ure, C., *The British Press and Broadcasting Since 1945*, 2nd edn. (Oxford: Blackwell, 1996). On global developments, see Herman and McChesney, *The Global Media*.

five of the seven owners controlled less than half of the titles, leaving 63 per cent of circulation in the hands of two controlling groups, Mirror Group and News Corporation.[153] While the UK regulatory system, with powers shared between the Secretary of State and the Monopolies and Mergers Commission (MMC) under the Fair Trading Act 1973 (FTA), appeared to pay detailed attention to take-overs and mergers in the newspaper sector in the 1980s and 1990s, it might be concluded that this was to little purpose. Curran and Seaton identify some 120 newspaper take-overs from 1965 to 1993, of which 29 were referred to the MMC for consideration.[154] The fact that 23 of the 29 references were ultimately cleared led Ainsworth and Weston to doubt whether the, apparently minimal, practical effect justified the laborious FTA system.[155] However, the trend of concentration does not only exist in relation to individual sectors, but also on a cross-media basis. The important and fast-growing satellite television market in Britain is, of course, wholly dominated by Rupert Murdoch's BSkyB, part of the same News Corporation group which controls over one-third of newspaper circulation. The degree of concentration which was allowed to occur might be thought to illustrate a failure to view the bigger picture, and it seems that while every small step was undertaken with the utmost care and caution, Elliott's bus was pulling rapidly away into the distance.

While the 1980 Act can be said to have *assumed* an ongoing justification for regulation of media markets and failed to make adequate provision for the rapid changes taking place, so, it might now be concluded, did the 1990 Act. The 1990 Act was, however, particularly noteworthy for its radical reform of licence allocation for terrestrial commercial television broadcasting. Replacing a system criticized as long ago as 1975 by Lewis,[156] in terms of its failure to incorporate legal or other institutional restraints on the discretion exercised by the IBA[157] in allocating licences, the 1990 Act introduced a system of hybrid franchising, in which those seeking licences would make competitive bids and be required to meet two criteria: financial sustainability and a programme quality threshold. In the event of competitors meeting these baseline standards, the franchise would normally be awarded to the higher bidder. Under Section 17 the ITC was empowered to accept a lower price bid in place of a higher one 'where there are exceptional circumstances which make it appropriate for them to award to licence to another applicant'. The practical reality of the first round of franchising under this system was that only half of the licences awarded actually went to the highest bidder, undermining the supposed emphasis on price

---

[153] See Department of National Heritage, White Paper, *Media Ownership: the Government's Proposals* (London: HMSO, 1995) Cm. 2872.

[154] Curran, J. and Seaton, J., *Power Without Responsibility: the Press and Broadcasting in Britain*, 5th edn. (London: Routledge, 1997), 294.

[155] Ainsworth, L. and Weston, D., 'Newspapers and UK Media Ownership Controls', *Media Law and Practice*, 16/1 (1995) 2.

[156] Lewis, N., 'IBA Programme Contract Awards', *Public Law*, 1975, Winter, 317.

[157] The predecessor of the ITC.

bidding, and presumably emphasizing either programme quality or some other 'exceptional circumstance'. There is a suggestion underlying the exercise of this discretionary power that it may be serving some value related to a concept of 'the public interest'. Certainly Harlow and Rawlings believed that giving preference to factors other than the size of the bid 'underscores the continuing relevance of "public interest" ',[158] yet it remains unclear what might be intended by the term in this context. While 'programme quality' may seem an attractive option in this sense, ensuring perhaps range and diversity of programming in the service of conventional PSB expectations, the concept of 'quality', without further elaboration, remains in itself hopelessly subjective and nebulous, and essentially serves to confirm wide and unstructured discretion in the hands of the ITC.

Unsuccessful legal challenges to the exercise of the licensing power under this provision in 1992[159] and 1996[160] illustrated and confirmed a marked judicial reluctance in Britain to interfere with the discretion of 'expert' bodies and failed to enlighten as to the conception of public interest applied by the regulator. Harlow and Rawlings are left to conclude their discussion of these cases by asking whether, in light of this degree of judicial deference, there are actually *any* grounds on which the ITC's discretionary powers in this context could be successfully challenged.[161] Interestingly, in the course of the first of these judicial review actions, in a dissenting judgment in the Court of Appeal, Lord Donaldson MR, stated that, 'Judicial review was a supervisory jurisdiction exercised in the public interest', and that, 'There was a public interest in ensuring that the prescribed method of allocating licences be followed whatever criticisms might be made of that method.'[162] Though Lord Donaldson did not elaborate on exactly what was intended by 'the public interest' in this context, it seems reasonable to conclude that he was referring to no more than the necessity to ensure that the decision was taken within the procedures established in the statutory measures which granted the ITC the power to allocate franchises. Thus, the term 'the public interest' here seems to imply simply adherence to legal requirements, rather than any other principle or value.

To return to the position under the 1990 Act, while the franchising provisions had sought to introduce a form of market accountability, via price bidding, into the licensing procedure for broadcasting, and was in keeping with the Thatcherite emphasis on market forces as a solution to social issues, it can be argued that the Act as a whole failed to engage in any effective anti-concentration regulation of the market as a whole, as illustrated vividly by the extent of the Murdoch

---

[158] Harlow, C. and Rawlings, R., *Law and Administration* (2nd edn.) (London: Butterworths, 1997), 277.
[159] *R v. Independent Television Commission, ex parte TSW Broadcasting* (1992); (CoA) Times Law Reports, 7th February 1992; (HoL) *The Independent*, 27th March 1992.
[160] *R v. Independent Television Commission, ex parte Virgin Television Ltd.* [1996] EMLR 318.
[161] Harlow and Rawlings, *Law and Administration*, 272–82.
[162] Times Law Reports, 7 February 1992.

empire's cross-media holdings. A further major reform was required only six years later.

The Broadcasting Act 1996 was preceded by three government White Papers the previous year, covering media ownership,[163] privacy and media intrusion,[164] and digital terrestrial television,[165] demonstrating the range of ongoing issues left unresolved by the existing statutory framework. The White Papers and the Act threw up some interesting examples of how concepts of public interest may inform debate in this area, and, arguably, how they are inadequately developed.

For example, the White Paper on media ownership stated three objectives for the regulation of cross-media ownership:

- the promotion of diversity in media material, and the expression of a range of views;
- the maintenance of a strong media industry, 'for the economic benefit of the country'; and
- ensuring the proper operation of markets, including access for new entrants to markets, and the prevention of cross-media subsidies or predatory pricing.[166]

While all of these considerations may establish perfectly legitimate 'public interest' objectives for the regulatory regime, there are likely to be many situations in which they conflict, raising questions as to how one should be prioritized over another. The White Paper[167] proposed simply that, in relation to television broadcasting, or cross-media holdings including interests in television, the ITC would be expected to balance these three criteria, raising again the spectre of unstructured and potentially unchecked discretion, identified above in the context of franchising. Elsewhere, the same White Paper states that,

Television, radio and the press have a unique role in the free expression of ideas and opinion, and thus in the democratic process. The main objective must therefore be to secure a plurality of sources of information and opinion, and a plurality of editorial control over them. Another important objective is to provide an environment to enable United Kingdom broadcasters, equipment manufacturers and programme makers to take full advantage of major market opportunities.[168]

Echoing this wide range of priorities, in the specific context of the acquisition of national newspaper titles by those already holding broadcasting licences, Schedule 2 to the 1996 Act established criteria to be indicative of the public interest

---

[163] Department of National Heritage, *Media Ownership*.

[164] Department of National Heritage, White Paper, *Privacy and Media Intrusion* (London: HMSO, 1995), Cm. 2918.

[165] Department of National Heritage, White Paper, *Digital Terrestrial Television: the Government's Proposals* (London: HMSO, 1995), Cm. 2946.

[166] Department of National Heritage, *Media Ownership*, Para. 6.19   [167] Ibid., Para. 6.25.

[168] Ibid at Para. 16.

in the following terms:

  a) the desirability of promoting –
     i) plurality of ownership in the broadcasting and newspaper industries, and
     ii) diversity in the sources of information available to the public and in the opinions expressed on television or radio or in newspapers,
  b) any economic benefits ...
  c) the effect of the holding of the licence by that body on the proper operation of the market within the broadcasting and newspaper industries or any section of them.[169]

Again, while these might all be thought to be perfectly legitimate examples of public interest claims, the substantial potential for tension and conflict between these priorities is apparent. Most obviously, against the value of pluralism of ownership and diversity of output, may be pitched economic benefits, perhaps in allowing a UK-based media giant to grow to such a size that it may dominate the home market, in order that it can compete effectively on the global stage, and act as a 'national champion', winning for the UK economy the financial benefits that would accrue.

This potential for plurality and diversity to be compromised, in order to allow UK media corporations to be able to compete effectively in the global context, illustrates very clearly the problem passed to regulators of the media. They are asked to weigh such competing claims one against the other, and in the absence of any system of principles to structure their discretion. Potential problems in this respect are compounded if the courts continue to show the kind of deference to 'expert' decision-makers suggested in the litigation over franchise allocation. In such statutory provisions which incorporate but do not resolve or reconcile tensions between claims, and in the absence of an organizing principle, or clear prioritization of these competing objectives, the risks are clear: inconsistency and unpredictability in regulatory interventions, largely unstructured and unchecked regulatory discretion, and the overriding of long-term citizenship interests by short-term economic factors.

Meanwhile, a degree of myopia, or at least excessively narrow focus, can also be seen in relation to the 1996 Act. In part apparently as an effort to stimulate a competitive market in digital television, and in part to convert as many households as possible to digital television in order eventually to allow the analogue service to be switched off (and presumably the valuable asset of the analogue spectrum to be sold), the government adopted a policy of supporting the principle of developing an alternative digital 'delivery platform' to BSkyB's direct-to-home satellite transmission. Digital terrestrial television (DTT) was the 'big idea' in the mid-1990s, at least in the eyes of legislators, with the result that the first thirty-nine sections of the 1996 Act were given over to regulation of this new medium. In a welcome recognition of the realities of technological convergence, Oftel, primarily the regulator of telecommunications, was given

---

[169] Broadcasting Act 1996, Schedule 2, Para. 13.

certain powers in relation to regulation of conditional access decoding systems for DTT.[170] However, the ITC was to be the principle regulator in relation to DTT, having responsibility for allocating broadcasting licences, and 'multiplexes', blocks of the digital spectrum sufficient to carry a number of channels. Section 8(1) illustrated the government's policy of establishing this new platform, requiring the ITC, when considering the grant of a licence, to satisfy itself that such a decision 'would be calculated to promote the development of digital television broadcasting in the United Kingdom other than by satellite'. Clearly, despite its stated preference for deregulation, the government of the day saw the need for active intervention in order to seek to achieve a more competitive market in digital television.

Such intervention may seem to run counter to the impression given earlier that regulatory activity in relation to the media has been essentially reactive. Certainly, such a legislative endorsement of the nascent DTT technology seems to represent an exception to this norm. However, while establishing extremely detailed provisions relating to the arrival of DTT, the legislative framework might be thought to suffer from the same narrowness of focus, to the exclusion of the broader picture, as was noted earlier in relation to the FTA provisions on take-overs and mergers in newspapers. In particular, conspicuous by its absence from the 1996 Act provisions on DTT was any measure which integrated control of DTT multiplexes into the maximum cross-media holdings established in Schedule 2. If DTT was to take off as the government appeared to hope, logic would require that control of the digital spectrum in this important new medium should be factored in to any overall calculations of cross-media power. Of course, with the benefit of hindsight, and knowledge of the failures of ITVDigital, ONDigital, and the very limited uptake of the latest incarnation of DTT in the form of the Freeview service, the issue may now seem less important. Despite the ability to view a somewhat expanded range of channels after a one-off payment for a decoder, the public has not been sufficiently impressed by the range of channels on offer, many already offered via analogue, an extended range of BBC channels, and some second-string offerings from Sky, to take up this new system. It would seem that those who want digital television are more inclined to opt for the digital satellite system operated by Sky, with its wider range of channels and greater interactive facilities. It may simply be that DTT arrived in the digital television marketplace too late to upset the position of dominance already achieved by Sky. Thus, even the apparently proactive legislation on DTT arrived too late to catch Elliott's bus.

The Broadcasting Act of 1996 was the last substantial piece of legislation on media regulation brought in by the Conservative administrations. Elsewhere,

---

[170] Largely reflecting the requirements of the Advanced Television Standards Directive (Directive 1995/47).

I have described this Act in terms of 'a holding operation',[171] which might just have bought enough time for a more radical overhaul of the regulatory structure in order to build an edifice sufficiently robust to deal effectively with the new challenges posed by technological and market changes. The Conservative governments from 1979 to 1997 had overseen the regulation of the media in a period of massive and rapid change, yet at the end of their period in office, the institutional structure of media regulation was essentially unchanged other than certain changes of nomenclature, and though intervention continued despite the government's emphasis on deregulation and market forces, there was no more clarity as regards objectives or principles than there had been when they came to power. The failure to address, or offer mechanisms or principles to assist in resolving rationally the kind of conflict between public interest claims identified above, is a substantial part of what Hitchens[172] identified in the mid-1990s as the absence of any planned medium- or long-term media policy, or even planning process. Certainly, the frequent need for wholesale review and reform of the statutory basis for media regulation would seem to bear this out, and Elliott's bus still seemed to be pulling further away into the distance with the regulators languishing in its wake.

New Labour: Same Old Story?

With eighteen years in opposition in which to develop policies in relation to the media, it might have been expected that when New Labour came to power in 1997, they might have brought with them a more considered set of responses to the underlying issues. However, the change in party of government did not see any immediate change in the regulatory structure applicable to the media, or even any apparent significant changes in government policy. That said, it is clear that the New Labour government's media policy was influenced heavily by the output of the 'think-tank' the Institute for Public Policy Research (IPPR). The agenda developed by the IPPR, for the media, as presented by Collins and Murroni,[173] drew substantially upon the findings of the IPPR's Commission on Social Justice, where aspects of citizenship were emphasized, and found to underlie and justify regulation of the media. The key statement identified from the Commission's findings, that 'the foundation of a free society is the equal worth of all citizens',[174] serves as an overarching objective for specific areas of social policy, translated into the context of media regulation in the following terms: 'Freedom of access to the information necessary to full participation in economic, political and social life is a central element of citizens' entitlements in modern societies.'[175] In theory, this looks like a welcome attempt to establish a clearly principled and proactive agenda, breaking with the reactive and *ad hoc*

---

[171] Feintuck, M., 'The UK Broadcasting Act 1996: a Holding Operation?', *European Public Law*, 3/2 (1997), 201.   [172] Hitchens, 'Get Ready, Fire, Take Aim'.
[173] Collins, R. and Murroni, C., *New Media, New Policies* (Cambridge: Polity Press, 1996).
[174] Ibid., 13.   [175] Ibid., 76.

traditions of the past, and one which recognizes the centrality of citizenship concerns which has been observed in this book.

Collins and Murroni also pointed towards the desirability of establishing a single 'super regulator' to reflect the realities of the increasingly convergent and conglomerated media industries. Their proposal for 'Ofcom' became the central feature of the Blair government's 2000 White Paper,[176] with the statutory foundations for Ofcom, and its financial basis, being introduced in 2002[177] in advance of the more far-reaching reforms first introduced into Parliament in the form of a draft Communications Bill in May 2002.

Given the realities of modern media markets and technology, the introduction of one regulator to take on many of the functions of five existing bodies[178] seems to be eminently sensible. In particular, given the reality of close intertwining between delivery mechanism and product in broadcasting markets, it may well be that one super-regulator is indeed better placed to take an overview of market realities as opposed to a range of regulators focusing on different aspects. In general the logic of a single media regulator and the rationalization resulting from its introduction is to be supported, though not without reservations. Simply put, replacing many regulators with one does not *in itself* guarantee either more consistent or more principled regulation, or regulation which necessarily better serves objectives which might be associated with the public interest. In addition, it should be noted that, predictably, New Labour has declined to address the perennial question of self-regulation of the press industry.

While the influence of the IPPR agenda, with its emphasis on citizenship concerns, might be expected to be of assistance, much would depend on how the 'spirit' of this agenda was translated into legislative and administrative reality. If the central, informing concept remained undefined or inadequately specified and prioritized, it may be that the underlying values would be no better protected. It was in the Communications Bill 2002 where any specification of the values which would inform the new regulator's activities could be expected to be found.

The draft Bill, and the Communications Act 2003 which it ultimately became, are vast documents, and it is both impossible and unnecessary to offer a complete summary of them here. However, it is worth noting that while one of the primary purposes of the legislation was undoubtedly to rationalize the media regulation system in the UK, this was not the only motivating force driving the legislation forward. Indeed, it is arguable that two other factors were of at least as great a significance in drafting the Bill as the desire to rationalize the regulatory structure. First, it is clear that the Bill formed part of a wider reform of competition law and regulation, relating closely to the Competition Act 1998 and Enterprise Act 2002, introduced in pursuit of a markedly deregulatory agenda.

---

[176] Department of Culture, Media and Sport, White Paper, *A New Future for Communications* (HMSO: London, 2000), Cm. 5010. [177] Office of Communications Act 2002.

[178] Broadcasting Standards Commission, Independent Television Commission, Radio Authority, Radiocommunications Agency, and Oftel.

Tessa Jowell, Secretary of State for Culture, Media and Sport made this abundantly clear at the Bill's launch, when she stated that, 'We intend to remove or relax most rules concerning media ownership', while adding the intention to keep those rules 'necessary to promote the public interest'.[179] To this end, the original Draft Bill contained a provision titled explicitly 'Duties to secure light touch regulation',[180] and though, following pre-legislative scrutiny[181] and the brokering process of parliamentary debate, this became 'Duties to review regulatory burdens',[182] the message and intention, illustrating the government's 'deregulatory impulse',[183] remains clear and very much the same. Second, it is equally obvious that the introduction of the legislation was influenced significantly by the need to give effect to a package of EU Directives issued in early 2002,[184] aimed at harmonization of the basis for media regulation across the internal market.[185] In the face of limits on the competence of the EU to regulate in respect of cultural issues, the measures were the result of long deliberation, and were considered to be the best available means to address the risk identified by Humphreys of 'competitive deregulation' between Member States in pursuit of attracting inward investment;[186] a trend which would threaten to undermine the internal market.

Thus, the Communications Act 2003 can be seen to incorporate responses to a range of different influences:

- the pressure to reform and rationalize the pre-existing regulatory structure in the face of technological development, media convergence and corporate conglomeration;
- the pressure to encourage growth in the, economically important, media sector;
- the pressure to pursue, as a matter of government policy and ideology, a deregulatory agenda; and,
- the pressure to comply with European harmonization requirements, in pursuit of a single-market agenda.

From the perspective adopted in this book, the key question must remain whether the new arrangements, driven by this diverse range of factors, make any significant difference, for better or for worse, on the protection of citizenship values or other versions of the public interest. The Report of the Parliamentary Joint Committee, which scrutinized the Draft Bill, chaired by the renowned former film-maker Lord David Puttnam, expresses significant reservations as

---

[179] *The Guardian*, 8 May 2002.   [180] Clause 5.   [181] Puttnam Report, Para. 67.
[182] Communications Act 2003, s.6.   [183] Puttnam Report, Para. 64.
[184] Framework Directive, Directive 2002/21/EC OJ 2002 No. L108/33, 24 April 2002; Access Directive, Directive 2002/19/EC, OJ 2002 No. L108/20, 24 April 2002; Authorization Directive, Directive 2002/20/EC, OJ 2002 No. L108/21, 24 April, 2002; Universal Service Directive, Directive 2002/22/EC, OJ 2002 No. L108/51, 24 April 2002.
[185] See Feintuck, 'Walking the High-Wire', 108–11 for an overview of the Directives.
[186] See, generally, Humphreys, *Mass Media*.

regards the original Draft Bill's content in this respect. The Puttnam Report constitutes a wide-ranging, well-informed and in-depth critique of the Draft Bill as a whole: an example of pre-legislative scrutiny at its very best, with questions of 'public interest' and 'citizens' interest' to the fore.

The Report notes a trope from 'consumer' to 'customer' between the 2000 White Paper and the Draft Bill of 2002,[187] and also observes that while the concept of 'citizens' interests' had been given a high profile in the White Paper,[188] it had failed to appear as part of Ofcom's proposed duties in the Draft Bill. While Clause 4 of the Draft Bill sought to give effect to the EU Framework Directive, incorporating a wide range of potentially competing objectives contained therein, it contained no indication of how Ofcom should prioritize these factors in the case of their coming into conflict. Likewise, Clause 3 imposes on Ofcom some fifteen general, and again potentially conflicting, duties, with the regulator permitted to resolve any conflicts between them 'in the manner they think best in the circumstances'. The Puttnam Report identified as 'an abdication of responsibility' the failure by Parliament to specify a hierarchy of duties for the new super-regulator, and recommended explicitly the establishment of a 'principal duty' embodying specifically and explicitly 'the long-term interests of all citizens'.[189]

After much tense and high-profile parliamentary wrangling, the Communications Act 2003 as it finally emerged did incorporate some of the Puttnam Report's recommendations. In some senses, the final form of Section 3(1) may appear to be a major victory:

It shall be the principal duty of Ofcom, in carrying out their functions –

(a) to further the interests of citizens in relation to communications matters; and
(b) to further the interests of consumers in relevant markets, where appropriate by promoting competition.

Certainly, this reference to 'the interests of citizens' is to be welcomed, though the subsequent list of 'things which Ofcom are required to secure',[190] and to which they 'must also have regard'[191] totals some nineteen factors, which, under Section 3(7), if these duties conflict, Ofcom must, in the original words of the Bill, resolve 'in the manner they think best in the circumstances'. Thus, though Section 3(6) does establish a priority for EU obligations, the clear hierarchy of duties sought by Puttnam otherwise remains absent, just as it did under the 1996 Act, leaving wide-ranging and largely unstructured discretion in the regulator's hands, and citizenship interests vulnerable to defeat by other factors. In practice, it may well be that the deregulatory agenda established by Section 6, which requires Ofcom in effect to ensure the lightest feasible level of regulation, might prove a major factor in directing Ofcom's approach to such matters, and may certainly be expected to discourage the kind of active intervention required

---

[187] Puttnam Report, Para. 20.   [188] Ibid., Para. 24.   [189] Ibid., Para. 26.
[190] Section 3(2).   [191] Section 3(4).

to ensure the protection of citizenship interests. Though requirements of transparency via reasoned decision-making are imposed in relation to 'important cases',[192] potentially contributing to the accountability of the regulator, this is not the same thing as establishing a statutory priority for citizenship-related interests.

At the most general level, it therefore seems that the vulnerability of broad public interests in media regulation has not been satisfactorily remedied by the Communications Act 2003. That said, writing in early 2004, and with Ofcom only having taken up its powers at the very end of 2003, it is too early to say precisely how things will work out. It is clear though that, in general, any improvement in such respect is not guaranteed by the statutory framework, but is dependent upon the exercise of the regulator's broad discretionary powers. However, it is also necessary to consider, if briefly, some more specific examples of areas in which Ofcom will have responsibility for matters which may raise particular 'public interest' issues.

Public Service Broadcasting

Most obvious amongst such issues in the context of British broadcasting is the question of the role and future of PSB. This is not the place to discuss in detail the historical development of the British PSB tradition in television broadcasting,[193] though two things will surely be understood. First, that the model noted earlier, dominated by the publicly owned BBC, and commercial, though heavily regulated ITV (Channel 3) and more recently Channel 4 and Channel 5, has represented the mainstream broadcasting tradition in Britain, and arguably the archetypal version of the Western European tradition. Second, it will be known that in the post-Thatcher/Reagan market-oriented political environment, and with the advent of new technology, especially digitalization, the PSB tradition has come under ever-increasing challenge.

The government's response to this situation in the 2003 Act is interesting. Under Section 264, Ofcom is required to review and report, one year after its establishment, on the extent to which public service broadcasters have 'provided relevant television services which (taking them together over the period as a whole) fulfill the purposes of public service television broadcasting in the UK',[194] with a view to 'maintaining and strengthening the quality of public service television broadcasting in the UK'.[195] In perhaps the most direct and authoritative statement of what constitutes PSB values since Lord Reith's famous, almost totemic, mission statement for the BBC of the 1920s of 'informing, educating, and entertaining', the Act goes on to specify the purposes of PSB in the UK. Though the list of factors incorporated in Sections 264(4) and (6) do include

---

[192] Sections 3(11) and 3(12).
[193] See Curran and Seaton, *Power Without Responsibility*, Ch. 22; also Feintuck, *Media Regulation*, Ch. 2.   [194] S.264(3)(a).
[195] S.264(3)(b).

Lord Reith's phrase almost verbatim,[196] the list is extensive. It includes relatively conventional public service qualities such as range of subject matter, appeal to and meeting the needs of a range of audiences, the maintenance of high standards as regards content and quality of programme-making, and, 'facilitating civic understanding and fair and well-informed debate on news and current affairs'.[197] However, it also goes beyond such predictable matters to provide additional, very specific indicators of PSB qualities, such as the support and stimulation of cultural activity via broadcasting of drama, comedy and music, 'what appears to Ofcom to be a suitable quantity and range of programmes dealing with … science, religion and other beliefs, social issues, matters of international significance or interest and matters of specialist interest',[198] and, 'an appropriate range and proportion of programmes made outside the M25 area'.[199] Such criteria are certainly much more reminiscent of the requirements generally found in the licences of commercial television broadcasters in Britain than the broad terms of reference against which the BBC operates under its Charter.

There are at least three possible responses to such a specific and relatively detailed enumeration of public service qualities. One is to welcome it, as a means of providing performance indicators against which the BBC and licensed broadcasters can be measured, and a means of structuring the discretion vested in Ofcom. A second is to wonder whether such definitions are already outdated, perhaps like the Reithian vision, serving to mask 'a concept replete with definitional difficulties',[200] failing to take into account the substantial changes to the broadcasting landscape created by the introduction of new technology, especially interactive digital television services. The third response, is to wonder why, if it is possible to list in such detail the values of public service broadcasting, it is not equally desirable and possible in this context to list what is intended by 'public interest' or 'the interests of citizens' and to integrate them into the listing of PSB qualities or indeed articulate them fully at the forefront of Ofcom's overall responsibilities. Of course, it may be that the public interest values are considered by the legislators to be coterminous with PSB qualities, a position which is perfectly possible, but should perhaps be clearly stated rather than left to assumption, if this is indeed the intention.

It seems significant that these requirements are to be considered by Ofcom across the range of public service broadcasters 'taken together' rather than being read as specific requirements or quotas being imposed upon individual broadcasters. Indeed, the final abandonment of any attempt to impose strict specific requirements or programme quotas on any one individual licensed broadcaster is signalled clearly in Sections 265 and 266, which state objectives in the broadest possible terms, and places reliance on the requirement imposed on licence

---

[196] S.264(6)(a).   [197] S.264(6)(c).   [198] S.264(6)(f).   [199] S.264(6)(j).

[200] Harrison, J., 'Interactive Digital Television and the Expansion of the Public Service Tradition', *Communications Law*, 8/6 (2003), 401. See Liddiment, D., 'One Person's Public-Service Gem is Another's Garbage', *The Guardian*, 12 January 2004, for a discussion of some of the indefinable qualities that lurk beneath the apparently straightforward concept of PSB.

holders to produce a 'statement of programme policy', against which they must monitor their performance, subject to oversight by Ofcom. This must be seen as a clear example of 'light touch' regulation, in practice if not in name.

However, Ofcom's ability to regulate PSB as a whole may be faced with a different, potentially more significant problem. While its powers are reasonably extensive in relation to licensed broadcasters, its relationship with the BBC is far from clear. The BBC has not been brought fully within the scope of Ofcom's regulatory brief, but will instead remain subject to the terms of its Charter and Licensing Agreement,[201] supervised by its Governors, and subject to backstop powers exercised by the Secretary of State for Culture Media and Sport. The Puttnam Report raised queries concerning both the BBC's role in the competitive marketplace of public service broadcasting and Ofcom's role in relation to the Corporation.[202] Such factors are likely to be significant in the context of the wholesale review of the BBC's Licensing Agreement and Charter renewal, to be completed by 2006, and into which Ofcom's first review of the PSB landscape, due out early 2005, is likely to make a significant input. The ability of the BBC currently to operate outside the direct ambit of Ofcom's powers appears anomalous, not just from the perspective of its commercial competitors, who feel that by virtue of its funding through the compulsory licence fee the Corporation enjoys unfair advantages in the marketplace, but also, logically, from the point of view of regulating the *sector as a whole*. Any realistic claim to oversee the public service landscape must be fundamentally weakened if the largest, best-established, and most high-profile public service broadcaster in the world is not fully included within that view. In reality, in the wake of the Hutton Report,[203] it may be that it would actually serve the BBC's best interests, in terms of establishing independence from government influence, for it to find itself fully under Ofcom's regulatory umbrella. In this context, much seems to rest on Ofcom's first report into PSB, and the ensuing review of the licence fee and the BBC's Charter.

Merger Control 'in the Public Interest'

Finally at this stage, one further, vitally important, area of Ofcom's powers under the 2003 Act must also be commented on: the regulation of competition and especially mergers within the media industries under Part 5, Sections 369–389. Of course, takeovers and mergers within the media industries have always proved controversial and high-profile. Whether it be repeated struggles over control of broadsheet newspaper titles in the 1970s and 1980s, or the presently ongoing merger of Carlton and Granada, the two giants of Channel 3, such mergers are always viewed in relation to the potentially important, if strictly contingent,

---

[201] See S.198.   [202] Puttnam Report, Paras. 212–15 and 325.

[203] Hutton Report, *Report of the Inquiry into the Circumstances Surrounding the Death of Dr David Kelly, C.M.G.* (London: The Stationery Office, 2004).

relationship between concentration of ownership of media outlets and control over what is communicated through them, and ultimately the range of views in circulation in society.

Much of the press coverage in the immediate aftermath of the Draft Bill's publication in May 2002 focused on aspects of merger control. In particular, emphasis was given to two possible consequences – the potential for a single owner to dominate Channel 3 (which the Carlton/Granada merger will now bring about) and the possibility of Rupert Murdoch making further inroads towards the domination of the UK media scene as a whole. The broadsheets ran with headlines such as 'Easing the reins on media moguls',[204] and somewhat more explicitly, 'Government clears way for Murdoch to buy Channel 5',[205] referring to the proposed abolition of the previous position under which owners of national newspapers with more than 20 per cent of circulation could not control a national radio or television licence.[206] On the day following publication of the Draft Bill, *The Telegraph* (in 2004 itself to be subject to a high-profile change of ownership regime) observed that 'Despite government claims about the importance of "diversity, plurality and democracy", the decision to relax ownership will lead to far greater concentration of media power.' In a similar vein, *The Independent* noted 'So much talk of diversity but so little desire to stop Mr. Murdoch's dominance.' The Murdoch-controlled *Times* emphasized 'a better, freer marketplace', while *The Guardian* concluded, bluntly, that 'Murdoch must have done a deal'!

The substance behind such headlines is that many of the complex range of provisions applicable specifically to the media, mostly originating from Schedule 2 of the Broadcasting Act 1996, establishing maximum holdings and intervention thresholds, are swept away, being replaced by general competition provisions under the Competition Act 1998 and the merger provisions in the Enterprise Act 2002. Under Sections 369–372 of the Communications Act, Ofcom acquires concurrent powers with the Office of Fair Trading (OFT) under these Acts, with the potential for further grants of power by the Secretary of State. Under Sections 373 and 374, the provisions of the FTA that had provided specific measures for take-overs and mergers in newspapers are replaced by the general provisions of the Enterprise Act.

A particular point of interest here is the language used both in the Enterprise Act and the Communications Act, where reference is made, respectively, to 'Public Interest Cases' and 'Media Public Interest Considerations'. The provisions allow reference by the Secretary of State to the OFT via an 'intervention notice' where a public interest consideration is relevant to a merger situation.[207] Incorporated into Section 58 of the Enterprise Act by Section 375 of the Communications Act are detailed specifications of what constitutes 'the public interest'

---

[204] *The Guardian*, 8 May 2002.   [205] *The Independent*, 8 May 2002.
[206] See Stewart, P. and Gibson, D., 'The Communications Act – a New Era', *Communications Law*, 8/5 (2003), 357.   [207] Enterprise Act 2002, S.42(1).

in relation to mergers between newspapers, between broadcasters, or mergers which cross the two sectors.

These provisions were added late in the parliamentary process as something of a concession in the Lords, and as Ofcom notes, are 'often described as the plurality test'.[208] Ofcom summarizes the public interest criteria as follows:

In the case of a newspaper merger, the public interest considerations, as defined by the Act, are:

- The need for accurate presentation of news in newspapers;
- The need for free expression of opinion in the newspapers involved in the merger;
- The need for, to the extent that is reasonable and practicable, a sufficient plurality of views expressed in newspapers as a whole in each market for newspapers in the UK or part of the UK.

In the case of a broadcasting merger or a cross-media merger, the pubic interest considerations as defined by the Act, are:

- The need for there to be a sufficient plurality of persons with control of the media enterprises serving that audience in relation to every different audience in the UK or a particular area/locality of the UK;
- The need for availability throughout the UK of a wide range of broadcasting which (taken as a whole) is both of high quality and calculated to appeal to a wide variety of tastes and interests;
- The need for persons carrying on media enterprises and for those with control of such enterprises to have a genuine commitment to the attainment in relation to broadcasting of the standards objectives set out in Section 319 of the Communications Act 2003 (for example governing matters of accuracy, impartiality, harm, offence, fairness and privacy in broadcasting).[209]

Clearly, the precise way in which such broad provisions will be interpreted is subject to substantial discretion on Ofcom's behalf. In Stewart and Gibson's terms, 'It is in essence for Ofcom to objectively consider whether the new company would have too prominent a voice across all sectors of the media.'[210]

Especially in the early years of the new regulator exercising this jurisdiction, companies involved in actual or proposed mergers will require guidance as to how the powers will be used. Produced in light of DTI guidance as to when intervention will take place, and with the intention of mirroring the OFT's guidance, Ofcom moved quickly after taking up its powers to indicate how it would go about offering general advice as regards proposed mergers. In essence, Ofcom's advice[211] amounts to little more than a re-statement of the provisions summarized above, and identifies its role as being one of applying the tests, and reporting the results to the Secretary of State with a recommendation as to whether the

---

[208] Ofcom, 'Ofcom announces guidance on media mergers' public interest test', http://www.ofcom.org.uk/media_office/latest_news/nr_nr_20040105, accessed 7 January 2004.
[209] Ibid.   [210] Stewart and Gibson, 'The Communications Act', 358.
[211] Ofcom, 'Ofcom guidance for the public interest test for media mergers', http://www.ofcom.org.uk/codes_guidelines/ofcom_codes_guidance/pi_test/pi_legal, accessed 8 January 2004.

merger should be referred to the Competition Commission for further consideration. As *The Guardian* reported,[212] though Ofcom will be prepared to amplify the general situations in relation to a party considering a proposed merger, such advice or guidance will not ultimately bind Ofcom or any of the other authorities involved in the process.

Though Ofcom only plays one part in a process which is triggered and concluded by the Secretary of State, and with the Competition Commission playing a significant role, Ofcom's advice will surely be influential. While suspicions have been voiced by some media owners, that the provisions continue to permit an unhealthy degree of political influence over the sensitive issue of media takeovers and mergers,[213] in fact, the range of public interest criteria established under Section 375 and subsequent Sections do outline some key factors which might usefully form the basis for a meaningful version of the concept in this context and which may establish a framework against which decisions must be justified. Though there is clearly scope for interpretation in individual cases, they do provide a structure to the regulator's discretion. However, one is left with a feeling that, although the Secretary of State will now operate within the context of more transparent advice from the Competition Commission, the political role will indeed remain significant, just as it did under the former FTA provisions regarding take-overs and mergers in the newspaper sector. As critics of the new regime can argue,

Ofcom's public interest test cannot be applied in every takeover because its inquiries can only be triggered by the trade and industry secretary. This means that a government, of whatever hue, can decide which bidder should undergo such a test and which should not. That decision will, of course, be subjective. However remote the possibility, it allows a government to make a political judgment about referral which could be based, not unfeasibly, on a bidder's attitude towards its administration.[214]

In addition to such factors, which serve to place reliance upon the accountability of party politicians, there are, of course, some serious technical–legal difficulties in establishing competition rules in relation to media markets. In particular, problems of market definition,[215] and measuring market share (for example, comparing readership and audience on national and local bases), which form prior questions to scrutinizing dominance within a market, comprise serious obstacles to a rational and predictable system. That said, the degree of transparency imported into the regime under the new provisions may make a substantial difference in adding credibility and legitimacy to the system. Clearly, the new merger provisions do go some way towards identifying a public interest test for take-overs and mergers in the media, but not, as just noted, one that

---

[212] *The Guardian*, 6 January 2004.
[213] See, for example, 'Shouldn't this man be worried?' *The Guardian*, 12 January 2004.
[214] Ibid.
[215] See, for example, Carter, E. J., 'Market Definition in the Broadcasting Sector', *World Competition*, 24/1 (2001), 93.

will be applied in every case, and it should be noted that these public interest criteria apply *only* to that part of Ofcom's brief which relates to take-overs and mergers. The regulator's responsibilities, of course, extend far beyond this, and even include a degree of content regulation, taking over from the ITC and BSC responsibilities in relation to taste and decency on radio and television. In this perennially problematic context, the statutory provisions which empower Ofcom to establish its 'Content Board',[216] unsurprisingly, offer much less by way of guidance or structure as to the standards to be applied.

Commercial Freedom and Democratic Values

On the whole, from the kind of public interest agenda pursued in this book, it might be thought that the arrival of Ofcom and the 2003 Act offers much to be enthusiastic about. In some senses, this conclusion is reasonable. However, inevitably there must also be reservations. Indeed, at the very point of Ofcom taking up its powers at the end of 2003, certain bodies were quick to voice concerns as to whether the new regulator would really serve either consumers or citizens, or whether 'Ofcom is serving industry's self-regulatory ambitions' on matters such as broadcast advertising.[217] Only limited reassurance can be gained from an examination of Ofcom's summary of its roles, which it states as being to:

- Balance the promotion of choice and competition with the duty to foster plurality, informed citizenship, protect viewers, listeners and customers and promote cultural diversity.
- Serve the interests of the citizen-consumer as the communications industry enters the digital age.
- Support the need for innovators, creators and investors to flourish within markets driven by full and fair competition between all providers.
- Encourage the evolution of electronic media and communications networks to the greater benefit of all who live in the United Kingdom.[218]

Such a summary of the regulator's position inevitably raises at least as many questions as it answers. Do such statements amount to more than platitudes? Do they reassure us as to which values will be preferred when decisions have to be made, as on occasion they inevitably will, which require Ofcom to determine whether industry interests must be privileged over consumer interests, or con-sumerist interests over citizen-related interests, or private, commercial interests should prevail over 'public interests'? The ambiguities and conflicts which are central to a brief as wide as that enjoyed by Ofcom are substantial, and they cannot be resolved satisfactorily by the simple use by Ofcom of the hyphen, in

---

[216] Communications Act 2003, S.12 and S.13.

[217] Consumers' Association spokesperson, quoted in *The Guardian*, 29 December 2003.

[218] Ofcom, 'Home Page, About Ofcom', http://www.ofcom.org.uk/about_ofcom/?a=87101, accessed 8 January 2004.

summarizing its brief in terms such as 'serving citizen-consumers in the digital age'.[219]

In Harrison's terms, the Act as it ultimately emerged from Parliament, incorporating references to citizens as well as consumers, represented 'a change of emphasis from the Bill's main aim to enhance the economic performance of British media through deregulation and consolidation, towards a more deliberate attempt to preserve the British tradition of public service in broadcasting'.[220] However, though the change in language from Bill to Act might be welcome, problems remain, especially in terms of 'how the economic interests of the commercial sector will in practice be compatible with the public interest and the interests of the citizens', leading to questions as to 'how successful the regulator will be in balancing conflicting forces'.[221]

I have argued at length elsewhere as regards the significance of the media in relation to citizenship,[222] and, specifically in relation to the then Draft Communications Bill, have noted the delicate balance required by Ofcom 'between a degree of commercial freedom and the defence of democratic values'.[223] Though the parliamentary process, and especially the excellent pre-legislative scrutiny carried out by the Puttnam Committee, resulted in concessions being made, and positive changes being made from the original form of the Draft Bill, many problems seem to remain. To a significant extent, these result from a failure to meet the Puttnam Report's fundamental recommendation that a clear hierarchy of values should be established within the statutory framework, rather than leaving such values vulnerable to market forces and the exercise of regulatory discretion.

Regulating the media poses significant problems, in terms of conceptual definition and techniques for achieving identified objectives. In particular, the picture may become clouded by technical difficulties in establishing rules as regards ownership or control, and market definition, in relation to an increasingly convergent and conglomerated set of industries. However, as any student of media regulation should be aware, attempts to design institutional structures which produce outcomes which are effective in terms of protecting or furthering underlying values are unlikely to be successful unless the prior task of identifying and articulating those values with reasonable clarity is properly undertaken. Technical regulatory difficulties, such as identifying market share of cross-media organizations, are compounded, and effective action perhaps rendered impossible, when no clear hierarchy of principles or objectives are established. In this sense, though the Puttnam Committee's work represented a valiant effort, both the Communications Act and the European Directives which influenced significant parts of it, represent missed opportunities. The Act, and Ofcom offer no guarantees that citizenship interests will be given adequate protection in the face of commercial pressures. In this sense, a substantial part of the stated rationale for the Act in its

---

[219] Ibid.   [220] Harrison, 'Interactive Digital Television', 401.   [221] Ibid.
[222] See generally, Feintuck, *Media Regulation*.   [223] Feintuck, 'Walking the High-Wire', 124.

final form may not be translated into practical outcomes; public interest values beyond those attaching to commercial interests may not be protected.

It seems that the lack of a rational policy-making process in relation to media regulation, which Hitchens noted in 1995,[224] the result perhaps of the absence of sufficient clarity as regards any fundamental, animating value-base, is still hindering the development of meaningful protection for democratic interests in the area. Of course, an alternative perspective would suggest that the Communications Act 2003 and current regulatory framework for the media in fact represent a very clear translation of government policy into practice; the policy, on this view, being that of allowing economic concerns to be prioritized over citizenship values. Meanwhile, the market and technology moves on, and Elliot's 'bus' seems to continue to pull away, leaving those concerned for citizenship interests hoping, perhaps in vain, that some alternative will come along shortly.

CONCLUSIONS

The conclusion reached in the first Part of this book was that the fulfilment of the promises contained in anything but the narrowest vision of democracy required the establishment of normative standards which related directly to inherent, fundamental values contained within the liberal–democratic settlement. Even where, as in Britain, clear statements of the values underpinning the polity are hard to come by, there is no doubt that they exist, and that central amongst them are expectations related to citizenship.

What emerges, from the work of the likes of Fisher or Hitchens, referred to earlier in this chapter, is a clear impression that in the regulation of matters crucial to expectations of citizenship, standards and practices have emerged in a haphazard and piecemeal fashion. As is illustrated by Elliot's vision of the receding bus, or Campbell and Lee's account of the FMD crisis, the absence of a principled and rational basis on which to act has led to reactive regulation, rather than regulatory activity which articulates, reflects, and serves fundamental principles. In the absence of the development of a clear foundation of principle on which to build a regulatory edifice, it has been possible for regulatory policies and practices to emerge which reflect only one part of the set of values which we might expect them to reflect. The total predominance of the 'blackboard economics' approach to regulating FMD noted by Campbell and Lee, and the priority apparently given to narrow consumer interests within the FSA's activities, may both serve as examples of this phenomenon. It must surely be of democratic concern if the government's policy on matters such as food supply or the media was indeed shaped primarily by macroeconomic factors. The risks associated with such a one-dimensional approach, in the absence of a rational and rigorous policy-making and regulatory framework of principle, should be

---

[224] Hitchens, 'Get Ready, Fire, Take Aim'.

obvious: other values outside this perspective will be marginalized or overridden. This may be especially true in an era where technological change, whether it be GMOs or digital broadcasting, and increasingly globalized and conglomerated markets, combine and serve to appear to increase the need for action to protect non-commodity values of the kind historically associated with, say, PSB or the utilities.

Certainly, the kind of transparency and efforts at encouraging participation associated with the FSA's activities are to be welcomed. Likewise, the structural reforms in media regulation, with Ofcom potentially better able to respond to the convergent media markets than its multiple predecessors, seem to be a step forward. Such procedural and structural reform, may offer significant improvements in constitutional and democratic terms, enhancing rationality, accountability, and hence legitimacy in the regulatory endeavour. However, such matters, though of great democratic significance in themselves, are not the whole of the story. These, essentially procedural, expectations are not ends in themselves, but rather should be seen as institutions which are supposed to serve the kind of substantive democratic values which attach to citizenship, and which seem to require enhanced protection, by way of resistance to the influence of powerful, sectional economic interests. If the liberal–democratic settlement is not to be quietly replaced by what Leys refers to as 'neoliberal democracy',[225] with its much narrower set of market-oriented economic values, the quest must be for principles or devices which themselves have democratic legitimacy, are legally enforceable, and which serve the broader democratic value-set.

The amendments made to the Communications Bill in an attempt to protect 'the public interest', though they may represent the result of valiant efforts, ultimately must be seen not to go far enough. In particular, the Communications Act as it stands does not fulfil the Puttnam Committee's desire to see a clear hierarchy of values established with public interest values given an appropriately secure and high statutory priority. Instead, such vulnerable values must compete for recognition with others, deriving from powerful producer and consumer expectations within the increasingly commodified media market, with the eventual priority between them resting on the wide-ranging and relatively unstructured discretion provided to the regulatory authorities. In such a situation, though pursuing a claim of 'public interest' may seem unsatisfactory and unattractive, it does, at least if linked explicitly to citizenship claims, serve to draw attention to the existence of a range of democratic values beyond the economic. It may, especially in the absence of clear statements of constitutional principle, and in an increasingly deregulatory and market-oriented Britain, offer the best available game in town.

---

[225] See, generally, Leys, *Market Driven Politics*.

4

The Public Interest in Regulatory Practice: the USA

The Constitutional and Administrative Context

In language, culture, common law heritage, and, democratic tradition, there is sufficient shared between the UK and US to make comparison, in relation to a phenomenon such as 'the public interest', immediately attractive. In both countries, as in all modern, capitalist democracies, the relationship between private property interests and claims of public interest or general welfare must be resolved within the context of liberal market economies. However, it is also immediately apparent that there are substantial differences.

The federal and fiercely republican context in which regulation of private activity takes place in the US, has led to a very different administrative tradition from that of the UK. Though Schuck identifies a secure *legal* foundation for the activities of regulatory agencies,[1] within an arguably much more developed administrative law tradition than that in Britain, he notes also that the *political* legitimacy of such agencies and their actions is constantly challenged. However, as we will see in relation to the public interest brief pursued by the Federal Communications Commission (FCC), even the legal and constitutional basis of such powers is on occasion subject to challenge. Despite a degree of constitutional security provided by judicial confirmation of the scope for agencies to be granted authority by Congress,[2] within a context in which what is recognized as the public sector – and certainly state provision of social welfare – is much smaller than that traditionally associated with Western European democracies, US administrative agencies with responsibilities to intervene in private activity are faced with a constant 'burden of justification'.[3]

Given the substantial differences in constitutional, political and administrative traditions just identified, prudence demands a degree of caution in making direct comparisons between the jurisdictions. Certainly, the British system, within which regulators, empowered by often broad statutory terms, are treated with a high degree of deference by the judicial system, looks very different from the situation in the US, where an apparently highly developed and proactive

---

[1] Schuck, P. H. (ed.), *Foundations of Administrative Law* (Oxford: Oxford University Press, 1994), 9–11. [2] *Mistretta v. United States*, 488 US 361 (1989).
[3] Schuck (ed.), *Foundations of Administrative Law*, 10.

administrative law system might be expected to have played a very significant role in seeking to ensure that administrative agencies operate within the requirements of the federal, republican constitutional tradition.[4] Simply put, it seems to be the case that in the US, to a far greater degree than in the UK, 'The judiciary not only helped define the terms of internal governmental activity, it also helped define relations between state and society.'[5] However, trans-Atlantic comparisons remain of potential utility, especially given the fact that it might be reasonably expected that clearer answers and principles are likely to emerge from the 'perennial democratic discourse over the nature of the good society, the proper conception of the public interest, and the appropriate domains of law, politics and the administration'[6] found in the US. In addition, as noted in Chapters One and Two, the shared common law heritage and the sheer similarity in issues emerging in relation to regulatory activity, make comparisons both attractive and inevitable.

The bulk of the direct comparative work will be undertaken in Chapter Five, while the purpose of the present chapter is to seek to understand how concepts of public interest have developed in, and have informed, the American regulatory system. Paralleling the subject matter of Chapter Three's study of the UK, the focus here will be primarily on the key regulators of broadcasting and of food supply; the FCC, and the Federal Food and Drug Administration (FDA).

As Harris and Milkis note in their study focused on two other federal agencies, the Federal Trade Commission (FTC) and the Environmental Protection Agency (EPA), 'the study of contemporary regulatory affairs offers a distinctive opportunity to grapple with weightier questions of democracy, citizenship, the evolution of an administrative state, and the role of ideas in American politics'.[7] They also comment, however, that 'in an effort to arrive at policy-relevant considerations', studies of regulation too often 'gloss over more profound questions'.[8] Central to these seems to be how 'the public interest' is interpreted and applied in the activities of regulatory agencies and the courts which oversee them.

However, in order to consider the role of a concept such as public interest in the context of regulation, it is also necessary to understand the changing visions of the role of regulation within a society such as the US. Studies of the modern American regulatory system invariably start from Franklin Roosevelt's New Deal, the 1930's response to the 1929 crash and the depression that followed. The pre-existing order is summarized by Harris and Milkis:

The earlier political economic order was predicated on the twin assumptions that the general welfare was best served by individuals pursuing their particular economic interests

---

[4] See generally, Craig, P. P., *Public Law and Democracy in the United Kingdom and the United States* (Oxford: Clarendon, 1990).

[5] Skowronek, S., *Building a New American State: the Expansion of National Administrative Capacities, 1877–1920* (Cambridge: Cambridge University Press, 1982); excerpt in Schuck, (ed.), *Foundations of Administrative Law*, 34.   [6] Ibid.

[7] Harris, R. A. and Milkis, S. M., *The Politics of Regulatory Change: a Tale of Two Agencies*, 2nd edn. (Oxford: Oxford University Press, 1996), 3.   [8] Ibid.

and that those individuals ultimately and justly could be held responsible for their own economic position.[9]

Thus, despite Keynes's unambiguous statement in the 1920s that 'it is not a correct deduction from the Principles of Economics that enlightened self-interest always operates in the public interest',[10] and Stewart's identification within the civic republicanist tradition of 'a more ample vision based upon associational values',[11] the development of a new public philosophy in the 1930s, the start of 'social regulation', can be said to have marked a distinct shift in the relationship between the American corporation and the state, and the start of the modern era of regulation. While the origins of social regulation in the New Deal era might be thought of as a pragmatic attempt to reform capitalism, in order to save it, in terms of its aims and institutions it might be thought of as relying on deeper historical and constitutional foundations. Indeed, in some senses the case of *Munn v. Illinois*,[12] referred to in Chapter One, seems to confirm the presence of a concept of public interest regulation over fifty years earlier, albeit one capable of being limited to the context of what would come to be referred to as 'essential facilities'.

It must be acknowledged that agencies are the product of their social and political historical context as much as the constitutional and legal, and it can be argued that within agencies, at least as regards their internal operation, 'the administrative process owes more to experience than doctrine'.[13] However, regulatory activity must also be viewed in the context of the system of checks and balances, within the US presidential, bicameral and federal structure, the strong separation of powers model, and a Supreme Court fiercely protective of the Constitution. These arrangements might properly be thought to reflect a series of values which underlie the constitutional settlement, and which, drawing on Madisonian concerns, include a strong degree of resistance to the risk of a tyranny of the majority; 'the prospect of a majority faction subordinating the policy process to its own interests and against the public interest or minority rights'.[14] Though this inevitably results in tensions, and may even risk a degree of inertia, it has a potential advantage in ensuring that underlying constitutional values cannot be readily overridden or discarded. In addition, as Harris and Milkis make clear, the US Constitution, whether viewed from the perspective of those pursuing the development of social regulation in the 1920s and 1930s, or from the country's eighteenth-century founders, is not only about limiting government activity and powers. It also embodies a vision of 'positive government', with a proper

---

[9] Ibid., 58.

[10] Keynes, J. M., *The End of Laissez Faire* (London: Hogarth Press, 1927), quoted in Harris and Milkis, *The Politics of Regulatory Change*, 58.

[11] Stewart, R. B., 'Regulation in a Liberal State: the Role of Non-Commodity Values', *Yale Law Journal*, 92 (1983), 1537, at 1543.   [12] *Munn v. Illinois*, 94 US 139 (1877).

[13] Breger, M. J. and Edles, G. J., 'Established by Practice: the Theory and Operation of Independent Federal Agencies', *Administrative Law Review*, 52/4 (2000), 1111, at 1234.

[14] Harris and Milkis, *The Politics of Regulatory Change*, 33.

role in 'promoting the public interest over particular interests'.[15] In Sunstein's terms, 'the liberal republicanism of American constitutional thought' is premised on 'a set of ideas treating the political process not as an aggregation of purely private interests, but as a deliberative effort to promote the common good'.[16]

The move to social regulation from the 1930s onwards may be viewed in light of these underlying values and tensions; in particular though, a concern that the untrammelled pursuit of profit by powerful and organized corporate interests should not be allowed to override the citizenship expectations of others. However, whether the programme of regulation originating from the New Deal is viewed either as mere ventilation of pressure, in defence of the continuation of capitalism, or as an embodiment of fundamental constitutional expectations, it established the modern basis for the American regulatory state that persisted through the remainder of the twentieth century and into the present.

There can be no doubt that the development of American public interest regulation owes at least as much to the writing of political economy as to legal thinking. Writers such as Mitnick[17] and Breyer[18] provide a politico-economic perspective that has a much higher profile in the American literature than the British.

Breyer[19] sets out by establishing a categorization of economic rationales for regulation: control of monopoly power; rent control, avoiding excess profits; dealing with externalities or spillovers; inadequacy of information; and addressing excessive competition. Beyond these main justifications for regulation, he notes a secondary range of issues, including inequality of bargaining power, rationalization, moral hazard, scarcity, and paternalism. Factors deriving from these various secondary economic rationales often form part of the justification for what is referred to as 'social regulation', but these issues, in their economic sense, only form part of the mixture of rationales. Thus, when Breyer later moves on to consider allocation under a public interest standard,[20] for example the processes followed by the FCC when licensing, it becomes clear that justifications from pure economics comprise only one factor in the regulatory process. Indeed, far from the apparently objective criteria of economics being the dominant feature, the potential for a large degree of subjectivity in the criteria adopted and applied is inevitable. Substantial tensions arise, between the desirability of rules, standards and consistency, as opposed to flexibility and responsiveness in the individual case. Of course, the interests of 'justice' point in both directions, revealing, says Breyer, an underlying tension which he characterizes as similar to that between law and equity.[21] In the case of US regulatory agencies, the set of factors just outlined has tended to result in a heavily legalized and

---

[15] Harris and Milkis, *The Politics of Regulatory Change*, 13.

[16] Sunstein, C. R., *After the Rights Revolution: Reconceiving the Regulatory State* (Cambridge, Mass.: Harvard University Press, 1990), 12.

[17] Mitnick, B. M., *The Political Economy of Regulation* (New York, N.Y.: Columbia University Press, 1980).

[18] Breyer, S., *Regulation and its Reform* (Cambridge, Mass.: Harvard University Press, 1982).

[19] Ibid., Ch. 1.   [20] Ibid., Ch. 4.   [21] Ibid., 74.

adversarial model of regulatory practice, which relates less and less directly to any underlying economic rationales, and may also lose sight of other informing values. It may, as will become clear, offer little assistance in terms of conceptual development of the supposedly central value of the public interest.

As Rabin notes, even the massive and rapid development of US administrative law in the 1970s 'provided no key to a substantive definition of the public interest'.[22] However, what is abundantly clear is that the public interest, and regulation undertaken in its name, lies at the very intersection of law, politics and economics, and is, quite properly, subject to critique from scholars within all these disciplines. In the terms of Baldwin et al., the public interest approach 'has been said to understate the extent to which regulation is the product of clashes between different interest groups and (alternatively) the degree to which regulatory regimes are established by, and run in, the interests of the economically powerful'.[23] Whatever angle it is approached from, the chance is that regulation is unlikely ever to be found to be delivering fully the public interest outcomes which it seems to promise. Of course, this should be relatively unsurprising if an awareness is maintained of the lack of definition of the concept within the regulatory context.

Mitnick is quite clear that a theory of interest is required if the policy-making and regulatory processes are to be properly understood. While unwilling to associate with 'perspectives that assume regulation is instituted either to serve public interests or private, regulated-industry interests',[24] he is clear that 'unless one assumes that the state or public mystically acts for itself in seeking the regulation, public interest theories require, in effect, that parties seeking regulation be *agents* for the public interest'.[25] Though helpful in potentially reasserting the pursuit of public interest regulatory objectives as above and beyond the interest-group fray, this does not in itself help in establishing a core meaning for the concept. However, Mitnick's study of public interest theories is important both in providing an overview of a range of perspectives, but also more specifically in identifying the tendency for public interest theory to be 'implicit'.[26] This may go some way to explaining why he finds little help in seeking a normative statement of the public interest from legal history, and is instead drawn into the literature of philosophy.

Mitnick's work is also important in drawing attention directly to a phenomenon which though on one level obvious, is worthy of clear re-statement. One of the complications in discussion of public interest theory, and regulation in its name, is the presence of multiple versions in play at the same time. Thus, as Mitnick illustrates, while Posner might conceive of public interest regulation as serving the public finance function of taxation, he notes that others will use

---

[22] Rabin, R., 'The Administrative State and its Excesses: Reflections on The New Property', *University of San Francisco Law Review*, 25 (1990) 273; extracts reproduced in Schuck, *Foundations of Administrative Law*, 123.

[23] Baldwin, R., Scott, C., and Hood, C., *A Reader on Regulation* (Oxford: Oxford University Press, 1998), 9.   [24] Mitnick, *The Political Economy of Regulation*, 86.

[25] Ibid., 91, original emphasis.   [26] Ibid., 97–9.

'public interest' primarily by way of emphasizing the statutory power of those entrusted with regulatory authority to define the term.[27] Meanwhile, others will present ' "public interest" theories of a highly specialized character', such as the economist's sense of 'optimal resource allocation, given the existing income distribution',[28] or, with echoes here of the discussion of the UK's Food Standards Agency in the previous chapter, use ' "consumer interest" as synonymous with, part of, or an indicator for the "public interest" '.[29] As he correctly notes, it is impossible to compare conclusions based on such specialized models of the public interest with those reached via other more general approaches.

In terms of the main agenda of this book, considering whether a normative concept of public interest may have a presently unfulfilled function as an interpretative principle which meshes with the values which underlie the liberal–democratic settlement, such a conclusion is unpromising. Yet it is quite clear that despite the absence of a real dialogue between speakers of different 'languages of public interest', versions of the concept have consistently informed debate over regulation in the US. Mitnick refers to Herring's approach, viewing the public interest as subjective, and something to be determined by each civil servant on a case-by-case basis, and therefore by default inevitably associated with group interests relevant to each individual decision.[30] However, he also quotes Fainsod, who, considering the Interstate Commerce Commission and FTC, concluded that 'In theory at least, and frequently in practice, they are capable of recognizing some interests as more "public" or more "general" than other interests and of adapting, fusing, and directing group pressures towards such a recognition.'[31]

Though the activities of the federal regulatory agencies in relation to this brief have always been subjected to criticism and challenge, they may be thought to be supported strongly by the civic republican current that continues to run through American political philosophy. Take for example Seidenfeld, who argues that,

On the whole civic republicanism is consistent with broad delegations of political decision-making authority to officials with greater expertise and fewer immediate political pressures than directly elected officials or legislators. Moreover, given the current ethic that approves of the private pursuit of self-interest as a means of making social policy, reliance on a more politically isolated administrative state may be necessary to implement something approaching the civic republican ideal... [H]aving administrative agencies set government policy provides the best hope of implementing civic republicanism's call for deliberative decision-making informed by the values of the entire polity.[32]

---

[27] Mitnick, *The Political Economy of Regulation*, 106–7.

[28] Ibid., 108, quoting Russell, M. and Shelton, R. B., 'A Model of Regulatory Agency Behavior', *Public Choice*, 20/Winter (1974), 47.   [29] Ibid., 108.

[30] Ibid., 104, referring to Herring, P. E., *Public Administration and the Public Interest* (New York, N.Y.: McGraw-Hill, 1936).

[31] Ibid., 103, quoting Fainsod, M., 'Some Reflections on the Nature of the Regulatory Process', in Friedrich, C.J. and Mason, E.S. (eds.), *Public Policy: a Yearbook of the Graduate School of Public Administration* (Cambridge, Mass.: Harvard University Press, 1940).

[32] Seidenfeld, M., 'A Civic Republican Justification for the Bureaucratic State', *Harvard Law Review*, 105/7 (1992), 1511, extract in Schuck, *Foundations of Administrative Law*, 26.

The 'faith in the ability of experts to develop effective solutions to the economic disruptions created by the market system' to which Rabin refers,[33] was not, of course, unchallenged, even in the heyday of the regulatory state, from the 1940s to the 1970s. Rabin identifies criticism in particular from two perspectives, concerned first with the absence of clear and consistent policy guidelines, leading to *ad hoc* policy development on a case-by-case basis, and second, about the 'oppressive tendency of the regulatory system'.[34] This contributed, inevitably, to the development of a prominent role for the courts in resolving issues arising from regulatory activity. The courts went through a long period of expanding their demands, far beyond the basic set of requirements set out in the Administrative Procedure Act (APA), concerned no doubt that 'Deference to traditional processes of informal rulemaking and adjudication in such cases appeared to be tantamount to surrendering the function of judicial review.'[35] The interventionist judicial trend as regards agency rule-making, however, went into reverse following *Vermont Yankee*,[36] when 'There was a retreat along all of the major fronts of judicial review to the more secure ground of requiring only that the regulatory agencies offer some assurance of good faith consideration of the issues.'[37] The much discussed case of *Chevron*,[38] six years later, seems to confirm an unusually deferential judicial position towards agencies:

When a challenge to an agency construction of a statutory provision, fairly conceptualized, really centers on the wisdom of the agency's policy, rather than whether it is a reasonable choice within a gap left open by Congress, the challenge must fail. In such a case, federal judges – who have no constituency – have a duty to respect legitimate policy choices made by those who do. The responsibilities for assessing the wisdom of such policy choices and resolving the struggle between competing views of the public interest are not judicial ones: 'Our Constitution vests such responsibilities in the political branches.'[39]

While such judicial statement may offer an appearance of unambiguous support for the activities of regulatory agencies, the situation in reality is, inevitably, much less clear than that. As the litigation in *FDA v. Brown and Williamson Tobacco Corp.*[40] demonstrates, the judiciary continue to patrol the boundaries

---

[33] Rabin, R., 'Federal Regulation in Historical Perspective', *Stanford Law Review*, 38 (1986), 1189; in Schuck, *Foundations of Administrative Law*, 42.

[34] Ibid., 43. See related discussion of Charles Reich's 'New Property' thesis, Ch. 7, below.

[35] Ibid., 47.

[36] *Vermont Yankee Nuclear Power Corp. v. Natural Resources Defense Council Inc.* 435 US 519 (1978). See Stewart, R. B., 'Vermont Yankee and the Evolution of Administrative Procedure, *Harvard Law Review*, 91 (1978) 1805.   [37] Rabin, 'Federal Regulation', 47.

[38] *Chevron, USA, Inc. v. Natural Resources Defense Council Inc.* 467 US 837 (1984). See a summary of the issues raised by this important and much discussed case in Strauss, P. L., *Administrative Justice in the United States*, 2nd edn. (Durham, North Carolina: Carolina Academic Press, 2002), 368–75. For a particular take on the case, see Sunstein, C. R., *Designing Democracy: What Constitutions Do* (Oxford: Oxford University Press, 2001), 146–8.

[39] *Chevron*, 467 US 837 (1984), 866, quoting *Tennessee Valley Authority v. Hill*, 437 US 153 (1978), 195.   [40] 529 US 120 (2000).

of agency discretion with some vigilance. Apparent fluctuations in judicial attitude to agencies may explain why Mitnick concludes that the legal history offers
'little in the form of basic criteria that can be taken to determine the desirability of regulation and to permit choice among alternative regulatory means'.[41]
In fact, from the perspective of considering the underlying values inherent in
systems of regulation, the more deferential judicial approach, and its tendency
to focus on narrow technical issues to the exclusion of conceptual analysis may
seem particularly unhelpful: 'In this "deferential model," the agency's function
is to give meaning to the statute: the court determines only whether the interpretation the agency has chosen is a "rational" reading, not whether it is the
"right" reading.'[42] While consistent with constitutional visions of the rule of
law and separation of powers, the lay person might be surprised and disappointed to discover that the apparently dynamic US administrative law system has
offered so little, and perhaps missed opportunities, in relation to forcing regulatory agencies to operate within a framework of defined principles. Again, when
we turn shortly to consider the activities of the FCC, readers may be surprised as
to the extent to which, despite consistently close political and judicial scrutiny
over a period of some seventy years, the fundamental principle which informs the
Commission's activities, 'the public interest, convenience and necessity', remains
remarkably undefined.

Mashaw reminds us that the legal debate in such areas is likely in itself to
contain contradictory emphases and demands: '[W]hile focusing on the rule of
law and its undeniable importance in maintaining liberty, we should not forget
the apparent equal importance of a contradictory demand: the demand for justice
in individual cases.'[43] Thus, though judicial review of administrative action may
provide us with more or less clear-cut answers as to the legality of the actions
of regulatory agencies in specific cases, this focus may lead to neglect in terms
of the provision of enlightenment as regards the fundamental legitimacy claims of
schemes of regulation as a whole. However, as we will consider in the conclusion
to this chapter and in later chapters, it may be that the apparent conflict between
broad delegations of power to agencies, and legal certainty – in Mashaw's terms
the question of 'vagueness and legitimacy' – may be capable of being rendered
less problematic than first appearance would suggest.

Given the range of conflicting political, economic, legal and constitutional
claims and perspectives just summarized, it is hardly surprising if the judiciary
and/or the regulators themselves are viewed as having failed in terms of establishing, or requiring the establishment of clear principles which underpin, explain
and justify regulatory action. As we will see in relation to the activities of the

---

[41] Mitnick, *The Political Economy of Regulation*, 259.

[42] Farina, C., 'Statutory Interpretation and the Balance of Power in the Administrative State',
Columbia Law Review, 89 (1989), 452; in Schuck, *Foundations of Administrative Law*, 193.

[43] Mashaw, J., 'Prodelegation: Why Administrators Should Make Political Decisions', *Journal of
Law, Economics and Organization*, 1 (1985), 81; in Schuck, *Foundations of Administrative Law*, 177.

FCC as regards its 'public interest' brief, those seeking to challenge its activities may express frustration at the degree of judicial deference shown, and consider this to be a missed opportunity to extrapolate and develop principles to structure agency discretion, or indeed to strike down broad delegations of authority as unconstitutional. Ultimately, however, such judicial deference may be seen to reinforce the established position of regulatory agencies within the American constitutional schema.

That said, the deregulatory agenda of the Reagan era, Clinton's attempt to 'reinvent government',[44] and Bush's return to an overtly deregulatory agenda collectively serve to pose strong challenges to the regulatory perspective developed since at least the 1930s, and may be thought to present clear and present dangers to the values underlying it: in particular, the animating force of the public interest. With that in mind, it becomes all the more important to explore the extent to which the concept is adequately defined, and whether it can, and should be defended. It can plausibly be argued that 'the regulatory process is one of conflict and bargaining rather than clear matching of ends and means',[45] yet it is possible that it may, beyond simply reflecting pluralism, still usefully serve the overarching value system of liberal–democratic society, though probably only if it is informed by adequate, normative, interpretative principles. The following case studies will seek to explore the extent to which this is, and might be, the case in specific contexts.

Food and Drug Administration

Constitutional and Historical Context

Just as in the UK and elsewhere, regulating for safety in the supply of food would seem to constitute the pursuit of an obvious 'public interest'. As was noted in the previous chapter, however, beneath this superficial level, there exists a range of interests competing for recognition, which agencies, and the framework within which they operate, must accommodate. In the case of the FDA, it is necessary and proper to draw illustrations from both branches of its brief – food, and pharmaceutical drugs. There exist immediately apparent parallels between the course of events which led to the establishment of Britain's FSA, discussed in the previous chapter, and the establishment, early history, and subsequent reform of the FDA.[46]

The FDA today describes itself as the Federal Agency responsible, *inter alia*, 'for ensuring that foods are safe, wholesome and sanitary' and 'that these

---

[44] See the influential Osborne, D. and Gaebler, T., *Reinventing Government* (New York, N.Y.: Addison-Wesley, 1992).   [45] Harris and Milkis, *The Politics of Regulatory Change*, 7.

[46] See generally Swann, J. P., *History of the FDA*, at FDA website, http://www.fda.gov/oc/historyoffda/fulltext.html (accessed 7 November 2003), extracted from Kurian, G. (ed.), *The Historical Guide to American Government* (Oxford: Oxford University Press, 1998).

products are honestly, accurately and informatively represented to the public'.[47] The Agency's brief also extends to biological material, cosmetics, drugs, medical devices and veterinary products. The FDA's Mission Statement makes clear that this brief is viewed as not only being that of 'protecting the public' but also of 'advancing public health', and 'helping the public get the accurate, science-based information they need to use medicines and food to improve their health'.[48]

Though with historical origins traceable back to mid-nineteenth century activity in the field of chemistry within the Department of Agriculture (USDA), what is today recognized as the FDA dates back to the passing of the Food and Drugs Act 1906. Often referred to as 'the Wiley Act', after Harvey Washington Wiley, chief chemist within the Division (later Bureau) of Chemistry of the USDA, the Act introduced a regulatory aspect to what had hitherto been seen primarily as a scientific mission. While maintaining a dual focus, on food and on drugs, the new regulatory agency, under Wiley's leadership, developed a concern in particular with chemical additives to food.

However, the 1906 Act also needed to address some legal and constitutional issues. In the nineteenth century, though the federal authorities maintained oversight of imported food, it was the individual states which exercised control over domestically produced food and drugs, resulting in potential and actual inconsistencies in standards and enforcement. In addition, both in the years immediately before the 1906 Act, and afterwards, the Bureau of Chemistry and later the FDA had been developing informal standards for foods: standards, the applicability of which courts differed on.

By the 1930s, in the wake of a range of scandals regarding ineffective or dangerous medical products, especially the death in 1937 of more than one hundred people following use of the untested and highly toxic drug Elixir Sulfanilimide, and ongoing concerns over deceptively or wrongly labelled food, not covered by the existing law, Congress passed the Food, Drug and Cosmetic Act 1938. Just as the disastrous consequences of Elixir Sulfanilimide had been the proximate cause of the introduction of the 1938 Act, so major reform occurred again in 1962 arising out of concerns over the drug Thalidomide. The reform included strengthening the regulation of drug trials, and transferring responsibility from the FTC to the FDA. Perhaps like moves in the UK to transfer responsibility for food safety away from MAFF following BSE and foot-and-mouth, the intention was to shift responsibility to a body perhaps more focused on the public interest and somewhat more insulated from industrial and commercial issues.

Though it may be that these high profile problems over pharmaceutical drugs may catch the headlines, Swann[49] observes that by the 1960s, following a series of expansions of the law in the 1950s, about half of the food supply had become

---

[47] FDA website, http://www.fda.gov/comments/regs.html (accessed 7 November 2003).

[48] FDA website, http://www.fda.gov/opacom/morechoices/mission.html (accessed 7 November 2003).   [49] Swann, 'History of the FDA'.

subject to a recipe standard established by the FDA, determining ingredients that could be lawfully included in a product. Though more mundane in some senses, this function implies a more direct and widespread regulatory intervention in the nation's diet. However, in 1976, Congress was moved to limit the expansion of the FDA brief as regards vitamins and dietary supplements, prohibiting the Agency from controlling the potency of dietary supplements, though allowing the agency to continue to exercise powers in relation to enriched foods. Though the FDA was permitted from 1958 to enforce a ban on any carcinogenic additives, Strauss notes how Congress specifically prohibited the FDA from banning saccharin, despite evidence indicating its carcinogenic effect in animal experiments.[50] The potential for tension between Congress and an agency such as the FDA is obvious.

However, a further tension inherent within the FDA's role is also worth noting at this point. Inevitably, the public relations consequences of permitting a seriously harmful drug to be released cannot be over-estimated, and this may lead to an overly defensive attitude within the Agency. The other perspective, regarding the application of precaution and the hidden risks it may bring in retarding the development of potentially valuable products, will be returned to in the context of 'the precautionary principle' later in this chapter.

Inevitably, the FDA operates within the web of constitutional and administrative law which establishes the limits on the duties and powers of government agencies. Thus, its activities in relation to both food and drugs have been regularly scrutinized by the courts, and indeed have formed the context for significant case law development. Though certain high-profile issues such as the FDA's attempts to regulate in relation to tobacco products have captured the headlines, as Gilhooley observes,[51] issues have arisen in the full range of typical US administrative law contexts, relating to both substance and procedures. Addressing such issues is an ongoing process, involving the resolution of competing claims from manufacturers, consumer and 'public interest' pressure groups, and the FDA itself, and each new piece of legislation inevitably throws up its range of new issues to be resolved.[52] New legislation may establish a new matrix in which issues will arise, and, as Littlefield and Hadas comment,[53] may often compel the FDA to question established policies and practices.

Of course, the most recent high-profile action challenging the extent of the FDA's powers arose in the context of the Agency's attempts to further regulate the tobacco industry. We will return to this later in this chapter, in the context of

[50] Strauss, *Administrative Justice*, 166, at fn. 51.

[51] Gilhooley, M., 'The Administrative Conference and the Progress of Food and Drug Reform', *Arizona State Law Journal*, 30 (1998), 129.

[52] See, for example, Becker, K. M., Flannery, E. J., and Henteleff, T. O., 'Scientific Dispute Resolution: First Use of Provision 404 of the Food and Drug Administration Modernization Act 1997', *Food and Drug Journal*, 58 (2003), 211.

[53] Littlefield, N. and Hadas, N. R., 'A Survey of Developments in Food and Drug Law from July 1998 to November 1999', *Food and Drug Law Journal*, 55 (2000), 35.

a more general discussion of the way agencies' jurisdictions may be determined. It is sufficient to note for the moment, that, despite dissent from Breyer, J., who was prepared to take a more expansive view, the majority opinion of the Supreme Court in *FDA v. Brown & Williamson Tobacco Corp.*[54] was to place a narrower construction on the scope of regulatory agencies' public interest powers, to the effect that an administrative agency's power to regulate in the public interest must always be grounded in a valid grant of authority from Congress.

The interplay of statute law, administrative procedure, and in particular con-stitutional rights does, though, raise a series of issues relatively unfamiliar to British eyes. It can be persuasively argued that, in connection with regulators in the US, the courts should avoid deciding cases on broad constitutional grounds, and instead seek to proceed on the basis of 'harder' standards of review deriving from statutory and administrative grounds whenever possible.[55] However, an alternative perspective would see the ability of the courts to focus on consti-tutional expectations, such as commercial free speech, as proper, and a useful mechanism for avoiding problems of inconsistency which may otherwise arise from differences in the standards of review.[56] While such arguments might on occasion serve as no more than convenient cover for those seeking a particular outcome in a particular case, or may indeed have an esoteric air to those other than the administrative law cognoscenti, they do raise the important issue of the applicability of general principles and standards, such as constitutional rights, in the context of regulatory activity: whether there exists a 'higher order' of principles which may trump 'ordinary' legal rights. However, it is questionable whether such legal actions or debates either shed much light on, or indeed draw upon, a coherent concept of public interest which might help in resolving, and establishing a sense of legitimacy in the resolution of, the issues raised.

Interestingly, though the US food market and its regulation might seem to be of a scale so large as to be immune to external influence, Gilhooley[57] notes how legislation from 1997 supports efforts at measures seeking to harmonize regu-lation with the practices of other jurisdictions, where this is consistent with the purposes of US food and drug legislation, and, in the interest of trade, encour-ages the Agency to move toward mutual recognition agreements with the EU. Whether such moves help in the development of underlying principle, or are only adopted where they mesh comfortably with the existing framework of policy and practice, remains to be seen.

---

[54] 529 US 120 (2000). See Boeckman, A. M., 'An Exercise in Administrative Creativity: the FDA's Assertion of Jurisdiction Over Tobacco', *Catholic University Law Review*, 45 (1996), 991. See also Croley, S. P., 'Public Interested Regulation', *Florida State University Law Review*, 28 (2000), 7, for a succinct summary of the litigation.

[55] Gilhooley, M., 'Constitutionalizing Food and Drug Law', *Tulane Law Review*, 75 (2000), 815.

[56] Noah, L., 'What's Wrong With "Constitutionalizing Food and Drug Law"', *Tulane Law Review* 75 (2000), 137; and in reply to this, Gilhooley, M., 'Constitutionalizing Food and Drug Law: When Avoidance is Right', *Houston Law Review*, 38 (2002), 1383.

[57] Gilhooley, 'The Administrative Conference', 139.

Risk and Precaution

Though there is an increasing presence of international bodies such as the WTO, and conventions regulating international trade in food such as the Application of Sanitary and Phytosanitary Measures,[58] harmonization of food regulation between the EU and US is not always straightforward, as illustrated in the recent dispute between the two trade areas over the use of growth hormones in cattle.[59] Echols[60] observes a trend within the EU towards defence of traditional foodstuffs and manufacturing processes, protecting local cultures and traditions; the kind of raw milk cheeses and certain cured meats found in European markets may be thought to present health risks which US regulators would not countenance. In part, the EU approach may be explained as an embodiment of subsidiarity, and a symbol or symptom of the absence as yet of a true single market, at least when compared with the apparently more unified or homogenous US market.

In addition, however, Echols also identifies a further trans-Atlantic difference which may reflect more deep-seated differences in the approach to regulating the food supply. She notes a marked reluctance on the part of European authorities to accept new technologies and novel foods, while US regulators are more willing to embrace processes such as genetic engineering or irradiation of foodstuffs. Echols points towards a partial explanation of this difference, in terms of the US administration's preference for an exclusively science-based approach, as compared with the European Commission's willingness to take into account what she terms a 'social factor', referring perhaps to cultural diversity and tradition.[61]

As was seen in the discussion of the UK's FSA in the previous chapter, the idea of a precautionary principle is increasingly influential in European discourse on regulation of risk in this field, and is considered by some to be a version of a public interest approach to regulation. Given the principle's high profile in a wide range of international treaties and declarations, especially in the environmental field, and suggestions that in this context it is 'ripening into an enforceable norm of customary international law',[62] it might be expected that the principle would offer an area of common ground where trans-Atlantic harmonization might take place.

In a telling analysis which in many ways picks up where Echols's description leaves off, Wiener seeks to find a deeper understanding of the similarities and differences in US and EU approaches to precautionary regulation in, amongst other areas, food standards. He identifies as thin stereotyping a vision which portrays Europeans as 'risk-averse, . . . afraid of new technologies . . . and of global

[58] See Salmon, N., 'A European Perspective on the Precautionary Principle, Food Safety and the Free Trade Imperative of the WTO', *European Law Review*, 27 (2002), 138, at 146–8.

[59] Ibid., 148–50; also Hood, C., Rothstein, H., and Baldwin, R., *The Government of Risk: Understanding Risk Regulation Regimes* (Oxford: Oxford University Press, 2001), 6.

[60] Echols, M. A., 'Food Safety Regulation in the EU and the US: Different Cultures, Different Laws', *Columbia Journal of European Law*, 4 (1998), 525.   [61] Ibid., 530.

[62] Wiener, J. B., 'Whose precaution after all? A comment on the comparison and evolution of risk regulatory systems', *Duke Journal of Comparative and International Law*, 13 (2003) 207, at 212.

markets, jumping to adopt precautionary regulations against even the most remote and speculative risks', and Americans as 'risk-indifferent or even risk-preferring, ... confident that new technology ... and the power of ... markets will solve every problem and that precaution is a waste of time and a hindrance to progress'.[63] Instead, he develops a more sophisticated picture, which does identify elements of the two systems which diverge, but also illustrates areas where convergence can be seen, and also sees areas of complex interaction, including processes of ' "hybridization", in which both systems borrow legal concepts from each other in a complex and continuous mutual evolution'.[64]

While the EU has formally articulated and endorsed the precautionary principle, in relation to environmental and food issues,[65] and has taken strong preventive action, for example on GM food, the difference between Europe and the US is illustrated in the trade dispute over growth hormones in cattle. Wiener quotes EU Trade Commissioner Pascal Lamy as expressing a version of the conventional wisdom: '[I]n the US they believe that if no risks have been proven about a product, it should be allowed. In the EU we believe something should not be authorized if there is a chance of risk.'[66] It is, of course, possible to view this difference in more pragmatic, economic terms. As Salmon observes,

Europe, being a major consumer rather than major exporter of GM foods does not have the same financial interest in promoting a rapid and widespread acceptance of these products as some other WTO Members. Individual States within Europe may well favour a stronger precautionary approach to the marketing of GM products than that enforced by the European framework. However, the official European stance has to be reconciled with that of the WTO, which is, of course heavily dominated by major GM exporting states such as the USA, who inevitably have a strong interest in promoting a minimal approach to the regulation of their products.[67]

Wiener, however, goes on to identify what he sees as a more complex reality underlying differences of approach, deriving from a wide range of variables, ranging from how the issues are framed, through risk assessment and management methods and standards, through to choice of which risks to regulate and of policy instruments and enforcement mechanisms, and differences in hierarchical structures of government. We will return to Wiener's analysis in the next chapter, but for the moment can summarize his conclusions in terms of a complex picture in which 'the pattern is not of increasing European precaution and declining US precaution, but rather simultaneous precaution against different risks'.[68]

Thus, while the EU regulators and policy-makers may pronounce the precautionary principle more publicly, this is not to say that a precautionary approach

---

[63] Wiener, J. B., 'Whose precaution after all? A comment on the comparison and evolution of risk regulatory systems', *Duke Journal of Comparative and International Law*, 13 (2003) 208.

[64] Ibid., 209.

[65] See McNelis, N., 'EU Communication on the Precautionary Principle', *Journal of International Economic Law*, 3/3 (2000), 545.   [66] Wiener, 'Whose Precaution?', 213.

[67] Salmon, 'A European Perspective', 154.   [68] Wiener, 'Whose Precaution?', 230.

is totally alien to the US, as Applegate indicates,[69] drawing on the 1976 DC Circuit judgment in *Ethyl Corp. v. EPA*,[70] relating to 1970 amendments to the Clean Air Act. Though the judicial approach adopted in *Ethyl* as regards the extent of requirements that could be enforced in relation to rule-making procedures were repudiated by the Supreme Court in *Vermont Yankee*,[71] it does not seem that the substantive principles set out in *Ethyl* as regards precautionary action have been overturned. In essence, as Applegate observes, *Ethyl* may be seen as authority for permitting regulation in the face of uncertainty. He quotes the following passage:

Where a statute is precautionary in nature, the evidence difficult to come by, uncertain, or conflicting because it is on the frontiers of scientific knowledge, the regulations designed to protect the public health, and the decision that of an expert administrator, we will not demand rigorous step-by-step proof of cause and effect. Such proof may be impossible to obtain if the precautionary purpose of the statute is to be served.[72]

However, the precautionary principle generally remains at the margins of US regulatory activity, in relation to food supply at least. In Wiener's terms, 'Mistrust of governmental power may itself be a reason for US reluctance to embrace the precautionary principle, while European legal culture may be more comfortable with principles of obligatory regulatory action.'[73] A similar conclusion as regards different trans-Atlantic attitudes of distrust towards public officials and hence towards discretionary powers and their regulation, is reached by Asimow.[74]

The dialogue between Gilhooley and Noah as regards 'Constitutionalizing Food and Drug Law', noted earlier, seems to illustrate the complexity of the situation in the US, where the 'proper' legal mechanism for resolving such issues must be chosen from a highly developed structure of administrative procedure, statute, and constitutional law, and with the potential on occasion for additional tensions arising between federal and state jurisdictions. In Europe meanwhile, despite some complications arising from the principle of subsidiarity, resulting in 'considerable variety in regulatory approaches across member states',[75] Wiener draws on two Court of First Instance decisions in September 2002,[76] to conclude that it is increasingly clear that where regulatory authority is vested in EU bodies, 'when . . . institutions act under the precautionary principle, judicial review is to be very deferential'.[77]

In the US, in the high-profile context of GMOs, it appears that regulatory institutions may already possess powers which could enable them to proceed on

---

[69] Applegate, J. S., 'Sustainable development, agriculture, and the challenge of genetically modified organisms', *Indiana Journal of Global Legal Studies*, 9 (2001), 207.
[70] 541 F.2d 1 (DC Cir) (1976). [71] 435 US 519 (1978).
[72] Applegate, 'Sustainable Development', 256. [73] Wiener, 'Whose Precaution?', 247.
[74] Asimow, M., 'Delegated Legislation: United States and United Kingdom', *Oxford Journal of Legal Studies*, 3/2 (1983), 253, 272–3. [75] Wiener, 'Whose Precaution?', 230.
[76] *Pfizer Animal Health SA v. Council of the EU*, Case T-13/99; *Alpharma Inc. v. Council of the EU*, Case T-70/99. [77] Ibid., 219.

a precautionary basis. Applegate observes that the three bodies covered by the 1986 Coordinated Framework for Biotechnology, the EPA, FDA and USDA, already had legislation available to them which could allow them to intervene in relation to uses of biotechnology. He finds a fundamental assumption at play, that GMOs are not so new as to require new principles, embodied in new legislation, to control them, and that therefore regulation of GMOs should proceed on the established product-by-product basis. He notes specifically how the FDA's statement of policy on new foods 'adopts a general presumption that GM foods are not different from their non-GM counterparts',[78] and goes on to quote the FDA's 1992 Statement of Policy:[79]

[T]he regulatory status of food, irrespective of the method by which it is developed, is dependent upon objective characteristics of the food and the intended use of the food (or its components) ... [T]he key factors in reviewing safety concerns should be the characteristics of the food product, rather than the fact that the new methods are used.

Applegate's account seems to confirm very real differences in approach taken in the US and EU. The US authorities adopt an approach which is essentially product- and science-based, echoed in the WTO agreements which require that GATT applies to products (and not their production processes) and that trade restrictions be based on 'science'. Though, as Applegate observes,[80] in adopting the precautionary principle the European Commission has repeatedly emphasized the need to perform traditional risk assessment based on available information, and the EU treaty requires reliance on 'available and scientific data', the EU authorities adopt a more process-based, flexible, and certainly more interventionist approach, which draws on the precautionary principle's origins in a German concept of *Vorsorgeprinzip*, or 'foresightedness principle' – 'a process for taking environment- and health-protective actions while the dangers of not taking such protective action remain uncertain'.[81] The trans-Atlantic divergence of approach, observes Applegate, derives from the adoption of different competing narratives; the US and WTO being informed by a narrative of progress, and the continuation of traditional processes of breeding via new means, while the EU model relates to a narrative of concerns as to the unknown, and unintended consequences. In terms of the central narrative of this book, either could conceivably constitute the basis for a unitary claim of the public interest.

From the perspective adopted in this book, it might be expected that the adoption of a precautionary principle should be strongly welcomed. Indeed, in terms of it apparently providing a relatively clear and consistent value base which might be expected to orientate regulatory activity, and thereby structure discretion, it seems to have much to recommend it. In terms of seeking to protect the interests of the current and future community, via adopting a clear preference for a value system which permits proactive or pre-emptive regulation in the

[78] Applegate, 'Sustainable Development', 232.   [79] Ibid., 233.   [80] Ibid., 250.
[81] Ibid., 209.

absence of absolute proof of risk, it does have some of the characteristics of many constructs of the public interest identified in Chapter One. It may even be thought to share some of the characteristics of what Sunstein refers to as an 'interpretative principle', giving certain values a high priority in terms of factors which are to be taken into account when making regulatory decisions. Used in this way it might be viewed as a doctrine of restraint, with the potential to curb potential excesses in the exercise of private property power, in pursuit of the protection of fundamental community values; reasserting the legitimacy of regulation of private activity in pursuit of the polity's overarching value system. However, doubts regarding the precautionary principles value-base were raised in the previous chapter, and Sunstein, from his civic republicanist position which might be expected to endorse such developments, also expresses some significant reservations about the use of the precautionary principle.[82]

Drawing on a typology established by Stewart,[83] Sunstein identifies a continuum of understandings of the principle. At one end are the most cautious and 'weak' versions, amounting to no more than a suggestion that 'Regulation should not be precluded by the absence of scientific uncertainty about activities that pose a risk of substantial harm.'[84] At the other end of the continuum are the 'strongest', whereby 'Prohibitions should be imposed on those activities that have an uncertain potential to impose substantial harm, unless those in favour of those activities can show that they present no appreciable risk.'[85] The latter test clearly imposes a heavy, and potentially undischargeable, burden of proof on those wishing to undertake activities.

Sunstein finds weak versions of the principle to be 'unobjectionable and important': 'The weak versions of the precautionary principle state a truism, one that is uncontroversial and necessary only to combat public confusion or the self-interested claims of private groups demanding unambiguous evidence of harm.'[86] Sunstein acknowledges that 'the precautionary principle has strong moral goals', and, 'To the extent that [it] is a reminder of obligations to the future, it is entirely salutary.'[87] This has clear echoes of versions of public interest which emphasize protection of broader societal interests, and especially the interests of future generations, from the special interests of particular groups; indeed, it may seem to have the potential to function as an interpretative principle.

In essence, Sunstein's concerns relate to adverse consequences which he suggests flow from the application of 'strong' versions of the precautionary principle. He is concerned that the 'presumption in favour of stringent regulatory controls'[88] that such versions incorporate, amounts to risk aversion and as such

---

[82] Sunstein, C. R., 'Preferences and Rational Choice: New Perspectives and Legal Implications: Beyond the Precautionary Principle', *University of Philadelphia Law Review*, 151 (2003), 1003.
[83] Stewart, R. B., 'Environmental Regulatory Decision Making Under Uncertainty', 2002, in Swanson, T. (ed.), 20 *Research in Law and Economics* 71 (2002), 78.
[84] Sunstein, 'Preferences and Rational Choice', 1014.   [85] Ibid.   [86] Ibid., 1016.
[87] Ibid., 1035.   [88] Ibid., 1018.

carry associated social costs: 'such regulation might well deprive society of significant benefits'.[89] He provides examples which demonstrate that expensive regulation may have adverse effects on life and health, and may have what would be perceived as negative outcomes in terms of the distribution of costs. Ultimately, his concerns regarding the application of the precautionary principle relate to the narrowness of the perspective – its focus on risk to the exclusion of potential benefits, its blindness to consideration of trade-offs which, rationally, ought to be taken into account, and of distributional consequences which flow from its application. As McNelis confirms, in the context of biotechnological research into medicines or new foodstuffs, 'It would be unfortunate if investment in such research was discouraged by an overly restrictive reaction from authorities.'[90] The problem, from this perspective is that a strongly precautionary approach may tend to focus on one set of immediately apparent risks, while ignoring other risks that may be present, and indeed any risks which may flow from its application. In essence, Sunstein's critique of the approach rests largely upon the risks of unintended negative consequences, perhaps of the kind envisaged by McNelis, which might attach to strong versions of the precautionary principle. There is a certain irony here, given that avoidance of adverse unintended consequences is exactly what underlies many arguments in favour of the precautionary principle.

Though Sunstein's critique of applications of strong versions of the principle are powerful and in some ways persuasive, Applegate establishes sound arguments in favour of the adoption of what is a more common and 'weaker' version of the precautionary principle. He observes 'a caricature which depicts a draconian, unreasoning, inflexible command that rejects all technologies that have emerged since the Industrial Revolution',[91] a version of the principle which, as Applegate notes, has been adopted by some zealots, but is far from the vision of most serious proponents of the principle, and far from the model incorporated in many treaties. The model Applegate advocates, he describes as 'the foresight principle, not the Luddite Principle'.[92] It does seem only proper to emphasize that Sunstein's critique is clearly not based on the kind of caricature which Applegate identifies, and is indeed applied primarily to 'stronger' proposed versions of the precautionary principle than that considered by Applegate. However, Applegate is very clear that the model of the precautionary principle generally advocated and implemented is 'neither rigid, nor the enemy of serious scientific inquiry'.[93] It does not fall foul of Sunstein's proper concerns about narrowness, as it emphasizes a holistic vision, employing an apparently healthy scepticism, generally absent from both pro- and anti-GM literature, applied equally to claims as regards potential risks and potential benefits. Drawing on the Prometheus myth relating to the tendency of humankind to 'misuse' technology, Applegate

---

[89] Sunstein, 'Preferences and Rational Choice', 1023.
[90] McNelis, 'EU Communication on the Precautionary Principle', 551.
[91] Applegate, 'Sustainable development', 248.   [92] Ibid.   [93] Ibid.

finds that the precautionary principle emphasizes a social critique as well as 'scientific' and economic approaches:

Most GM investment is in technologies that improve profits rather than relieve human suffering. The value of the investment, in turn, is based on the continuing domination, through intellectual property, of the next generation of agriculture by a small number of already wealthy American and European corporations. Greed makes new technology dangerous and warrants caution in adopting it.[94]

From this perspective, the adoption of a precautionary principle helps in providing justification for not postponing regulatory action, thereby buying time for further investigation and clarification. In both these senses, it seems at least as 'scientific' as the science-based approach upon which US regulators of biotechnology may seem to operate, and which may, given its tendency to exclude a wider vision of socio-economic and environmental consequences of legitimate public concern, actually prove to be narrower than an approach based on a precautionary principle. Indeed, the precautionary principle may be thought to be serving the sort of goals associated with certain visions of the public interest in Chapters One and Two. In being properly protective of long-term community interests in the face of profit-driven activity by private parties which has uncertain consequences, and, in providing the time for more complete assessment of the pros and cons, it might provide for a more informed approach to the trade-offs to which Sunstein refers. A problem noted in the previous chapter, however, was that the more holistic the precautionary principle becomes, in terms of encompassing the widest range of factors, the less distinct it becomes from conventional cost/benefit analyses and the problems associated with them.

Certainly, the precautionary principle may seem to offer potential problems, as regards the degree of discretion it would grant to regulators. Yet as should be clear, 'discretion' is not in itself a problem, but rather may become a problem, sliding into arbitrariness, when it is not properly 'confined, structured and checked'.[95] In reality, the structure of administrative procedures, statutory requirements, and constitutional rights which form the frame within which US regulation takes place seems to offer some reassurance in this respect. Indeed, the absence of a precautionary principle may constitute a more real threat to underlying values. Denial of a precautionary principle may actually facilitate the victory of private interests over public interests, cutting across purposive constructions of precautionary powers, such as those referred to in *Ethyl*,[96] which appear to be intended to protect vulnerable public interests. Once in place, it may offer some resistance to the acceptance of the pragmatics of economics.

---

[94] Ibid., 262.
[95] Davis, K. C., *Discretionary Justice: a Preliminary Inquiry* (Urbana, IL.: University of Illinois Press, 1971). [96] 541 F.2d 1 (DC Cir.) 1976.

A Structure of Principles?

We will return to debate further the precautionary principle in Chapter Seven. However, notwithstanding approval or reservations that might be expressed regarding the application of versions of the precautionary principle, there remains a strong case for the establishment of some kind of general principles which might serve to orientate regulatory activity in areas such as food supply, whether imposed upon regulators from the outside, or developed internally alongside more specific rules and practices. As Asimow states in relation to rule-making (although this could potentially have broader application): 'Interpretive rules and policy statements are indispensable to proper administration. Agencies cannot perform effectively unless they clarify the law through interpretive rules and channel their discretion through policy statements.'[97]

However, though agencies such as the FDA may claim to act in pursuit of public interest objectives, there is little to suggest that in doing so they utilize, or even seek to work towards, a developed conception of what the public interest may mean within their sphere of activity. Certainly the literature seems to suggest that there is much to be done in respect of establishing the public interest as a coherent principle, not just in the FDA but in other federal agencies also. In a study of three such agencies, the Office of the Comptroller of the Currency, and the EPA, in addition to the FDA, Croley[98] appears to mirror the agencies' actions in apparently avoiding the issue. In a piece in excess of 50,000 words, considering the legal and political conditions in which agencies are likely to deliver what he terms 'public interested' as opposed to 'special interest' regulation, Croley deals directly with what might be meant by 'the public interest' in this context only in one footnote, commenting that 'a publicly interested regulator is motivated to advance some conception of the general welfare'. As Garrett observes in her telling critique of this approach, Croley 'has declined to answer perhaps the most fundamental questions: What is the public interest? Against what baseline should we judge regulatory outcomes to determine whether they are normatively desirable or not?'[99] In the absence of answers to these questions, Garrett argues that it is impossible to tell whether agencies' actions align with the public interest.

To British eyes, often struck by the dense framework of administrative law created by US legislators, judges and indeed agency rule-makers, it might be surprising to find Garrett[100] observing that Croley's case studies reveal that the framework established by the APA and judicial activity in interpreting and developing its principles in fact serve to 'insulate regulators from Congress and frees them to pursue their own agendas'. It seems that while an absence of definition for a concept potentially as central as 'the public interest' might appear to be helpful to an agency, in maximizing the scope of discretion available to it, the

---

[97] Asimow, M., 'Public Participation in the Adoption of Interpretive Rules and Policy Statements', *Michigan Law Review*, 77 (1975), 520.   [98] Croley, 'Public Interested Regulation'.

[99] Garrett, E., 'Interest Groups and Public Interested Regulation', *Florida State University Law Review*, 28 (2000), 137, at 143.   [100] Ibid., 145.

same absence may contribute to the failure to establish regulatory objectives, or to establish the legitimacy of agency action, and may indeed contribute to leaving its agenda vulnerable to interest-group capture. It may be that the establishment of a developed, normative construct of the public interest, by providing part of the 'structuring' of discretion which Davis[101] and others indicate the need for, may help in both these senses.

FEDERAL COMMUNICATIONS COMMISSION

Statutory Brief and Constitutional Context

The democratic significance of media industries, and their regulation, was noted in the previous chapter in the context of considering Ofcom's activities in Britain. In the US, the same issues apply, in relation to the media's role as a crucial part of the 'public sphere', and its ability to impact upon citizenship interests. However, debates over media regulation in the US take place in a markedly different constitutional context, in which the starting point is the apparently unambiguous terminology of the First Amendment to the Constitution, guaranteeing freedom of speech. Of more direct significance for the present study, though, is the power granted under the Communications Act 1934, originally to the Federal Radio Commission (FRC), and subsequently inherited by the FCC, to regulate in pursuit of 'the public interest, convenience, and necessity'. While the presence of such a phrase alone does not signify in itself the establishment of a strong normative concept, it might be expected that in the seventy years in which the phrase has been in use, in the context of US administrative procedure and law, steps would necessarily have been taken to define it in substantive terms. On inspection, it soon becomes apparent that though the FCC's actions have indeed been the subject of fierce debate, both in relation to the First Amendment, and the statutory brief to act in the public interest, only limited, if any, progress has been made in terms of developing a coherent, normative model of the public interest. As with other US administrative agencies, the dominant vision of the appropriate extent of the FCC's powers and roles has fluctuated historically, and, inevitably, the public interest brief has come under particular pressure in the modern technological context and deregulatory climate.

As already indicated, the FCC's brief must be viewed in its constitutional setting. The First Amendment guarantee that 'Congress shall make no law ... abridging freedom of speech or press', provides a starting point of positive liberty, very different from that historically found in the UK. This starting point may form part of the reason why the 'public service' tradition in broadcasting, so common in Western European democracies, is so manifestly absent in the US. It would seem constitutionally unthinkable for a US regulator to

---

[101] Davis, *Discretionary Justice.*

intervene to set and enforce detailed programme standards or quotas on independent broadcasters, or impose strict requirements of balance in news reporting, in the way that the ITC has until recently done in the UK. However, it is also clear that the First Amendment promise of freedom of speech is not as absolute as it might superficially appear, and US courts have repeatedly found circumstances in which they were prepared to find regulation of print, and especially, broadcast media to be constitutional in spite of arguments to the contrary based on the First Amendment.

At the broadest level, a majority of the Supreme Court in *FCC v. Pacifica Foundation*,[102] confirmed that it was lawful for a higher degree of regulation to be applied to broadcast as opposed to print media, on the basis that broadcasting's uniquely pervasive influence and intrusive potential; its direct reach into the home, and ready accessibility by children, was found to justify greater state intervention than in relation to print media.[103] In fact, heavier regulation of broadcast media is the norm in all comparable states, and though a variety of explanations for this phenomenon can be offered, including broadcasting's origins as a military resource, it may be not unconnected with the advent of broadcasting coinciding historically with the growth of the 'big', interventionist state.[104]

In relation to the licensing powers of the FCC, crucial in establishing lawful access to broadcasting frequencies, *Red Lion Broadcasting v. FCC*[105] confirms the authority of the FCC to license broadcasters. Barendt summarizes the position arrived at in terms of a judgment that 'Freedom of speech did not entail a right to broadcast without a licence or unconditionally with one'.[106] The FCC's rules aimed at prohibiting exclusive tie-ups between local broadcasters and national networks were also found not to interfere with the freedom of speech of licensees in *NBC v. US*.[107] The courts have remained clear, however, that the FCC does not have unlimited powers in such areas. Ramberg notes how in *Red Lion*, and previous decisions, the court has expressed its willingness to strike down 'arbitrary' or capricious decisions, or an 'idiosyncratic conception of the public interest'.[108]

However, the courts will generally seek to maintain a clear line between regulation of media markets, and regulation which imposes restrictions on content published or transmitted, though it is clear that there will be occasions, albeit very limited ones, where the courts will find grounds for intervention as regards non-market-related media activity. At the sharp end of journalistic practice, in *Dietemann v. Time Inc*,[109] the court was willing to permit

[102] 438 US 726 (1978).
[103] See Barendt, *Broadcasting Law: a Comparative Study* (Oxford: Clarendon, 1993), 6.
[104] Ibid., 3–10.   [105] 395 US 367 (1969).   [106] Barendt, *Broadcasting Law*, 30.
[107] 319 US 190 (1943).
[108] Ramberg, B., 'The Supreme Court and Public Interest in Broadcasting', *Communications and the Law*, (1986), 11, at 22–3, referring to *Red Lion*, and to *Federal Radio Commission v. Nelson Brothers Bond and Mortgage*, 289 US 266 (1933).   [109] 449 F.2d 244 (1971).

the imposition of restrictions on techniques used in 'news gathering', while *Near v. Minnesota*[110] and the historic Pentagon Papers litigation[111] appear not to rule out entirely the possibility of the imposition of prior restraint, though only in very limited circumstances. The case of *Red Lion*[112] in 1969 did confirm the lawfulness of the FCC's 'Fairness Doctrine', which required licensed broadcasters 'to devote some time to the discussion of important issues and to present contrasting views on controversial topics',[113] though this requirement was subsequently largely abandoned during the Reagan administration.[114] These are, however, clearly very narrow exceptions to the general position, and the courts are at pains to demonstrate that they are not permitting abridgement of the First Amendment freedom over which they act as guardian. *Turner Broadcasting v. FCC*[115] perhaps best represents the typical position in relation to regulation of content, with the courts limiting legitimate regulatory intervention to circumstances in which such actions 'are justified on grounds unrelated to the content of expression',[116] while in 1997,[117] the Supreme Court was willing to strike down a measure contained in the Telecommunications Act 1996 which was intended to prohibit 'indecent transmission' and 'patently offensive display'.

Thus, the general position is that, though confirming the FCC's power to intervene in media markets in pursuit of its regulatory brief, the starting point for the US courts remains a strong presumption in favour of the First Amendment freedom, with a heavy burden of proof resting on the executive, the legislature, or regulators when seeking to reverse this presumption. In this sense, the FCC operates within reasonably clear bounds; in so far as it regulates in pursuit of social objectives, it must find mechanisms largely unrelated to broadcast content in order to achieve them. This amounts to a task of achieving its objective, in terms of ensuring a range of broadcast product via surrogate means (structural regulation of the market), rather than direct, content-related, regulation. Again, this is not an uncommon approach, even outside the constitutional context of the US, with structural regulation often found to be in effect the best available surrogate for what might otherwise be considered illegitimate regulatory interference with

---

[110] 283 US 697 (1931).

[111] *New York Times v. US*, 403 US 713 (1971). See Rudenstine, D., *The Day the Presses Stopped: a History of the Pentagon Papers Case* (Berkeley, C.A.: University of California Press, 1996).

[112] 395 US 367 (1969).

[113] Barendt, *Broadcasting Law*, 29; see also Hoffman-Riem, W., *Regulating Media: the Licensing and Supervision of Broadcasting in Six Countries* (New York, N.Y.: Guilford Press, 1996).

[114] Sunstein, C. R., *Designing Democracy: What Constitutions Do* (Oxford: Oxford University Press, 2001), 35.

[115] 114 S Ct 2445 (1995). See also Vick, D., 'The First Amendment Limitations on Broadcasting in the United States After *Turner Broadcasting v. FCC*', *Media Law and Practice*, 16/3 (1995), 97.

[116] See Klingler, R., *The New Information Industry: Regulatory Challenges and the First Amendment* (Washington DC: Brookings Institute Press, 1996).

[117] *Reno v. ACLU*, 117 S Ct 2329 (1997).

the operations of markets in free speech even if the ultimate objective is diversity of media content.[118]

However, inevitably, that is not to say that the FCC's actions or the scope of its substantive powers are uncontroversial. From at least three perspectives, its activities in pursuit of 'the public interest, convenience and necessity' are subject to vehement criticism. First, the exercise of its powers is attacked on the basis that it has been ineffective, having patently failed to avoid a situation of oligopoly within US media markets, potentially a problem from the point of view of the interests of competition, consumers and citizens. Related to this is a second line of criticism that states that the Agency's agenda is too vulnerable to capture, through political appointment of Commissioners, and/or by powerful media business lobbies. The third critical line, attacking its regulatory power as unconstitutional, by virtue of being too extensive or too ill-defined, is adopted primarily by those who seek to pursue a deregulatory agenda. It is this third line of argument that perhaps most clearly raises questions over what is to be understood as 'the public interest' in this context.

The first of these arguments can be summarized very briefly, as there is already an extensive, powerful and well-known literature on the subject.[119] Essentially the story told is one of vertical and horizontal integration within the media industries so that the US market is dominated by a small number of giant conglomerates, a situation which, from a number of perspectives, identified in Chapter Three, is seen to run counter to perceived public interests while serving the commercial interests of those who control these corporations. Part of an increasingly global phenomenon,[120] this concentration of power within the media industries is seen as contrary to the effective operation of markets. In addition, though the relationship between concentration of ownership and lack of diversity of views expressed in the media should, strictly speaking, be seen as a contingent rather than necessary connection, by potentially limiting the range of material available to individuals with which to engage in triangulation of their view of the world, concentration of control over media outlets appears to threaten citizenship and hence democratic interests.[121] It may be thought to amount to the increasing privatization of an aspect of the public sphere.

The second line of argument also need not detain us unduly. Though the power of appointment rests with the President, subject to the advice and consent

---

[118] See Congdon, T., Graham, A., Green, D., and Robinson, B., *The Cross Media Revolution: Ownership and Control* (London: John Libbey, 1995), 70; also Feintuck, M., *Media Regulation, Public Interest and the Law* (Edinburgh: Edinburgh University Press, 1999), 53.

[119] See Bagdikian, B., *The Media Monopoly* (6th edn.) (Boston, Mass.: Beacon Press, 2000); Herman, E. and McChesney, R., *The Global Media* (London: Cassell, 1997); Champlin, D. and Knoedler, J., 'Operating in the Public Interest or in Pursuit of Private Profits? News in the Age of Media Consolidation', *Journal of Economic Issues*, 36/2 (2002), 459.

[120] Herman and McChesney, *The Global Media*.

[121] Keane, J., *The Media and Democracy* (Cambridge: Polity Press, 1991); McQuail, D., *Media Performance, Mass Communication and the Public Interest* (London: Sage, 1992); Schiller, H., *Information Inequality* (New York, N.Y.: Routledge, 1996).

of the Senate, the President may appoint only a bare majority of the Agency's five Commissioners from within their party. However, as Breger and Edles note, the Congressional influence over appointments is also significant,[122] and the result is that the Commission is rendered subject to the volatile party political fray. It should not be unexpected that 'political appointees', including the FCC's Chair, will be appointed with an awareness of their political outlook in mind, as an aspect of a 'spoils' system, and will inevitably tend to pursue policies which fit with their political orientation. However, it is not only from this direction that the FCC is vulnerable to interest group pressure. Barendt points very clearly towards the FCC's vulnerability to lobbying by powerful interest groups,[123] while Schiller, in somewhat polemical mode, observes that 'anyone familiar with the industry-serving commission [has] to regard its alleged role as a protector of the public interest, and a scourge of the broadcasters, as a fantasy'.[124] If true, this is clearly problematic, though, like Croley's discussion of 'publicly interested regulation',[125] it ultimately does little to illuminate as to what the public interest might be, other than to suggest that it is something different from private commercial interests.

This leads us naturally into an inquiry as to what normative values 'the public interest' might represent in this context, and whether it is, or can be, adequately defined so as to defeat arguments that consider it 'too indeterminate to be constitutional',[126] or simply so vague as to render it largely meaningless. Barendt is very clear in his condemnation of 'the public interest, convenience and necessity' as a 'vacuous formula'.[127] This may not be that surprising, if Ramberg is right in suggesting that the concept as applied in the communications field was in fact 'borrowed' from the rather different context of utilities law, where 'necessity' and 'convenience' may carry some concrete meaning which does not transplant readily into the new context.[128] Meanwhile, current FCC Chair, Michael Powell has been quoted as referring to the public interest as 'an empty vessel into which people pour whatever their preconceived views or biases are'.[129] Such comments do not bode well for those going in search of substantive values, and it is therefore unsurprising to see the quest compared to that for the mythical 'Holy Grail', the image used by Krasnow and Goodman[130] in their survey of the development of the concept in the context of the FCC's activities.

---

[122] See Breger and Edles, 'Established by Practice', 1139–40 and 1250.

[123] Barendt, *Broadcasting Law*, 85.   [124] Schiller, *Information Inequality*, 53.

[125] Croley, 'Public Interested Regulation'.

[126] May, R. J., 'The Public Interest Standard: Is it too Indeterminate to be Constitutional?', *Federal Communications Law Journal*, 53 (2001), 427.   [127] Barendt, *Broadcasting Law*, 29.

[128] Ramberg, 'The Supreme Court and Public Interest', 16 May, 'The Public Interest Standard', 445, observes a direct line of usage of the term, from *Munn v. Illinois*, to a subsequent Illinois statute, to the Federal Transportation Act 1920, and thence into subsequent Acts.

[129] Quoted in Champlin and Knoedler, 'Operating in the Public Interest', 459.

[130] Krasnow, E. and Goodman, J., 'The Public Interest Standard: the Search for the Holy Grail', *Federal Communications Law Journal*, 50 (1998), 605.

The Public Interest Standard

Though formally originating from sections 307 and 309 in the Communications Act 1934, versions of the concept can be seen to be informing debate over regulating the airwaves earlier still. Krasnow and Goodman quote Secretary of Commerce Herbert Hoover, in 1925 as stating 'The ether is a public medium, and its use must be for the public benefit. The use of a radio channel is justified only if there is a public benefit.'[131] Though statements such as this express sentiments from which it is difficult to dissent, they offer little or nothing in terms of definition of the concept. They must also be read in the context of limited frequencies within the then available radio spectrum: 'spectrum scarcity', which, as was noted in the previous chapter, justified regulation on the simple basis of effective transmission.

Drawing upon this rationale for regulatory intervention, we find statements such as that from Congressman White, in 1927, in the run-up to the Radio Act of that year, stating that 'the broadcasting privilege will not be a right of selfishness. It will rest upon an assurance of public interest to be served.'[132] Krasnow and Goodman helpfully emphasize the development indicated by such an approach adopted in the 1927 and 1934 Acts: 'broadcasters were deemed "public trustees" who were "privileged" to use a scarce public resource',[133] a model effectively confirmed by the Supreme Court as recently as 1969, when they stated that 'It is the right of the viewers and listeners, not the right of broadcasters, which is paramount.'[134] In practice, just as the 'privilege' of incorporation through charter has been translated into corporate rights,[135] so the analogy with 'trusteeship' in this context has broken down. Indeed, there is significant doubt about the extent to which this theoretical position is translated into reality.

A more aggressively sceptical approach to the trusteeship model than that set out by Fowler and Brenner,[136] discussed below, could not be imagined. Another example comes from Krotoszynski,[137] who finds fundamental contradictions beneath this apparently settled position. He believes that the public interest duty 'rests on an untenable premise: that broadcasters will act in ways inconsistent with their financial self-interest';[138] 'that the "trustee" will act as a fiduciary for the benefit of the viewing public'.[139] He believes also that it is 'virtually incapable of being vigorously enforced',[140] given what he sees as the inherent subjective element in the Commission's judgments over, say, children's programming, and also the FCC's lack of true independence from Congress. Krotoszynski believes that 'Congress will never willingly surrender its leverage over the broadcasting industry, and the public interest standard is a key component of this leverage.'[141]

---

[131] Krasnow, E. and Goodman, J., 'The Public Interest Standard: the Search for the Holy Grail', *Federal Communications Law Journal*, 50 (1998), 608.   [132] Ibid., 609.   [133] Ibid., 610.
[134] *Red Lion Broadcasting v. FCC*, 395 US 367 (1969).   [135] See below, Ch. 7.
[136] Fowler, M. S. and Brenner, D. L., 'A Marketplace Approach to Broadcast Regulation', *Texas Law Review*, 60 (1982), 207, especially 213 *et seq*.
[137] Krotoszynski, R. J., 'The Inevitable Wasteland: Why the Public Trustee Model of Broadcast Regulation Must Fail', *Michigan Law Review*, 95 (1997), 2101.   [138] Ibid., 2109.
[139] Ibid.   [140] Ibid., 2122.   [141] Ibid., 2137.

He argues that 'At the end of the day, the "public interest" standard serves the interests of Congress, the Commission, and the broadcasting industry very well indeed. The only unserved constituency is the public.'[142] Ultimately, he seems to believe that structural and behavioural regulation directed unambiguously at aspects of the operation of market forces, such as spectrum auctions and/or common carrier obligations, would actually better serve the objectives of public interest regulation than the current regulation in its name.

There are, however, clearly risks attached to such an approach. Parallel issues may be seen to exist in relation to telecommunications, where the Telecommunications Act of 1996 can be seen as 'the replacement of regulation with competition'.[143] It is worth noting that McFadden indicates that, by contrast, historically, 'The FCC has consistently held that its public interest standard and the antitrust laws exist to protect the public's interests, not the economic interests of competitors.'[144] The implicit statement here is that though it may be believed that competition law measures are ultimately likely to benefit citizens (as consumers) via a sort of trickle-down process, the primary beneficiaries, and focal point of the measures, are those players in the market who would otherwise suffer as a result of anti-competitive behaviour. The focus of such measures is economic, and any social benefits therefore strictly contingent.

However, it might be thought that in relation to the FCC's regulation of broadcasting, the Rubicon was already crossed some years ago. The general direction to be taken could not have been indicated more clearly than when Mark Fowler, the then-Chair of the Commission, co-authored an article stating that 'in light of the First Amendment's heavy presumption against content control, the Commission should refrain from insinuating itself into program decisions made by licensees',[145] and that 'regulators and others have become increasingly aware that regulatory processes have infringed the first amendment rights of broadcasters without a sufficiently compelling justification'.[146]

Such a paradigm shift to a market-based, competition law approach certainly does not guarantee, any more than the (questionably effective) former public interest regulation, to serve well the ultimately social interests which underlie intervention in such fields. It may generally be expected to protect such values even less.

The 'public trustee' model will be returned to, and reviewed in later chapters, in the context of discussions of stewardship approaches to the public interest, but for the moment it is important to note that the 1927 Act made clear that despite being in the position of 'trustees', broadcasters were not to be censored by the regulatory authorities:

Nothing in this Act shall be understood or construed to give the licensing authority the power of censorship over the radio communications or signals transmitted by any

---

[142] Ibid., 2138.
[143] McFadden, D. B., 'Antitrust and Communications: Changes after the Telecommunications Act of 1996', *Federal Communications Law Journal*, 49 (1997), 457, at 457.   [144] Ibid., 464.
[145] Fowler and Brenner, 'A Marketplace Approach', 210.   [146] Ibid., 209.

radio station, and no regulation or condition shall be promulgated or fixed by the licensing authority which shall interfere with the right of free speech by means of radio communications.[147]

This clause, essentially re-emphasizing the constitutional centrality of freedom of expression, inevitably served to encourage challenges to the FRC's licensing activities, though the courts were quick to support the Commission's licensing activities and subsequently those of the FCC, as not being an abridgement of freedom of speech but merely the proper pursuit of the public interest role granted to them by Congress. As relatively recently as 1981, the Supreme Court noted that 'The Commission's judgment regarding how the public interest is best served is entitled to substantial judicial deference.'[148]

However, beyond the, at best marginally helpful and at worst misleading, analogy of the position of broadcasters as trustees, relatively little definition has been achieved in relation to how 'the public interest' is to be understood. In a sense, it might be argued that the degree of judicial deference shown has resulted in missed opportunities to clarify the notion. In 1940, the Supreme Court identified the public interest standard as being 'as concrete as the complicated factors for judgment in such a field of delegated authority permit', and 'a supple instrument for the exercise of discretion',[149] and three years later affirmed that the public interest standard is the touchstone of FCC authority to exercise broad regulatory powers, and held that the public interest standard was not unconstitutionally vague.[150] As we shall see shortly, however, this has not stopped critics from attacking the use of the concept on precisely this ground.

Demonstrating the fluctuating scope of perceptions of the extent of intervention permitted under the concept, in 1960, the FCC did publish a Programming Policy Statement which provided an indicative list of the range of programming which broadcasters should carry in order to meet the public interest requirement.[151] The list of 'major elements necessary to meet the public interest' including news, public affairs, weather, educational, children's and religious programmes, is in fact very close to the qualities traditionally associated with the Western European public service broadcasting tradition. However, the approach was already coming under pressure from changes in the market and the technology of broadcasting, and the spectrum scarcity justification would soon be severely challenged, in the US as elsewhere, by the advent of digitalization.

Krasnow and Goodman chart how, as early as the 1970s, the FCC started, within the flexibility granted to it under the public interest standard, to

---

[147] Radio Act 1927, S.29.
[148] *FCC v. WNCN Listeners Guild*, 450 US 582 (1981), 596, quoted in Krasnow and Goodman, 'The Public Interest Standard', 625.
[149] *FCC v. Pottsville Broadcasting*, 309 US 134 (1940), at 138.
[150] *NBC v. US*, 319 US 190 (1943). See Krasnow and Goodman, 'The Public Interest Standard', 621.
[151] Quoted in Krasnow and Goodman, 'The Public Interest Standard', 615.

shift towards a 'marketplace' approach to regulation. By 1981, they note FCC Chair Mark Fowler as stating that 'we are at the end of regulating broadcasting under the trusteeship model',[152] and quote the DC Circuit Court of Appeals as confirming that the FCC 'may rely upon marketplace forces to control broadcast abuse if the Commission reasonably finds that a market approach offers the best means of controlling the abuse'.[153] Essentially amounting to deregulation, remanding regulation substantially to market forces is viewed as being within the flexibility of approach granted to the FCC by Congress.[154] Flexibility may or may not be viewed as a virtue in this context:

Since Congress has found it inadvisable or impossible to define specifically for future situations exactly what constitutes the public interest, the political problem of achieving consensus as to the case-by-case application of this standard has been passed to the FCC. The flexibility inherent in this elusive public interest concept can be enormously significant to the FCC not only as a means of modifying policies to meet changed conditions and to obtain special support but also as a source of continuing and sometimes hard-to-resolve controversy.[155]

In the mid-1980s, Ramberg concluded that 'All too often the court uses the public interest in a manner that is vague and undefined', that 'There is not one public interest', and, that though 'What emerges is a standard applied in peculiar ways and in various circumstances', this 'does not suggest that the phrase is without content, that is, a worthless concept'.[156] This is not a hugely positive and not untypical conclusion to reach. However, Krasnow and Goodman ultimately find that 'the genius of the public interest standard is its breadth and flexibility',[157] though they also note that, especially in the digital era, in the absence of spectrum scarcity justifications for regulation, 'the constitutional foundation for renewed extensive content regulation has become increasingly uncertain'.[158] Thus, both direct regulation of content and its surrogate in the form of structural regulation are found to be of doubtful legitimacy. However, noted earlier was the ongoing claim, despite the findings of the Supreme Court in *NBC*,[159] that the vagueness inherent in the concept raises questions of its constitutionality. Commenting extra-judicially, Judge Henry Friendly is found to be extremely critical of the concept as used in the Communications Act, finding it as 'drained of meaning'[160] and there are still voices that consider the public interest standard 'too indeterminate to be constitutional'.[161]

---

[152] Krasnow and Goodman, 'The Public Interest Standard', 616.
[153] Ibid., 618, referring to *Telecommunications Research and Action Center v. FCC*, 800 F.2d 1181 (DC Cir) (1986).   [154] Krasnow and Goodman, 'The Public Interest Standard', 617.
[155] Ibid., 626.   [156] Ramberg, 'The Supreme Court and Public Interest', 27.
[157] Krasnow and Goodman, 'The Public Interest Standard', 630.   [158] Ibid., 633.
[159] 319 US 190 (1943).
[160] Quoted in Krasnow and Goodman, 'The Public Interest Standard', 626.
[161] May, 'The Public Interest Standard'.

The latter phrase is one used by May, writing from his position within the Progress and Freedom Foundation. May's perspective is strongly deregulatory[162] arguing that the FCC's Commissioners should 'make it a priority to pull back the dogs of regulation and let the market work',[163] and hoping that the arguments he supports will be sufficient to persuade Congress to provide more specific guidance to the FCC that will 'provide an unmistakable roadmap toward a deregulatory end game consistent with a competitive marketplace'.[164]

Moving beyond such deregulatory polemic, he locates his concerns regarding the unconstitutionality of the concept of public interest in the context of Montesquieu's separation of powers doctrine which underlies the US Constitution, and argues from this base that 'nondelegation boundaries have been transgressed when Congress authorizes its delegate ... [the FCC] ... to simply act in the "public interest" '.[165] He is able to draw on some recent academic support,[166] and some minority judicial comments, but has to go back to 1935 to find examples of the higher US courts being prepared to enforce the nondelegation doctrine in this kind of context.[167] He notes though that the Supreme Court 'has never formally abandoned the doctrine', which he hopes will be resuscitated. He goes on to identify a 'softer' version of the doctrine, which seems to amount to the ability of courts not to strike down federal legislation in broad terms as excessively open-ended, but to 'hold that federal administrative agencies may not engage in certain activities unless and until Congress has *expressly authorized* them to do so'.[168] This view does appear to be reasonably consistent with that of the Supreme Court's 2000 decision in *FDA v. Brown and Williamson Tobacco Corp.*,[169] referred to earlier. Indeed, not all judicial opinion is entirely against the notion, with Justice Rehnquist, in *Benzene*,[170] a case relating to the exercise of statutory powers by the Occupational Health and Safety Administration, prepared to find the relevant statutory position unconstitutional, as a standardless, and hence unlawful, delegation.[171] However, as May accepts, the reluctance of the courts to intervene by way of reviving the non-delegation doctrine is generally apparent. In particular, May concedes that the *American Trucking* case,[172] in which the court required that delegation be based on an intelligible principle, but gave very wide latitude as to what this implied, 'did not breathe much new life into the nondelegation doctrine'.[173] He does note though,

---

[162] See May, R. J., *A Reform Agenda for the New FCC* (Washington DC: Progress and Freedom Foundation, 2001), and 'Call Them Off', *Legal Times*, 4th June 2001.
[163] May, 'Call Them Off'.   [164] May, 'The Public Interest Standard', 432.
[165] Ibid., 428.   [166] Ibid., 444.
[167] *Panama Refining Co. v. Ryan* 293 US 388 (1935); *Schechter Poultry Corp. v. US* 295 US 495 (1935).
[168] Sunstein, C. R., 'Nondelegation Canons', *University of Chicago Law Review*, 67 (2000), 315, quoted in May, 'The Public Interest Standard', 438, emphasis added.   [169] 529 US 120 (2000).
[170] *Industrial Union Department v. American Petroleum Institute* 448 US 607 (1980).
[171] See Strauss, *Administrative Justice*, 165–8.
[172] *Whitman v. American Trucking Associations*, 2001 US LEXIS 1952 (2001).
[173] May, 'The Public Interest Standard', 442.

optimistically from his point of view, that none of the case law entirely forecloses the possibility that challenges on the basis of non-delegation may succeed in the future.

He goes on to quote a range of scholars who urge a revival of the non-delegation doctrine, to deal with statutory delegation of power via the public interest standard which 'says practically nothing at all' about Congress's goals, or 'leave basic normative issues unanswered and thus within the realm of the delegate', or grant 'nearly absolute discretion'.[174]

Though May is clearly swimming with a fashionable deregulatory current at his back, he is clearly going against a strong judicial tide which, as he illustrates, appears to recognize the necessity of confirming the discretion of specialist administrative agencies empowered by deliberately broad Congressional grants of power. The underlying problem is one of ensuring the constitutionality of agency action under Congressional grant of authority, while permitting the agency sufficient room for manoeuvre in which to act effectively. Beyond the broad, overarching non-delegation doctrine, which courts may appear unwilling to apply, Sunstein does point towards a range of 'hidden', 'constitutionally inspired', and, 'sovereignty-inspired' non-delegation canons which he identifies as avoiding the blanket nature of the traditional doctrine and offering promising ways out of the impasse.[175]

In essence, the question here is one of identifying jurisdictional bounds: the extent of legitimate agency discretion within the larger constitutional scheme. Seeking to maintain a focus on what can be viewed as the central issue, the initial delegation of authority from Congress, Noah considers the application of three different metaphorical accounts of the issue. He discusses the enabling statute as being (1) akin to a corporate charter, or (2) a constitution, with its inevitable dynamic element, or (3) as a source of common law norms with all the resulting flexibility in terms of future development.[176] Each of these metaphors, he writes, 'suggests a distinct relationship between administrative agencies and the courts, accompanied by different expectations about the degree of fidelity government officials must accord to their delegations of legislative authority from Congress'.[177] He notes how, if we consider these from first to last in the order presented, they tend to indicate a more flexible, less confined interpretation of the extent of agency powers, and one which is less susceptible to judicial review, more deserving of judicial deference. The difference between the majority judgments, and Breyer's in *FDA v. Brown and Williamson Tobacco Corp.*,[178] referred to earlier, perhaps illustrates the debate most clearly. Noah's conclusion is that the narrowest construction, deriving from the analogy with a corporate

---

[174] All ibid., 444.

[175] Sunstein, C. R., *Designing Democracy: What Constitutions Do* (Oxford: Oxford University Press, 2001), 145–53.

[176] Noah, L., 'Interpreting Agency Enabling Acts: Misplaced Metaphors in Administrative Law', *William and Mary Law Review*, 41 (2000), 1463.   [177] Ibid., 1468.

[178] 529 US 120 (2000).

charter, is the most constitutionally appropriate:

> If ... we conceive of organic statutes as charters, or as constitutions of specifically enumerated powers that can be embellished somewhat by a necessary and proper clause but not significantly expanded, then agencies will not as easily upset the balance of power among the three main branches of government.[179]

The perspective adopted here is very different to Sunstein's, to which we will turn shortly, which Noah characterizes as being based upon the 'common law' metaphor, implying wide agency power. Whether or not we agree with Noah's conclusions, his work helpfully illustrates the tension created by different visions of the US constitutional settlement. His observation that 'undue reliance on such metaphors may suggest overly facile answers to difficult legal questions'[180] is well made, though the comparison of grants of authority as 'charters' has something of the ring of the 'trustee' analogy in broadcasting, which has been shown to have manifestly failed to achieve its apparent objectives. Similarly, whether or not we agree with May's deregulatory perspective, it is worth taking note of a perspective raised in his conclusions. He states that,

> Congress must ask itself anew whether the public interest standard is indeed sufficiently 'concrete' to fulfil Congress's responsibility to set communications policies for the Information Age, or whether it is so vague that it can mean whatever three FCC Commissioners say it means on any given day.[181]

This serves as a vivid illustration of a fundamental issue, referred to earlier in Chapters One and Two, in terms of the likely inability of an inadequately defined construct of the public interest to achieve anything worthwhile. If it is the empty vessel that May, Fowler, and, others suggest, then it is indeed vulnerable to capture, and filling with whatever values those in power decide to fill it with. It may then even run the risk, as Krotoszynski suggests,[182] of serving more the political and bureaucratic interests of Congress and the FCC than it does the public it is meant to serve. Even if we do not share May's deregulatory perspective, his message has import. Greater clarity, greater normative specificity is necessary in usage of the term 'the public interest', as otherwise the (too) malleable concept may fail to serve any useful function, and in particular will fail to serve the values it purports to protect in the name of the public interest. It will be a straw in the wind, rather than a force of resistance.

UNFULFILLED POTENTIAL, OR JUST A BLIND ALLEY?

While the foregoing should have illustrated the apparent *potential* for 'the public interest' to represent important but vulnerable values within the American polity,

---

[179] Noah, 'Interpreting Agency Enabling Acts', 1530.   [180] Ibid.
[181] May, 'The Public Interest Standard', 453.
[182] Krotoszynski, 'The Inevitable Wasteland'.

two different conclusions might be drawn from consideration of the concept's application in relation to food supply and the media industries. It might be thought either that there remains a significant untapped or unfulfilled potential for the concept, or that it is a vision which has been tried but has failed and is beyond salvation.

Without doubt, a significant problem is the multiple, often competing meanings which are attached to, or contained within, the concept of 'public interest'. The range of economic meanings, identified by Breyer, in combination with the vast array of models in play in political philosophy, and changing visions of the state and society, form a burden that would strain to bursting even the best designed portmanteau term. In Stewart's terms, the range of values at stake within the regulatory endeavour in a liberal democracy, and the administrative law which applies to it, include not only 'the protection of entitlements' and 'the promotion of production', but also 'non-commodity values'.[183] The pursuit by society of values beyond the economic, such as 'Aspiration, Diversity, Mutuality and Civic Virtue',[184] which form part of Stewart's vision of a 'more ample liberalism', imply the need for a deliberative system which relates to certain visions of the public interest, but places enormous demands on such a concept. The FDA's, and other agencies' response to GM food seems to illustrate perfectly further underlying tensions, relating to the competing scientific and economic, as opposed to social, factors which all may make claims to represent central public interest values.

There are, occasional glimmers of hope, such as Fainsod's claim, noted earlier, that 'frequently in practice [regulatory agencies] are capable of recognizing some interests as more "public" or more "general" than other interests and of adapting, fusing, and directing group pressures towards such a recognition'.[185] However, ultimately, the concept appears desperately unclear, even in terms of whether its purpose is simply to assist in softening the hard edges of raw capitalism, or whether it does in reality represent or seek to advance within the polity some other (perhaps 'higher') values or ideals, such as those of civic republicanism. As things stand, the presence or absence of the term's usage may, in itself, signify very little, even in relation to regulators thought to act as 'agents of the public interest'. While the FDA clearly pursues what at the broadest level are examples of public interest regulation, the term is hardly used, while the FCC, with the term at the heart of its remit, may be thought to have singularly failed to protect certain values which would generally be thought central to any meaningful version of the concept, and is constantly subjected to challenge when it does seek to pursue them. In relation to non-commodity values such as diversity and civic virtue, found within many constructs of the public interest, Stewart noted in 1983, in the deregulatory era epitomized by the thoughts set out in Fowler

[183] Stewart, 'Regulation in a Liberal State', 1537.   [184] Ibid., 1568.
[185] Fainsod, 'Some Reflections'.

and Brenner's piece,[186] that,

For over 30 years, the FCC, with considerable judicial prodding, has instituted a wide variety of program measures to promote such values. Even in their prime, such efforts were widely condemned by critics as ineffective. Today, the FCC with the administration's encouragement and Congress' acquiescence, is abandoning most of those efforts in the name of deregulation.[187]

Stewart's conclusions in relation to such (arguably failed) regulatory pro-grammes, is that 'the record of these and other regulatory efforts underscores the need for specifying non-commodity objectives, determining whether regu-lation is likely to advance them, and designing effective measures to promote them'.[188] It seems clear, however, that a regulatory regime based on an 'empty vessel' construct of the public interest, which is capable of capture by interest groups, offers no more protection to non-commodity values than do market forces; it may seem to go beyond potentially useful flexibility, into unhelp-ful fluidity. It is, of course, the central thrust of this book to determine whether a developed, normatively clear, concept of public interest might assist with an agenda such as Stewart's, by providing a robust conceptual basis for regulation.

It is clear that the legal realm is extremely significant, in terms of under-standing and applying the concept of public interest in the US context. Though finding the issues presented in different forms, ranging across disputes framed by constitutional terms, or application of the APA, or specific statutory terms, the US judiciary has repeatedly been required to pronounce on the concept's application by regulatory agencies. The court's attitude, in terms of adopting a more interventionist or more deferential stance, may be seen as critical in determining the scope of agency power. In the post-*Chevron* era, Noah cites the FDA's announcement that it does not need new powers to restrict human cloning experiments, and the FCC's consideration of requiring broadcasters to provide free air-time to election candidates, as evidence that 'the judiciary's rush to defer to reasonable agency interpretations of ambiguous statutory language has emboldened agencies to push to the outer limits of their jurisdiction'.[189]

Whether or not we accept Noah's perspective, or whether we prefer Sunstein's vision in which regulatory agencies have an important role to play in the pur-suit of the objectives of deliberative democracy, and must therefore be granted appropriately broad powers,[190] what is clear is that, ultimately, judicial activ-ity has tended, inevitably, to focus on highly technical legal matters, to the exclusion of offering assistance in defining public interest values. Even where legal and academic disputes are presented in the context of broad constitutional

---

[186] Fowler and Brenner, 'A Marketplace Approach'.
[187] Stewart, 'Regulation in a Liberal State', 1580.   [188] Ibid., 1581.
[189] Noah, 'Interpreting Agency Enabling Acts', 1466.
[190] See Sunstein, *After the Rights Revolution*, Ch. 2.

theory, such as the non-delegation doctrine,[191] the adversarial nature of process inevitably focuses primarily on determining the instant case, resolving the argument presented in favour of the immediate interests of one of the litigants or academics, rather than development of the underlying concept.[192] The nature of debate, of adversarial process, in any particular case may result in such larger questions being buried beneath narrower legal issues, or indeed the focus shifting to different, but equally broad, legal issues such as appropriate methods and extent of judicial interpretation of statutes.[193]

Disputes arising out of the activities of regulators such as the FDA or FCC essentially raise questions regarding the legality of agency action, yet underlying these 'technical' issues are much larger questions relating to the *legitimacy* of such actions within the polity. Inevitably, in constitutional terms, questions arise also as the constitutionality of judicial role. Shapiro highlights this question of legitimacy, stating that 'Judicial review of delegated legislation always raises the question of the relative legitimacy of two agents, the initial delegate and the judicial reviewer.'[194] In reviewing delegated powers, the judiciary, understandably, and concerned for the perceived legitimacy of their own actions, will tend to focus on the technical/legal level rather than the more abstract constitutional question of legitimacy. They will, predictably, tend to become involved in the construction of the problem within the legal framework presented to them. Whether consciously or not, the judiciary will therefore tend to further the bifurcation of technical issues from moral matters.[195] The reason why this process may have failed to result in the development of a meaningful construct of the public interest, or any clear vision of the values which underlie it, may well relate to the failure of law to develop an adequate and appropriate terminology, which fully incorporates and articulates the underlying conceptual framework deriving from democratic expectations rather than relying on analogy and metaphor. This appears to indicate a need for the development of precisely the kind of 'Interpretative Principle' which Sunstein advocates,[196] of which the public interest could be one such.

It might be reasonably concluded at this stage that all the judicial activity referred to above has done little to illuminate or develop the concerns and values which underlie the concept's use. It may be that the high degree of judicial deference shown to regulatory discretion in the post-*Chevron* era is particularly

---

[191] For an overview of the doctrine, and some comparative context, see Asimow, M., 'Delegated Legislation: United States and United Kingdom', *Oxford Journal of Legal Studies*, 3/2 (1983), 253; Craig, *Public Law and Democracy*, 116–27; Shapiro, M., 'Judicial Delegation Doctrines: the US, Britain and France', *West European Politics*, 25/1 (2002), 173.

[192] See Sunstein, *Designing Democracy*, 184, for discussion of how *Bowers v. Hardwick* was decided on due process, not equal protection.

[193] For a conventional account of statutory interpretation in US administrative law, see Strauss, *Administrative Justice*, 349–365.   [194] Shapiro, 'Judicial Delegation Doctrines', 179.

[195] Minor, W. S., 'Public Interest and Ultimate Commitment', in Friedrich, C. J. (ed.), *Nomos V: The Public Interest* (New York, N.Y.: Atherton Press, 1962).

[196] Sunstein, *After the Rights Revolution*, Ch. 5. Discussed below, Ch. 6.

problematic in this respect, though in reality the previous case law offered little more by way of amplification of 'the public interest'. It is arguable that, within the constitutional scheme, this is exactly as it should be, the alternative seeming to be the judiciary becoming immersed in the political and policy fray which underlies the difficult subjects delegated to agencies via statute. In Shapiro's terms, 'Given the best will in the world by judges to avoid imposing their own policy preferences, interpretation of such statutes necessarily and unavoidably involves judicial policy choices because the statutes themselves frequently had not clearly, consistently, and completely made such choices.'[197] However, from the point of view of the development and protection of potentially important democratic norms such as the public interest, the combination of lack of statutory clarity, any failure by agencies to act consistently and clearly, and ultimately, the failure of the judiciary to articulate and enforce such values, is disappointing, and may appear as a series of missed opportunities. As Shapiro observes, 'The bulk of US jurisprudence ... does not concern the constitutionality of delegating legislation but the lawfulness, as opposed to the constitutionality, of the delegated legislation.'[198] The risk is the ongoing 'defective translation'[199] of democratic values into legally recognized and enforced principles.

Though the constitutional settlement may seem, from some perspectives, to debar judicial action in this area, it is clear that the boundaries of legitimate judicial intervention are flexible and subject to change, as cases such as *Vermont Yankee*[200] and *Chevron*[201] illustrate. Also, as Sunstein suggests, less blunt instruments than the all-or-nothing non-delegation doctrine may be available.

To be sure, perceptions of the legitimate extent of judicial intervention as regards the interpretation of the US Constitution will ultimately depend upon whether an interpretivist or non-interpretivist position is adopted. In other words, the proper scope of judicial authority will be determined by a consideration of whether the view taken of the judicial role in relation to the Constitution is one whereby the judiciary may intervene to strike down decisions of the executive or its agencies only when, using Ely's terms, 'proceeding from premises that are explicit or clearly implicit in the document itself',[202] (interpretivist), or whether the judiciary may act on a broader basis, drawing upon, in Ely's striking phrase, 'society's "fundamental principles" or whatever'[203] (non-interpretivist). While interpretivism may appear attractive on the one hand, being closely associated with a classical if narrow portrayal (or perhaps caricature) of how judicial decisions are or 'should be' taken, it also has significant problems in terms of being 'clause-bound'; restricting activity in relation to contemporary

---

[197] Shapiro, 'Judicial Delegation Doctrines', 184.   [198] Ibid., 181.

[199] Teubner, G., *Juridification of Social Spheres* (Berlin: Walter de Gruyter, 1987), extracts in Baldwin, R., Scott, C., and Hood, C. (eds.), *A Reader on Regulation* (Oxford: Oxford University Press, 1998).   [200] 435 US 519 (1978).

[201] 467 US 837 (1984).

[202] Ely, J. H., *Democracy and Distrust: a Theory of Judicial Review* (Cambridge, Mass.: Harvard University Press, 1980), 12.   [203] Ibid., 4.

re-interpretation of constitutional terms. On the other hand, non-interpretivism, granting apparently broad powers to the judiciary to overturn the decisions of bodies which may claim a more obvious democratic mandate, 'seems especially vulnerable to a charge of inconsistency with democratic theory',[204] and Ely's sceptical 'or whatever' should be indicative of the heavy burden of specification and justification placed on those who wish to argue such a line. Repeatedly in this book, phrases such as 'fundamental values' and 'democratic principles' have been used, and it is clear that a non-interpretivist line is being advocated. It will therefore be necessary to bear in mind the problems identified by Ely in the final part of this book, when an attempt will be made to uncover such values and principles. The task will be to consider whether the problems of non-interpretivism can be alleviated, by the establishment of a framework of principle within which judicial power, extending beyond clause-bound interpretation, can be legitimately exercised, and to reflect on whether the concept of public interest may have a role to play in the fulfilment of these principles or values.

On balance, the interim conclusion to be drawn at this stage should not be that the public interest represents a conceptual dead end, and that we should abandon its usage, but rather that it appears to represent a missed opportunity. In particular, it seems possible within the matrix of US administrative and constitutional law, that application of a developed version of the concept of public interest could assist substantially in establishing and confirming on an ongoing basis the legitimacy of the actions of regulatory agencies. It is possible that the constitutional concerns raised over broad delegations of power to them, in the name of the public interest, could, logically, be reduced by the application of a normative version of the concept as an interpretative principle, serving to structure their discretion. Such principles would have the potential to provide both a structure within which discretion could legitimately be exercised, and standards against which regulators could be effectively held to account by the judicial system. Though this would probably not satisfy those coming from a strong ideological predisposition towards deregulation, a concept which embodied clear and unambiguous statements as to the goals and purposes of the grant of discretion could be judicially applicable, and would, in providing a more effective judicial check on public interest powers than that provided by the current law, help to remedy any genuine, constitutionally derived, concerns regarding broad grants of discretion.

Yet on a Madisonian construction of the Constitution, such as Sunstein adopts, it seems already clear that regulation of private property power is a legitimate state activity: he refers to 'the republican account', on which 'self-interest is an insufficient basis for political advantage; it must be translated into some broader conception of the public interest'.[205] However, a chronic problem seems to be the difficulty in recognizing the status of norms such as 'the public interest' which are not easily captured by conventional rules of construction

---

[204] Ibid., 5.   [205] Sunstein, *After the Rights Revolution*, 12.

generally used in legal discourse, which apply more readily to more specific terms. The failure of the 'public trustee' model in broadcasting, truly the failure of reasoning from analogy or metaphor, demonstrates the weakness of working from approximations and analogy in the absence of more precise legal concepts which fully capture the nature of the competing interests under consideration.

In the final two chapters of this book, some consideration will be given both to further exploration of the meaning and function of the public interest in such contexts, and to the extent to which the development of constructs such as 'stewardship' may facilitate the concept's effective application, enabling it to serve better the democratic values it represents. However, before turning to such matters, it is important to see what similarities and differences emerge, and what lessons can be learnt, from drawing together the material from this chapter on the US and the previous one on the UK.

5

Anglo-American Comparisons

At first sight, the substantial differences in constitutional form may be thought likely to render comparisons between the UK and the US difficult or impossible. However, similarities in the fundamental purposes of the regulatory regimes that have been considered, and the issues they address and raise, may be seen to outweigh the contextual differences. In this chapter, the findings from the previous two will be reviewed, key issues highlighted, and comparative conclusions drawn. The act of comparison will serve to confirm and clarify the nature of problems which underlie regulating in 'the public interest', but may also suggest avenues worthy of further exploration in pursuit of devices which serve the values and goals which the regulatory regime purports to further.

In both the UK and the US, the regulatory endeavour in relation to fundamentals of citizenship, such as food and media, seeks to protect democratic expectations from threats posed by raw market forces. In both cases, regulatory activity is confined, albeit in different ways, by a constitutional and administrative law framework which imposes outer limits on regulators' powers. In both cases, we can see examples of how the systems respond to the influence of technical legal constraints, and to scientific and economic arguments, yet may often seem to fail to reflect fully or adequately the set of non-commodity values on which such regulation is premised. By way of confirming the agenda for the final part of this book, this chapter will suggest that regulatory failure, in terms of the apparent lack of mesh between the outcomes of regulation and the apparent objectives, derives to a significant extent from the failure to identify, and articulate with reasonable clarity, the underlying rationales for intervention, combined with the failure to give them legal form.

In essence, the agenda is opened up by the question asked directly by Garrett, referred to in the previous chapter: 'Against what baseline should we judge regulatory outcomes to determine whether they are normatively desirable or not?'[1] Though this question clearly relates to the *legitimacy* of regulatory interventions, the solutions found in constitutional and administrative law appear, unsurprisingly, to relate primarily to *legality*. A parallel, but connected, issue is that while the values being pursued are substantive, and therefore can be said to be more or less effectively pursued, the administrative law system tends to emphasize procedure, and accountability, rather than effectiveness in relation to substantive

---

[1] Garrett, E., 'Interest Groups and Public Interested Regulation', *Florida State University Law Review*, 28 (2000), 137, at 143.

objectives. In both jurisdictions considered, scrutinizing 'effectiveness' is con-sidered to be essentially the responsibility of the political realm rather than the legal, with the judiciary, to a greater or lesser degree, disabled from intervening in relation to such substantive matters. It will be suggested that a normative vision of 'the public interest' may serve as an interpretative principle, focusing regulatory and judicial activity properly on such values, and helping to avoid the risk of a technical, legal or scientific emphasis prevailing over achievement of social objectives. It may serve as an otherwise missing link, requiring continu-ity of emphasis throughout regulatory practice, and offering a potential standard of review which retains a focus on the underlying democratic values rather than an otherwise disconnected set of technical legal norms which may relate poorly to the animating democratic rationales for regulation.

Of course, even a quick glance at the previous two chapters will reveal marked differences in the degree to which regulatory action is subjected to judicial scrutiny. It is quite clear that US regulators and their actions are much more frequently challenged in the courts than their British counterparts.[2] The problem just referred to though, is that all this judicial activity may achieve relatively little in terms of ensuring that regulatory outcomes mesh properly with regulatory rationales.

In both jurisdictions, it appears that some idea of 'public interest' lies at the heart of the regulatory endeavour. Though it may not be described in those precise terms in either the FDA or UK FSA statutory briefs, it is clear that the intention is for such agencies to pursue some notion of general, as opposed to individual, welfare, which is at the core of any mainstream construct of the public interest. In some cases, this will be distorted or weakened somewhat, via a trope from 'citizenship interests' to far narrower, and atomistic, 'consumer interests',[3] or via the application of imprecise and inadequate metaphors such as 'trusteeship'. In other cases it will be entirely explicit, such as in the FCC's brief, yet will remain ill-defined and subject to continuous challenge. The problem here is that even repeated legal challenges to such a term do not necessarily help with elucidation of its meaning, or assist in focusing attention on the extent to which the regulatory reality conforms to its theoretical basis. Fascinating and scholarly as it may be, the legal discourse does little to assist in relation to the (arguably more fundamental) question of democratic legitimacy.

In one sense, this is not a criticism of the legal realm. The first 'Law Job',[4] 'disposition of the trouble case' is, arguably, being more or less successfully fulfilled. However, it is not possible to be so sanguine as regards the remaining

---

[2] For a useful, if now dated account of the relationship between the courts and regulatory agencies in the UK, see Baldwin, R. and McCrudden, C., *Regulation and Public Law*, (London: Weidenfeld and Nicolson, 1987), Ch. 4. More up-to-date coverage is in Prosser, T., *Law and the Regulators* (Oxford: Clarendon, 1997), and Graham, *Regulating Public Utilities: a Constitutional Approach* (Oxford: Hart Publishing, 2000), but is limited, indicating the lack of influence the UK courts have in this respect.   [3] See discussion of the FSA, and Ofcom in Ch. 3.

[4] See above, Ch. 2.

three essentially legal tasks set out by Harden and Lewis,[5] based on Llewellyn's formulation. If the lawyer has a role in establishing norms and institutions for the ordering of social activity, and establishing the location of legitimate institutional power, and developing processes for determining the direction society will take, then failure to identify adequately, or to articulate and institutionalize, the fundamental values which inform the institutions which act in pursuit of social objectives, ultimately suggests significant failings in the legal system.

While the principles of the Rule of Law and separation of powers may be thought to restrict the propriety of judicial intervention in relation to the normative underpinnings of regulation, the integration of explicit values into the basic statutory, administrative, and constitutional law which forms the context for regulation could create a more permissive role, bringing such tasks legitimately within the judicial ambit. Though no single vision of the role of administrative law will be found, whether in examining the UK or other liberal democracies, it is clear that administrative law is intimately linked to, and in many ways can be viewed, as the application of constitutional law and principle, and hence to the democratic value-base.

Though many will have reservations relating to the judiciary 'meddling' in such matters as 'public interest' values, the alternative, the present reality, is that there is no body within the institutional structure charged specifically with the task of protecting these fundamental values. If legislators abdicate their responsibilities to establish a hierarchy of values, as illustrated by the UK's Communications Act 2003, and regulators, for whatever reason, seem to fail to pursue adequately the objectives which underlie their role, in the absence of normative clarity as to these rationales and objectives it is impossible to remedy the situation. If there are values which inform regulation which transcend the party political and interest group fray, such as those commonly associated with concepts of the public interest, or with deliberative constructs of democracy, the legal system must be equipped to protect them. However, as Baldwin and McCrudden observe, judicial decision-making in such cases sometimes simply seems to miss the point. Though written in a British context, and some years ago, they make a point which still seems pertinent, and may be equally applicable beyond Britain. They state that, in reviewing regulators' actions, 'The judges appear to decide such cases without an agenda. They tend either to locate one dominant rule and apply it, or to react to the factual circumstances of the particular case.'[6]This leads to the broader constitutional context being ignored, and in order to permit a proper 'constitutional conversation' to take place, involving the regulator and those affected, Baldwin and McCrudden find that:

A better way to decide such cases may be to deal with the array of relevant arguments and to choose on the basis of articulated principles. In order to set standards, judges should

[5] Harden, I. and Lewis, N., *The Noble Lie: The British Constitution and the Rule of Law* (London: Hutchinson, 1986). [6] Baldwin and McCrudden, *Regulation and Public Law*, 71.

instead identify more clearly their value premises and articulate which values they adopt in particular situations.[7]

The issue highlighted by this perspective relates closely to that identified by Sunstein, when he observes how 'well-functioning constitutional orders try to solve problems ... through reaching incompletely theorized agreements'.[8] Of course, it may not seem desirable for democratically unaccountable judges to be given, or take for themselves, the power to identity the values to be applied in matters of social regulation, and it would indeed seem preferable for the principles and values to be established elsewhere. A further potential problem or limitation, this time relating to the efficacy of the courts in supporting public interest objectives, is that, both in the UK and the US, a high degree of judicial deference is seen to be shown towards the decisions of 'expert' regulators. Again, within the existing constitutional and legal framework, this is arguably as it should be. However, where the premises upon which these expert bodies act remain inadequately defined, this raises all kinds of problems in relation to their effectiveness, their vulnerability to capture, and, as a result of the lack of accountability inherent in such a situation, ultimately, their constitutional legitimacy. It is necessary for regulators to be both effective, in terms of the objectives they are established to pursue, and accountable within the democratic schema, and the problems identified in this respect seem to transcend the constitutional differences between the UK and US.

While it is proper to note that the UK's FSA clearly represents an improvement on what went before, in terms of transparency of operation and distance from governmental pressure, it is far from clear that the change has resulted in any improvement as regards protection of public interest values. Though accountability may have been significantly enhanced, it is clear that the trope from 'citizen' to 'consumer', as in the FSA's interpretation of its role, serves to confirm the vulnerability of public interest concerns, and hence raises serious questions as regards the effectiveness of the Agency's activities.

While the FSA may set great store on the adoption and application of the precautionary principle, in terms of protecting public interest values, the conclusion reached in the previous two chapters was that in reality the principle was something only slightly removed from conventional cost–benefit risk analysis techniques, failing to import into the decision-making process any clear structure of values beyond 'precaution'. In addition, the scope of the precautionary principle must presumably be subject, in the European context, to the application of the principle of proportionality,[9] taking the least restrictive alternative available, which may further limit its impact. Chapter Four illustrated how debate over the precautionary principle plays out in the US, with significant concerns expressed about how it fails to fit with what has been identified as the

---

[7] Baldwin and McCrudden, *Regulation and Public Law*, 71.

[8] Sunstein, C. R., *Designing Democracy: What Constitutions Do* (Oxford: Oxford University Press, 2001), 50.   [9] See below, Ch. 7.

dominant 'progress through markets' narrative. Ultimately, however, the key problem with the precautionary principle in the context of this book's agenda is that it remains, or at least is too easily reduced to, a procedural device. Of course, this should not be under-valued. Versions of it may conveniently serve to promote pauses for thought, and more fully rounded consideration of potential consequences of action, thereby potentially improving the quality of decision-making and, by imposing structure, enhancing the accountability of those who take such decisions. However, the limitation of the principle (besides controversy over stronger and weaker versions) remains that, ultimately, it fails to import any values into the debate, other than precaution itself. Though this, like the enhanced structure, accountability and perhaps transparency it brings should probably be welcomed, it does not, in Fisher's terms speak to 'the nature of what is being held to account'.[10] It does not help to establish alternative values, or an alternative democratic narrative which can compete with currently dominant politico-economic perspectives, which favour justifications for decisions offered in the name of 'science' or markets. In failing to import a normative content, it may be indicative of a more general limitation of procedural safeguards in relation to promoting the public interest.

When an agency has broad statutory discretion, in a context of judicial deference towards expert bodies, it becomes exceedingly difficult to launch a challenge against the legality of its actions or indeed inaction. When within that discretionary realm, heavy reliance is placed on implicit faith in 'science', or economics, or perceived need for a product, or faith in markets, or indeed too much emphasis on 'risk', it is virtually impossible, in the absence of some alternative established value-set, to challenge the legitimacy of agency actions, in the absence of some significant procedural failing. While legitimacy might be thought to be the proper responsibility of the political rather than the legal domain, political systems and institutions dominated by the party of government are not likely to be very responsive to such challenges. This may well be why so much emphasis is placed on the pursuit of judicial review as a 'surrogate political process'.

In relation to both of our key focal points, food supply and the media, it is clear that there is an almost constant reform of regulatory arrangements, to address new technological and market developments. The establishment of the UK's FSA and America's FDA both took place in response to a series of specific occurrences, perceived as threats to the actual safety, or public perceptions of safety, in the food supply. In relation to the media, the Act which established the FCC was a response to the then new technology of radio broadcasting, just as the series of reforms in the statutory framework for the regulation of the British media, in 1990, 1996 and 2003, constituted a response to the rapid technological and market changes in recent years. The essentially reactive nature of such change should again be noted here, but it is also worth reflecting on the

---

[10] Fisher, E., 'Drowning by Numbers: Standard Setting in Regulation and the Pursuit of Accountable Public Administration', *Oxford Journal of Legal Studies*, (2000), 109, at 129.

extent to which these reforms have assisted or hindered in respect of establishing a clear understanding of the rationales for regulation. There can be no doubt that, after decades of reform and debate on both sides of the Atlantic, we are no nearer a normatively meaningful construct of the public interest which is embedded in the regulatory process.

One likely conclusion to be drawn from such reflections must be that, like the outcomes of judicial scrutiny, the reforms of the statutory basis for regulatory activity can be considered missed opportunities to reappraise, clarify and reassert the objectives of public interest regulation. Certainly the brief established for the Food Standards Agency, in terms of its consumer orientation points in that direction, and though Section 3 of the Communications Act 2003 does explicitly incorporate a concept of citizenship, all the signs are that this is vulnerable to being smothered by the same Section's other general duty for Ofcom, 'to further the interests of consumers in relevant markets, where appropriate by promoting competition',[11] and the Section 6 emphasis on minimizing regulatory impact.

Based upon an examination of the UK's Communications Act 2003 and the Food Standards Act 1999, and the US Communications Act 1934, the conclusion must be that primary legislation is unlikely to establish a framework which supports public interest values, at least unless it specifies explicitly a hierarchy of values. For whatever reasons, legislators in both jurisdictions seem unwilling to do so. While the measures which result could be viewed as defective translations of democratic, constitutional norms into legal form, an alternative perspective would emphasize the significant impact that such reforms have had on the regulatory rationale: discarding historical concepts of general welfare via social regulation for one of the public good as manifested in the operation of market forces, and representing something of a return to the pre-New Deal situation identified in Chapter Four. Typified by the emphasis in Britain of the competition-oriented Enterprise Act, and the lighter touch to be applied to commercial public service broadcasters under the Communications Act, this parallels the shift in approach advocated by Fowler and Brenner in the US,[12] from the historical 'trusteeship' model, to a situation where the market is seen as the only legitimate force in shaping the media. Such a move does nothing to arrest trends towards commodification of the media, and may be thought to manifest, rather than resist, the process of competitive deregulation. Seen in this light, the legislation which has reformed regulatory agencies and their powers in recent years may be viewed not so much as a defective translation of political norms into legal form, but a very effective and accurate translation of a politico-economic philosophy, based on the primacy of market forces, into regulatory reality. If there is a truly 'defective' element, it lies in the failure to translate and incorporate

---

[11] S.3(1)(b).

[12] Fowler, M. S. and Brenner, D. L., 'A Marketplace Approach to Broadcast Regulation', *Texas Law Review*, 60 (1982), 207.

democratic ideals into regulatory mechanisms, and the absence of constitutional mechanisms which require this.

It is clear that in so far as regulation in such fields in both jurisdictions once revolved around a more or less vague concept of public interest, this has now been marginalized, with centre stage taken by an apparently clearer, and certainly more fashionable, market-oriented approach. Yet lip-service at least is still paid to a public interest ideal. It remains at the heart of US FCC's brief, controversial as that may be, and is used, apparently as a term-of-art in the UK's Enterprise Act and in the Communications Act in relation to merger control. It is also central to the rhetoric of the UK's FSA, even if the reality suggests that it is a much attenuated version, focused heavily on consumer interests, that is applied in practice. Though social regulation rationales and objectives might be expected to arise from such public interest starting points, the reality is that such values are poorly protected, if at all, with market-oriented regulation being focused on the interests of competitors and consumers, rather than citizens. The absence of a specific value-laden content for the 'empty vessel' of 'the public interest' results in the absence of an organizing principle which might serve the vulnerable democratic values. Indeed, the evidence from the last two chapters seems to serve to confirm what I have written previously, in relation to the media specifically, but seeming to be of wider application:

> Much regulatory activity ... is justified by reference to a claim of the public interest. It might be expected that this basic justification would be clarified by reference to objectives that are deemed to further this concept. However, where the concept is itself inadequately defined, it is difficult to assess whether outcomes are meeting the various criteria which may be embodied in 'the public interest'.[13]

In such circumstances, it is hardly surprising if 'the public interest perspective is prone to attack on the basis that regulation often seems to fail to deliver public interest outcomes'.[14]

In the absence of effective regulation in pursuit of such objectives, what is left is the freedom of private parties to pursue their own interests within the context of the market or the political marketplace of 'public choice'.[15] Increasingly, this means the exercise of private property power by large, often international, corporations. It is not necessary to subscribe fully to the somewhat polemical theses of the likes of Monbiot[16] or Hertz,[17] as incisive as they might sometimes be, in order to acknowledge the potential for such corporate activity to impact on citizenship interests within liberal democracy. In the fields of food and media,

---

[13] Feintuck, M., *Media Regulation, Public Interest and the Law* (Edinburgh: Edinburgh University Press, 1999), 57.

[14] Baldwin, R. and Cave, M., *Understanding Regulation: Theory, Strategy and Practice* (Oxford: Oxford University Press, 1999), 20. [15] On public choice, see above, Ch. 1.

[16] Monbiot, G., *Captive State: the Corporate Takeover of Britain* (London: Macmillan, 2000).

[17] Hertz, N., *The Silent Takeover: Global Capitalism and the Death of Democracy* (London: Arrow Books, 2002).

focused on in the previous two chapters, the potential is especially clear. Whether or not Friedman was right to argue that 'The social responsibility of business is to increase its profits',[18] it is clearly true to state that, despite the rhetoric or realities of 'corporate social responsibility', to be considered in Chapter Seven, the *primary purpose* of business corporations is the pursuit of profit; in relation to developments in genetically modified foodstuffs, Applegate must surely be right to state that 'Most GM investment is in technologies that improve profits rather than relieve human suffering.'[19] It is equally clear that, as the American television market is usually held to exemplify, a broadcasting system free of public service obligations will, in pursuit of commercial objectives, fail to deliver many of the qualities traditionally associated with the heavily regulated, Western European public service model. Though the threat to other interests, often associated with citizenship, but perhaps more generally located within the kind of 'ample vision of democracy', to which Stewart refers,[20] is readily apparent, it is necessary to justify strongly and precisely any incursions into the realm of private property power, especially when the *zeitgeist* demands priority for market forces.

Of course, as Krasnow and Goodman[21] observe in relation to the FCC's public interest power, it is equally possible to construe the pursuit by regulators of consumer interests, or of market forces, as being action taken in the public interest, within the broad terms of the power to pursue the 'public interest, convenience and necessity' granted to the Agency by Congress. What this illustrates vividly is the vulnerability of the concept to capture, and subversion to sectional interests at the expense of the collective or general interests it seems meant to serve. Certainly, the failure on numerous occasions, in administrative action, in legislation and in judicial decision-making, to define with any degree of clarity what the term implies in any particular context, has made it all the more vulnerable to capture or subversion. Yet in a sense it is difficult to lay the blame at any particular door. It may well be that it is indeed in the interests of politicians within the legislature or in the executive, or in the interests of powerful lobbies within trade and industry, that the concept remains vague and open to capture. It may be in the perceived interests of regulators that it remains undefined, as a means of maximizing the discretion available to them, though Baldwin and McCrudden do identify difficulties which may arise for agencies, apparent from the study of the FCC in Chapter Four, from 'broad mandates which are difficult

[18] Friedman, M., 'The Social Responsibility of Business is to Increase its Profits', *New York Times Magazine*, 13th September 1970, reproduced in Hoffman, W. M. and Frederick, R. E. (eds.), *Business Ethics: Readings and Cases in Corporate Morality*, 3rd edn. (New York, N.Y.: McGraw-Hill, 1995).

[19] Applegate, J. S., 'Sustainable Development, Agriculture, and the Challenge of Genetically Modified Organisms', *Indiana Journal of Global Legal Studies*, 9 (2001), 207.

[20] Stewart, R. B., 'Regulation in a Liberal State: the Role of Non-Commodity Values', *Yale Law Journal*, 92 (1983), 1537.

[21] Krasnow, E. and Goodman, J., 'The Public Interest Standard: the Search for the Holy Grail', *Federal Communications Law Journal*, 50 (1998), 605.

to cite as convincing defences when they are under attack'.[22] As Krotoszynski observes, it may be that 'The only unserved constituency is the public.'[23] If this is so, it may be that the judiciary, as guardians of the constitution and with the explicit brief to pursue the 'Law Jobs', should be expected to offer assistance to this weak and vulnerable concept. Yet the lawyers seem no more able or willing to assist in finding and protecting meaning within the concept than any other party.

Though noted in Chapter Two was Dworkin's observation that '[A]n accurate summary of the considerations lawyers must take into account, in deciding a particular issue of legal rights and duties, would include propositions having the form and force of principles',[24] it seems that the concept of public interest which underlies much social regulation cannot, or will not, be recognized as one such. Its absence of clear definition, even when used in statutes such as the US Communications Act 1934, render it effectively outside the scope of usual practices of statutory interpretation. In the US context the absence of any direct reference to the public interest in the Constitution or Bill of Rights, suggests that only lawyers of a significantly non-interpretivist leaning are likely to pursue the value. In Britain, the absence of clear constitutional terms and executive dominance of the 'supreme' legislature inevitably make such matters more complex, and in general might be thought to have contributed historically to a judicial reluctance to intervene in relation to 'expert' administrators, in the absence of clearly defined constitutional principles on which to draw.

In both jurisdictions it appears that the judiciary have been prepared to determine individual cases, to construe aspects of particular statutes, and even in the US to consider, in light of the Constitution, the extent of the powers granted by Congress in the name of the public interest, without significantly adding to our understanding of what the concept actually means. It appears that, notwithstanding the common law roots of certain versions of the concept, embodied in the US case law drawing on previous British cases,[25] which led to the establishment of the 'essential facilities' doctrine, modern judges cannot recognize anything approaching a legal principle which can be called 'the public interest'.

In some ways recourse to the overarching terms of the US Constitution seems to offer the potential for greater clarity of principle than is found in the UK cases. That said, it is clear that the Constitution does not provide ready-made answers. Indeed, as was illustrated in Chapter Four, complex disputes over the application of the non-delegation doctrine may ultimately appear to muddy the waters, and distract from the substantive questions at hand. The perennial risk becomes that of the tendency to determine such matters based on decisions as regards technical

---

[22] Baldwin and McCrudden, *Regulation and Public Law*, 34.
[23] Krotoszynski, R. J., 'The Inevitable Wasteland: Why the Public Trustee Model of Broadcast Regulation Must Fail', *Michigan Law Review*, 95 (1997), 2101.
[24] Dworkin, R., *Taking Rights Seriously* (London: Duckworth, 1977), 71.
[25] See above, Ch. 1.

legal matters, rather than the substantive issues. Again, the apparent need for some form of improved linkage between democratic questions of legitimacy, and the technical legal issues, appears to be indicated.

As things stand, the legitimacy of judicial intervention into agency action is always under question as soon as it ventures any way towards the substance of the agency decision. Considering judicial delegation doctrines in the UK, US and France, Shapiro notes that 'The more obvious it becomes that the judicial reviewer is second-guessing the administrative agency, and the more obvious it is that the guesses concern matters about which the agency knows far more than the judicial reviewer, the more the favourable legitimacy balance of the court is depleted.'[26] There may be proper constitutional limits on the extent to which the judiciary can be expected to create such links via case law, given the apparent proximity of such matters to the merits of individual cases. The line between merits and procedure can be a fine one, as will be seen in Chapter Seven when tests of 'proportionality' are considered. However, in the US courts, the creation of the 'Hard Look' doctrine appears to provide a more intense standard of review than traditionally found in either US or UK courts, while seeming to remain focused on procedure rather than merits.[27] First canvassed in the UK by Harden and Lewis in the mid-1980s, the essence of the test was set out in *Greater Boston Television Co. v. FCC*:

The function of the court is to ensure that the agency has given reasoned consideration to all material facts and issues. This calls for insistence that the agency articulate with reasonable clarity its reasons for decision, and identify the significance of the crucial facts, a course that tends to assure that the agency's policies effectuate general standards, applied without unreasonable discrimination.[28]

Craig views this as 'a *via media* between judicial deference to agency discretion and more intensive judicial review',[29] and by focusing on requiring that agencies demonstrate the rigour of their decision-making process, that they have taken a 'hard look' at all relevant matters and options, the courts can scrutinize the quality of decision-making without appearing to encroach, improperly perhaps, on the merits of the decision as such. Where the range of relevant factors and principles is reasonably clearly established, it may offer some significant leverage to the judiciary in ensuring that agencies have acted according to them, and may contribute significantly to achieving democratic expectations of accountability. However, a problem seems to remain where values or principles are not specified in the grant of authority to the agency, or established in advance by the agency itself. In addition, where the agency's authority is clearly expressed,

[26] Shapiro, M., 'Judicial Delegation Doctrines: the US, Britain and France', *West European Politics*, 25/1 (2002) 173, at 179.

[27] See Harden and Lewis, *The Noble Lie*, 272–5; Craig, P. P., *Administrative Law* (5th edn.) (London: Sweet and Maxwell, 2003), 635–8; Craig, P. P., *Public Law and Democracy in the United Kingdom and the United States of America*, (Oxford: Oxford University Press, 1990), 182–7.

[28] 403 US 923 (1971), 851.   [29] Craig, *Public Law and Democracy*, 182.

but in terms which deny or de-prioritize democratic values, it does not offer the judiciary a means of striking down decisions by reference to democratic fundamentals. Thus, if citizenship values are not clearly expressed as being a factor which ought to be taken into account, the agency will be within its powers not to take them into account; indeed, it may be vulnerable to challenge in such circumstances if it *did* take them into account. Where an agency is granted the power to determine between competing factors 'in whatever manner it thinks fit', as in the UK's Communications Act 2003,[30] and no clear hierarchy of values is established, the Hard Look doctrine might seem to offer relatively little. Again, the need seems to be indicated for some form of overarching, judicially enforceable, interpretative principle, requiring decision-makers to demonstrate that they have given due weight to fundamental democratic values even where legislation does not specifically require it.

Shapiro notes how, in seeking to avoid the restraint imposed on the judiciary by legislative supremacy, reviewing courts increasingly rely on 'law "higher" than that of the delegating statute, be it constitution, common law, general principles of law, reasonableness, justice, fairness, or international agreements',[31] and in particular concepts of human rights. In concluding his comparative study, Shapiro comments that 'the administrative review courts of all three countries [UK, US and France] seem as anxious, or more anxious, to ask whether delegated legislation meets various judicial criteria of goodness, fairness, justice, reasonableness and rights protection as they are to ask whether delegated legislation is in accord with the will of the primary law making delegator or principal'.[32] If this is right, it appears that judges are already applying a range of interpretative principles, but perhaps in such an unstructured manner as to risk inconsistency and unpredictability, and indeed threaten the legitimacy of their activities. In the regulatory contexts explored in this book, it would seem far preferable for judges to act in accordance with a clearly enunciated interpretative principle which granted express authority for them to review decisions in accordance with established public interest values.

In the absence of such a mechanism, attempts to interpret measures such as the grant of powers to the FCC under the Communications Act tend to adopt analogies or metaphors such as a 'corporate charter'[33] to describe the terms of reference of regulators, or 'trusteeship'[34] to characterize the position of broadcasters in a regulated marketplace. Though arguments from analogy and metaphor are attractive, and common enough in legal discourse, they also have a significant potential to mislead. The corporate charter analogy is exceedingly difficult to apply in relation to the specific circumstances of the FCC. Though

---

[30] Communications Act 2003, S.6, discussed above, Ch. 3.
[31] Shapiro, 'Judicial Delegation Doctrines', 195.   [32] Ibid., 198.
[33] Noah, L., 'Interpreting Agency Enabling Acts: Misplaced Metaphors in Administrative Law', *William and Mary Law Review*, 41 (2000), 1463.
[34] See Krasnow and Goodman, 'The Public Interest Standard'; Krotoszynski, 'The Inevitable Wasteland'; Fowler and Brenner, 'A Marketplace Approach'.

its application would certainly remove any risk of excessively broad grants of discretion, surely no meaningful charter, which Noah implies grants specified and limited powers, could permit sufficiently wide discretion to allow an agency such as the FCC to engage effectively in its activities? In reality, it amounts to something close to an argument for clause-bound regulation by rule, rather than discretion. As for 'trusteeship', problems arise in relation to the expectation of the powers of a trustee, under which, though they may exercise discretion, they should act exclusively in the interests of the 'beneficiaries'. Clearly, even within a regulated, public service-oriented broadcasting sector, commercial broadcasters must have a major and legitimate concern for their profitability, in addition to the interests of the 'beneficiaries', the public. This latter factor, the unlimited number of unspecified or global category of beneficiaries, would also pose difficulties for trusts lawyers. While a quest for accurate, technical legal language in relation to public interest values may at one level be criticized in terms of appearing to be seeking narrow, technical answers to broad socio-political questions, it is apparent that the absence of adequate legal principles, terminology, or categorization, seems to render the constitutional authorities, the judiciary, impotent in protecting such democratic values.

Discussed earlier were problems in terms of the limitations of procedural measures in protecting substantive interests. Baldwin and McCrudden make clear the limits of due process requirements, which lie at the heart of administrative law applicable to regulatory agencies. Though procedural requirements relating to, for example, participation, consultation and openness are very significant, in terms of contributing to ensuring the accountability of agencies, they do not provide 'a complete basis on which to build legitimacy',[35] and will not necessarily ensure that effective outcomes occur, in terms of outcomes being consistent with underlying regulatory rationales. Yet it is clear that in many ways procedural law is the trade-craft of administrative lawyers, and provides the context in which the judiciary may be able to get some purchase on questions arising out of regulation. This is especially so in Britain, where judges have not historically been able to act with reference to the relatively clear statements of value and intent found in a single constitutional document such as the US Constitution.

Such a difference is clearly of some potential significance, given the central role of administrative law in devising and applying principles against which administrative bodies can be rendered accountable in a manner consistent with democratic expectations. However, the *differences* in constitutional form are perhaps not so significant, in relation to Anglo-American comparisons in our present context, as *similarities* of fundamental purpose for the two administrative law regimes, and of the problems encountered in terms of protection of public interest values. Though British administrative law may be thought to lack the central focal point found in the US system in the form of the APA, it nonetheless

---

[35] Baldwin and McCrudden, *Regulation and Public Law*, 45.

addresses the same central theme: namely the objective of maximizing the benefits of discretion while minimizing the potential risks associated with it. As already indicated, this results in administrative law placing a heavy emphasis on procedural measures, rather than the establishment of substantive norms, and the possible limitations of such a procedural approach have just been noted.

If we return to the differing US and European approaches to the precautionary principle noted in previous chapters, we find that both regulators and lawyers will differ dramatically in their attitude towards the utilization of this particular approach to risk. Nonetheless, it is clear that regulators on both sides of the Atlantic must address risk, and, in accordance with democratic expectations, must be held accountable via political and legal mechanisms, for the actions they take. As was noted in Chapter Four, in the context of risk regulation, Wiener identifies 'a process of "hybridization" in which both systems borrow legal concepts from each other in a complex and continuous mutual evolution'.[36] Disabusing us of the simple vision often portrayed of a risk-averse EU and a progress-oriented US, Wiener notes how, when the question is framed differently, in reality, both jurisdictions are, from a broader perspective, at 'the highly precautionary end of the global scale'.[37] He notes also how, in terms of risk assessment, the jurisprudence of the ECJ revealed in the decision on the French refusal to end the ban on the import of British beef, 'that Member State governments may not invoke precaution to regulate risks that the Commission has deemed insignificant', is 'quite reminiscent of *Benzene*'.[38] He observes that the stereotypically described differences in approach to risk is in fact better portrayed as precaution against different risks,[39] and also how 'both are federations of subsidiary jurisdictions, with considerable variety in regulatory approaches across member states'.[40] He goes on to suggest the likelihood of greater structural similarity or convergence, at least as regards environmental regulation, as while the US policy had traditionally been firmly located at the federal level, and the competence of the EU had taken some time to be established, now, 'the EU [is centralizing] toward a stronger role for the Commission in Brussels and ... [the US is decentralizing] toward a greater role for the states',[41] with the likely result that the two systems will at some point share broadly similar matrices of power.

In addition to such claims as to similarities, Wiener also challenges the conventional view as to differences in the approach to enforcement of regulation. As he notes, the traditional differences in procedure can be characterized as 'adversarial legalism' in the US, as opposed to the European approach which 'invites more negotiation of policy development'.[42] Again, he suggests that in the context of

---

[36] Wiener, J. B., 'Whose Precaution After All? A Comment on the Comparison and Evolution of Risk Regulatory Systems', *Duke Journal of Comparative and International Law*, 13 (2003) 207, at 209. [37] Ibid., at 216.
[38] Ibid., 216, referring to *Industrial Union Department v. American Petroleum Institute*, 448 US 607 (1980). [39] Ibid., 229.
[40] Ibid., 230. [41] Ibid., 248. [42] Ibid., 246.

environmental regulation, moves in opposite directions, with Europe becoming more formal and legalistic, and the US becoming less adversarial, there is some likelihood of convergence in some middle ground.

However, Wiener's thesis is not one of simple convergence, but 'hybridiz-ation: the exchange of legal concepts across systems',[43] which result in new variations when transplanted into their new context. He cites examples of, amongst others, how Europe has 'borrowed' from the US approaches on emissions trading, product liability law, the proposed environmental liabil-ity directive, environmental impact assessments, and an increasingly federal approach to environmental regulation, while traded in the opposite direction have been the Dutch practice of environmental covenants and related voluntary negotiated agreements, and the concept of precaution drawn from the Ger-man *Vorsorgeprinzip*. He identifies hybridization as deriving from a range of factors, including the increasingly integrated world economy, and global corpor-ations, creating pressure for harmonization, the development of trans-national networks of NGOs and policy specialists, and, based presumably on modern communications techniques, greater interchange between government officials and academics.

Wiener's thesis is challenging and important. It does not, however, have much to say as regards how such hybridized concepts bed down, a potential problem given the differences in constitutional context and administrative law practice identified earlier.[44] It might be expected that problems could arise in relation to the ability of local administrative law systems to operate effectively in relation to policies and practices resulting from cross-fertilization or hybridization, which introduce 'alien' concepts into the domestic legal and administrative systems. Clearly, there are both similarities in terms of common law tradition, and differ-ences in constitutional context as between the UK and US which must be taken into account. However, the potential for problems might be expected to be even more significant in relation to legal 'transplants' between different legal families, such as between the traditions of common law and civil law:[45] a potentially significant issue in the context of the development of administrative law within the EU.

This theme is picked up and developed by della Cananea who, following in the footsteps of MacCormick,[46] succinctly summarizes a shift from 'adminis-trative law as a "province" of the state',[47] to a new situation where 'procedural administrative law cannot be understood on the basis of the traditional paradigm

---

[43] Wiener, J. B., 'Whose Precaution After All? A Comment on the Comparison and Evolution of Risk Regulatory Systems', *Duke Journal of Comparative and International Law*, 13 (2003) 207, 258.

[44] See discussion of public service law, below, Ch. 7.

[45] See Zweigert, K. and Kötz, H., *An Introduction to Comparative Law*, 3rd edn. (Oxford: Clarendon, 1998).

[46] MacCormick, N., 'Beyond the Sovereign State', *Modern Law Review*, 56 (1993), 1.

[47] della Cananea, G., 'Beyond the State: the Europeanization and Globalization of Procedural Administrative Law', *European Public Law*, 9/4 (2003), 563, at 565.

founded on the state', and, 'instead of identifying administrative law with the State ... we find a more complex world in which the state is just one of several public organisations existing alongside legal orders operating outside its borders'.[48] He points towards not only the EU, but also the Council of Europe, the organs of the European Convention on Human Rights,[49] and indeed, reflecting the increasingly globalized nature of capital, the WTO, all as being instrumental in this paradigm shift.

Although the context in which administrative law is understood must therefore be changed, as della Cananea observes, its functions should remain essentially the same: it must continue to serve as, in the classic formulation which he quotes from Stewart, a 'surrogate political process'.[50] In other words, in devising and applying procedural principles, the administrative law system must ensure that agencies, when exercising their powers, act in accordance with fundamental constitutional and democratic expectations even if the political system fails to so ensure.

So, the shift away from a nation-state based conception of administrative law does not subvert the fundamental purpose of the legal system in relation to the maintenance of the separation of powers and democratic checks and balances. Nor does it, in della Cananea's striking phrase, subvert what he finds to be one of administrative law's 'underlying and cultural premises', the theory of "'the public interest" as inherently different from other interests, of either collective or individual character'.[51]

Clearly therefore, administrative law, whether viewed within the traditional sense of the law of the nation-state or within the context of della Cananea's new paradigm, has a potential role to play, seemingly beyond procedural matters, in relation to furthering a set of values often referred to as 'the public interest'. Nehl notes how, in the specific context of the administration of the supra-national EU, 'it does not seem too daring to speak of an ongoing process of "constitutionalisation" with respect to procedural requirements'.[52] However, whether in its distinctive national form, at the supra-national level, or in some hybridized version, administrative law has limitations in this respect. Though potentially very strong in terms of affording procedural protection, the statement or establishment of core democratic values is not generally within its compass. Thus, in so far as administrative law may, via its procedural focus, support those liberal–democratic values of accountability embedded in the constitution, it is unlikely to contribute significantly to the normative development of a concept of public interest, or the protection of the values which might be included within the term. If this is so in the US, despite concrete constitutional terms on which to

---

[48] Ibid., 577.

[49] See generally, Beatson, J. and Tridimas, T. (eds.), *New Directions in European Public Law* (Oxford: Hart, 1998).

[50] Stewart, R. B., 'The Reformation of American Administrative Law', *Harvard Law Review*, 88 (1975), 1670.   [51] della Cananea 'Beyond the State', 576.

[52] Nehl, H. P., *Principles of Administrative Procedure in EC Law* (Oxford: Hart, 1999), 1.

rely, there seems very little chance that this will occur in the UK in the absence of such defined constitutional principles and with the development of administrative law principles having been perhaps retarded historically by the Diceyan inheritance,[53] unless, perhaps, the influence of European jurisprudence serves to push the UK legal system in this direction.

Despite significant differences in the constitutional and administrative law contexts in which regulation takes place in the UK and US, the limitations of administrative law in this respect, and more generally the problems in developing, defining and upholding a concept of the public interest, are common to both. Though fluent in statute, constitution and common law, judges seem unable to understand or speak the language of the public interest. It does not appear to fall into any category which they recognize as being within their competence.[54] The consequent risk is that where politicians, either because the issues appear difficult or intractable, or by virtue of a political choice in favour of market mechanisms, do not frame legislation in such a way as to require regulators to prioritize and protect basic democratic expectations, such as equality of citizenship, the administrative law system will not be able to fulfil its potential as a 'surrogate political system', leaving the values extremely vulnerable. While the administrative law system may, at its best, form a potent mechanism for ensuring that democratic expectations of accountability are met, it will rarely be focused on the effectiveness of regulators in relation to substantive values. In Harlow and Rawlings's well-known terms, its 'Red Light' function of stopping excesses of power or jurisdiction can be said to be much more developed than its 'Green Light' function of encouraging and facilitating good administration.[55]

While those seeking to defend public interest values may find themselves forced to support a broad, purposive approach to judicial interpretation of statutory and constitutional terms, they must do so in the knowledge that this approach, in the absence of some clarity in the normative values to be upheld, risks tipping the constitutional balance, embodied in the separation of powers, too far in the judicial direction. Simply encouraging the judiciary to be more active in pursuit of public interest values does not help, if there is no clear conception of what those values are. One constitutional problem, the lack of protection for fundamental values, is replaced by another, if excessive power, unstructured by clear constitutional principle, rests with the relatively unaccountable judiciary.

If nothing else is clear from this and the preceding chapters, it is that the precise normative content of 'the public interest' is far from a truth which could be held self-evident. Indeed, much of the evidence presented in this and the previous two chapters might seem to suggest a bleak prospect for the development of a

---

[53] See Tomkins, A., *Public Law* (Oxford: Clarendon, 2003), 23; or Craig, P. P., *Administrative Law* (5th edn.) (London: Sweet and Maxwell, 2003), 4.

[54] For a succinct study on the adaptation of the concepts and language of administrative law to different social circumstances, see Loughlin, M., *Public Law and Political Theory* (Oxford: Clarendon, 1992), 184–90.

[55] Harlow, C. and Rawlings, R., *Law and Administration*, 2nd edn. (London: Butterworths, 1997).

meaningful concept of public interest in regulation. At best, it might be viewed as a repeatedly missed opportunity, and in terms of the alternative agendas set out in Chapter One, abandoning the concept may seem to make more sense than persistent attempts to revive or reinvigorate it.

Yet within any vision of democracy which extends beyond the mere aggregation of individual interests, if, in Sagoff's terms, 'the public realm is not empty of values',[56] it seems that there must be norms which transcend those currently pursued by regulators and recognized by judges. They are still commonly referred to as 'public interest values', even if they are not currently effectively defined or enforced. The twin challenges to be taken up in the concluding Part of this book, are to seek to establish what the content of such values might be, and how they might be given a legally recognizable form.

---

[56] Quoted in Steele, J., 'Participation and Deliberation in Environmental Law: Exploring a Problem-Solving Approach', *Oxford Journal of Legal Studies*, 2001, 415, at 424.

PART III
SYNTHESIS AND CONCLUSIONS

6

A Coherent Concept of the Public Interest in Regulation

This chapter will review the themes and issues presented in Parts One and Two and seek to establish an argument for the advisability, or even the necessity, of the adoption of a value-laden concept of public interest, and to establish the content and purpose of such a construct in the context of regulation. This is, of course, no easy task, given that Part One of this book identified problems relating to the theoretical basis for the public interest in regulation, and Part Two went on to illustrate some of the additional problems associated with the use of the concept in its practical context. The two sets of difficulties are, inevitably, intimately connected, and it is necessary to start here by highlighting the key findings as to problems which must be addressed if a concept of the public interest is to be developed which might inform meaningfully, and assist in, the regulatory endeavour.

WHY PUBLIC INTEREST REGULATION FAILS

Readers will recall the focus of this book, established in Chapter One, derived from Selznick's definition[1] of regulation: 'the use of the concept of the public interest as a justification for regulatory intervention into private activity, limiting the exercise of private power, in pursuit of objectives valued by the community'. It is, of course, now necessary to observe and acknowledge at the outset of this chapter that 'failure' or 'success' in terms of 'regulation in the public interest' is extremely difficult to measure with precision. This is a direct consequence of the lack of any unitary or precise vision as regards the content or extent of the values implied by the term 'public interest' or even perhaps 'objectives valued by the community'. This problem will be returned to in later sections of this chapter, but for present purposes it will be assumed, as has been suggested earlier, that there are a range of values associated with liberal democracy, especially relating to citizenship expectations and collective interests, which are commonly associated with the concept of 'public interest' and which are left vulnerable to

---

[1] Selznick's original version is 'Sustained and focused control exercised by a public agency over activities that are valued by a community'; Selznick, P., 'Focusing Organizational Research on Regulation', in Noll, R. (ed.), *Regulatory Policy and the Social Sciences* (Berkeley, CA.: University of California Press, 1985).

social and economic forces if not adequately protected. In the absence of such valued objectives, regulation would be without justification.

Why then, are such values not well served by existing regulation pursued in the name of 'the pubic interest'? The case study material presented in Chapters Three to Five indicates a number of recurrent problems.

Certainly, the problem of diverse claims and constituencies may seem to provide a significant obstacle to effective regulation. The existence of competing individuals and groups, often with overlapping and multiple interests, may make it difficult for regulators to identify clearly or consistently the interests and values they are aiming to serve. Thus, for example, wider, legitimate, but sometimes nebulous, public interests such as those relating to citizens, may too easily be lost when regulators focus more narrowly on the rather clearer and better-defined claims of consumers or producers. At a broader level still, in an era in which certain of the value-sets underpinning liberal democracy, namely market economics and individualism, predominate over all others, in the absence of any popular ideological alternative emphasis, the other 'non-commodity values'[2] and collective values which underlie the polity may become distinctly marginal to regulatory activity. Even where citizenship interests are recognized, both the dominant ideology, and, in Britain at least, the legal system, is likely to recognize primarily the atomistic, individual aspects of citizenship as opposed to any collective aspects.

There is also a suggestion that the desire to demonstrate short-term results may lead to regulators focusing on immediate, measurable outcomes, to the exclusion of longer-term agendas. In addition, in the quest to justify regulatory intervention, there is an observable tendency to rely, perhaps excessively, on apparently objective, technical data, deriving from science, or economics, or hard law, by way of justification for decisions. Though a fundamental democratic expectation is that of legitimacy via rational justification, the risks of excessive reliance on a single set of such factors is illustrated vividly in the account provided by Campbell and Lee[3] of the role of 'blackboard economics' during the foot and mouth disease (FMD) epidemic in the UK. Concepts such as 'the precautionary principle',[4] though apparently to be welcomed as offering informing principles for decision-making, may properly be viewed as little more than procedural revisions of previous modes of cost–benefit analysis, and may operate in the absence of a system of informing, substantive values.

Further obstacles to effective public interest regulation may arise as a result of continuing emphasis on the nation-state as the primary focus of regulatory activity and source of regulatory authority. The growth of global capitalism,

---

[2] Stewart, R. B., 'Regulation in a Liberal State: the Role of Non-Commodity Values', *Yale Law Journal*, 92 (1983), 1537.

[3] Campbell, D. and Lee, R., 'Carnage by Computer: The Blackboard Economics of the 2001 Foot and Mouth Epidemic', *Social and Legal Studies*, 12/4 (2003), 426.

[4] See discussion in Chs. 3, 4, and 7.

to which we will return shortly, may render regulation at this level difficult or impossible. However, national politics which persist in defending the sovereignty of nation-states, can serve to further trends towards competitive deregulation, and, through an emphasis on subsidiarity, can potentially undermine the effectiveness of trans-national bodies such as the EU, which may actually be better placed to address such issues.[5]

Related to the first set of problems identified above, is a fundamental issue, identified throughout the case studies, of a lack of structuring of regulatory discretion by reference to any clear system of principle. The failure of primary legislation to impose upon regulators a clear hierarchy of values,[6] to guide the exercise of the wide discretion granted to them, is compounded both by the failure of regulators themselves to provide such internal structuring and the failure of the legal system to require such structuring and rationalizing of decision-making. Though more obvious in the UK,[7] the phenomenon of judicial deference to 'expert' regulatory agencies where broad discretion has been granted is also apparent in the US in the post-*Chevron* era.[8] While a basic level of procedural safeguards is maintained, and even improvements achieved in relation to matters such as transparency and political independence in the operation of the UK's FSA, this is not the same as the establishment of substantive, normative provisions which refer directly to the objectives of regulation. In essence, the systemic problem here is the failure to identify and articulate with reasonable clarity the rationales and values which underlie public interest regulation, which has the inevitable consequence of leaving any such values vulnerable. Such a task seems to lie beyond the limits of proceduralism. It relates to Sunstein's suggestion that, though 'people can often agree on constitutional *practices*, and even on constitutional *rights*, ... they cannot agree on constitutional *theories*', with the result that 'constitutional orders try to solve problems ... through reaching *incompletely theorized agreements*'.[9]

Lack of clarity over such values often leads to uncomfortable and ineffective adoption and adaptation of metaphors and analogies, such as 'trusteeship' or 'corporate charters',[10] to describe the activities of regulators and those regulated, in the absence of legal terminology which captures effectively, or relates directly to, the particular relationships and issues involved.[11] Without bespoke legal concepts relating to such relationships, judges are left to determine issues via extrapolation and interpretation, and though this is very much the tradecraft of the judiciary, this leads into difficult debate, in the context of the US especially,

---

[5] See discussion of EFSA, above Ch. 3.

[6] See discussion of pre-legislative scrutiny of Communications Bill 2002, above, Ch. 3.

[7] See discussion of ITC decisions, Ch. 3.

[8] *Chevron, USA Inc. v. Natural Resources Defense Council Inc.*, 467 US 837 (1984). See above, Ch. 4.

[9] Sunstein, C. R., *Designing Democracy: What Constitutions Do* (Oxford: Oxford University Press, 2001), 50, original emphasis.   [10] See above, Ch. 4, and below, Ch. 7.

[11] See generally Sunstein, *Designing Democracy*, Ch. 2.

as regards the constitutional propriety of interpretivist and non-interpretivist approaches,[12] compounding the uncertainty as regards the protection of such values.

In essence, the range of problems which seem to underlie the failure of regulation to protect public interest values, identified in the case studies in Part Two, can be summarized briefly in terms of the following four interconnected issues which form the basis for much of the discussion in the rest of this chapter:

- the failure to identify with any degree of precision the range of collective values (and hence policy objectives) associated with the concept, which are the subject of regulatory intervention;
- the failure to orientate and structure effectively, by reference to a system of substantive principle or values, the broad grants of discretion to regulators made in the name of 'the public interest', leaving the process open to interest group capture, and difficult to hold to account;
- the tendency to adopt, in practice, partial versions of the concept which reflect one sub-set of values (such as the economic), but exclude other legitimate democratic considerations (such as equality of citizenship); or alternatively to use over-extended versions of the concept which lack meaning, credibility, and legitimacy; and,
- the failure of the legal system to develop a conceptual framework which, within the local constitutional context, recognizes and offers effective and democratically legitimate protection for public interest values.

The lack of conceptual clarity as regards the public interest is especially problematic where the social values it is supposed to refer to and serve, such as citizenship or collective claims in the UK, remain poorly specified. The pursuit of somewhat vague social aspirations via an ill-defined and weakly enforced concept of public interest may certainly seem like a quest doomed to failure. However, if there are any social values worthy of protection, and if regulation is to be used in pursuit of them, it remains possible that, in the absence of any obvious alternative construct or device which encompasses and serves these goals, it is worth pursuing further the possibility of progress via a developed and defined concept of the public interest. Inevitably, it must be accepted that the use of such a concept must in itself, after Davis's discussion of discretion,[13] be 'confined' to those realms where it is appropriate (where more specific concepts are not available[14]) and 'structured' via a transparent framework of principle which, in fulfilment of democratic expectations, aids accountability in its exercise.

---

[12] See Ely, J. H., *Democracy and Distrust: a Theory of Judicial Review* (Cambridge, Mass.: Harvard University Press, 1980).

[13] Davis, K. C., *Discretionary Justice: a Preliminary Inquiry* (Urbana, IL.: University of Illinois Press, 1971).

[14] See Held, V., *The Public Interest and Individual Interests* (New York, N.Y.: Basic Books, 1970), 163, discussed above, Ch. 1.

The remainder of this chapter will seek to address the kind of issues just identified, and to consider whether the concept's potential can be fulfilled in the context of regulation. Possible legal forms in which public interest values may be applied beyond this field will be addressed briefly in Chapter Seven, before the arguments are summarized and conclusions reached in Chapter Eight.

PUBLIC INTEREST VALUES AND THE CHALLENGES TO THEM

In many ways, the challenges posed to public interest values should be apparent from the preceding chapters. However, it is helpful to reconsider them directly at this stage, if only briefly, by way of clarifying the nature of the values being discussed.

Chapter Two identified three threads interwoven to form the fabric of liberal democracy: capital and the market, personal freedom and individualism, and collective values. From this it is clear that values beyond the economics of market exchange and private profit form an integral part of the foundations of our polity. The key tension, as identified in Chapter Three, was the relationship between commercial freedom and other democratic values.

As was discussed in Chapter One, it is often argued that market economics serve the public interest, via wealth maximization. However, it was also observed there that the implication of this is that the assignment and recognition of property rights which permit such activity is in effect legitimated, at least in part, by the associated benefits for society which are said to derive from their exercise. Thus, as was seen in Chapter Four, Sunstein seeks to legitimate regulation of private property power by arguing that 'self-interest is an insufficient basis for political advantage; it must be translated into some broader conception of the public interest'.[15] From this perspective, as Stewart argues, there is a strong case for regulation and administrative law playing an important role in protecting and promoting not only entitlements and production, but also what he refers to as 'non-commodity values',[16] in which he includes 'Aspiration, Diversity, Mutuality and Civic Virtue'.[17]

Though the values he expresses may stand in need of further definition, Stewart's vision of a 'more ample liberalism' has strong claims to represent more accurately the totality of the liberal–democratic settlement than do perspectives which give what might be thought of as undue or excessive prominence to a purely economic vision. Yet it is abundantly clear that such broader democratic values are increasingly under challenge.

The role of the state, legitimated by its claims to represent the democratic settlement, is being threatened by the forces of private capital: 'Corporations,

---

[15] Sunstein, C. R., *After the Rights Revolution: Reconceiving the Regulatory State*, (Cambridge, Mass.: Harvard University Press, 1990), 12.   [16] Stewart, 'Regulation in a Liberal State', 1537.
[17] Ibid., 1568.

the contraptions we invented to serve us, are overthrowing us. They are seizing powers previously invested in government, and using them to distort public life to their own ends.'[18] While the blame for allowing this to happen may be placed at the door of individual governments, it is also clear that forces beyond the nation-state are at play. The power of global capital, manifested in multinational corporations, is a fundamental challenge to the ability of governments to carry out the functions traditionally expected of them: 'The role of nation states has become to a large extent simply that of providing the public goods and infrastructure that business needs at the lowest costs, and protecting the world free trade system.'[19] Though the work of the likes of Monbiot and Hertz, from which the quotations above are drawn, may be considered by some to be overly polemical, the trends and themes they identify and consider so vividly cannot be ignored. The major thrust of their argument is that what Hertz refers to as 'the "democratic" elements of liberal democracy' are being marginalized as governments of 'Western' states, not just the US, have become increasingly preoccupied only with 'the "liberal" element, or even more narrowly, just the economic element of liberalism'.[20] Potentially unlimited power would seem to be equally problematic in democratic terms, whether exercised by government or private corporations.

These themes are developed further by Leys, who identifies in the market-driven politics of recent British governments, from the Thatcher administration onwards, policies which have resulted in a process of 'de-democratisation of the state'[21] and heavy social costs. In exploring the implications of such trends for 'democracy and the collective values on which it depends', Leys notes how governments, in order to survive in office while operating in the context of the global economy, 'must increasingly "manage" national politics in such a way as to adapt *them* to the pressures of transnational market forces'.[22] The resulting trend towards competitive deregulation was noted in Chapter Three. Leys observes that,

Contrary to the impression given by neoliberal ideology and neoclassical economics textbooks, markets are not impersonal or impartial but highly political, as well as inherently unstable. In the search for survival, firms constantly explore ways to break out of the boundaries set by state regulation, including the boundaries that close non-market spheres to commodification and profit-making. This is a crucially important issue since it threatens the destruction of non-market spheres of life on which social solidarity and active democracy have always depended.[23]

In concrete terms, Leys identifies trends of increasing differentials in income between richer and poorer, resulting in part from the wages of unskilled and

---

[18] Monbiot, G., *Captive State: the Corporate Takeover of Britain* (London: Macmillan, 2000), 4.

[19] Hertz, N., *The Silent Takeover: Global Capitalism and the Death of Democracy* (London: Arrow Books, 2002), 9. [20] Ibid., at 102.

[21] Leys, C., *Market-Driven Politics: Neoliberal Democracy and the Public Interest* (London: Verso, 2001), 71. [22] Ibid., 1, original emphasis.

[23] Ibid., 3.

semi-skilled workers being squeezed down within a global market, an increase in child poverty, an increase in crime rate and the prison population, and an increasing official exploitation or condonement of racism. He also identifies clearly a process of commodification in the media, discussed previously in Chapters Three and Four, whereby public service values are replaced by market values.[24] Leys concludes that governments have seen some of these social costs, resulting in inequalities both in economic and citizenship terms, amounting to very real forms of social exclusion, as inevitable consequences of a political agenda pursuing macroeconomic policies related to 'the tendency towards a "market society"'.[25] He observes that 'The facts suggest that market-driven politics can lead to a remarkably rapid erosion of democratically determined collective values and institutions.'[26]

While Sunstein is surely right to argue that 'free markets are a tool, to be used when they promote human purposes, and to be abandoned when they fail to do so',[27] the ideological dominance of market-driven politics is such that the preservation of the wider liberal–democratic value-set stands desperately in need of protection. Thus, although we may agree that 'Achievement of social justice is a higher value than the protection of free markets',[28] finding devices through which to pursue such an agenda effectively, in the face of the hegemony of market values, is no easy task. In this connection, Sunstein identifies one possible approach premised on the claim that 'constitutions should be "countercultural", in the sense that they should protect against those aspects of a country's culture and traditions that are most likely to produce harm'.[29] This offers an intuitively attractive proposition, and one that relates closely to the possible function of a concept of public interest, suggested previously in Chapter Two, as a counterbalance to the excessive dominance of any one sub-set of values within the liberal–democratic settlement.

While a case can therefore be constructed which argues for a constitutional response to the dominance of market economics, the case will be weak for so long as there is no clear specification of the precise values which are threatened. It must be conceded that, generally, the values of 'social justice', or 'ample liberalism', or, of course, 'the public interest', will appear much less clearly defined than those of the market. If we are to argue for constitutional protection of such values, it is necessary to try to pin down what is meant. As was discussed in the first Part of this book, it is not possible to identify an uncontested account of public interest principles, though to some extent it is possible to identify common underlying threads. Attempts to address the question frontally, listing clearly what the principles are, are, perhaps unsurprisingly, few and far between,

---

[24] Ibid. Ch. 5.   [25] Ibid., 74.   [26] Ibid., 4.
[27] Sunstein, C. R., *Free Markets and Social Justice*, (Oxford: Oxford University Press, 1997), 7.
[28] Ibid., 9.   [29] Ibid., 8.

though both Bell[30] and Milne,[31] referred to previously in Chapter Two, make brave and helpful attempts to do so.

Bell argues that the 'public interest emerges as a set of fundamental values in society',[32] identifying as public interest arguments 'values . . . which are no more contestable or difficult to state than are arguments about rights'.[33] He identifies matters such as 'protecting government institutions, protecting recourse to the courts, protecting the institution of the family, protecting economic institutions, protecting certain constitutional values such as race equality, protecting certain moral values, and preventing fraud', and, 'In the wider political debate, . . . values such as providing for national security, providing for public order, providing for basic educational and welfare needs, and providing humanitarian help to those in need at home and abroad.'[34] Though it might be thought that this list falls foul of the caveat issued earlier, as regards avoiding the concept of public interest being too all-encompassing, and being used where alternative, more precise concepts could be employed, Bell is surely right to consider that 'Such fundamental values characterise the basic structure of society', and 'In that they have a firm basis in the existing character of social and political institutions, the difficulty of stating their content is reduced.'[35]

Milne discusses how 'Certain conditions which are necessary for a community's continued existence are clearly not only in every member's interest qua member but also qua individual person.' He goes on to argue that in a modern democracy, such conditions include, 'not only security of person and property but such things as efficient sanitation and hygiene provisions' and 'efficient means of transport and communication'.[36]

Though the lists provided by Bell and Milne are clearly not, and not intended to be, exhaustive, and certain aspects of them, inevitably, may be contestable, they do specify with some clarity a range of matters which are central to many constructs of the public interest, and which are clearly vulnerable to the kind of market-driven agenda just discussed. It should be obvious that the kinds of values, or interests, or claims, to which they point, also fall within the bounds of modern constructs of social citizenship and have, in recent history, been closely associated in Britain and elsewhere with the activities of 'the Welfare State' and social regulation.

Clearly, the kind of trends identified by Leys and others as deriving from market-driven politics pose a direct threat to the values of citizenship, and in particular the social aspect of citizenship.[37] Morgan notes how 'a presumption

---

[30] Bell, J., 'Public Interest: Policy or Principle?', in Brownsword, R. (ed.), *Law and the Public Interest* (Proceedings of the 1992 ALSP Conference) (Stuttgart: Franz Steiner, 1993).

[31] Milne, A. J. M., 'The Public Interest, Political Controversy, and the Judges', in Brownsword, R. (ed.), *Law and the Public Interest* (Proceedings of the 1992 ALSP Conference) (Stuttgart: Franz Steiner, 1993). [32] Bell, 'Policy or Principle?', 30.

[33] Ibid., 34.   [34] Ibid.   [35] Bell, 'Policy or Principle?', 34.

[36] Milne, 'Political Controversy', 42.   [37] See above, Ch. 2.

in favour of market governance', leading to the absence of thinking beyond a competition paradigm, can lead to the translation of 'aspects of social welfare that previously may have been expressed in the language of need, vulnerability or harm into the language of market failures or market distortion'.[38] The prospect of losing sight of the social consequences deriving from market-oriented activity suggests, in the context of the US, a return towards a society based upon pre-New Deal principles, and in the context of Britain, to a situation reminiscent of that before the twentieth-century development of the welfare state which ran hand-in-hand with the expansion of expectations of social citizenship. We will turn later in this chapter to consider the possible relationship between the welfare state and the public interest but for the moment will simply note Spicker's observation that 'Markets are insufficient to guarantee welfare.'[39] It is, however, possible to conclude on an interim basis that the kind of values identified by Bell and Milne as being essentially elements of 'the public interest' within liberal democracy, though they might indeed represent 'objectives valued by the community', are, demonstrably, highly vulnerable and in need of further protection. Leys quotes from Karl Polyani, writing in the 1940s, on the consequences of allowing market forces to operate uncontrolled:

To allow the market mechanism to be the sole director of the fate of human beings and their natural environment . . . would result in the demolition of society. Robbed of the protective covering of cultural institutions, human beings would perish from the effects of social exposure; they would die as the victims of acute social dislocation through vice, perversion, crime and starvation. Nature would be reduced to its elements, neighbourhoods and landscapes defiled, rivers polluted, military safety jeopardized, the power to produce food and raw materials destroyed.[40]

While this may appear a somewhat apocalyptic vision, Leys examines the issues in the modern British context in a more measured manner, and concludes that,

What the British case shows is that party politics and state policy-making are themselves now powerfully market-driven and less and less likely to defend, let alone renew and revitalise, the prerequisites of democracy. We need to understand this in order to develop an effective alternative politics.[41]

Though Leys's focus is on the escape of capital from *political* control, it is obvious that the legal and regulatory institutions will inevitably also have a potential role

---

[38] Morgan, B., *Social Citizenship in the Shadow of Competition: the Bureaucratic Politics of Regulatory Justification* (Aldershot: Ashgate, 2003), p. 3.

[39] Spicker, P., *The Welfare State: a General Theory* (London: Sage, 2000), 97.

[40] Polyani, K., *The Great Transformation: the Political and Economic Origins of Our Time* (Boston, Mass.: Beacon Press, 1957 [1944]), quoted in Leys, *Market Driven Politics*, 6.

[41] Leys, *Market Driven Politics*, 6.

to play, as what Stewart refers to as a 'surrogate political process',[42] in protecting democratic and constitutional values beyond those of the market. The potential importance, but also flimsiness of the protection offered to such values by the legal system is suggested by Morgan, when she notes that 'The shadow of competition gives social relations a texture imparted by the influence of not legal, but *economic* rationality.'[43] Clearly, economic activity, market forces, have the potential to impact significantly on the ability of all to act as citizens, especially in terms of social citizenship. If Morgan, drawing on Weber, is correct to consider that 'law is, from the perspective of political economy, instrumental in facilitating capitalism',[44] and if it were true to any significant extent that the legal system has failed to acknowledge values beyond the economic, this would suggest a failure of the legal system to incorporate, or give adequate weight to, the wider set of substantive values which can be identified within the liberal–democratic settlement. Law should also be expected to facilitate democracy. We will consider this issue shortly, when addressing the Rule of Law more directly, but for the moment will simply suggest that a significant part of the problem might arise from the failure to establish a conceptual framework, recognizable by lawyers, which incorporates, and attaches due weight to, liberal–democratic values beyond the economic.

It was suggested in Chapter Two that the precise content of what constitutes a meaningful construct of 'the public interest' might change according to which elements of the democratic value-set are under threat in any particular era, in fulfilment of what Sunstein identifies as a 'countercultural' role.[45] It is now clear that there are democratic features of our society that we value which do extend beyond the economic but which are significantly marginalized by the present-day dominance of market economics. It seems apparent that non-commodity values such as those suggested by Stewart, and in particular fundamental democratic expectations such as equality of citizenship, all of which have collective as well as individual aspects, are under threat from the unregulated, or inadequately regulated exercise of private power. If this is the case, it may be properly said that a legitimate public interest exists in furthering those parts of the basis of social life which are valued, and in protecting them if under threat. Though the legitimacy of such claims can be stated plainly, there remains a substantial problem, however, of giving such concepts forms which are recognizable and enforceable in law.

THE NEED FOR INTERPRETATIVE PRINCIPLES

To a significant extent, the apparent failure of regulation to protect public interest values results from the absence in the legal system, and hence the

---

[42] Stewart, R. B., 'The Reformation of American Administrative Law', *Harvard Law Review*, 88 (1975), 1670. [43] Morgan, *Social Citizenship*, 8.
[44] Ibid., 19. [45] Sunstein, *Free Markets and Social Justice*, 8.

regulatory system, of an adequate conceptual framework, which draws on the
values inherent in the constitution to establish enforceable norms and practices which fulfil democratic expectations. The task in hand is therefore, in
essence, that of seeking to resolve problems referred to in Chapter Two, where
it was noted that Teubner[46] observes the weaknesses in structural coupling
between politics, law and social life: in Minor's terms,[47] the bifurcation of legal-
technological concerns from moral values. As already suggested, a normatively
based concept of public interest may appear intuitively attractive in this respect.

   This is not say, however, that any such intuitive attraction exists in the absence
of more concrete foundations. Klosko comments on Rawls's approach whereby
'Rawls believes that principles of justice should be developed from selected "intuitive ideas" latent in the public culture of democratic societies'.[48] There is a real
sense though in which the premises on which Rawls seeks to build a theory of
justice are not quite so 'intuitive', or at least are not as problematic, as the use of
that term might suggest. Klosko goes on to quote Rawls in the following terms:

> [T]he political culture of a democratic society, which has worked reasonably well over a
> considerable period of time, normally contains, at least implicitly, certain fundamental
> intuitive ideas from which it is possible to work up a political conception of justice suitable
> for a constitutional regime.[49]

Thus the suggestion is that though of 'intuitive' origins, the legitimacy of such
ideas derives from their widespread, long-term and ongoing acceptance as the
basis for the organization of society, and their refinement, definition, acceptance,
and institutionalization. The principles, practices and institutions deriving from
such 'intuitive ideas' which have become embedded in the polity form much
of the substance which cements society together qua society; they serve as a
source of legitimacy for the institutions of governance. They are not timeless or
wholly unchanging, as demonstrated by the growth of the range and inclusivity of
citizenship expectations within liberal democracy. Though potentially subject to
review where the sense of legitimacy becomes challenged, as perhaps in the New
Deal process in the US, this is merely to 'renew the cement' with an alternative
set of arrangements and institutions more appropriate to current conditions,
themselves, inevitably, originating from a different set of 'intuitive ideas'. Of
course, some might seek to argue that if such a transformation is acceptable,
then the more recent swing to market-oriented values can also be viewed as
legitimate. The difference, however, as has been illustrated over the last few

---

[46] Teubner, G., *Juridification of Social Spheres* (Berlin: Walter de Gruyter, 1987), extracts in
Baldwin, R., Scott, C., and Hood, C. (eds.), *A Reader on Regulation* (Oxford: Oxford University
Press, 1998).

[47] Minor, W. S., 'Public Interest and Ultimate Commitment', in Friedrich, C. J. (ed.), *Nomos V:
The Public Interest* (New York, N.Y.: Atherton Press, 1962).

[48] Klosko, G., *Democratic Procedures and Liberal Consensus* (Oxford: Oxford University Press,
2000), 193. See generally Ch. 7 and especially 193–198.

[49] Rawls, J., *Political Liberalism* (New York, N.Y.: Columbia University Press, 1993), quoted in
Klosko, *Democratic Procedures*, 193.

pages, is that while New Deal arrangements in the US and the British welfare state may be viewed as attempts to fulfil or reflect the *whole range of values* accepted as underlying the liberal–democratic settlement, the current market-driven arrangements recognize and further only *one sub-set of these values*, and can be seen to cut across the legitimate democratic expectations of many citizens. Indeed, the narrower, currently dominant, sub-set of values might even seem to represent not a form of social 'cement', but rather a 'solvent' which seems likely to contribute to social disintegration.

Inevitably, and perhaps properly, some lawyers find some difficulty in working from ideas which are not given recognizable legal form. Statutes and cases seem to be sources which are the very stuff of lawyering, while constitutional principles are also familiar to legal discourse in most democracies; broad, primordial, ideas lacking legal form, whether described as 'intuitive' or not, are, inevitably, often treated with some scepticism. Only when such ideas become fully fledged, institutionalized in legal form, will they be integrated fully into legal discourse. This seems to reconfirm the problems identified by Teubner, of the self-referential nature of law, whereby the legal system tends to respond to social and political issues on its own terms, to the exclusion of the democratic context from which the issues, and the law, derive their claims for legitimacy. It certainly suggests problems in terms of giving legal effect to a concept as nebulous as the public interest usually is. The argument being pursued here, of course, is that the values associated with the public interest, as just discussed, seem to fall precisely into the category of fundamental ideas which Rawls recognizes, or which, as was noted in Chapter Two, Dworkin identifies as 'propositions having the form and force of principles' which form part of 'the considerations lawyers must take into account in deciding a particular issue of legal rights and duties'.[50]

However, such principles may frequently fail to get support from the legal system. They may be overlooked, or discarded in technical legal debate, especially in an adversarial context, and where they do not feature explicitly in recognized sources of law may be subject to the uncertainty as to recognition which derives from the kind of debate over 'interpretivist' and 'non-interpretivist' approaches referred to in Chapter Four. Certainly an overly clause-bound approach to the consideration of democratic values will lead to the marginalization of what readers will perhaps recall Ely referring to as 'society's "fundamental principles" or whatever'.[51]

An associated risk, especially apparent in the discourse of administrative law, and noted in Chapter Five, is that of social values being translated into procedural rather than substantive norms. While institutional arrangements ensuring fair procedure and accountability are certainly crucial to maintaining the legitimacy of constitutional, administrative and regulatory process, and are generally the

---

[50] Dworkin, R., *Taking Rights Seriously* (London: Duckworth, 1977), 71.
[51] Ely, *Democracy and Distrust*, 4.

focal point of administrative law, even strong adherence to procedural expectations does not guarantee that legitimate, substantive, democratic expectations
will be met. Though it is clear that administrative law can on occasion develop
in such a way as to recognize substantive claims in limited circumstances,[52]
this remains very much the exception rather than the norm. Generally speaking, the legal system applicable to regulation seems much more comfortable
with procedural rather than substantive issues, form and procedure being central, characteristic, elements of *Gesellschaft* and bureaucratic-administrative law
systems.[53] It is therefore hardly surprising if the regulatory systems considered
in previous chapters, and the legal instruments which inform them, fail to give
adequate recognition or protection to the kind of social values which they are
supposed to be pursuing. While potentially strong in relation to expectations of
accountability, the system may remain weak as regards substantive democratic
values.

This approach may reflect what is sometimes described as a 'thin' version of
the Rule of Law, 'a formalist conception, referring to the relatively modest claim
that state power is exercised according to law, no matter what the content'.[54]
This contrasts sharply with a 'thicker' version of the concept, which 'refers to the
existence of a particular set of substantive guarantees that accrue to citizens by
virtue of legal mechanisms'.[55] Morgan, from whom these definitions are drawn,
goes on to identify the potential for application of the Rule of Law in the bureaucratic regulatory setting. After considering briefly a model which gives emphasis
to a range of fundamental political liberties and human rights, she then identifies a model which may reflect 'market liberalism', a perspective which supports
only 'the kinds of substantive guarantees considered to be essential preconditions
for the smooth functioning of a market economy', and which would therefore
emphasize particularly rules relating to property ownership and contract. Such
a model might not seem at odds with expectations relating to what Marshall[56]
describes as the 'civil' element of citizenship, but would fail to recognize the
broader sets of claims associated with his construct of 'social' citizenship. In this
connection, Morgan goes on to identify a different perspective which can underlie versions of the Rule of Law, which she terms 'tempered market liberalism',
and which 'connotes a set of substantive guarantees frequently associated with

---

[52] An example may be the development in Britain of 'substantive legitimate expectation' in cases
such as *R v. North and East Devon Health Authority ex parte Coughlan* [1999] L.G.R. 703. See
Craig, P. P. and Schønberg, S., 'Substantive Legitimate Expectation after *Coughlan*', *Public Law*,
2000, Winter, 684; also Craig, P. P., *Administrative Law* (5th edn.) (London: Sweet and Maxwell,
2003), Chapter 19.

[53] Kamenka, E. and Tay, A. E. S., 'Beyond Bourgeois Individualism – the Contemporary Crisis
in Law and Legal Ideology', in Kamenka, E. and Neale, R. S., *Feudalism, Capitalism and Beyond*
(London: Arnold, 1975).   [54] Morgan, *Social Citizenship*, 32.

[55] Ibid., 33.

[56] See Marshall, T. H., *Citizenship and Social Class* (Cambridge: Cambridge University Press,
1950), and *Sociology at the Crossroads and Other Essays* (London: Heinemann, 1963), discussed
above, Ch. 2.

the various facets of the welfare state, guarantees that aspire to promote social citizenship, in addition to civil and political citizenship'.[57]

There are, of course, very obvious risks associated with 'thinner' visions of the Rule of Law, which may offer an air of legitimacy to the exercise of power while guaranteeing only legal formalism. In Turpin's words,

> The rule of law in its minimal sense of government according to law may seem to be a relatively unexacting principle, which is satisfied by any state that has taken the trouble to invest its officers with legal authority to do what is required of them. The rule of law in this limited sense is not inconsistent with despotic government, if the despot is scrupulous about using the forms of law.[58]

It is clear that a 'thin', proceduralist, approach to the Rule of Law is less contentious, in the sense of lending itself more easily to conventional legal analysis and argument. However, it may, by itself, have little effect in terms of protecting the values which underlie the democratic settlement; in Lewis's terms, 'Few now pretend that procedural democracy of a somewhat skimpy kind will of itself deliver substantive rights and freedoms.'[59] It is therefore readily apparent that any meaningful discussion of the Rule of Law must include discussion of the value system upon which legitimate exercise of power ultimately depends. This was precisely the approach taken by Harden and Lewis, in their 1986 analysis of the British constitution, 'The Noble Lie'.[60] Here, in considering the constitution in terms of a legitimate framework for governance, they identify as central to the legitimacy claims a value-laden vision of the Rule of Law, based on the expectations contained within the British constitutional schema. Again, the issue we are faced with, especially in the British context, is the relatively inexplicit nature of the values which inform and legitimate the constitutional, and hence administrative and regulatory institutions.

Inevitably, the less explicitly the underlying values are expressed, the greater the need for extrapolation and interpretation. This may pose problems for lawyers, but it is not to deny the existence of a value-base. In this connection it is also worth repeating Bell's assertion, noted earlier in this chapter, regarding public interest claims as being 'no more contestable or difficult to state than are arguments about rights'. It remains necessary, however, to equip the legal and regulatory systems with devices which require and facilitate the recognition, and thus enforcement, of such values and claims. This theme will be pursued further

---

[57] Morgan, *Social Citizenship*, 34.

[58] Turpin, C., *British Government and the Constitution: Text, Cases and Material*, 4th edn., (London: Butterworths, 1999), 76.

[59] Lewis, N., 'Markets, Regulation and Citizenship: a Constitutional Analysis', in Brownsword, R. (ed.), *Law and the Public Interest* (Proceedings of the 1992 ALSP Conference), (Stuttgart: Franz Steiner, 1993), 112.

[60] Harden, I. and Lewis, N., *The Noble Lie: The British Constitution and the Rule of Law*, (London: Hutchinson, 1986).

in Chapter Seven; however, it is also very much Sunstein's focus when he develops a thesis on 'interpretative principles', in order to 'show how background norms might vindicate underenforced constitutional norms, respond to changed circumstances within the constraints of text, and use notions of regulatory failure so as to achieve legislative goals'.[61] His dual concerns are that either such background norms might be ignored in judicial or regulatory decision-making, or that historically defined, but now anachronistic norms might be applied, which could undermine the regulatory purpose. Sunstein categorizes his menu of interpretative principles in terms of 'Constitutional Norms', 'Counteracting Statutory Failure', and, 'Institutional Concerns'. Though he mostly locates his discussion in the specific context of judicial construction of statutes, many of the interpretative principles which Sunstein sets out may be thought to apply equally to regulators interpreting and pursuing their brief.

As regards his first category, 'Constitutional Norms', Sunstein notes how 'Constitutional law is an uneasy amalgam of substantive theory and institutional constraint, and the constraints properly lead courts to be reluctant to uphold constitutional principles with complete vigour.'[62] That said, he then identifies a range of factors which do or could aid the fulfilment of constitutional and democratic expectations. These include the reference to the federal basis of the US Constitution, the expectation of political deliberation, or deliberative democracy, which he finds 'traceable to the origins of the Constitution and firmly rooted in current law',[63] principles of accountability and non-delegation, and principles relating to property and contract rights, and indeed welfare rights. He locates and exemplifies these principles in the context of specific legal disputes, or areas of regulatory practice within their social and historical context.

He then identifies more briefly interpretative principles relating to 'Institutional Concerns', arising in the context of judicial control of agency powers, highlighting concepts such as presumptions in favour of judicial review, presumptions against implied repeals, and deferral by the courts to administrative agencies in relation to policy and fact. In general, these principles seem less controversial, in the sense that they are perhaps more clearly established, and relate less to specific substantive issues than to the relationship as a whole between the judiciary and agencies.

Finally, Sunstein turns to interpretative principles relating to 'Counteracting Statutory Failure'. He argues here that 'In light of the conventional difficulties in the implementation process, courts should generously construe statutes designed to protect traditionally disadvantaged groups and noncommodity values.'[64] Beyond this, he identifies a range of principles relating to issues such as promoting political accountability, the problem of statutory obsolescence, where 'a statutory provision may no longer be consistent with widely held social norms' or

---

[61] Sunstein, C. R., *After the Rights Revolution: Reconceiving the Regulatory State* (Cambridge, Mass.: Harvard University Press, 1990), 161. [62] Ibid., 163.
[63] Ibid., 164.   [64] Ibid., 171.

'the legal background may have changed dramatically as a result of legislative and judicial innovations',[65] understanding and accounting for the systemic effects of regulatory action, and the principle of 'proportionality', to which we will return in the next chapter.

Sunstein concedes that there is an inevitable potential for conflict between some of these principles in particular cases, and with that in mind he proposes a 'hierarchy of interpretative principles',[66] with, in essence, what he views as high and well-embedded constitutional principles, such as political accountability and deliberation at the top, and those without such well-established or clear constitutional roots, such as proportionality, at the bottom. In establishing this hierarchy, Sunstein refers to a purpose which seems closely related to the themes explored earlier in this chapter in relation to the ongoing challenges to democratic and public interest values: '[T]he overriding goal is to promote the purposes of constitutional democracy while taking account of the changes introduced by the rise of the regulatory state.'[67]

It should be said that much of what Sunstein advocates here is far from revolutionary, at least in the context of the US, as evidenced by the examples he is able to cite of cases where the application of such interpretative principles have been, or could reasonably have been, applied. Rather, it is the drive towards a self-conscious or considered adoption and application of the principles which is significant. However, it should be remembered that Sunstein is writing from within a very different constitutional tradition from that of Britain. As he properly observes, 'Background norms vary from one country to another; the relevant principles diverge sharply in accordance with assumptions that prevail in the nation's legal culture.'[68] It is therefore necessary to explore the extent to which the approach he takes can be applied in Britain. However, it is first necessary to say a little more about the civic republicanist tradition from within which he writes, as it seems to offer insights into a democratic vision which, though related to, is markedly different from the tradition of the UK. In particular, it appears to offer a very different perspective on the relationship between the citizen and the political community.

THE CIVIC REPUBLICANIST APPROACH AND ITS ATTRACTIONS

As is clear from even the briefest survey of literature on the civic republicanist tradition, this is no more of a single school of thought than is liberalism, or socialism, or communitarianism. As Honohan makes clear from the very start of her lucid and accessible study, modern proponents of, and commentators on civic republicanism, vary in terms of the lineage they claim for this

[65] Sunstein, C. R., *After the Rights Revolution: Reconceiving the Regulatory State* (Cambridge, Mass.: Harvard University Press, 1990), 174.   [66] Ibid., 186–7.
[67] Ibid., 187.   [68] Ibid., 160.

approach: 'While all recognise Machiavelli as central, some trace the tradition from Aristotle through Rousseau; others see the thread as linking Cicero to Locke and then Madison, thus overlapping with the stars of the liberal firmament.'[69] While it is apparent that some of the most prominent modern proponents, such as Sunstein, draw particularly on the Madisonian tradition, seeking to locate their arguments within the context of principles prominent in the founding era of American democracy, as Craig observes, 'How far republican ideals permeated the thinking of the framers of the Constitution is a topic on which there has been much disagreement.'[70] It is, however, helpful to take a more rounded, if brief, overview of the republicanist tradition, and how it relates to the major alternative threads of modern political theory.

Honohan is able to trace the development within civic republicanist thinking of four key ideas, which are emphasized in different historical eras. *Civic virtue* is the focal point of 'the precursors of this tradition'[71] in ancient Athens and Rome: 'Citizen participation within the political process was the highest form of active life, and the object was the pursuit of the pubic good which must take precedence over the good of a particular individual.'[72] By the fifteenth to seventeenth century, thinkers identified *freedom* as the primary value, with virtue as being more instrumental. Subsequently, in the eighteenth century, *participation* and the complications of larger-scale societies with greater numbers of citizens comes to the fore, though the likes of Madison and Rousseau are found to offer radically different approaches. The more modern, twentieth-century, approaches to civic republicanism have, of necessity, to consider a still larger number, and more inclusive set, of citizens. Honohan sees these as 'Reacting to totalitarianism and neutralist liberalism', highlighting 'the ways in which self-realisation requires public recognition', seeing 'freedom in positive terms as realised in political action', and reaffirming 'the role of politics in realising shared goods'.[73] This produces in Honohan's terms, a focus on *recognition*. She uses 'recognition' to signify, 'that politics is an arena of personal expression and self-realisation'.

For individuals to flourish, their most central concerns need some kind of confirmation in the public arena. This is in contrast to the widely prevailing view which sees politics as a mechanism for reconciling diverging interests more or less peacefully, and for which self-realisation and recognition are private or social, not political, matters.[74]

Contrary to libertarian approaches, civic republicanism looks beyond individual rights. Contrary to pluralist visions, the republican requirement that 'there be some independent "public interest", and not just naked political bargain, exemplifies the republican concern with pursuit of the public good'.[75]

---

[69] Honohan, I., *Civic Republicanism* (London: Routledge, 2002), 4.

[70] Craig, P. P., *Public Law and Democracy in the United Kingdom and the United States of America* (Oxford, Oxford University press, 1990), 331.　　　[71] Honohan, *Civic Republicanism*, 13.

[72] Craig, *Public Law and Democracy*, 319.　　　[73] Honohan, *Civic Republicanism*, 111.

[74] Ibid., 112.　　　[75] Craig, *Public Law and Democracy*, 335.

Contrary to 'value neutral' accounts of liberalism, it confirms and indeed emphasizes the existence of a system of values beyond personal autonomy underlying the constitutional settlement: 'Republican politics is concerned with enabling interdependent citizens to deliberate on, and realise, the common goods of an historically evolving political community, at least as much as promoting individual interests or protecting individual rights.'[76]

In this sense, civic republicanism appears to stand in marked contrast to the liberal–democratic tradition. However, Honohan identifies two different strains within republican thinking: an 'instrumental republican strain' which views citizenship as primarily a means of serving individual freedom, and a 'strong republican' strain, which, drawing perhaps more on the older set of republican roots, emphasizes 'the inherent value of participating in self-government and realising certain common goods among citizens'.[77] The combination of factors which underlies 'stronger' civic republicanist thought therefore distinguishes the approach most clearly from liberalism. Liberalism will emphasize individual rights, interests and freedoms, with politics merely instrumental in the service of such objectives, while civic republicanism will observe that 'without a political structure there is no basis on which people can form an agreement to live together', and thus 'they must cultivate civic virtue, or a commitment to the common good'.[78] Though viewed by Honohan as 'a specific variant of communitarianism',[79] civic republicanism can be distinguished from communitarianism by virtue of the former's clear emphasis on citizenship, membership of a specifically *political* community, as opposed to the latter's more general notion of membership of a community.

Within the civic republicanist tradition, private interests are said to be served by membership of the political community, as such active membership facilitates the achievement of common goods. Thus, civic republicanism, in its modern application in large-scale societies, as perhaps typified by Sunstein's approach, will emphasize participation and deliberation, within a political framework, in pursuit of and protection of common goods. This, however, is not necessarily a comfortable or unproblematic position.

The deliberative nature of the republic seems to derive from a classical vision of a small number of citizens actively engaged in a process of discourse which may eventuate in outcomes which transcend factional interests, or, alternatively and problematically, may be captured by a majority interest group. Though the larger scale of the American political community, even at the nation's birth, may seem to militate against the republican expectation of citizen participation in the deliberative process, it can also be presented as advantageous. Madison identified virtue in a larger-scale model of social affairs, provided that institutions are designed in such a way as to guard against a tyranny of the majority, in effect

---

[76] Honohan, *Civic Republicanism*, 1.   [77] Ibid., 9.   [78] Ibid., 5.   [79] Ibid., 8.

arguing that,

[I]n a large state with an economy based on the pursuit of private wants, there is inevitably great social diversity and, therefore, less chance of a tyrannous majority forming either among the electorate or elected. Social diversity helps create political fragmentation which prevents an excessive accumulation of power.[80]

A federal structure, combined with a strong separation of powers model is said to further protect freedom, and in particular, the freedoms and interests of minorities. In terms of the central Madisonian concern with avoiding the tyranny of any one faction, the benefits of the 'extended republic' are relatively clear. However, it is not necessarily obvious how the deliberative aspects of civic republicanism can be maintained or furthered. As David Held notes, 'Madison's extended republic is a far cry from the classical ideals of civic life and the public realm. The theoretical focus is no longer on the rightful place of the active citizen in the life of the political community; it is instead, on the legitimate pursuit by individuals of their interests and on governments as, above all, a means for the enhancement of these interests.'[81] Thus Madison's vision of the republic, with its significant emphasis on pluralistic struggle, Held believes 'signals the clear interlocking of republican with liberal preoccupations.'[82]

Guarding against domination by any one interest group, is a central issue in the Madisonian tradition. The concern, in Madison's words, is that of 'a number of citizens, whether amounting to a majority or minority of the whole, who are united and actuated by some common impulse of passion, or of interest, adverse to the rights of other citizens, or to the permanent and aggregate interests of the community.'[83] Thus, 'a fundamental purpose of government is to protect the freedom of factions to further their political interests while preventing any individual faction from undermining the freedom of others.'[84] The response to this adopted by the founders of the US was to establish a system of fundamental rights, in the Constitution and Bill of Rights, which have supra-legislative status,[85] and which are protected by the Supreme Court as guardian of the constitution: a position contrasting sharply with the traditional British position of a supreme legislature which can be portrayed as having the ability to make or unmake any law.[86]

Beyond the question of deliberation, and the need to guard against a tyrannous majority, two further issues raise obvious problems. The identification of 'common goods' may seem to raise difficulties apparently very similar to those considered in Chapter One in relation to identifying 'the public interest'; it might

---

[80] Quoted in Held, D., *Models of Democracy*, 1st edn. (Cambridge: Polity Press, 1987), 65.

[81] Held, D., *Models of Democracy*.   [82] Ibid.

[83] From Madison, J., *Federalist* No. 10, quoted in Loveland, I., *Constitutional Law: a Critical Introduction* (London: Butterworths, 1996), 10.   [84] Held, *Models of Democracy*, 187.

[85] See Loveland, *Constitutional Law*, 11–25.

[86] Bradley, A., 'The Sovereignty of Parliament', in Jowell, J. and Oliver, D. (eds.), *The Changing Constitution*, 4th edn. (Oxford: Oxford University Press, 2000), 23.

be thought one thing to identify pursuit of 'common goods' as an objective, but quite another to specify the substance of 'common goods'. In addition, the civic republicanist position clearly requires certain preconditions to be met if individuals are to be able to act as citizens, fully engaged in the deliberative political process. Honohan addresses both of these issues in detail; we will briefly consider her responses to each of these two sets of problems in turn.

Honohan observes that 'The common good is a concept that is not popular today', and indeed is one which 'may be resisted as collectivist and potentially oppressive'.[87] In Sunstein's terms, 'the republican belief in the subordination of private interests to the public good carries a risk of tyranny' and is 'threatening to those who reject the existence of a unitary public good, and who emphasize that conceptions of the good are plural, and dependent on perspective and power'.[88] Understandably, Honohan identifies the kind of common good in the sense of 'the corporate good of a social group' as having been 'justly criticised as intrinsically hostile to individual freedom and self-determination'.[89] If, however, the common good is thought of as simply the aggregate of the goods or interests of atomistic individuals, then the problems identified as associated with common interest constructs of the public interest observed in Chapter One reappear, and, indeed, as Honohan observes, 'There is no sense here in which goods are shared.'[90]

However, she goes on to argue that though there may be no single 'common good' which can be identified, there may yet be 'common goods'. What she calls 'the ensemble of conditions for individual goods'[91] may properly be considered 'common concerns', yet ultimately are established by reference primarily to an instrumental vision rather than a 'strong' civic republicanist belief in their inherent value. From this latter perspective, it is probably proper to think of common goods in terms of 'What is good for each person as a member of a society or group',[92] emphasizing the centrality of the group:

> The republican tradition has emphasised the interdependence of citizens, in its material, moral, psychological and ontological dimensions. Humans carry on their lives only in a range of practices in which they interact with others, and which give (or fail to give) public recognition to certain goods.[93]

Here we have, in terms of Virginia Held's typology of public interest accounts discussed in Chapter One,[94] rather than a common interest or preponderance account, a unitary theory premised explicitly upon the inherent value of membership of a political community. While liberal theories focus on individual

---

[87] Honohan, *Civic Republicanism*, 150.

[88] Sunstein, C. R., 'Beyond the Republican Revival', *Yale Law Journal*, 97 (1988), 1539, at 1540.   [89] Honohan, *Civic Republicanism*, 151.

[90] Ibid.   [91] Ibid., 151.   [92] Ibid., 152.   [93] Ibid., 153.

[94] Held, *The Public Interest*.

freedoms in pursuit of self-fulfilment, the civic republicanist account of common goods emphasizes the necessity of politically organized society for fully
human existence, whereby there exists a set of values in the republic which is
beyond, and greater than, the aggregate of individual interests; 'many such common goods cannot be realised independently by citizens'.[95] Echoing some of the
voices heard earlier in this chapter, Honohan observes that 'citizens have an
interest in common goods which are not realised by the market alone'.[96]

As was noted in Chapter One, a major problem of common interest and
preponderance accounts of the public interest is their potential failure to take
account of the interests of future generations. Honohan notes how, within the
civic republicanist vision, 'because the market is better at meeting current effective demand than providing for future or collective goods, the state may also
sustain possibilities and valuable options currently undervalued by, or under
pressure from, the market or other forces in society'.[97] The civic republicanist
expectation of deliberation is important here, and argues Sunstein, was a vision
which, though not uncontested, played an important role in the framing of the
US Constitution.[98] According to this vision, as stated by Sunstein,

The purpose of politics is not to aggregate private preferences, or to achieve an equilibrium
among contending social forces. The republican belief in deliberation counsels political
actors to achieve a measure of critical distance from prevailing desires and practices,
subjecting these desires and practices to scrutiny and review ... The republican position
is ... that existing desires should be revisable in light of collective discussion and debate,
bringing to bear alternative perspectives and additional information.[99]

We have already noted the practical difficulties of establishing deliberative mechanisms in large-scale communities, which often seem to revolve around factional
interests at least as much as any conception of common good. It is also possible
at this point to question Sunstein's republican approach in terms of his concurrent objectives of broad participation and the need to 'insulate political actors
from private pressures'. Certainly Powell seems to consider the consequence of
this conjunction of claims to result in the need for strong external scrutiny to
ensure that legislative autonomy does not overwhelm the deliberative desire.[100]
He observes that 'Sunstein's argument for deliberative politics unintentionally
sounds very much like an argument for government by an independent judiciary,
which is scarcely a program for broad political participation.'[101] Certainly, there
is an issue here of institutional design, which civic republicans must address, and
on which the Madisonian 'extended republic' seems to place great emphasis.

---

[95] Honohan, *Civic Republicanism*, 203.   [96] Ibid.   [97] Ibid., 198.
[98] Sunstein, 'Beyond the Republican Revival', 1558 *et seq.*   [99] Ibid., 1548.
[100] Powell, J., 'Reviving Republicanism', *Yale Law Journal*, 97 (1988) 1703, at 1708.
[101] Ibid.

Though it may not in reality go as far as amounting to an argument for 'government by the judiciary', it certainly does attach substantial significance to the judicial role. In turn, this must suggest a need for the establishment of principles by which, in order to ensure accountability, judicial discretion, like any other discretion, must be adequately structured.

It is clear that in order for such potential values or 'common goods' to be served, and for meaningful 'deliberation' to take place, civic republicanism has to assume the ability of all citizens to engage in the political processes around which society is organized. In addition, the civic republicanist expectation of freedom in the form of political autonomy seems to look further than non-domination, which certain schools of liberal thought may not extend beyond.[102] In Honohan's terms, citizens need a material basis, not just 'social capital' or civic virtue to be able to act as active and independent citizens. Extremes of economic inequality, which may often be found to underlie social exclusion, present a serious obstacle to the possibilities for political equality and freedom.[103] In particular, as she goes on to note, 'the degree of equality required may be greater if . . . political autonomy means having an equal voice in a deliberative politics'.[104]

Though the precise degree of economic equality needed is contentious, and republicanist thought does not always place the same degree of emphasis on the need for freehold property as does Harrington,[105] Honohan is clear that 'it requires more than a basic threshold of resources or capabilities, as economic inequalities tend to translate into possibilities of domination and unequal exercises of political power'.[106] Thus, given existing social and economic inequalities, in order to seek to facilitate the required extent of political autonomy necessary in pursuit of civic republicanist ideals, the need for a substantial amount of state intervention, including some redistribution of resources, may be indicated.

Thus, the civic republicanist agenda seems to advocate both a high degree of political autonomy, and a relatively high degree of state intervention if its objectives are to be realized. Though apparently contradictory, each is rationally necessary, and their co-existence is no more problematic than the acknowledgment in liberal thought of the necessity of market forces being subjected to regulation if the perceived benefits of their exercise are to be realized. Indeed, at this point the civic republicanist approach seems to begin to run parallel with the liberal–democratic agenda, not least as regards ensuring that government powers do not become so extensive as to become oppressive, and hence lose legitimacy within the political settlement. In considering a vision of 'liberal republicanism', Sunstein identifies a perhaps surprisingly high degree of overlap between the two

---

[102] The classic account of 'negative' and 'positive' freedom is found in 'Two Concepts of Liberty', in Berlin, I., *Four Essays on Liberty* (Oxford: Oxford University Press, 1969). See also 'Berlin's Division of Liberty', in Macpherson, C. B., *Democratic Theory: Essays in Retrieval* (Oxford: Oxford University Press, 1973).   [103] Honohan, *Civic Republicanism*, 191.

[104] Ibid., 192.   [105] Craig, *Public Law and Democracy*, 325.

[106] Honohan, *Civic Republicanism*, 192.

philosophies:

Some elements of the liberal tradition are highly congenial to republican conceptions of politics. In their emphasis on the possibility of forming public policy through deliberation, on political equality, on citizenship, and on the salutary effects of publicity, republicanism and liberalism are as one. All four of the basic republican commitments find a home within the liberal tradition.[107]

Indeed, he goes on to note how although 'The most collectivist forms of republican thought are of course at odds with the most atomistic versions of liberalism, ... Republican thought, understood in a certain way, is a prominent aspect of the liberal tradition.'[108] Whether this classification is more or less helpful than Honohan's, noted above, of republicanism as a 'specific variant of communitarianism', is debatable.[109] What is clear, however, is that, as is commonplace in mainstream modern discourse on liberal democracy, great emphasis must be placed within civic republican thinking on the fact that 'freedom requires a strong institutional structure of accountability and transparency within which the government exercises its power'.[110] This implies an emphasis on the legitimacy of state power, and, as a consequence, a strong separation of powers model, and a high-profile and constitutionally powerful role for the judiciary: features much more apparent in the US constitutional scheme than in Britain.

In the concluding section of this chapter and in Chapter Eight, we will return to consideration of the application of a civic republicanist approach in the context of public interest regulation. However, in terms of the agenda established in previous chapters, the potential attractions of this perspective should already be apparent. It clearly has the potential to move beyond the most unattractive aspects of liberal/pluralist perspectives which take 'the existing distribution of wealth, existing background entitlements, and existing preferences as exogenous variables', which are simply accepted as forming 'a kind of prepolitical backdrop for pluralist struggle'.[111] While seeking to avoid collectivist and oppressive tendencies, and resting firmly on principles of constitutional democracy, the civic republicanist approach also seems to remedy a more specific, oft-noted, weakness of liberal–democratic approaches, in terms of their failure to acknowledge or protect values beyond those of the individual and the market. In acknowledging the existence of, and justifying state intervention in pursuit of, the furtherance of 'common goods', values which extend beyond the aggregation of individual interests, civic republicanism seems to emphasize the polity as a whole more strongly than liberal–democratic thought, offering the enhanced potential to establish and reflect, in the terms of this book's agenda, 'objectives valued by the community'. In addition, in the emphasis it places on active citizen participation

---

[107] Sunstein, 'Beyond the Republican Revival', 1567. [108] Ibid., 1569.

[109] For a detailed study of the relationship between Communitarianism and Liberalisms, see Mulhall, S. and Swift, A., *Liberals and Communitarians*, 2nd edn. (Oxford: Blackwell, 1996).

[110] Honohan, *Civic Republicanism*, 206.

[111] Sunstein, 'Beyond the Republican Revival', 1543.

in deliberative processes, civic republicanism might seem to offer a legitimate and definite orientation for regulatory activity in the public interest, seeing regulation in effect as a 'surrogate deliberative process', while simultaneously requiring the accountability of those who exercise such power.

None of this is to claim that existing political practices, whether in the US or elsewhere, necessarily embody or reflect fully a civic republicanist vision of rising above the aggregation of individual interests via deliberative processes. Inequalities in political influence, arising from social and economic inequalities which may undermine expectations of equality of citizenship, are of course clearly evident in the US and other democracies.

Nor is it to claim that in the context of the US or other democracies, judicial practice consistently upholds civic republicanist norms. As Michelman seems to suggest, though seminal cases such as *Brown v. Board of Education*,[112] which led to the desegregation of schooling, might be thought to represent successes on the road to fulfilment of expectations of equality of citizenship via law, other decisions, such as *Bowers v. Hardwick*,[113] upholding the state of Georgia's law which criminalized homosexual acts between consenting adults in their home, might indicate the clear failure of the legal system to protect such principles.[114] Abrams suggests that though it formed an apparently flourishing area of scholarship amongst historians and political scientists from the 1960s to the 1980s, the republican strain in American politics when adopted by legal scholars was 'straitened by the distinctive problems and perspectives of liberal legalism', reflecting the fact that legal scholars' 'assumptions have been shaped by a liberal, pluralist institutional structure, in which collectivism and affirmative citizenship are at best minor themes'.[115] Echoing Powell's comment,[116] noted above, Abrams identifies an over-emphasis or over-reliance on the judicial role in Michelman's work, and in Sunstein's writing a wariness in relation to the coercive potential of deliberatively arrived at substantive norms, both perhaps arising from their concerns as regards 'collectivist' forms of republicanism. Abrams's concerns are picked up also by Epstein, who argues that 'No political theory can concentrate on process and deliberation to the exclusion of substantive concerns. Yet that is precisely what Michelman and Sunstein heroically try to do.'[117] The limits of proceduralism have been referred to already, earlier in this chapter and in Chapter Five, and though Epstein may be right to argue that their approach fails to develop any completely clear vision of substantive values, Michelman and Sunstein seem to do more than most in this respect, and do so explicitly. In fact, it becomes apparent on reading further, that Epstein's critique

[112] 347 US 483 (1954).   [113] 478 US 186 (1986).

[114] Michelman, F., 'Law's Republic', *Yale Law Journal*, 97 (1988), 1493.

[115] Abrams, K., 'Law's Republicanism', *Yale Law Journal*, 97 (1988) 1591, at 1591 and 1592.

[116] Powell, 'Reviving Republicanism'.

[117] Epstein, R., 'Modern Republicanism – Or the Flight From Substance', *Yale Law Journal*, 97 (1988) 1633, at 1633.

derives from a very different vision in which 'Limited government, public choice, and private property all can be integrated into a single theory that incorporates some portion of the revived republican tradition.'[118] It is hard to be clear exactly which portion of the republican tradition he is proposing incorporating, though it is certainly not one focused on citizenship or common goods. His approach, which he claims to be, 'much richer, for it recognizes that individual self-interest is the engine both of economic and social advancement and political intrigue',[119] seems to bear much more resemblance to the 'public choice' theories referred to in Chapter One than anything resembling civic republicanism properly-so-called. That said, we have already noted the extent to which the Madisonian vision of the republic does incorporate concepts more closely associated with liberal/pluralist thinking than classical republicanism, and that even Sunstein's 'liberal-republican' thinking does indeed place heavy emphasis on the value of pluralism and markets.

Though civic republicanism is therefore, like any grand theory, susceptible to criticism on grounds of inconsistency, it is no more inconsistent than liberal thought, and offers important insights into the relationship between citizen and state. None of the above means that it is not proper to seek to aspire to conditions which fulfil civic republicanist objectives within a modern democratic setting. Indeed, Sunstein argues that 'The fact that the American constitutional regime at its outset owed a great deal to republican thought is an important corrective to approaches that purport to speak for the American constitutional tradition, but proceed from pluralist premises or invoke prepolitical rights.'[120]

In Sunstein's terms, the central civic republicanist expectations of 'the belief in political deliberation and the belief in political accountability', which he traces back to Madison and others framers of the US Constitution, 'are . . . closely allied in American constitutionalism'.[121] He is properly conscious of the potential difficulties inherent in appealing to principles contested more than two hundred years ago at the founding of the US, and identifies as a principal task the need to 'move beyond the republican revival by integrating aspects of traditional republican thought with the rise of the modern regulatory state'.[122] In pursuit of civic republicanist objectives via mechanisms which emphasize 'the basic republican commitments – to political equality, deliberation, universalism and citizenship',[123] his arguments for the application of interpretative principles, discussed earlier in this chapter, look powerful. The agenda he draws from his 'overriding goal . . . to promote the purposes of constitutional democracy while taking account of the changes introduced by the regulatory state',[124] seems relevant within any democratic context, yet its application may be thought to be particularly problematic in the setting of the UK.

---

[118] Ibid., 1650.   [119] Ibid.   [120] Sunstein, 'Beyond the Republican Revival', 1563.
[121] Sunstein, *After the Rights Revolution*, 187.
[122] Sunstein, 'Beyond the Republican Revival', 1589.   [123] Ibid., 1590.
[124] Sunstein, *After the Rights Revolution*, 187.

CIVIC REPUBLICANISM, UK STYLE?

While the civic republicanist mode of thinking is clearly well established, if far from uncontested, in the American context, it is much less obviously within the mainstream of British political thought. It may be that Harrington, writing in the constitutional ferment of the seventeenth century,[125] provided 'the crucial link in the transfer of republican thought from England to the US colonies, where it exercised considerable influence on the revolutionaries and upon the framers of the constitution'.[126] In addition, Wollstonecraft in the eighteenth century,[127] and 'social liberal'[128] T. H. Green, in the early years of the twentieth century, who has been described as one of the few liberals who 'are best seen as covert republicans',[129] also make British contributions to what can be viewed as a republican tradition. However, their influence was limited and they do not form anything approaching a continuous chain of republican thought.

In part, the absence of a republican tradition in Britain might seem inevitable, given republicanism's inherent associations with opposition to the concept of monarchy, which remains an institution strongly embedded in British traditions. The constitutionally limited power of the monarchy post-1688 may itself be seen as forming the basis for a move away from republican thought to what, as we shall see, became a central constitutional reliance on the Rule of Law: 'In a sense, the idea that those who are subject to laws should make them was superseded by the idea that those who make the law should be subject to it.'[130] However, the concerns of civic republicanism extend far beyond the question of monarchy, and it is on occasion possible to discern aspects of the British polity which seem to share a degree of functional equivalence with its broader principles.

Though the US may be characterized as a 'capitalist democracy' and Britain a 'social democracy',[131] it can be argued that the difference is less marked in the post-Thatcher/Reagan era than previously, and in any case, the claim of *democracy* remains a constant and central claim in legitimating the exercise of power in both. Though the forces of capital and individualism may appear increasingly to dominate both societies, and the pluralist vision may be thought to have triumphed over any sense of common good, it remains appropriate to ask 'whether any society may not need a degree of unity in order to be a society at all, or how much diversity even a liberal society can tolerate without falling apart'.[132] This

---

[125] See Honohan, *Civic Republicanism*, 63–75.

[126] Craig, *Public Law and Democracy*, 323.

[127] See Honohan, *Civic Republicanism*, 99–102; also Held, *Models of Democracy*, 79–85.

[128] Goodwin, B., *Using Political Ideas*, 4th edn. (London: John Wiley, 1997), 47. Loughlin, M., *Public Law and Political Theory* (Oxford: Clarendon, 1992), refers to Green in terms of 'New Liberalism'.

[129] I am grateful to Colin Tyler for this quotation, drawn from Braithwaite, J. and Pettit, P., *Not Just Deserts: a Republican Theory of Criminal Justice* (Oxford: Clarendon, 1990), 57.

[130] Honohan, *Civic Republicanism*, 76.   [131] Klosko, *Democratic Procedures*, 176.

[132] Arblaster, A., *Democracy*, 3rd edn. (Buckingham: Open University Press, 2002), 65.

returns us very directly to the overarching 'Law Job' identified in Chapter Two, the idea that there are certain tasks required to be undertaken in any group, large or small, in order to allow it to continue to function as a group. Maintenance of the conditions which fulfil the polity's claims of legitimacy appears to be one such fundamental task, and central to such claims is the series of expectations which flow from the concept of 'democracy'. Of course, this begs the question of what the expectations and values are which form the basis of democracy in the modern British context. Only once this question has been considered is it meaningful to move on to consider the functions that law and regulation might fulfil, and the forms they may take.

As noted previously, in seeking out the values or principles which underlie the British democratic settlement, the task is notoriously hampered by the absence of a single constitutional statement of the kind found in the US Constitution and the Amendments to it. Though the incorporation of the ECHR via the Human Rights Act may give the appearance of clarifying certain fundamental liberties, this does not take us far down the road of exploring the broader, fundamental basis of the constitutional settlement. The absence of a developed concept of 'state',[133] and a limited sense of 'citizenship', alongside a reliance on a combination of convention, tradition, statute, case law and treaties, have an effect of rendering the clear identification of constitutional principles peculiarly difficult. In the context of the present inquiry, it is necessary to seek to identify what within British constitutional arrangements legitimate the polity, or serve as the 'social cement' which allows the society to continue qua society, and indeed whether any values or interests are recognized beyond the aggregation of individual interests and in particular how the polity identifies and protects any such 'common goods'.

Though Dicey's vision of a British constitution premised on twin pillars of the Rule of Law and Sovereignty of Parliament is open to ready criticism in terms of its descriptive accuracy, its relevance today, and, its logical inconsistency,[134] it remains an influential account in terms of providing a starting point for constitutional discussion. It is unnecessary to rehearse criticisms here, but it is worth noting that few if any critics within the political mainstream would argue against some version of the Rule of Law, even if they might be at pains to distance themselves from Dicey's vision. Noted earlier was Turpin's commentary on the vacuous nature of a vision of the Rule of Law premised only on legal formalism, yet, like most commentators, he offers little by way of an alternative vision. This task is, however, very much at the heart of Harden and Lewis's work on the British constitution, which identifies a very definite normative content

[133] See Prosser, T., 'Towards a Critical Public Law', *Journal of Law and Society*, 9/1 (1982), 1.

[134] In addition to the Harden and Lewis, *The Noble Lie*, for an excellent overview, see Jowell, J., 'The Rule of Law Today', in Jowell, J. and Oliver, D. (eds.), *The Changing Constitution*, 4th edn. (Oxford: Oxford University Press, 2000).

for a meaningful concept of the Rule of Law:

> The rule of law is a highly connotative, value-laden idea and as such must be sharply differentiated from *a* rule of law, a specific norm or guide to action. It speaks to a belief in the kind of polity which seeks to subordinate naked power and to elevate civic order and rational progress. It implicitly rejects the idea of immunity from criticism, of being above collective institutions rather than facilitating their operation. ... [I]t is the central legitimating feature of organized public life – the supreme constitutional principle.[135]

Though the Harden and Lewis vision is far from uncontested,[136] and raises major challenges in terms of designing and maintaining institutions which serve effectively the 'supreme constitutional principle', alternative perspectives which deny, or fail to identify normative foundations of the legitimacy claims for constitutional arrangements, seem to leave the existence of the polity at the mercy of the pluralist fray. The risk, raised in Chapter Two, is that within a 'liberal democracy' lacking in a set of institutionally grounded legitimating values, the settlement may be quietly overthrown by a hegemonic ideology, such as that representing the preference for market forces seen today. The clear and present danger is that Britain may become highly 'liberal', but not at all 'democratic'. In Arblaster's terms, 'There are those ... for whom democracy and the freedoms which often accompany it are an inconvenience, an obstruction to the uninhibited pursuit of wealth and profit.'[137] In resisting such forces, in preserving society qua society, in protecting the democratic element of liberal democracy, the institutions of regulation and the legal system have potentially critical roles to play, via 'assuring the larger constitutional values inherent in the rule of law to promote rational civic discourse'.[138] This can be seen to parallel the deliberative element of civic republican thought, and is at least as problematic in the British context as the US, in terms of giving it practical effect. What is clear, however, is that such institutions which might be charged with producing deliberative outcomes will be disabled from doing so if they are not in themselves able to identify the basis for their legitimacy within the larger political settlement and its value system.

Of course, given the current hegemony of liberal-individualism, regulatory interventions stand under a constant and peculiarly weighty burden of justification. When, as discussed in Chapter Three, the Communications Act or Enterprise Act empower regulators to act 'in the public interest', or when the Food Standards Agency (FSA) identifies the public interest as its objective, if it is not possible to identify the legitimate basis for such activities then intervention is likely to be perceived as illegitimate, is likely to be subject to legal challenge, and is unlikely to be effective in terms of achieving its objectives. Here we return to the link referred to by Sunstein, between questions of 'the

---

[135] Harden and Lewis, *The Noble Lie*, 19.
[136] See Loughlin, M., 'Tinkering with the Constitution', *Modern Law Review*, 51/4 (1988), 531.
[137] Arblaster, *Democracy*, 55.   [138] Harden and Lewis, *The Noble Lie*, 263.

regulatory state' and 'the purposes of constitutional democracy'. Though it will be recalled that he identifies 'political equality, deliberation, universalism and citizenship' as amongst 'basic republican commitments', these are also amongst the features which he identifies as consistent with liberalism. As such, they may be expected to be present as much in British democratic arrangements as in America. In pursuing their regulatory agendas, and in serving to 'promote social justice through public action', bodies such as Ofcom or the FSA[139] appear to have the potential to further such democratic expectations, especially that of citizenship.

Ofcom's powers, in seeking to ensure a degree of diversity in media output via maintenance of pluralism in ownership and control,[140] are clearly intended to serve all three elements of Marshall's construct of citizenship.[141] The expectations of citizenship, and of equality of citizenship, are now considered so fundamental as to be considered an essential element of the modern democratic settlement, and can indeed be said to form a significant part of the value system, or 'social cement', which binds society together. The kind of Universal Service Obligation which may be imposed on utility providers by way of 'social regulation',[142] seems closely related to the kind of 'basic threshold of resources and capabilities' referred to by Honohan in her discussion of modern republicanism.

It is not, of course, only through such forms of regulation that equality of citizenship is pursued. Historically, the welfare state tradition of the twentieth century also sought to pursue democratic inclusivity directly through the pursuit of social citizenship, via ensuring what Marshall referred to as 'a modicum of economic welfare'.[143] However, such interventions are not easily squared with classical liberalism. As Goodwin notes,[144] Lloyd George's introduction in 1909 of limited pension schemes and sickness and unemployment benefits 'had to be reconciled with the liberal creed, since they represented intervention in the market system and, further, interfered paternalistically with individual freedom'. As Goodwin recounts, Hobhouse[145] sought to justify this in terms of a contribution to pursuing a liberal value in equality of opportunity, thus 'ushering in a period of social liberalism'.[146] Loughlin notes how Green's vision of 'society not as an aggregate of isolated atoms but as an organism for the realization of common purposes',[147] contributed to forming the foundation of an approach which developed a more positive conception of liberty, resulting in the situation whereby 'The function of law, then, was to provide the conditions

---

[139] Young, I. M., *Inclusion and Democracy* (Oxford: Oxford University Press, 2000), 117.
[140] See above, Ch. 3.   [141] See above, Ch. 2.   [142] See above, Ch. 3.
[143] Marshall, T. H., *Citizenship and Social Class* (Cambridge: Cambridge University Press, 1950), 11.   [144] Goodwin, *Using Political Ideas*, 57.
[145] Hobhouse, L. T., *Liberalism* (London: Williams and Norgate, 1911).
[146] Goodwin, *Using Political Ideas*, 57.
[147] Loughlin, *Public Law and Political Theory*, 121.

for the development of our capacities and powers towards the moral end of self-realization.'[148]

However, the drive in post-war Britain towards Marshall's expectation of guaranteeing all the 'essentials of a decent and secure life at every level, irrespective of the amount earned',[149] encapsulated an unresolved tension in liberalism. In Jordan's terms,

Its [liberalism's] concern for the moral quality of the lives of full citizens forbade it to attempt to raise up the deprived by material means alone. Yet it never discovered how to give social benefits in other than the material terms it so deeply distrusted; thus it was constantly caught between assisting the poor and needy, and reminding them of the unworthiness of requiring assistance.[150]

Of course, throughout its history, the welfare state was challenged not only from within the liberal establishment but also from the Left. George and Wilding succinctly summarize a position adopted within the socialist tradition:

While supporting the aims and purposes of the welfare state, socialists have remained aware of its limitations and its dangers. They voice four general fears – that it is concerned with injustice rather than justice, that it can be used as a substitute for necessary preventive action, that it can be limited to seeking equality of opportunity, that it is concerned with poverty not with inequality.[151]

From further Left, 'Marxists are agreed that in spite of its origins, the social reform movement has delayed and perhaps averted for good the collapse of capitalism.'[152] By 'humanising' capitalism and 'by reducing tensions', the welfare state through social policy legislation 'promotes social cohesion and thus makes continuity and stability of the social system possible'.[153]

However, it was not from the Left that the significant attack on the welfare state was ultimately to come. Nor was it directly as a result of the inconsistencies inherent in the new Liberal philosophies of the early twentieth century. Jordan noted the risks attaching to excessive intervention, especially when ultimately premised upon liberal paternalism,[154] but was also able to observe, as early as 1976, the very different challenge to the welfare state coming from the Conservative Party of that time. He quotes Sir Keith Joseph as stating that 'When you take responsibility away from people, you make them irresponsible. Hand in hand with this you break down traditional morals.'[155] However, though it was 1979 when the first Thatcher government came to power, it was arguably not until after the third election victory in 1987 that the true extent of the Party's

---

[148] Loughlin, *Public Law and Political Theory*, 122.

[149] Marshall, T. H., *Citizenship and Social Class* (Cambridge: Cambridge University Press, 1950), 82.

[150] Jordan, B., *Freedom and the Welfare State* (London: Routledge and Kegan Paul, 1976), 204.

[151] George, V. and Wilding, P., *Ideology and Social Welfare* (London: Routledge and Kegan Paul, 1976), 80.   [152] Ibid., 101.

[153] Ibid.   [154] Jordan, *Freedom and the Welfare State*, 213, and Ch. 15 generally.

[155] Ibid., 205.

anti-collectivist sentiment, based upon a version of Hayek's market liberalism, was fully unleashed. In addition to a consistent policy of seeking to reduce public expenditure, which impacted on public services as a whole, key public services such as health and education were reformed in such a way as to introduce quasi-market forces.[156] In essence, any concept of equality of citizenship that had informed the establishment and running of welfare state services was changed to a notion that 'citizenship is based upon participation in markets'.[157] In parallel with attacks on the trade union movement, and the ongoing disablement of local government which was a hitherto significant, if always vulnerable, power bloc presenting a potential degree of balance to central government power, reducing the meaning of citizenship in this way served as a significant aspect of the process of establishing a system of government which Gamble has discussed in terms of being premised on the idea that only two forces were to be perceived as legitimate: the free market and the strong central state.[158] The success of the Thatcher legacy can be seen in the extent to which the Labour Party was forced, in order to obtain office, to abandon its historic associations with the broader conceptions of citizenship and the welfare state and instead adopt a mode of thinking premised on a market vision, which though forming a variant on it, remains within the orthodoxy established in the Thatcher years.

It can therefore plausibly be argued that the last twenty-five years have seen a withdrawal of the British state from certain of the welfare functions associated with its height in the thirty years following the Second World War. However, in so far as it continues to engage in some welfare functions which serve the needs of citizenship, whether in the interests of damping down pressure for real reform and maintaining class domination, as Marxists critics would have it, or as a result of some more altruistic motive such as the furtherance of liberty and equality, it is fair to conclude still that 'government relates to a political community'[159] to which citizenship expectations are inextricably linked. The welfare state tradition, the social regulation of utilities, and, indeed, the public service broadcasting tradition, all manifested much more strongly in the UK than the US, provide evidence of this phenomenon and demonstrate a strong, if often poorly articulated, concern for the issue of citizenship. Even if participation in markets is presented as the modern manifestation of citizenship, the essential Thatcherite promise, represented in policies such as sale of shares in privatized utilities and right-to-buy in relation to council houses, was that *all* could participate fully in the (market-driven) society. In its rhetoric at least, Thatcherism

---

[156] See generally, Johnson, N., *Reconstructing the Welfare State: a Decade of Change 1980–1990* (Hemel Hempstead: Harvester Wheatsheaf, 1990). On education reform, see Feintuck, M., *Accountability and Choice in Schooling* (Buckingham: Open University Press, 1994). On quasi-markets, see Le Grand, J., *Quasi-Markets and Social Policy* (Basingstoke: Macmillan, 1993).

[157] Johnson, *Reconstructing the Welfare State*, 197.

[158] Gamble, A., *The Free Economy and the Strong State: the Politics of Thatcherism* (Basingstoke: Macmillan, 1994). [159] Spicker, *The Welfare State*, 128.

did not deny the claim of equality of citizenship, and indeed to some extent can
be seen to have rested on the claim of universality.

However, do any such actions in pursuit of equality of citizenship imply values
of the kind associated with a civic republican tradition, which extend beyond
the aggregation of individual interests? While Thatcher's oft-quoted claim that
'there is no such thing as society' constitutes an extreme vision, it is little more
than the logical conclusion of a strong emphasis on liberal individualism. In
Goodwin's terms, 'the counterpart of the strong conception of the individual
is a weak conception of the nature and purpose of society and in particular of
government, which is seen as a device for performing the residual tasks which
individual self-interest leaves undone'.[160] She continues that,

> This means that liberal theorists are unwilling to invoke concepts such as the common good
> or the public interest, which are predicated of society as a whole, and would circumscribe
> their use in justifying state intervention. The only common good which classical liberals
> would recognize is the maximization of the aggregate of individual benefits.

This seems to place a liberal democracy such as Britain far outside the civic
republican tradition and to cast doubt on Sunstein's claim of a degree of common ground between the republican and liberal traditions. However, Young
seems right in confirming that, at the very least, 'workable democratic politics
requires of citizens some sense of being together with one another in order to
sustain the commitment that seeking solutions to conflict under circumstances of
difference and inequality requires'.[161] As she continues, 'political co-operation
requires a less substantial unity than shared understandings or a common good',
but does require, *inter alia*, 'that those who are working together . . . understand
themselves as members of a single polity'.[162] By definition, citizenship, though
perhaps a less prominent constitutional feature in Britain than elsewhere, seems
to imply membership of a political community, the continuation of which can be
considered to be a value greater than and beyond the aggregated interests of individuals. This appears to be a common thread which does bind civic republicanism
and anything but the most extreme vision of liberalism.

While we have seen how the Madisonian civic republican tradition in the
US incorporates many values associated with liberal pluralism, we have also
noted the existence and acceptance within British 'social liberalism' of features
which appear to reflect values within the polity which extend beyond liberal-
individualism and market exchange. In both cases, the adoption of ideas which
diminish ideological purity can be viewed as pragmatic measures adopted in
pursuit of *democratic* values. Though they may appear to emphasize different
aspects of citizenship, it remains a central focal point for both. The claim of
equality of citizenship both pre-dates the Welfare State era (though admittedly
then based on a less extensive membership), and survives into the current era

---

[160] Goodwin, *Using Political Ideas*, 38.   [161] Young, *Inclusion and Democracy*, 110.
[162] Ibid.

in the Thatcherite emphasis on citizenship through participation in markets and the post-Thatcherite, New Labour, rhetoric on social exclusion.

For the avoidance of any doubt, it should be stated at this point that none of this is to assert a case for communitarianism, or a Rousseau-like vision of the general will, or even a broad thesis of common goods. Neither is it to suggest the necessity of adopting somewhat alien civic republican traditions in Britain, though to some extent these seem to highlight and speak more directly to some of the democratic issues and concerns identified in this chapter than does much current domestic political thought. Certainly, the civic republican approach seems to recognize, and address more clearly, the democratically necessary concept of a political community, than does the liberal tradition. That said, the reality is that British democracy, despite its strong liberal influence, has incorporated, and indeed requires for its continued existence, a concept of political community, manifested in the social welfare and social regulation traditions which service and reflect the democratic expectation of equality of citizenship, providing a degree of functional equivalence with the emphasis placed on citizenship in the civic republican tradition. It does also assume a preference for the continuation of society qua society, and the avoidance of allowing, in Polyani's phrase, 'the market mechanism to be the sole director of the fate of human beings',[163] and the nightmare scenario which he suggests would flow from this. In turn, this appears to necessitate the maintenance of legitimacy of the polity via ensuring the delivery of democratic expectations. In so far as the law and regulation must play a part in this process, it is hampered by the absence in Britain of clarity over the fundamental norms which underlie the constitution, which in turn results in the absence of, but also the heightened need for, interpretative principles of the kind envisaged by Sunstein. Though Britain may not have a strong republican tradition, it does claim to have a lengthy history of democracy. It can now be argued that regulation 'in the public interest' has the potential to play a crucial role in furthering this democratic agenda.

---

[163] Quoted in Leys, *Market Driven Politics*, 6.

7

Wider Applications of the Public Interest

Previous chapters have emphasized the potential significance of the concept of 'public interest' in the field of regulation, and have sought to define it in this context. They also indicated the need to consider the legal forms in which the concept might be manifested in the context of regulation. It is inevitable, however, that consideration will be given to the concept's application beyond regulation as defined. Before reaching conclusions on the book's main arguments, it is therefore necessary to consider these matters.

In certain specific contexts, such as government control of information,[1] in particular in relation to the activities of 'whistleblowers' who bring information into the public domain via 'public interest disclosures', the term is already used.[2] More commonly, it is often applied in connection with attempts to obtain leave to pursue, or costs related to, litigation seeking to pursue group or collective interests: 'public interest litigation', where the concept's implications will be primarily procedural.[3] Though the use of the term 'public interest' in these situations is certainly intended to raise an appeal to values relating to the general interests of the community, it can be readily distinguished from the regulatory context explored in earlier chapters by reference to the absence of sustained intervention, and there is a sense in which the application of the concept in these contexts fails to capture its essence as it has been defined here, in terms of it serving as an embodiment of the principle of equality of citizenship.

It is necessary to remain aware of the acknowledged risks associated with over-extended versions of the concept, or attempts to apply it as a panacea. Inevitably, such approaches tend to return the concept into the nebulous form from which this book has sought to shift it. However, in this final chapter, consideration is given to other areas in which the concept might be used to facilitate the legal system's potential to reflect fundamental, substantive, democratic expectations. Clearly, the areas covered here do not constitute an exhaustive catalogue, but suggest some preliminary thoughts and agendas for future research, where public

---

[1] See Feintuck, M., 'Government Control of Information: Some British Developments', *Government Information Quarterly*, 13/4 (1996), 345.

[2] See Birkinshaw, P. J., *Freedom of Information: the Law, the Practice and the Ideal*, 4th edn. (London: Butterworths, 2001).

[3] See Cooper, J. and Dhavan, R. (eds.), *Public Interest Law* (Oxford: Basil Blackwell, 1986); also Chakrabarti, S., Stephens, J., and Gallagher, C., 'Whose Cost the Public Interest?', *Public Law*, 2003, Winter, 697.

interest values arising from expectations of equality of citizenship may appear to relate closely to existing or nascent legal principles, both in public and private law, and where such a concept might have a role to play in legitimating and furthering their development. In essence, the agenda identifies a range of areas in which private property power is, or might be, limited by reference to non-commodity values, and invites the question of whether a concept of the public interest, as developed in previous chapters, might be relevant or of assistance.

It was suggested in Chapter One that 'citizenship' might properly be characterized as 'the right to have rights': not an end in itself but rather a compact whereby the individual, in return for acknowledging responsibilities towards the collectivity that is society, can claim civil, political and social freedoms and powers to serve their own best interests. Of course, as has been illustrated in Chapter Six, a civic republicanist vision would place more emphasis on the role of the citizen within the democratic settlement, and on civic virtue. Ownership of property is clearly an important right associated with citizenship, well up the acknowledged hierarchy of interests recognized within democracies, yet it is also clear that interventions which limit the otherwise absolute nature of powers which derive from property ownership can on occasion be perceived as legitimate, where broader democratic interests would otherwise be threatened. However, as has been demonstrated throughout previous chapters, it is rarely the case that such interventions are founded upon a broad vision which incorporates the full range of democratic interests, but rather can be viewed more often as reflecting the much narrower values of capitalist economics; competition law is the *locus classicus* of this phenomenon. The apparent priority given to 'public *economic* interests' over 'public *democratic* interests', is in one sense simply a reflection of the *realpolitik* of the current hegemony of market values, but it also seems to reflect the greater difficulty inherent in stating precisely the nature of democratic values when compared with the values of the market.

The examples of regulation considered in Part Two all illustrate the use of public power with the apparent intention of constraining the power of individuals and private corporate entities which derives from ownership of property. Whether or not they are considered effective in this respect will be determined ultimately in relation to their terms of reference, or perhaps more realistically, the broader political perspective adopted in observing them. However, it is also important to remain aware that public bodies engaged in the regulation of private activity must themselves be limited in their actions by reference to democratic principles: the essential democratic promises of accountability, and the absence of arbitrary or unlimited power. The normative elements of our constitutional arrangements are expected to perform this restraining function, establishing the limits of legitimate power of public institutions. Thus, though governments may claim an electoral mandate which empowers them to develop and execute public policy, they remain subject to constitutional scrutiny, through political and legal mechanisms, and it remains possible that aspects of government behaviour may be challenged as illegitimate, in the sense of being anti-democratic, despite being legal, in the sense of having been carried out in accordance with formal legal requirements. Thus, reforms of the welfare state, if they were to have the consequence of denying adequate education or health care to some individuals, might be considered undemocratic and illegitimate, even if they have passed through all due legislative process. Likewise, measures which take previously public (collectively owned) property into private hands (for example through 'right to buy' policies in relation to public housing, or the selling-off of state-owned school playing fields), or which, in the pursuit of planning objectives, demand the compulsory acquisition of private property for public purposes, all have the potential to raise problems in this respect. All involve direct contests between individual and collective interests, and raise an apparent conflict between collective values associated with the democratic polity and the deeply entrenched values of private property ownership. As observed previously, they are unlikely to be resolved satisfactorily, or legitimately, by reference only to procedural expectations. In so far as such issues raise the possibility of diminishing equality of citizenship, both the exercise of private property rights and regulatory interventions can clearly be the proper subject of 'democratic impact assessment', against identified, substantive, public interest standards.

However, such matters essentially require the unpacking of constitutional values and arrangements relating to the legitimate extent of regulatory and other governmental powers. Though these matters should be, and indeed have elsewhere been, subject to close scrutiny, the focus of this book has been from the outset specifically on the impact of regulation in the name of the public interest rather than broader questions of the constitutional order. Thus, while acknowledging the existence and importance of wider concerns often associated with the public interest, the remainder of this chapter will focus on potential edifices for legitimate public interest intervention which highlight the actuality of, or potential for, the lawyer acting as institutional architect in pursuit of constitutional objectives. The concern will therefore be with the range of ways in which the power associated with private property might be limited by law in pursuit of non-commodity values. This requires consideration of both public and private law mechanisms, and the relationship between such devices and the objectives of public interest intervention discussed in previous chapters. In other words, the focus will be on the extent to which law may fulfil its potential as what Stewart calls a 'surrogate political process'[4] in relation to democratic values. In part, this will follow Craig's agenda in asking, 'How far the common law may have a role to play in controlling ... concentrations of power.'[5]

---

[4] Stewart, R. B., 'The Reformation of American Administrative law', *Harvard Law Review*, 88 (1975), 1670.
[5] Craig, P. P., 'Constitutions, Property and Regulation', *Public Law*, 1991, Winter, 538, at 538.

THE PRECAUTIONARY PRINCIPLE AND THE PUBLIC INTEREST

Discussed in Chapters Three and Four, the precautionary principle may be presented as being closely related to the public interest. In so far as it might be described as 'a rather shambolic concept, muddled in policy advice and subject to the whims of international diplomacy and the unpredictable public mood over the true cost of sustainable living', [6] or as 'too vague to serve as a regulatory standard',[7] it may certainly be thought to share some of the characteristic lack of definition associated with the public interest.

In terms of its practical effectiveness, the precautionary principle depends, of course, on its recognition and application, and given its best-established context, in environmental regulation, this means in practice its adoption in both national and international fora. While the concept's roots may generally be traced back to the German adoption of the *Vorsorgeprinzip* in the mid-1970s[8] it must be viewed in its original setting not as an entirely free-standing concept, but rather as part of a package of principles and practices concerned with protection of the environment, developed within the specific constitutional setting of Germany.[9] It must now properly be viewed as being applied in a potentially wide range of different 'regime contexts' and as a part of different systems, which will denote different drivers for the regulation of risk, applicable in different jurisdictions, reflecting different value bases, in different fields at different times.[10] Though the principle has now been increasingly widely adopted in international conventions and treaties,[11] and though it appears to seek to address problems arising from scientific uncertainty as to new or proposed developments, it can also be considered to suffer, in much the same way as some visions of the public interest suffer, from a lack of normative specificity which renders its application in itself uncertain, and hence perhaps lacking in legitimacy.

That said, some commentators on the precautionary principle do identify a value base which has a high degree of overlap with certain accounts of public interest values. References to global citizenship and collective interests in

---

[6] O'Riordan, T. and Cameron, J., 'The History and Contemporary Significance of the Precautionary Principle', in O'Riordan, T. and Cameron, J. (eds.), *Interpreting the Precautionary Principle* (London: Earthscan, 1994), 12.

[7] Bodansky, D., 'Scientific Uncertainty and the Precautionary Principle', *Environment*, 33/7 (1991), 5, quoted in Boehmer-Christiansen, S., 'The Precautionary Principle in Germany – Enabling Government', in Morris, J. (ed.), *Rethinking Risk and the Precautionary Principle* (Oxford: Butterworth-Heinemann, 2000), 52.

[8] For overviews of the principle's development, see Morris, *Rethinking Risk*, 1–7; O'Riordan and Cameron, *Interpreting the Precautionary Principle*, Ch. 1; Freestone, D. and Hey, E., *The Precautionary Principle and International Law* (The Hague: Kluwer, 1996), Ch. 1.

[9] See Boehmer-Christiansen, 'The Precautionary Principle in Germany', 31.

[10] See generally, Hood, C., Rothstein, H. and Baldwin, R., *The Government of Risk: Understanding Risk Regulation Regimes* (Oxford: Oxford University Press, 2001).

[11] See Freestone and Hey, *The Precautionary Principle*, Ch. 1 for examples up to the mid-1990s. For more recent accounts see Morris, *Rethinking Risk*; Harremoës, P. et al. (eds.), *The Precautionary Principle in the 20th Century: Late Lessons from Early Warnings* (London: Earthscan, 2002).

the global commons,[12] as well as obligations towards the interests of future generations,[13] implying a sense of stewardship, and concern for 'the emerging human rights of future generations',[14] suggest a set of values which inform debate over the principle. Certainly Attfield indicates a moral content, identifying in the principle 'a built-in hypothetical or conditional aspect, presumably answering, amongst other matters, to the importance of rights and of justice',[15] which requires consideration of what might be viewed as non-human, or at least non-immediately human, interests in other species and the ecosystem.[16]

It therefore seems that adoption of the precautionary principle imposes a requirement to take into consideration a range of values when regulatory intervention is being considered. However, it does not, in and of itself, seem to provide any guarantee as to the hierarchy of such values, and though at the simplest level it may be thought to state that 'we should resolve uncertainties in favour of the environment',[17] this does not assist in determining just how precautionary regulation must be,[18] or, in the terms of the debate discussed in Chapter Four, whether the principle is to be understood in its 'weaker' or 'stronger' sense. As use of the principle becomes extended so as to apply far beyond the environmental context, for example as in relation to the food industry,[19] or concerns over toxicity of plastics, or choking fears over novelty gifts included in food products,[20] or child protection,[21] the value base established in the environmental context may appear to become less relevant. As this happens, the principle appears to become increasingly procedural rather than substantive.

Though one approach, commonly asserted in Britain, is to 'seek to protect the integrity of "sound science" as the basis for considered action',[22] Freestone and Hey observe that the precautionary principle 'assumes that science does not always provide the insights needed to protect the environment effectively, and that undesirable effects may result if measures are taken only when science does provide such insights'.[23] There is indeed, as Fisher observes, an inevitability of regulation having to occur in circumstances of scientific uncertainty.[24] In such circumstances, application of the precautionary principle may be viewed as

---

[12] O'Riordan and Cameron, *Interpreting the Precautionary Principle*, 12–14.

[13] See Beckerman, W., 'The Precautionary Principle and our Obligations to Future Generations', in Morris, *Rethinking Risk*, 46.   [14] Freestone and Hey, *The Precautionary Principle*, 251.

[15] Attfield, R., 'The Precautionary Principle and Moral Values', in O'Riordan and Cameron, *Interpreting the Precautionary Principle*, 155.   [16] Ibid. 156–7.

[17] Bodansky, D., 'The Precautionary Principle in US Environmental Law', in O'Riordan and Cameron, *Interpreting the Precautionary Principle*, 203.

[18] See Haigh, N., 'The Introduction of the Precautionary Principle into the UK', in O'Riordan and Cameron, *Interpreting the Precautionary Principle*, 259.   [19] See Ch. 3.

[20] See Durodié, B., 'Plastic Panics: European Risk Regulation in the Aftermath of BSE', in Morris, *Rethinking Risk*.

[21] See Guldberg, H., 'Child Protection and the Precautionary Principle', in Morris, *Rethinking Risk*.   [22] O'Riordan and Cameron, *Interpreting the Precautionary Principle*, 23.

[23] Freestone and Hey, *The Precautionary Principle*, 12.

[24] Fisher, E., 'Is the Precautionary Principle Justiciable?', *Journal of Environmental Law*, 13/3 (2001), 315, at 317.

a process which facilitates or enables long-term planning,[25] preferring precaution to *ex post facto* resolution of problems, and which, in the environmental context, may complement other principles such as 'polluter pays', and indeed can provide an entry point through which governments can actually stimulate potentially valuable new markets such as those in clean technologies and recycling.[26] However, as was discussed in Chapter Four, it may alternatively be viewed as imposing regulatory delays which may stifle innovation.[27] Ultimately, in many contexts, it may seem that the precautionary principle does not provide an adequately clear framework of substantive values which permits the legitimate resolution of such competing claims. Rather, there may be perceived a tendency for the principle to morph into something not unrelated to conventional approaches to cost–benefit analysis.

The problems inherent in establishing levels of risk[28] relate to underlying questions as to the relationship between 'subjective' values and 'objective' science.[29] In Fisher's terms, 'The phrase, "scientific uncertainty" refers not simply to a "data gap" but to a whole series of methodological, epistemological and ontological problems in scientific practice which mean that science cannot provide the "complete truth".'[30] However, Fisher observes elsewhere,[31] how the British government's Cabinet Office Strategy Unit has produced a report which is underpinned by 'an unequivocal assumption that "risk" is a universal and fixed concept that is common to all public decision-making'. As she observes, 'This is not to say there is not a recognition that definitions of risk can vary but there is a presumption that a single definition can be arrived at.'[32] The implicit faith of a government in science to provide 'the right answer' might be seen to relate to the kind of emphasis on 'excessive reassurance' observed by Millstone and van Zwanenberg in relation to BSE,[33] but it may also, by instigating delays in preventive action pending conclusive scientific proof as to the nature and extent of risk, in effect lead to economic considerations, with the apparent interests of producers and users of a particular product being prioritized over public health concerns.[34] This would be decidedly problematic, undermining the chief

---

[25] See Boehmer-Christiansen, 'The Precautionary Principle in Germany'.

[26] See O'Riordan and Cameron, *Interpreting the Precautionary Principle*, 23.

[27] See discussion in Ch. 4. See also McNelis, N., 'EU Communication on the Precautionary Principle', *Journal of International Economic Law*, 3/3 (2000), 545.

[28] See Adams, J., 'A Richter Scale for Risk?', in Morris, *Rethinking Risk*.

[29] See Matthews, R. A. J., 'Fact Versus Factions: the Use and Abuse of Subjectivity in Scientific Research', in Morris, *Rethinking Risk*.

[30] Fisher, 'Is the Precautionary Principle Justiciable?' 317.

[31] Fisher, E., 'The Rise of the Risk Commonwealth and the Challenge for Administrative Law', *Public Law*, 2003, Autumn, 455, at 461.   [32] Ibid.

[33] See Millstone, E. and van Zwanenberg, P., 'The Evolution of Food Safety Policy-Making Institutions in the UK, EU and Codex Alimentarius', *Social Policy and Administration*, (2002), 593. Also Millstone, E. and van Zwanenberg, P., ' "Mad Cow Disease" 1980s–2000: How Reassurances Undermined Precaution', in Harremoës, P., *Late Lessons*.

[34] See Infante, P. F., 'Benzene: a Historical Perspective on the American and European Occupational Setting', in Harremoës, *Late Lessons* 35, at 43 in connection with *Benzene*, 448 US 607 (1980), referred to in Ch. 4.

attraction of the application of the precautionary principle, in its potential to serve as a measure which prevents damage as opposed to relying on *ex post facto* remedies.[35]

The application of the precautionary principle in these circumstances may facilitate effective responses to risk, or it may not. There are certainly historical examples of prophylactic measures being adopted long before the recognition of the precautionary principle,[36] but, as seems to be the case with many applications of the principle, such interventions are based on an implicit cost/benefit assessment, in which the relative weightings attached to the various factors remain unspecified and unpredictable. Though it is possible that interpretations of the precautionary principle may incorporate a specific set of values, and establish a hierarchy, this requires elaboration of the value-set in each context in which the principle is to be applied. The precautionary principle in itself does not import values other than 'precaution', and in the absence of clear specification of a value base can properly be viewed as not far removed from conventional cost/benefit analysis techniques.

Though the principle is now sufficiently clearly recognized in international treaties, including the EU's Maastricht Treaty,[37] to have apparently binding effect on state signatories,[38] its application in domestic courts may be more problematic. Fisher observes that 'while courts in the UK and other common law jurisdictions have been willing to recognise the principle and to uphold precautionary decisions [based upon it] they have not, in most cases, been willing to accept it as a justification for substantive and intensive review'.[39] She attributes reluctance to give full effect to the principle in part to a judicial view of the principle's application being within the competence of the executive or administrative discretion, the deference to administrative expertise noted in previous chapters, and therefore an area in which the courts must tread with great caution. In part, however, she indicates that judicial reluctance stems from doubts about the justiciability of the concept arising from its apparent vagueness, and the unfamiliarity of such broad concepts to British judges, who will generally seek to avoid any intervention which could possibly be construed as review of the merits, as opposed to procedural propriety, of an administrative decision. She does, though, note that in other common law jurisdictions, notably Australia, the principle has been recognized as a ground for review, though in circumstances where the principle has been embodied explicitly in legislation.[40] There may also

---

[35] See Freestone and Hey, *The Precautionary Principle*, 13.

[36] See for example Harremoës, *Late Lessons*, 5–8, discussing practical responses in the context of the cholera epidemic in London in 1854.

[37] See Haigh, 'The Introduction of the Precautionary Principle'.

[38] See Freestone and Hey, *The Precautionary Principle*, generally; also Cameron, J., 'The Status of the Precautionary Principle in International Law', in O'Riordan and Cameron, *Interpreting the Precautionary Principle*.   [39] Fisher, 'Is the Precautionary Principle Justiciable?', 315.

[40] See also Freestone and Hey, *The Precautionary Principle*, 255; Harding, R. and Fisher, L., 'The Precautionary Principle in Australia', in O'Riordan and Cameron, *Interpreting the Precautionary Principle*.

be a need to address questions of legal certainty and foreseeability arising out of the concept's application.[41]

As Fisher acknowledges, the distinction is not a clear-cut one, but in general terms it seems that the courts have been in essence only willing to review decisions as against precautionary principle standards when it is presented as a matter of procedural fairness, and therefore clearly within their competence, as opposed to a matter of substance or merit. As she properly concludes, this raises fundamental questions regarding the administrative law system, and the relationship between the courts and the executive, which go far beyond the context of environmental issues or the precautionary principle. In reality, it may also simply illustrate the currently limited extent of the concept's utility.

By way of conclusion, it can reasonably be stated that the precautionary principle does relate closely to many constructs of the public interest identified in Chapters One and Two, in its concerns for collective interests including those of future generations. In so far as it recognizes collective interests and has the potential to limit commercial activity which may otherwise diminish or compromise them, it may prove significant and should be welcomed. It may indeed be seen to relate to the specific vision of the public interest proposed in this book, in terms of its concern for the ability of all to act effectively as citizens. It is clear that from this perspective, there may well be a public interest in the adoption of precaution in relation to developments which otherwise risk long-term or irreversible damage to such interests. However, it can also be concluded that there are significant differences between the concept of public interest as developed in this book, and that of the precautionary principle. Given the precautionary principle's lack of inherent values beyond that of precaution, and the need for specification and elaboration of any values it implies, especially once it is taken beyond its home ground of environmental issues, it may be compared with the use of interim injunctions in legal proceedings, serving to do no more than attempt to preserve the *status quo* pending determination of substantive issues. Though such a function is important, from this perspective it differs markedly from the explicitly value-laden concept of public interest, which it may contingently serve. Indeed, in this sense its normative content may look rather more like some of the more vague versions of the public interest, and specifically, in the terms used in Chapter One, the public interest as a contested arena rather than as a unitary concept, with the associated risk of 'victory' being achieved by the party entering the arena with the greater power; in this case the powerful corporate bodies. In addition, there is, at present at least, a clear functional difference between the essentially substantive intent of the concept of public interest developed here, and the currently largely procedural effect of the precautionary principle.

There is little doubt that Freestone and Hey were right to state in 1996 that, 'the precautionary principle is here to stay'.[42] However, in so far as the

---

[41] Harding and Fisher, 'The Precautionary Principle in Australia', 252.
[42] Freestone and Hey, *The Precautionary Principle*, 249.

precautionary principle is at present reduced to a procedural rather than substantive norm, its impact is lessened. That is not to say that it may not still be important in decision-making, especially as noted by Freestone and Hey in terms of any contribution it may make to reversing the traditional burden of proof.[43] Application of the precautionary principle may serve to challenge a conventional approach which denies regulatory intervention until positive proof of harm is available, and instead seems to place an onus on those seeking to continue their activity where a *prima facie* case is established as to the harm they are causing. However, this implies a 'process of finding and applying "appropriate policy options" ',[44] and 'a balancing of the interests involved',[45] or consideration of 'proportionality of response or cost-effectiveness of margins of error to show that the selected degree of restraint is not unduly costly'.[46] This seems to reconfirm the precautionary principle's close relationship to traditional methods of cost/benefit analysis. Indeed, in so far as the policies and practices of bodies such as the EU and WTO reflect their vision of economic and political realities and priorities, and 'temper the precautionary frameworks governing [for example] the marketing of GMOs through a consistent preference for formulations incorporating a cost effectiveness proviso for precautionary action',[47] the precautionary principle's place in the hierarchy of relevant values is lowered, and the potential benefits of the principle's application may be significantly diluted.

PROPORTIONALITY

The process of weighing competing factors and taking decisions is the daily work of many public bodies, and debates over 'proportionality', referred to in passing in previous chapters, may form the public law forum in which public interest values may be fought over. It may be expected to run alongside and play an increasingly significant role in relation to, decisions taken with regard to the precautionary principle.

When engaged in decision-making and policy-setting, British regulatory and executive bodies exercising discretion have traditionally been, in general terms, subject to a flexible, and often loose, overarching concept of reasonableness based to a significant extent on that derived from the case of *Associated Provincial Picture Houses v. Wednesbury Corporation*.[48] Though the *Wednesbury* test, at its loosest, demands of decision-makers only that their decisions are not manifestly absurd, the intensity of the application of the test in judicial review is variable, and the broad test may be viewed as incorporating, or may be broken

---

[43] Ibid., 259.   [44] Ibid., 251.   [45] Ibid., 252.
[46] O'Riordan and Cameron, *Interpreting the Precautionary Principle*, 17.
[47] Salmon, N., 'A European Perspective on the Precautionary Principle, Food Safety and the Free Trade Imperative of the WTO', *European Law Review*, 27 (2002), 138, at 154.
[48] *Associated Provincial Picture Houses v. Wednesbury Corporation* [1948] 1 KB 223.

down into, a range of more specific factors.[49] In recent times courts have also begun to show some willingness to review the exercise of administrative discretion against a standard of 'proportionality', which may be thought generally to offer a more 'intensive' standard of review.[50] Though limited forms of this principle can be identified in British cases in the 1970s and 1980s,[51] as recently as 1991 the House of Lords was not willing to recognize or apply it as a separate head of review,[52] though acknowledged the possibility of its future development. It is only in the last fifteen or twenty years, as it has been increasingly influenced by European jurisprudence, that British administrative law has even begun to develop a more coherent and extensive vision of its application, and its nature and status remains a subject of controversy within administrative law circles.

A commonplace principle in certain European legal systems, though varying in its precise meaning, and prominent in the trans-national jurisprudence of the EU and ECHR, the concept of proportionality can be usefully summarized for present purposes in terms of a public body's decision being unlawful 'if its adverse effects on a legally protected interest or right go further than can be justified in order to achieve the legitimate aim of the decision'.[53]

While this principle may appear intuitively attractive, British courts remain reluctant to apply it directly in matters of wholly domestic law. However, in certain cases involving EU law or the ECHR via the Human Rights Act, it is clear that decision-making may be subjected to the somewhat more 'intensive' standard of review provided by a test of proportionality. Referring to the judgment of Lord Steyn in the case of *Daly*,[54] Craig summarizes the position thus:

Proportionality could, said Lord Steyn, require the reviewing court to assess the balance struck by the decision maker, not merely whether it was within the range of reasonable decisions. The proportionality test could, secondly, oblige the court to pay attention to the relative weight accorded to relevant interests, in a manner not generally done under the traditional approach to review. The proper intensity of review was, said Lord Steyn, guaranteed by the twin requirements that the limitation of the right was necessary in a democratic society, in the sense of meeting a pressing social need, and really was proportionate to the legitimate aim being pursued.[55]

Functionally, in terms of requiring decision-makers to demonstrate how they have weighed the various factors involved in their decision, the test of

[49] See Craig, P. P., *Administrative Law*, 5th edn. (London: Sweet and Maxwell, 2003), 553.
[50] Proportionality can itself be applied in varying degrees of intensity. See Craig, *Administrative Law*, 585–8 and 617–32.
[51] See Jowell, J. and Lester, A., 'Beyond *Wednesbury*: Substantive Principles of Administrative Law', *Public Law*, 1987, Autumn, 368.
[52] *R. v. Secretary of State for Home Department, ex parte Brind* [1991] 1 AC 696.
[53] de Burca, G., 'Proportionality and Wednesbury Unreasonableness: the Influence of European Legal Concepts on UK Law', *European Public Law*, 3/4 (1997), 561, at 562.
[54] *R. (on the application of Daly) v. Secretary for the Home Department* [2001] 2 AC 532.   [55] Craig, *Administrative Law*, 586.

proportionality may seem quite similar to the 'Hard Look' doctrine developed by the US courts in the 1970s,[56] discussed in Chapter Five.

Underlying legal disputes regarding proportionality, or indeed the precautionary principle, are questions regarding the constitutional relationship between the judiciary and the executive. Controversy over, and British judicial reluctance to adopt wholeheartedly, the potentially more intensive standards of review inherent in proportionality or Hard Look approaches, derives substantially from the proper, if in these circumstances arguably misguided, concern not to be seen to interfere with the merits of administrative decisions. The concern can be viewed as proper, in terms of such decision-making having been entrusted to democratically accountable bodies who must be permitted to exercise their discretion within reasonable bounds, but misguided, in that the focus of both proportionality and Hard Look can ultimately be seen to be on how a decision has been taken rather than the substance of the decision as such. Though the application of proportionality may suggest a higher degree of judicial intervention than the traditional approach based on *Wednesbury*, it does not even seem to come close to a judicial usurping of the constitutional allocation of the power of administrative bodies to determine matters on their merits.

In the US context, Sunstein observes that either excessive regulatory controls or inadequate implementation of regulatory objectives can result from 'the failure to import a proportionality principle into social and economic regulation'.[57] As he goes on to observe, 'Of course a proportionality principle contains no uncontroversial metric with which to measure social costs and social benefits',[58]; however, it does demand a reasoned and transparent mode of decision-making. Thus, in the case of *Brind*,[59] discussed in Chapter Three, application of a proportionality principle may, or may not, have produced a different outcome. Ultimately, this would seem to depend on the judicial weight attached to the fundamental, substantive, claim of freedom of expression. However, regardless of the difference it would have made in terms of the outcome, the application of a test of proportionality may well have served as a more rigorous standard of review. It may have also served the need, identified in Chapter Six, for judicial discretion, like any other discretion, to be properly structured by reference to clear principles.

Approaches such as Hard Look and proportionality may be seen to offer a structure in which proper consideration can be given to the relationship between administrative ends and means: certainly a more structured approach than generally found within the terms of review under *Wednesbury* reasonableness. Though the objectives underlying the application of such principles are therefore inherently unobjectionable, and may indeed serve well the purposes of ensuring

---

[56] See Harden, I. and Lewis, N., *The Noble Lie: The British Constitution and the Rule of Law* (London: Hutchinson, 1986), 272 *et seq.*

[57] Sunstein, C. R., *After the Rights Revolution: Reconceiving the Regulatory State* (Cambridge, Mass.: Harvard University Press, 1990), 181.   [58] Ibid., 182.

[59] *R. v. Secretary of State for Home Department, ex parte Brind* [1991] 1 AC 696.

rationality in administrative decision-making, in the absence of clear requirements as to the interests and values to be considered, and the weighting to be
attached to them, they will by themselves do little to ensure that the sort of vulnerable public interest values discussed in this book are adequately protected. By
assisting in the structuring of administrative discretion, proportionality services
the democratic expectation of accountability, and hence legitimacy, through
transparency of decision-making, but remains ultimately procedural, requiring
a demonstration of the proper assessment of relevant factors. However, it may
still fail, in Fisher's terms,[60] to speak to 'the nature of what is being held to
account'. In the absence of statutory or other measures which require that they
be taken into account, the application of either a concept of proportionality or
the Hard Look doctrine will fail to ensure a high priority for the consideration of
specific values such as equality of citizenship, which, as suggested earlier, seem
to lie beyond the limits of proceduralism and instead require direct recognition
and protection as *substantive* values. In this sense, a value-laden, citizenship-
oriented, construct of public interest such as suggested in this book might assist in
establishing a hierarchy of values which may inform the application of concepts
such as proportionality.

Corporate Social Responsibility and Corporate Citizenship

Raised repeatedly in previous chapters has been the democratically problematic
extent of corporate social power: the ability of corporate activity in pursuit of
profit to impact adversely upon the democratic and social expectations which
form the basis of the political community. The rhetoric of the 'Third Way', in
so far as it emphasizes social exclusion, and might be thought to draw to some
extent on the conceptual framework of market socialism,[61] might be expected to
offer means by which a rebalancing can be achieved between citizenship expectations and the power of corporations. However, given the current hegemony of
market values, it is inevitable that incursion into the realm of private property
and the regulation of powers associated with it will be limited.[62] That said, there
is an increasing presence in the literature on such topics of discussion of 'corporate social responsibility' (CSR) and 'corporate citizenship', which might appear
to offer 'Third Way' approaches which seek to avoid the perceived extremes of
capitalist and socialist responses, and may seem to serve underlying democratic

---

[60] Fisher, E., 'Drowning by Numbers: Standard Setting in regulation and the Pursuit of Accountable Public Administration', *Oxford Journal of Legal Studies*, (2000), 109, at 129.

[61] See, for example, Le Grand, J. and Estrin, S. (eds.), *Market Socialism* (Oxford: Clarendon, 1989); Roemer, J., A Future for Socialism (London: Verso, 1994); Wright, E. O. (ed.), *Equal Shares: Making Market Socialism Work* (London: Verso, 1996); Przeworski, A., *Capitalism and Social Democracy* (Cambridge: Cambridge University Press, 1985).

[62] See generally, Parkinson, J., *Corporate Power and Responsibility: Issues in the Theory of Company Law* (Oxford: Clarendon, 1996); also Parkinson, J., Gamble, A., and Kelly, G. (eds.), *The Political Economy of the Company* (Oxford: Hart, 2000).

values which relate closely to some visions of 'the public interest'. Consistent with the observation that 'corporate citizenship derives from and represents a particular version of the more generic concept [CSR]',[63] henceforth 'CSR' will be used here to encompass the whole range of initiatives being discussed, with the term 'corporate citizenship' used only where necessary to identify the specific characteristics associated with it and to distinguish it from CSR generally.

As with the concept of public interest, the first and most fundamental obstacle to exploring debates about CSR is that of definition. As Whitehouse notes, the literature in fact 'reveals a multitude of different meanings ascribed to the concept ranging from the implementation by companies of philanthropic ventures, to an obligation "to take proper legal, moral-ethical, and philanthropic actions that will protect and improve the welfare of both society and business as a whole" '.[64] She goes on to quote Votaw as observing, in a manner very reminiscent of some commentaries on the public interest discussed in Chapter One, that CSR 'means something, but not always the same thing to everybody'.[65]

However, such confusion has not prevented the concept being adopted by the United Nations, the European Union, and the UK's Department of Trade and Industry. By way of example, the EU's 2001 Green Paper states,

Most definitions of corporate social responsibility describe it as a concept whereby companies integrate social and environmental concerns in their business operations and in their interaction with their stakeholders on a voluntary basis.

Being socially responsible means not only fulfilling legal expectations, but also going beyond compliance ...[66]

Some key characteristics are revealed here. In particular, it is important to note, first, the essentially voluntary nature of CSR,[67] implying, beyond legal responsibility, a degree of corporate virtue, and second, the significance of 'stakeholders'. We will return to both, but must note immediately that though the Commission's statement may seem to offer a remarkably straightforward vision, it must properly be viewed as failing to take into account some genuine confusion, noted above, as regards the nature and extent of the implications of CSR.

Even the origins of the concept of CSR are somewhat unclear, being traceable certainly to Bowen's coinage in the 1950s, but arguably originating in the 1930s

[63] Whitehouse, L., 'Corporate Social Responsibility as Citizenship and Compliance', *Journal of Corporate Citizenship*, 11 (2003), 85, at 88.

[64] Whitehouse, L., 'Corporate Social Responsibility, Corporate Citizenship and the Global Compact', *Global Social Policy*, 3/3 (2003), 299, at 301.

[65] Ibid., quoting Votaw, D., 'Genius Becomes Rare', in Votaw, D. and Sethi, S. P. (eds.), *The Corporate Dilemma: Traditional Values and Contemporary Problems*, (Eaglewood Cliffs, NJ: Prentice Hall, 1973), 9.

[66] European Communities, Commission, *Promoting a European Framework for Corporate Social Responsibility*, Green Paper, COM (2001) 366 final, 6.

[67] Confirmed by Department of Trade and Industry, Business and Society: Corporate Social Responsibility Report (London: HMSO, 2002), 7; also United Nations, Global Compact Office, *The Global Compact: Corporate Leadership in the World Economy* (New York, N.Y.: United Nations, 2001), 1.

in the work of Berle and of Dodd,[68] and drawing on the seminal observations of Berle and Means on the separation of ownership and control.[69] It is, however, far from unchanging, and if Hemingway is right to suggest that 'the formal adoption of CSR by corporations is associated with the changing personal views of managers',[70] it must certainly be viewed as a slippery and flimsy concept. There is no doubt that measurable performance indicators in relation to CSR are difficult to find. While the organization Business in the Community may produce an annual Corporate Responsibility Index, this seems to focus on matters such as environmental performance and charitable giving, and it is much more difficult to assess or monitor performance in sectors such as the media, where companies may seek to emphasize their social responsibility by reference to their wider, but sometimes intangible, social role.[71] Though Carroll may identify four faces of a CSR pyramid, reflecting economic, legal, ethical and philanthropic aspects,[72] this vision is also clearly not uncontestable.

However, the waters appear to be muddied in particular by discussion of CSR and corporate citizenship, which are sometimes used interchangeably, and sometimes by way of distinction. As noted above, Whitehouse believes that 'corporate citizenship can best be explained as a version of CSR' in that it 'merely reflects some of the characteristics apparent within CSR'.[73] McIntosh et al., however, discuss a 'perceived transition from CSR to corporate citizenship', the latter term involving,

[C]orporations becoming more informed and enlightened members of society and understanding that they are both public and private entities. Whether they like it or not they are created by society and derive their legitimacy from the societies in which they operate. They need to be able to articulate their role, scope and purpose, as well as understand their full social and environmental impacts and responsibilities.[74]

On this construction, corporate citizenship may seem to set a more demanding burden on business than that suggested by statements on CSR of the kind quoted from the EU Green Paper, above. Rather than the voluntarism, emphasized in most visions of CSR, companies are in effect *required* to legitimate their

---

[68] See Wood, D. J. and Logsdon, J. M., 'Theorising Business Citizenship', in Andriof, J. and McIntosh, M. (eds.), *Perspectives on Corporate Citizenship* (Sheffield: Greenleaf, 2001); Whitehouse 'CSR as Citizenship and Compliance'; Hemingway, C., 'An Exploratory Analysis of Corporate Social Responsibility: Definitions, Motives and Values' 2002, *University of Hull Business School Memorandum*, 34.

[69] Berle, A. and Means, G., *The Modern Corporation and Private Property* (New York, N.Y.: Harcourt, Brace and World, 1932).   [70] Hemingway, 'An Exploratory Analysis', 19.

[71] See 'Communication with Care', *The Guardian*, 15 March 2004.

[72] Carroll, A. B., 'The Pyramid of Corporate Social Responsibility: Toward the Moral Management of Organizational Stakeholders', *Business Horizons* (Indiana University Graduate Business School) 34/4 (1991), 39. See also Carroll, A. B., 'The Moral Leader: Essential for Successful Corporate Citizenship', in Andriof, J. and McIntosh, M. (eds.), *Perspectives on Corporate Citizenship* (Sheffield: Greenleaf, 2001).   [73] Whitehouse 'CSR as Citizenship and Compliance', 88.

[74] McIntosh, M., Thomas, R., Leipziger, D. and Coleman, G., *Living Corporate Citizenship*, (London: Pearson Education, 2003), 16.

activity by reference to social values. However, Wood and Logsdon offer an alternative perspective, observing that the terms sometimes appear to be used synonymously, but suggesting that corporate citizenship may in fact suggest a narrower view, concerning 'a much smaller group of stakeholders and issues'.[75] They identify the potential for 'corporate social responsibility's emphasis on big sociopolitical issues' being replaced within corporate citizenship by 'a narrow focus on "sticking to the knitting" of business and getting involved in community affairs if the company wants to'.[76]

Corporate citizenship may therefore be viewed as either a narrower and better defined construct than CSR, or a thinner and still vague concept. However, Whitehouse seems to argue that neither construct pays sufficient attention to the need to harness an element of compulsion, or compliance, alongside the voluntarism that ultimately underlies most visions of CSR and corporate citizenship.[77] This weakness may be a result of inherent difficulties in pinning down the concept's normative content, or it may simply reflect the market-oriented *zeitgeist*.

Inevitably, the strongest proponents of market-liberalism, who emphasize that the primary responsibility of business is to increase its profits,[78] are likely to see in any vision of CSR, but especially a legally enforceable version, a 'fundamentally subversive doctrine'.[79] Henderson is only marginally less strident in his criticism of CSR and defence of profit-making:

> For a business enterprise, whether private or public, to concern itself directly and predominantly with profits is not to show undue regard for owners as distinct from 'stakeholders' in general, to slight other worthy objectives, or to allow greed to govern its actions. It means focusing on the most obvious measure of the value *to society* of what that enterprise is doing.[80]

Any apparent disregard of the social consequences of commercial activity together with the emphasis placed on the value *to society* of profit-making, especially when combined with a reliance on voluntarism, seems ultimately to imply a strong belief in what has recently been persuasively described as the 'superstition' of trickle-down or 'supply-side' economics.[81] This cannot be sufficient to discharge the burden placed on companies to establish, in Parkinson's terms noted in Chapter One,[82] that the possession of their social decision-making powers is

---

[75] Wood and Logsdon, 'Theorising Business Citizenship', 85.   [76] Ibid. at 86.

[77] Whitehouse 'CSR as Citizenship and Compliance', 94 *et seq.*

[78] Friedman, M., 'The Social Responsibility of Business is to Increase its Profits', *New York Times Magazine*, 13 September 1970, reproduced in Hoffman, W. M. and Frederick, R. E. (eds.), *Business Ethics: Readings and Cases in Corporate Morality*, 3rd edn. (New York, N.Y.: McGraw-Hill, 1995).

[79] Friedman, M., *Capitalism and Freedom* (Chicago, IL.: University of Chicago Press, 1969), 133, quoted in Whitehouse, 'CSR as Citizenship and Compliance', 87.

[80] Henderson, D., *Misguided Virtue: False Notions of Corporate Social Responsibility* (London: Institute of Economic Affairs, 2001), 158, original emphasis.

[81] See Wheen, F., *How Mumbo-Jumbo Conquered the World: a Short History of Modern Delusions* (London: Fourth Estate, 2004), 18.

[82] Parkinson, *Corporate Power and Responsibility*, 23.

in the public interest. However, debates over CSR must properly be viewed in the current context of the dominance of market values.

Based on their vision of corporate citizenship as a diluted version of CSR, Wood and Logsdon consider how the two concepts relate differently to the neo-classical economic model. They find CSR, which 'considers the moral and legal obligations to have precedence over self-interest' inevitably to be at odds with this economic vision, while corporate citizenship 'is compatible with standard economic analysis', in that '[i]t supports both "compassionate conservatism" and "constrained liberalism" given that voluntaristic charity is possible and supportable but not essential or obligatory'.[83] Meanwhile, Robert Reich identifies within the CSR debate a line of argument, apparently related to trickle-down approaches, as to 'long-term convergence' of corporate profitability and social objectives, though ultimately he finds it 'simply too broad and ill-defined'.[84] Whether or not we accept Wood and Logsdon's account of the contours of the two concepts, or Reich's conclusions, such analysis of CSR's relationship to market economics is extremely helpful, and may go some way towards explaining the lack of compulsion attaching to the concept(s) identified by Whitehouse, and hence its limitations.

It is surely right to observe that the absence of measures requiring compliance with expectations of CSR 'derives in part from the failure on the part of advocates of CSR to reach consensus as to the norms that should inform such a regime'.[85] However, statements such as the UN Global Compact and the EU's Green Paper make clear that CSR has 'a strong human rights dimension, particularly in relation to international operations and global supply chains',[86] highlighting a range of values that would generally be considered too fundamental to be left to voluntary initiatives alone. In addition, it is possible to observe a value base which underlies the concept in a general sense. It is commonly seen as enhancing the legitimacy of corporate activity,[87] and may be 'grounded in ethical theory' that implies 'obligations of fairness'.[88] However, there are a series of questions raised by such approaches, and indeed by the use of the concept of 'citizenship' in this connection. How is legitimacy to be established? To whom are obligations or responsibilities owed? Given that the concept of citizenship can only be made sense of within the context of a political community, what is the nature of the community within which the corporation is a 'citizen' and from which entitlements of citizenship derive, and to which duties of citizenship and expectation of virtue relate? The absence of adequate answers to these questions seems to underlie the lack of normative specificity which commentators identify.

---

[83] Wood and Logsdon, 'Theorising Business Citizenship', 86.

[84] Reich, R., 'The New Meaning of Corporate Social Responsibility', *California Management Review*, 40/2 (1998), 8, at 12.   [85] Whitehouse, 'CSR as Citizenship and Compliance', 95.

[86] Commission, *Promoting a European Framework for CSR*, 13.

[87] See Votaw, 'Genius Becomes Rare'.

[88] Van Buren III, H., 'Corporate Citizenship and Obligations of Fairness', *Journal of Corporate Citizenship*, 3 (2001), 55.

The fundamental issue underlying all of these questions seems to be that of understanding a concept of 'community', for it is from this basis that legitimacy, social obligations and 'citizenship' expectations flow. The EC Green Paper states that,

Corporate social responsibility extends beyond the doors of the company into the local community and involves a wide range of stakeholders in addition to employees and shareholders: business partners and suppliers, customers, public authorities and NGOs representing local communities, as well as the environment. In a world of multinational investment and global supply chains, corporate social responsibility must also extend beyond the borders of Europe.[89]

The difficulty in establishing the range of constituencies which might be expected to form a 'community' is, of course, especially problematic in the case of transnational corporations, which raise particular issues as regards the institutional framework, or legal order, within which they operate.[90] However, even the precise relationship between more local corporations, established nation-state legal orders, and ordinary citizens is in itself not unproblematic or settled. The historical transition from corporate status being acquired by grant of charter, to being simply formalized by legal incorporation was noted in Chapter One. Waddell comments on the early phase of this in the US context, noting how the Virginia Supreme Court in 1809 found that 'if the intention of the corporators is merely private or selfish; if it is detrimental to, nor not promotive of, the public good, they have no adequate claim upon the legislature for the privileges (of a corporate charter)'.[91] He goes on to note how '[s]ubsequent history is a contentious evolution of corporate rights and responsibilities', and how '[t]he corporation has fought to obtain the rights of a natural entity like a person, rather than be a creation of the state and subject to it'.[92]

As noted in Chapter Two, Craig provides a comparative commentary on the early development of UK and US law concerning the relationship between the private property interests of corporations and public interests in that property.[93] Though the context of much of the US case-law is that of positions of monopoly, and what was later to be described as 'essential facilities',[94] Craig notes how courts found that 'the possession of monopoly power, whether *de jure* in the form of a grant of a franchise, or *de facto*, placed constraints on the manner of its exercise'.[95] Though British cases must, of course, be considered outside the context of the US Constitution, Craig identifies the influence of British case law on the seminal US cases, and observes that the absence of a coherent body of

---

[89] Commission, *Promoting a European Framework for CSR*, 11.

[90] See Lewis, N. D., *Law and Governance* (London: Cavendish, 2001), especially Ch. 10.

[91] Waddell, S., 'New Institutions for the Practice of Corporate Citizenship: Historical, Intersectoral, and Developmental Perspectives', *Business and Society Review*, 105/1 (2000), 107, at 108. [92] Ibid.

[93] Craig, 'Constitutions, Property and Regulation'.

[94] See discussion of *Munn v. Illinois* (1877) 94 US 139, and related text in Chs. One and Two.

[95] Craig, 'Constitutions, Property and Regulation', 553.

more recent case law in this area in UK law 'should not ... be taken to mean that the common law is devoid of any notion of public property rights. As in many other areas of common law, we find strands of authority which may have been developed at different times and which only appear to encapsulate a broader principle when woven together.'[96]

In Waddell's terms, the changing relationship between state and corporation has been characterized by 'a corporate drive to maintain and increase its rights',[97] as part of what he calls 'this ad-hoc evolution of [a] corporate citizenship framework'.[98] Again, this implies a set of relationships of rights and responsibilities as between the corporation, the state, and other members of the community at large, and raises questions of legitimacy in relation to both corporate power and its regulation. However, there is a strong tendency in the literature of CSR to reduce debate over the scope of the corporation as citizen to one of discussion of stakeholders,[99] and to place emphasis on transparency of operation in relation to stakeholders in order that they can more effectively push corporations in the direction of CSR.[100] Unfortunately, the outer-bounds of 'stakeholders', that is, those with an interest in the activities of a corporation, are scarcely easier to draw, or any less contestable, than is the concept of the community within which the corporation might be considered a 'citizen'. Ultimately, debates over stakeholding have done little to enlighten as to the extent of the responsibilities of the 'corporation as citizen'.

It can reasonably be concluded that the ongoing debate over CSR has little to offer in this respect. Indeed, the appeal to voluntary action beyond legal requirements, which is perhaps the one genuine defining characteristic of CSR, may appear ultimately to be bolstered only by appeal to enlightened self-interest rather than any real sense of obligation, responsibility or virtue. As the EC Green Paper observes, reflecting the phenomenon of convergence of corporations' and society's interests considered by Robert Reich, noted above, 'A number of companies with good social and environmental records indicate that these activities can result in better performance and can generate more profits and growth.'[101] It is obvious that we are here on the very cusp of self-interest and virtue, and also that of the legal requirements and limitations placed upon citizens and the moral obligations which extend beyond them.

A cynical observer might reasonably conclude at this point that a concept of CSR properly-so-called would only start at the point where it actively cut across corporate interests, in pursuit of social values. A parallel might be drawn with

---

[96] Craig, 'Constitutions, Property and Regulation' at 555.

[97] Waddell, 'New Institutions', 109.   [98] Ibid., at p.110.

[99] See, for example, Waddock, S. and Smith, N., 'Relationships: The Real Challenge of Corporate Global Citizenship', *Business and Society Review*, 105/1 (2000) 47; also many of the other works on CSR referred to in this section.

[100] See Joseph, E., 'Promoting Corporate Social Responsibility: Is Market-Based Regulation Sufficient?', *New Economy* (Institute for Public Policy Research), (2002), 96.

[101] Commission, *Promoting a European Framework for CSR*, 7.

Bell's observation that, 'The public interest is used to describe where the net interests of particular individuals may not be advanced, but where something necessary to the development of the community is secured.'[102] However, it seems clear that as it stands, CSR, whether expressed under that name or that of corporate citizenship, which implies, but does not require, adherence to social duties and values, is essentially an appeal to some combination of altruism and enlightened self-interest. As such, it must be concluded that CSR initiatives fail to address to any meaningful extent the potentially damaging excesses of corporate power. Such initiatives may certainly be expected to have some impact in terms of enhancing perceptions of legitimacy in corporate activity, and may, in so far as they effectively encourage philanthropy, have some positive effects in relation to ameliorating social problems. However, their reliance on voluntarism, deriving to a large extent from a lack of normative clarity on which to legitimate more strident responses, combined with the current context of dominance of market values, leaves corporations essentially free to pursue their perceived self-interest, enlightened or otherwise. Just as it is inadequate in the market context to exhort monopolists not to take advantage of their dominant position, and instead the exhortation is given enforceable form in competition law, it is implausible and dangerous to leave the protection of democratic values, including on occasion fundamental human rights, to a regime based on voluntariness. Just as with 'the public interest', if CSR is to serve to protect democratic values such as equality of citizenship, these legitimate interests require clear articulation, and most likely need embodying in legal institutions which are designed explicitly to promote the polity's fundamental principles.

PUBLIC SERVICE LAW

Of all the subjects to be considered in this chapter, public service law appears to be most immediately related to the concept of public interest as defined in this book. In Chapter Three, reference was made to a reasonably well-established model of social regulation in the public interest, in the particular context of interventions into the provision of public utilities in the UK. Though such goods and services, considered fundamental to social and citizenship expectations, have, historically, in Britain and much of Western Europe, been delivered by publicly owned bodies, often with monopoly power, more recent times have seen a shift to their provision via private corporations subject to regulatory supervision, the latter, as noted by Majone,[103] providing a degree of 'functional equivalence' in the pursuit of social objectives. Though the shift towards privatized utilities

---

[102] Bell, J., 'Public Interest: Policy or Principle?', in Brownsword, R. (ed.), *Law and the Public Interest* (Proceedings of the 1992 ALSP Conference) (Stuttgart: Franz Steiner, 1993), 30.
[103] Majone, G., 'The Rise of the Regulatory State in Europe', West European Politics, 17 (1994), 77, reproduced in Baldwin, R., Scott, C., and Hood, C. (eds.), *A Reader on Regulation* (Oxford: Oxford University Press, 1998).

reflects the dominance of market ideology from the Thatcher era onwards, '[t]he theory of the social market economy, at its core, is that market institutions are always embedded in other social and political institutions, which both shape and legitimate them.'[104] If this is so, it might reasonably be expected that legal institutions would have an important part to play in ensuring that citizenship concerns are given due prominence alongside economic concerns when regulation is undertaken.

Graham addresses the issue via consideration of 'the growing importance of citizenship issues, rights issues, in utility regulation.'[105] He acknowledges the historical truism that 'British public law has been hostile to a rights-based discourse in the past',[106]; however, he then goes on to draw on general arguments as regards economic rights associated with conventionally expressed citizenship expectations, such as those identified by Marshall. He also considers the extent to which the Human Rights Act 1998, incorporating the ECHR into UK law (at least in respect of vertical effect), may impact upon regulatory intervention, and discusses how developments in European Union law in relation to utilities may contribute to regulation taking place within a framework of rights. The essence of his argument is that 'as well as being a consumer of utility services, the individual also has the rights of a citizen in regard to these services',[107] the claim which underlies the imposition of Universal Service Obligations and the like.

The recognition and embodiment in law of such rights is the perspective taken up by Prosser when he identifies and discusses 'a new growth of public service law in relation to the privatized utilities',[108] a body of law which 'is based on egalitarian rights derived from citizenship rather than an ability to bid in the marketplace'.[109] Prosser acknowledges though that such an approach is much less well embedded in British legal and constitutional thought than in other European states such as France or Italy, where well-established concepts of *service public* and *servizio pubblico* respectively, 'provide a strong jurisprudential base for social regulation'.[110] He finds that in French public law, 'public service is an activity in the general interest, provided by a public or private actor and subject to a special legal regime (requiring equality of treatment, adaptation to changing needs and security of supply etc.)',[111] and notes how the Conseil d'État has identified the essence of *service public* in terms of 'a means of consolidation of the social contract and of social solidarity, that it contributes to some types

---

[104] Gray, J., *The Moral Foundations of Market Institutions* (London: Institute of Economic Affairs, 1992), quoted in Lewis, N., 'Markets, Regulation and Citizenship: a Constitutional Analysis', in Brownsword, R. (ed.), *Law and the Public Interest* (Proceedings of the 1992 ALSP Conference) (Stuttgart: Franz Steiner, 1993), 116.

[105] Graham, C., *Regulating Public Utilities: a Constitutional Approach* (Oxford: Hart Publishing, 2000) at 129, and Ch. 7, generally.   [106] Ibid., 149.

[107] Ibid., 130.

[108] Prosser, T., 'Public Service Law: Privatization's Unexpected Offspring', *Law and Contemporary Problems*, 63/4 (2000), 63, at 63.   [109] Ibid.

[110] Prosser, T., *Law and the Regulators* (Oxford: Clarendon, 1997), at 287.

[111] Ibid., 288.

of redistribution and of transfers between social groups'.[112] He observes closely parallel legal responses in Italy.[113]

In considering such measures, Prosser observes that, when compared to the situation in Britain, these constitute 'a fuller recognition of the plurality of regulatory goals through the establishment of a relatively sophisticated case law dealing with the social requirements of public service, and suggesting that there is something different about basic services linked to citizenship'.[114] Despite the absence of a strong legal tradition of this kind in Britain, and despite conflicts within the EU which he identifies as arising out of differing degrees of legal protection of public services across the Member States, Prosser concludes that the introduction of independent regulators to oversee the privatized utilities in Britain, has combined with EU drives to open up utility markets and ensure the separation of regulation from operation of the enterprise, to create a space in which '[c]ontinental public service concerns have infiltrated this liberalization'.[115] By way of example, though he identifies limitations regarding the extent of application of the Utilities Act 2000, he notes that the overarching duty applying to energy regulators by virtue of Section 9,[116] which expresses the duty in terms of a broad definition of consumers, serves to permit (and indeed in some circumstances to require) regulators 'to take social considerations into account'.[117] He concludes that, 'It is clear that we are now seeing the beginning of the replacement of ineffective political controls over public enterprise by legal principles that include elements of social solidarity and rights of access to essential services.'[118]

From the perspective adopted in this book, and considered in Chapter Three particularly in relation to the range of interests associated with the public service broadcasting tradition, even fairly generous constructs of consumer interests cannot be expected to equate with the wider range of concerns associated with citizenship. That said, it is clear that the development of public service law, as described by Prosser, does have some potential in terms of serving the democratic expectation of equality of citizenship. It was suggested earlier in this chapter that the concept of public interest may have a role to play in relation to fostering nascent legal rights associated with citizenship. It is unclear whether the application of a concept of public interest of the kind advocated in this book, directly associated with such expectations, would bring anything of value to the debate in this particular context. If the prognosis arrived at by the likes of Prosser and Graham is right, that such interests may become adequately served by existing

[112] Ibid., 289.   [113] Ibid., 291.   [114] Ibid., 292.
[115] Prosser, 'Public Service Law', 82.
[116] The Section 9 duty requires regulators 'to protect the interests of consumers, wherever possible and appropriate, through promoting effective competition. The interests of consumers should be interpreted to include prices and conditions of supply, continuity and availability of supply, quality of supply, and, where relevant, the range of services offered. In defining the interests of consumers, due weight should be given to their long-term and medium-term interests as well as to their immediate or short-term interests.'   [117] Prosser, 'Public Service Law', 74.
[118] Ibid., 82.

and developing legal provisions relating to social regulation, and the development more generally of a rights-based discourse, then the answer is likely to be 'no'. However, if experience demonstrates that practical outcomes do not reflect the, still somewhat implicit, public service ideal reflected in the regulation of utilities, or if there are perceived problems observed with the development or bedding-down of public service law in Britain, it may be that the importation of a concept of public interest, explicitly linked to citizenship expectations, may yet have a salutary role to play.

PRIVATE PROPERTY AND THE PUBLIC INTEREST

Much of the debate in this book, including but going far beyond the questions of CSR discussed earlier in this chapter, has revolved around power associated with ownership of private property and the conflicts which arise between such power and democratic, often collective, interests. The relationship between the state and private interests expressed via property ownership has been raised repeatedly, in relation to the need, within and in pursuit of the objectives of liberal democracy, to ensure that the property rights associated with liberalism do not overwhelm the citizenship-related expectations of democracy. In Chapters One and Two, the debate was expressed largely in terms of the need to curtail property rights in pursuit of this agenda, yet the kind of social rights associated with public service law appear to suggest a different perspective which considers the development of a new series of *positive* rights.

In the context of regulation of utilities, access to which can be deemed essential to any meaningful construct of citizenship in modern times, Graham identifies two key questions: '[W]hat deal do we offer citizens in terms of access to utility services and to what extent are we prepared to interfere with private property rights to accomplish this deal and other public policy ends?'[119] The implication of this is the establishment within the political settlement of social rights that would not have existed, in terms of being recognized as such, a couple of generations previously. Graham considers arguments that amount to claims that 'social and economic rights have no place in a constitution',[120] but sketches out an opposing argument, drawing on Gewirth, which makes a case which amounts to a claim that 'every person has equal rights to freedom and well-being as the necessary conditions of action and successful action in general'.[121] While this abstract argument is in itself persuasive, and well worthy of further consideration and development in this context, Graham also seeks to ground his argument in more concrete terms, via an examination of the developing jurisprudence arising both from the HRA, which finally permitted UK courts to give effect to most of the provisions contained in the ECHR in the domestic setting,

[119] Graham, *Regulating Public Utilities*, 197.   [120] Ibid., and generally Ch. 7.
[121] Ibid., 134.

and from developments in EC law relating to utilities policy which appear to point towards the legal recognition of social rights and obligations. The key example he offers in relation to this latter area of development is the requirement imposed by the Voice Telephony Directive, relating to requirements as to universal service. Graham quotes the relevant provision,[122] and comments that

Member States are directed to maintain, in particular, the affordability of services for users in high cost or rural areas, those with disabilities and those with 'special social needs.' This last phrase is critical because, although it is not defined in the directive, it has been taken, by the Department of Trade and Industry, to refer to low-income consumers.[123]

Though Graham acknowledges the limited scope and development of such legal requirements to date, he also observes that 'their further elucidation may come in something akin to, if not identical with, a legally enforceable right'.[124] It could be added that the law relating to the EU's agenda on social policy may also, in general, be thought to point in this direction.[125]

Though less developed than the corpus of law within the French or Italian public service law tradition discussed by Prosser, it is clear that the sort of social regulation now associated with utility services in Britain looks remarkably like the legal recognition of a new series of enforceable rights. It can be argued that far from posing constitutional difficulties, the development and recognition of such rights even in the face of the dominance of market-liberal ideology, represents a proper constitutional response in recognition of democratic values. Indeed, this kind of development has some echoes of Charles Reich's innovative and provocative thesis on 'The New Property'.[126]

Reich's opening sentence observes that, 'The institution called property guards the troubled boundary between individual man and the state.' Thus, essentially constitutional questions regarding property must properly be considered in relation to citizenship, which patrols much the same zone, and hence the concept of public interest developed in previous chapters of this book. Though acknowledging the 'incomplete and tentative' nature of his thesis, in considering a shift from 'government largess' (*sic*) to the development of property rights in that which had previously been essentially considered grace and favour provision of social and economic benefits, Reich opens up a potentially significant perspective. From his viewpoint,

Ahead there stretches – to the farthest horizon – the joyless landscape of the public interest state. The life it promises will be comfortable and well planned – with suitable areas for work and play. But there will be no precincts sacred to the spirit of the individual man.

There can be no retreat from the public interest state. It is the inevitable outgrowth of an interdependent world. An effort to return to an earlier economic order would merely

---

[122] Directive 98/10/EC, *Revised Voice Telephony Directive*, Article 2.2(f).
[123] Graham, *Regulating Public Utilities*, 145.   [124] Ibid., at 146.
[125] See generally, Hervey, T., *European Social Law and Policy* (Harlow: Addison Wesley Longman, 1998).   [126] Reich, C., 'The New Property', *Yale Law Journal*, 73 (1964), 733.

transfer power to giant private governments which would rule not in the public interest, but in their own interest.[127]

Three aspects of this view are worthy of emphasis. First, it is clear that Reich's perspective is heavily based upon a perceived threat to individualism posed by a 'welfare state' in which government largesse 'must play a major role', indeed 'will be an ever more important form of wealth'. He notes and makes great play on the idea that just as all personal property in a sense derives from government largesse, in that grants of land originate from the largesse of the sovereign power, so it is possible to conceive of modern social and economic benefits also as examples of largesse which can (and should) be translated into, or encapsulated within, the idea of enforceable property rights. In serving the function of forming 'a boundary between public and private power' and by 'draw[ing] a circle around the activities of each private individual or organization',[128] such rights, suggests Reich, would promote individual freedom.

Second, in the context of this book, it is especially necessary to consider his use of 'the public interest', which, as noted in passing in Chapter One, he uses in essence as a synonym for the large, interventionist modern state, which he considers to have huge potential for negative impact upon the independence of the individual.

Third, and finally, the time in which Reich was writing was one of an apparently ever-expanding state, to which his writing was one response. However, his views on the consequence of any future withdrawal of the state, which would hand over power to private power blocs, can be seen, in light of the discussion in Chapter Six, to have demonstrated remarkable foresight.

The essence of Reich's argument is, of course, that of the necessity for social rights originating from largesse becoming 'vested' as property rights:

The concept of right is most urgently needed with respect to benefits like unemployment compensation, public assistance, and old age insurance. These benefits are based upon a recognition that misfortune and deprivation are often caused by forces beyond the control of the individual, such as technological change, variation in demands for goods, depressions, or wars. The aim of these benefits is to preserve the self-sufficiency of the individual, to rehabilitate him where necessary, and to allow him to be a valuable member of a family and community; in theory they represent part of the individual's rightful share in the commonwealth. Only by making such benefits into rights can the welfare state achieve its goal of providing a secure minimum basis for individual well-being and dignity in a society where each man cannot be wholly the master of his own destiny.[129]

Inevitably, over the forty years since it was written, Reich's approach has been subjected to criticism as it has gone in and out of fashion. The underlying emphasis on individualism can certainly be viewed as problematic, understating

---

[127] Reich, C., 'The New Property', *Yale Law Journal*, 73 (1964), 778.
[128] Ibid., 771.   [129] Ibid., 785.

the difficulties observed in Rabin's observation that 'Those who would exercise their individuality without constraint often would do so at the expense of others.'[130] As a result, it can be argued that his perspective understates the potential benefits which may accrue from the administrative law system, an aspect of the 'big state', which may, if subject to adequate procedural safeguards, actually be viewed as serving properly social and democratic objectives of limiting power, rather than undermining individual liberty:

> While government largess programs at times have been hedged with conditions the dominant purpose of which is to discourage nonconformist behaviour as an end in itself, other programs feature limitations designed to assure that largess will not be used in a fashion that poses risks to the health and safety of others. In the latter kind of cases, where the administrative program is designed to promote a conscientious pattern of conduct rather than a conformist mode of behaviour, a more refined conception of due process, as well as a system of internal bureaucratic controls, is essential to safeguard effectively against arbitrary official conduct.[131]

Sunstein notes that 'For the Supreme Court to undertake to protect welfare rights on its own would raise extremely serious questions of democratic legitimacy', but also that, where welfare rights are grounded in a statutory framework, 'Aggressive statutory construction ... might produce many of the advantages of recognition of constitutional welfare rights without imposing nearly so severe a strain on the judiciary.'[132]

In reality, it is Reich's use of the label 'property' which may be seen as the fundamental problem underlying his thesis. Harris observes that 'Even if there were sound public law strategic reasons for calling reformed largesse "property", we would still need to be clear that it is not property in the traditional sense.'[133] By this, Harris is asking whether the entitlements should be considered cashable or tradeable, or should form part of the individual's bankruptcy estate or be attachable by judgment creditors, and concludes that 'more confusion than light is achieved if we describe the entitlements themselves as "property", unless we really wanted them to take the form of cashable rights'.[134]

Reich's approach may also be considered problematic in terms of its failure to focus attention on the threat to individualist values posed *by* private property power. As Robertson states, 'This reflects the tendency of liberal thought to see the state rather than private property as the problem which needs to be dealt with when it comes to individual freedom.'[135] Curiously, of course, Reich's

---

[130] Rabin, R., 'The Administrative State and its Excesses: Reflections on The New Property', *University of San Francisco Law Review*, 25 (1990) 273; extracts reproduced in Schuck, P. H., *Foundations of Administrative Law* (Oxford: Oxford University Press, 1994), 123.

[131] Ibid., at 124.   [132] Sunstein, *After the Rights Revolution*, 168.

[133] Harris, J., 'Is Property a Human Right?', in McLean, J. (ed.), *Property and the Constitution* (Oxford: Hart Publishing, 1999), 74.   [134] Ibid.

[135] Robertson, M., 'Liberal, Democratic, and Socialist Approaches to the Public Dimensions of Private Property', in McLean, J. (ed.), *Property and the Constitution* (Oxford: Hart Publishing, 1999), 246.

approach also aligns in some ways with certain republican lines of thought, notably Harrington's, which emphasize the centrality of private property ownership to the citizen's autonomy.[136]

Though an important landmark in debates over property, Reich's challenging thesis has perhaps not received the attention it might deserve. Robertson observes how, though Reich 'fully embraces the core values of classical liberalism – the autonomy of the individual and the key role of private property in preserving that autonomy ... he has pushed against the structure of liberal thought to an extent which renders his work a provocative but marginal oddity to most mainstream liberal thinkers who remain more firmly embedded within that tradition'.[137] Though Reich's work is most obviously a response to what he perceived as problems arising out of 'the public interest state', it can also serve, when reflected upon, as a salutary warning to the risks of an alternative situation in which private property power is unconstrained. It is in this sense to a great degree consistent with the agenda established in this book in terms of a quest for a concept of public interest, within the mainstream of liberal–democratic thought, which serves the expectations of equality of citizenship within a political community. This value-set can be seen as represented, albeit in limited forms, by the ongoing recognition of social rights. Thus, despite his attack on 'the public interest state', in seeking to reconceptualize property rights in such a way as to incorporate within them expectations which serve equality of citizenship, Reich's line of argument might actually seem to offer some support for the construct of public interest proposed in this book, and seems worthy of further exploration.

PROPERTY AND STEWARDSHIP

As noted above, Reich's view can be seen as remaining solidly within a classical liberal view of property. In Robertson's terms, this means that, 'Property should be understood as belonging in the private zone where its owner decides how the asset is to be used. The state has a legitimate role in the separate public zone, but that role will only rarely require it to interfere with private property rights.'[138]

The liberal emphasis on the state as the major potential *obstacle* to individual freedom and fulfilment leads to a focus on defending property rights against state incursion. The risk here, as illustrated by Robertson's reflections on Reich, is the consequent lack of focus on adequate consideration for the threats to individual freedom, and hence equality of citizenship, posed not by the state but by concentrations in private hands of power derived from property ownership.

---

[136] See Craig, P. P., *Public Law and Democracy in the United Kingdom and the United States of America* (Oxford: Oxford University Press, 1990), 321.

[137] Robertson, 'Public Dimensions of Private Property', 245.   [138] Ibid., 241.

Alternative visions of property, reflecting collective rather than individualistic approaches can be found in the school of thought described as 'market socialism'. In general terms market socialist approaches, though emphasizing the problems posed by markets in terms of distributive justice, also identify benefits in the operations of markets with regard to information systems, incentive systems, and, overarching such matters, freedom. The essence of the market socialist approach is captured by Miller, when he notes that 'a market is a highly efficient mechanism for controlling the production of goods and services, but that the distribution of welfare that a market generates depends on the framework of public institutions – property rights, investment agencies, tax systems – which surrounds it'.[139] Such a formulation avoids what Roemer identifies as the 'fetish of public ownership'[140] associated with many schools of socialist thought, while emphasizing a significant role for the state in regulating private property in pursuit of egalitarian objectives. Interestingly, from the perspective adopted in this book, Roemer also emphasizes the role of the constitution in relation to property, observing that 'a regime of market socialism might well be characterized by its constitution, which might limit the permissible accumulation of private property in productive assets and perhaps explicitly describe other kinds of property that are (constitutionally) protected'.[141] Inevitably, Roemer's vision is not uncontested from within the socialist movement, with one critique being that of Levine, who observes that 'at least some socialists, those whose political and theoretical positions derive from Marx, want something that liberals do not and that liberal theory cannot properly accommodate: they want *communism*'.[142] Levine is left to doubt whether 'in the absence of a political vision that transcends the liberal egalitarian horizon, Roemer's proposed reforms, whatever their merits, can help get us from where we now are to where socialists ultimately want to be'.[143] To a significant extent, discontent with the market socialist approach, from the Left, derives from its development in association with a liberal tradition. Thus, though market socialists 'have developed many of the themes of the liberal egalitarian tradition, in particular reconciling the principles of social justice with those of market allocation',[144] the accusation levelled at market socialism from some quarters, in some ways similar to criticisms made of Reich's approach, is therefore that it fails to escape from the powerful gravitational hold of liberalism.

However, talk even of 'softer' forms of market socialism is considered akin to heresy under the current hegemony of market-liberalism, with New Labour's

---

[139] Miller, D., 'Why Markets?', in Le Grand and Estrin, *Market Socialism*, 32.

[140] Roemer, *A Future for Socialism*, 20.   [141] Ibid., 110.

[142] Levine, A., 'Saving Socialism and/or Abandoning It', in Wright, *Equal Shares*, 232, original emphasis. Levine makes clear in his footnote that in his conventional usage '(small-c) communism should not be confused with (big-C) Communism, the economic, social and political system formerly in place in the erstwhile Soviet Union and elsewhere'.   [143] Ibid.

[144] Gamble, A. and Kelly, G., 'The New Politics of Ownership', *New Left Review*, 220, (1996), 62. See also Gamble, A. and Kelly, G., 'Owners and Citizens', *Political Quarterly*, 69/4 (1998), 344.

'Third Way' politics appearing to be consciously distanced from the Party's socialist origins. Gamble and Kelly identify how 'there has long been a revisionist strand in the Labour Party which has rejected the traditional commitment to common ownership, but it has been generally uninterested in the question of private ownership'.[145] In pursuit of 'the project of an egalitarian market economy'[146] without recourse to public ownership of productive assets, Gamble and Kelly seek to undertake the necessary prior task of developing 'a distinctive approach to private ownership'.[147]

They observe that ownership of purely private property, goods of final consumption, is relatively uncontroversial, though even here, changing social norms and values may lead to arguments as to the appropriate legal response.[148] However, Gamble and Kelly are at pains to distinguish this kind of private property from 'impersonal or social property, which includes ownership of productive assets' and where the extent of 'ownership' can be contested. While in common usage, ownership may be thought to refer to unlimited 'full rights of use, of income, and of alienation', they observe that 'Such pure forms of ownership, however, are a rarity in modern economies'.[149] Noting in passing the possibility of different ways of classifying the rights associated with ownership,[150] they comment in particular on the consequences of 'the separation of legal ownership from control of productive assets caused by the rise of the joint-stock company as the dominant form of capital'.[151] Given the position which results, observed by Berle and Means[152] in the US over 70 years ago, that managers are thus 'the effective possessors of the company',[153] Gamble and Kelly go on to ask 'Does such legal ownership still matter? Or is the real issue ensuring that there is effective accountability and monitoring of corporate decision-making?'[154]

Their conclusion in effect is that any egalitarian market economy requires mechanisms of inclusion, 'that citizens acquire a stake in society by giving them opportunities and rights to participate through programmes which deliver employment, welfare and education'.[155] Via constructs such as stakeholder companies it is possible to implement such a vision, but 'if this vision is to have substance, then it requires utilizing the rights associated with ownership rather than seeking to suppress them'.[156] Inevitably, defining the range of stakeholders in companies providing 'public interest services'[157] is not without problems,

---

[145] Gamble and Kelly, 'The New Politics of Ownership', 63.   [146] Ibid., 64.
[147] Ibid., 63.
[148] See Storey, A., 'Compensation for Banned Handguns: Indemnifying "Old Property"', *Modern Law Review*, 61 (1998), 188.   [149] Gamble and Kelly, 'The New Politics of Ownership', 72.
[150] Ibid. They refer to Honoré, A., 'Ownership', in Guest, A. (ed.), *Oxford Essays in Jurisprudence* (Oxford: Oxford University Press, 1961); also Tawney, R. H., *The Acquisitive Society* (London: Collins, 1961).   [151] Gamble and Kelly, 'The New Politics of Ownership', 74.
[152] Berle and Means, *The Modern Corporation*.
[153] Hirst, P., 'Ownership and Democracy', *Political Quarterly*, 69/4 (1998), 354, at 361.
[154] Gamble and Kelly, 'The New Politics of Ownership', 74.   [155] Ibid., 80.
[156] Ibid., 81.
[157] Six (6), P., 'Ownership and the New Politics of the Public Interest Services', *Political Quarterly*, 69/4 (1998), 404.

and a conventional classification in terms of 'investors, workers, consumers and other interest groups',[158] is less than helpful, especially as regards the broad final category. Howsoever they are defined, in order to be meaningful, stakeholders' rights must be located *within* the legal relationships which constitute corporations, emphasizing the need 'to devise a set of rules and institutions which can facilitate more effective *governance* of the underlying productive assets'.[159] In effect, this amounts not to a rejection of private ownership of productive assets, but a construct of ownership which shares the benefits associated with ownership across a wider range of citizens. Thus, just as it was suggested earlier in this chapter that the voluntarism of CSR must be replaced by legally enforceable norms, so, any attempts to utilize stakeholding as a means of redressing the social inequalities arising from the existing distribution of ownership rights must also be embodied in a new range of legal principles and rules.

One such potential principle is that of 'stewardship', replacing the full set of 'incidents of ownership'[160] with a more limited set of rights. This approach has been persuasively canvassed by Lucy and Mitchell.[161] In relation to the specific context of the finite and non-renewable resource of land, the application of stewardship would serve to restrict the incidents of ownership in such a way as to recognize that 'the pursuit of individual economic interests in land must be secondary to alternative land use measures designed to satisfy social and ecological criteria'.[162] Thus, the expectations of absolute power engendered by claims of 'ownership' of property are replaced by a narrower set of expectations, which are less at odds with existing legal realities under which ownership rights may in fact be subject to some restrictions, and more consistent with a more inclusive vision which incorporates values beyond private economic interests. For example, this approach may be thought to have the potential to reconcile positive competing claims such as access to land in open country, with the rights of 'ownership' or 'stewardship'.[163]

Such an approach is not, however, to deny 'stewards' all of the benefits traditionally associated with the ownership of land. Lucy and Mitchell expressly observe that,

An abstract account of stewardship maintains that the holder, or steward, has some control and rights over the resource, but that control must in the main be exercised for the benefit of others. Since the steward's control must *in the main* be exercised in favour of others, it is not the case that he must be completely selfless, an island of altruism in a sea of self-interest.[164]

[158] Ibid., at 404.
[159] Gamble and Kelly, 'The New Politics of Ownership', 88, original emphasis.
[160] See Honoré, 'Ownership'.
[161] Lucy, W. N. R. and Mitchell, C., 'Replacing Private Property: the Case for Stewardship', *Cambridge Law Journal*, 55 (1996), 566.   [162] Ibid., 598.
[163] See Barker, F. and Lucy, W., 'Justifying Property and Justifying Access', *Canadian Journal of Law and Jurisprudence*, VI/2 (1993), 287.
[164] Lucy and Mitchell, 'Replacing Private Property', 584.

Though stewardship may be reminiscent of 'trusteeship', the two must be distinguished.[165] The problems of reasoning from approximate analogies or metaphors were commented on in Chapters Four and Five, and it is clear that stewardship, in the sense used by Lucy and Mitchell, is readily distinguishable from trusteeship. Given that trustees must act exclusively in the interests of a defined group of beneficiaries, on terms established by the trust, subject only to appropriate remuneration, the legal concept of trusteeship is rendered inappropriate in relation to the kind of public interest structure being considered here, both in terms of the degree of lack of self-interest required of trustees, and the large, potentially universal, group, the interests of which are to be served.

After brief consideration of the three different accounts of the public interest identified by Virginia Held,[166] Lucy and Mitchell conclude that 'although not without meaning, the public interest idea is probably best avoided by proponents of stewardship'.[167] However, the stewardship agenda they pursue seems wholly consistent with the approach to the public interest adopted in this book. In particular, in so far as 'it seems likely that the concept of land stewardship can more easily accommodate the possibility of duties to future generations than can private property',[168] it seems to relate to one of the basic core aspects of most accounts of the public interest, and in so far as it is 'particularly responsive to the problem of satisfying basic human needs under conditions of increasing scarcity',[169] it seems to align clearly with expectations of equality of citizenship.

I have argued elsewhere for the adoption of stewardship-type principles in the regulation of aspects of the mass media,[170] as a means of manifesting the public interest concerns associated with citizenship, and have noted the functional similarities between stewardship and the regulation of privatized utilities 'where the activities of the regulators serve to limit the freedom of companies to act entirely in pursuit of commercial interests'.[171] In areas such as debate over commercial exploitation of genetic material, a concept of stewardship, especially perhaps in conjunction with a developed version of the precautionary principle, might form an appropriate conceptual framework in which to resolve such matters legitimately. In the context of utilities, Graham also notes how 'a different concept of property rights', such as that suggested by Lucy and Mitchell, might reduce the readily apparent dissonance between ownership and regulation or limitation of the rights of ownership.[172] It might also be thought that the essential facilities

---

[165] The language of trusteeship is still often applied in some areas, notably in relation to 'public service' media such as the BBC, but also more generally; see discussion of 'trustee' model applied historically by the FCC in Ch. 4. Trusts in the strict legal sense are rare in such contexts, though note the Scott Trust in relation to *The Guardian* newspaper group; see http://www.gmgplc.co.uk/gmgplc/scottintro.

[166] Held, V., *The Public Interest and Individual Interests* (New York, N.Y.: Basic Books, 1970), discussed in Ch. 1.   [167] Lucy and Mitchell, 'Replacing Private Property', 588.

[168] Ibid., at 600.   [169] Ibid., at 599.

[170] Feintuck, M., *Media Regulation, Public Interest and the Law* (Edinburgh: Edinburgh University Press, 1999), 211–14.   [171] Ibid., at 213.

[172] Graham, *Regulating Public Utilities*, 197.

doctrine,[173] applied as a tool in the context of competition law, already shares some of the characteristics and objectives of stewardship.

Of course, application of stewardship principles, which Lucy and Mitchell consider exclusively, and in mostly abstract terms, in relation to land, like 'the public interest', must not be over-extended or treated as a panacea, and its practical, legal, application may contain many more potential pitfalls than its theoretical espousal. Some of these are considered by Varney, when he examines 'the practical application of stewardship and the interplay between sub-national, national and EU regulatory authorities' in the context of media regulation, and in particular key aspects of the modern, digital, media infra-structure.[174] In addition to problems with defining the precise range of interests to which the 'steward' must have regard, Varney sees difficulties in establishing representative and/or participatory mechanisms via which such objectives can be defined and pursued. It might be argued that some of these problems might be mitigated by the establishment of a high priority for citizenship interests, combined with more or less conventional mechanisms of accountability, trans-parency, and, especially, reasoned decision-making. However, significantly, and reflecting the emphasis offered by Gamble and Kelly in relation to product-ive assets, and some of the historical and current debate regarding the relative organizational positions of shareholders, managers and other interested parties in relation to corporate activity, Varney also observes the importance of mechan-isms of governance including the interests associated with civil society,[175] and in doing so reaffirms the significance of adequate accountability mechanisms in relation to discretionary powers. In many ways, such an approach suggests the potential for stewardship to serve as what Varney refers to as 'a guiding light', though it remains necessary to acknowledge practical difficulties in its legal implementation. We appear to have returned again to the problems, identi-fied in earlier chapters, of the legal system having some difficulty in recognizing and giving effect to broad principles, even where they are closely associated with fundamental constitutional and democratic values. This seems to reaffirm the sig-nificance of Sunstein's call for the recognition and application of interpretative principles.[176]

PROPERTY AND THE PUBLIC INTEREST: BEYOND REGULATION?

Whether viewed from a public or private law perspective, it is clear that the fundamental issue at the heart of this book has been the difficulty in reconciling private property ownership with the social, 'public interest', objectives which

---

[173] See Ch. 1.

[174] Varney, M. R. *Private Property and Competing Values in the Regulation of Digital Media*, Ph.D. thesis (Hull, 2004), forthcoming, Ch. 5.

[175] Here Varney draws on Lewis, *Law and Governance*.

[176] See Sunstein, *After the Rights Revolution*, Ch. 5.

underlie regulation. In Robertson's terms, the issue is, in essence, 'the public dimension of private power'.[177]

Robertson notes with approval observations made by Cohen in the 1920s that in exercising their economic power, 'the owners of large productive assets get not just *dominion over things* through their property rights, but also, and more importantly, *sovereignty over people*'.[178] There is, however, nothing inherent or immutable in this undermining of equality of citizenship; in Robertson's terms, 'The system of property arrangements in any society has to be consciously designed to maintain the proper form of political and social order.'[179] As Gamble and Kelly put it, 'if there is marked inequality in a society, it is a result of political choice, not of deterministic and irresistible economic logic'.[180] This is true both in relation to substantive, economic equality, and equality of citizenship.

Robertson summarizes succinctly the root cause of many of the difficulties inherent in regulating property power which have been encountered in this book. His important thesis is that,

[T]he democratic, rather than the liberal tradition, better highlights the public and constitutional aspects of private property. However, since the democratic tradition is less dominant in our culture than liberalism, its insights into the public dimensions of private property are more marginalised and muted.[181]

The development and use in this book of a concept of public interest explicitly linked to the value of equality of citizenship, which underlies liberal democracy, has been an attempt to address this issue. Noted in previous chapters was the problem of the bifurcation of technical legal responses from underlying moral questions, and an often inward-looking nature of the legal system, which results in a failure to translate the values inherent in the polity into enforceable legal forms: a failure in respect of the essential 'Law Jobs'.[182] Another problem is that of a model of legal scholarship which persists in pursuing agendas limited by sometimes artificial and rigid disciplinary divides. This is especially so as between public and private law, but also sometimes within public law, in relation to constitutional and administrative law. Such divisions can serve to limit the scope and exploratory potential of research. It is hoped that this book, and especially this chapter, have to some extent avoided this problem.

This book has sought to draw on both public and private law discourse, has considered British and American approaches, and has adopted a perspective which incorporates legal, political and economic material, in an effort to reflect the theoretical and practical context, and to emphasize the underlying constitutional values. In doing so, it has sought to point towards forms in which such values are or may be represented in law, within and beyond the core focus of regulation.

[177] Robertson, 'The Public Dimension of Private Power', 256.		[178] Ibid., 258.
[179] Ibid., 248.		[180] Gamble and Kelly, 'The New Politics of Ownership', 96.
[181] Robertson, 'The Public Dimension of Private Power', 246.		[182] See Ch. 2.

What has been suggested in this book is only one vision of what might be understood by 'the public interest'. It is, however, a vision which seems to reflect democratically central values. While it might reasonably be concluded that the civic republican tradition in many ways offers a more comfortable and conducive context in which such an agenda might be developed, it should be clear that the agenda relates primarily to the *democratic* context, and therefore is at least as relevant, maybe more so, within the UK's liberal democracy. Though to some extent looking beyond this book's core focus on regulation, it is hoped that the approach adopted in this chapter has suggested possible paths, worthy of further exploration, via which a concept of public interest, or something very like it in terms of orientation and content, may obtain meaning, and may be instrumental in facilitating, via law, the reassertion and defence of the fundamental democratic value of equality of citizenship.

8

Summary and Conclusions

The essential argument of previous chapters has been that 'the public interest' need not be a cover for ignorance, or an empty vessel, and that seeking to understand it need not be comparable with the mythical quest for the Holy Grail. Rather, the concept has the *potential* to serve fundamental democratic values. Whether this book's vision of the public interest is persuasive can only be decided by its readers. However, even if the main thrust of the argument is not accepted by all, a secondary agenda, of ensuring that use of the term 'the public interest' does not go unchallenged, must surely have been achieved.

In terms of the concept's place within the democratic scheme, it may well be that, as understood here, it sits somewhat more comfortably within a civic republicanist approach, which emphasizes community and common goods rather more than the British liberal–democratic tradition. The risk of 'legal transplants', without due regard to differences in social, political, constitutional and legal contexts of jurisdictions, was noted at the very start of this book,[1] and there will be no suggestion here of a wholesale adoption of civic republicanist principles in the UK. However, viewed holistically, both the American civic republican tradition and the British liberal tradition acknowledge democratic values beyond those of the market, and identify citizenship concerns as central to the democratic settlement. Indeed, both ultimately confirm that citizens form part of a whole which is larger than individual interests: a democratic political community. Where consideration of the perspective offered by Stewart's vision of 'more ample liberalism', or Sunstein's call to the civic republican tradition and the clear acknowledgment it makes of the existence of a political community beyond the aggregation of individual interests, is especially useful, is in the fact that they both serve to re-emphasize the democratic and collective elements of the polity in the face of increasing domination by the forces of individualism and the market. This is as relevant in Britain as in the US.

What becomes clear from consideration of such approaches, or in the British context the work of the likes of Leys, is that it is not just the hegemony of market-individualist ideology and the rise of global capital, but also a combination of other factors have led to the 'non-commodity values' contained within democracy being put under severe threat. We can observe in Britain in particular, a lack of clarity in relation to democratic and constitutional principles, a consequential lack of legal recognition or enforcement of the related values, and

---

[1] See Kahn-Freund, O., 'On Uses and Misuses of Comparative Law', *Modern Law Review*, 37/1 (1974), 1.

indeed a lack of structures which require a deliberative focus on aspects of the democratic settlement beyond individual and economic interests.

While there is no real possibility of either an early return to the height of the British welfare state, or the kind of deliberative democracy envisaged in classic civic republicanist thought, which may be thought to have reflected directly such concerns, there remains an expectation, deriving from democracy, that legal and regulatory instruments and practices will serve the end of equality of citizenship which is common to both. To a significant extent, the legitimacy of the state, and hence the legal and regulatory system, depends upon this expectation being met.

As Seidenfeld suggests, it may indeed be the case that in the modern context, administrative and regulatory agencies can be viewed as 'the best hope of implementing civic republicanism's call for deliberative decision-making informed by the values of the entire polity'.[2] We have seen how such values are being threatened by the ongoing hegemony of liberal individualism and the application of unmitigated market forces, and how the regulatory response looks unlikely to defend the polity's wider value set. It is clear, therefore, that though the regulatory system has a significant potential to act as a 'surrogate deliberative system', this potential remains largely unfulfilled. It can be argued that, to a great extent, this failure derives from the absence of clear orientation of the regulatory system towards democratic objectives, and a consequent actual or potential lack of a sense of legitimacy when it does intervene, resulting in a tendency for regulators to be left to focus on more immediate matters, more obviously within their understanding and the judicial construction of their statutory mandate.

There is no sense in which application of a concept of public interest by itself provides the answer to all the many problems identified previously. However, while in practice it is likely that the term will continue to be used loosely, and will carry a variety of meanings, a core meaning could be established in the context of regulation which identifies it closely with the values of equality of citizenship within democracy. The IPPR's finding that 'the foundation of a free society is the equal worth of all citizens'[3] seems to be equally relevant to liberal and republicanist democratic thought.

Serving as an 'interpretative principle', which permits and indeed requires those acting in the name of the public interest to be judged against such values, the concept of public interest may form a valuable adjunct to existing constitutional and legal principles and regulatory practices, and reinforce the democratic fabric of the polity. Indeed, in light of some of the threats to democratic values identified earlier, it may be thought that the application of the context in this way is not

---

[2] Seidenfeld, M., 'A Civic Republican Justification for the Bureaucratic State', *Harvard Law Review*, 105/7 (1992), 1511, extract in Schuck, P. H., *Foundations of Administrative Law* (Oxford: Oxford University Press, 1994), 26.

[3] Quoted in Collins, R. and Murroni, C., *New Media, New Policies* (Cambridge: Polity Press, 1996), 13.

only advisable, but necessary, in the absence of any other constitutional feature which effectively serves this function. The concept of 'public interest' viewed in this way can indeed be considered, as suggested in Chapter Two, to be 'a spur to conscience and to deliberation',[4] or as offering a 'moral intrusion'[5] into political discourse. However, the problem recognized previously in relation to such statements, of their failure to identify the values which should intrude or inform deliberation, is overcome if the concept is seen specifically as a call or requirement to deliberate on the fundamental democratic expectation of equality of citizenship, and to take those values fully into account when considering any regulatory action or inaction.

While some may suggest that a direct appeal to 'citizenship' might be preferable to the interposing of 'public interest' in this context, there seem to be good reasons why 'the public interest' might be preferred. In the UK, where a strong concept of citizenship is absent, the term may carry little weight or be of uncertain application. However, the use of a concept of 'public interest' which explicitly incorporates reference to *equality* of citizenship may be seen more obviously to link back to the underlying democratic values which are supposed to inform the polity. In addition, reference to 'citizenship' can all too easily be reduced to the concept's individualistic aspects, while the public interest should be seen to draw attention explicitly to the collective aspects embodied in community values. A concept of public interest used in regulation in the way suggested here, has a particular utility in providing a degree of linkage between the polity's fundamental value base and the institutions of law and regulation which are supposed to serve it.

It can be argued that Britain, indeed any democracy, has need of interpretative principles, by way of providing the 'structural coupling'[6] between the high democratic ideals and the constitutional, legal and regulatory realities, which may serve to reduce the problems arising from 'inadequately theorized agreements'.[7] By establishing the linkage between the fundamental premises on which the polity is established and the practice of regulation, by making explicit the values which it is purporting to pursue, the regulatory endeavour can be re-legitimated. In Virginia Held's terms, as was noted in Chapter Two, 'Acceptance of the existence of a political system may depend upon widespread acceptance of the ethical judgment that it is justifiable for the political system to use coercion to enforce its decisions. In this way the political system may be grounded upon an

---

[4] Pennock, J. R., 'The One and the Many: a Note on the Concept', in Friedrich, C. J. (ed.), *Nomos V: The Public Interest* (New York, N.Y.: Atherton Press, 1962).

[5] Bailey, S. K., 'The Public Interest: Some Operational Dilemmas', in Friedrich, C. J. (ed.), *Nomos V: The Public Interest* (New York, N.Y.: Atherton Press, 1962).

[6] Teubner, G., *Juridification of Social Spheres*, (Berlin: Walter de Gruyter, 1987), extracts in Baldwin, R., Scott, C., and Hood, C. (eds.), *A Reader on Regulation* (Oxford: Oxford University Press, 1998).

[7] Sunstein, C. R., *Designing Democracy: What Constitutions Do* (Oxford: Oxford University Press, 2001), 50.

ethical assumption that its existence is justified.'[8] While in many states, recourse can be made to clear statements of constitutional principle which serve as the foundation for the legitimacy of regulatory interventions, in Britain this is not the case, and given these circumstances, Britain stands particularly in need of such interpretative principles. Baldwin and McCrudden observe that, if a meaningful 'constitutional conversation' is to take place involving regulators and those affected by their actions, there is a need for the judiciary to 'identify more clearly their value premises and articulate which values they adopt in particular situations'.[9] It is clear that some body needs to do so. If the legal system does not adequately articulate and institutionalize the fundamental values which inform the institutions which act in pursuit of social objectives, not only will regulation be unlikely to achieve its apparent purposes, but, more broadly, the 'Law Jobs'[10] cannot be undertaken successfully. At present, as the case studies in Chapters Three to Five have illustrated, though 'the public interest' may continue to give the appearance of informing and justifying the regulatory endeavour, there is a real lack of clarity about what the term means, both in theory and in practice.

It must be accepted that the vision of the public interest being adopted here, as representing the democratic interests in equality of citizenship, is, inevitably, as contestable as any other such unitary approach. However, the strong democratic credentials of this claim are difficult to deny, and all the indications suggest that no other institution or principle is presently serving this value effectively. There is some strength in Sunstein's suggestion that what he refers to as 'politically contestable background principles', into which this construct of the public interest could be placed, might serve to 'vindicate underenforced constitutional norms',[11] such as the democratic expectations relating to equality of citizenship which appear especially neglected in recent years.

Sunstein warns that such principles should not be applied where statutory terms and priorities are clear.[12] In such cases, both judges and regulators must be expected to interpret powers by reference to statutory words, legislative intent, or in the US by reference to established constitutional standards. However, where statutory language or regulatory guidance is relatively imprecise, and especially where no clear hierarchy of values is established, it seems democratically appropriate to utilize a construct of public interest which represents democratic fundamentals as an interpretative aid. None of this should be read as an attempt to further what Harlow refers to as 'colonisation of the legal by the political'.[13] Rather, it is an attempt to ensure that the legal system, in serving as a 'surrogate political system', acts effectively so as to fulfil democratic promises.

---

[8] Held, V., *The Public Interest and Individual Interests* (New York, N.Y.: Basic Books, 1970), 189.

[9] Baldwin, R. and McCrudden, C., *Regulation and Public Law* (London: Weidenfeld and Nicolson, 1987), 71.   [10] See Ch. 2.

[11] Sunstein, C. R., *After the Rights Revolution: Reconceiving the Regulatory State* (Cambridge, Mass.: Harvard University Press, 1990), 161.   [12] Ibid.

[13] Harlow, C., 'Public Law and Popular Justice', *Modern Law Review*, 65 (2002), 1, at 2.

This is no more or less than what is required within the terms of the 'Law Jobs', in which it is, *inter alia*, necessary to establish norms and institutions which order social activity, establish the locus and legitimacy of institutional power, and develop processes for determining society's direction.

Of course, it may be argued that the use of interpretative principles is a novel introduction into the British legal system. However, in many ways the Rule of Law can also be seen in this light,[14] and indeed it seems to share many of the fundamental characteristics of the construct of public interest being advocated here. The Rule of Law, like 'the public interest', may be thought to fall within the category of 'contestable background principles', potentially useful in establishing linkage between grand democratic values and practical realities of the constitutional and legal systems. It certainly shares some of the fuzziness traditionally associated with the public interest, and the Rule of Law is essentially non-justiciable; although the public interest might on occasion form an issue to be tried, by itself it will rarely establish a cause of action. Certainly, both concepts, if understood in any meaningful sense, can be said to relate closely to the normative foundations of the polity, yet, though they remain persistent features in legal and political discourse, their precise content or meaning remains elusive. Both, however, have the potential to serve the greater democratic good.

There is, however, a risk associated with both, in that they can be too easily reduced to procedural requirements. The risks of a minimal model of the rule of law have been referred to in Chapter Six, while the limits of proceduralism have been noted in relation to the application of the precautionary principle as a manifestation of public interest values in the course of Chapter Seven. It is vitally important that if any concept is to serve effectively as an interpretative principle it must overtly incorporate, and explicitly refer to, the democratic values it is intended to serve. Given the threat to citizenship interests identified earlier in the trends towards commodification and marketization in relation to the media and food supplies, and for that matter a wide range of 'public services', the challenge to democracy, and hence the values which underpin the political community, is obvious. If such matters are not effectively regulated, the prerequisites of effective citizenship are left to the pull of market forces, threatening the legitimate democratic expectation of equality of citizenship. A significant role for regulators in this context is to consider the way in which their interventions will impact upon this expectation. The regulatory system already recognizes 'environmental impact assessments', and all new legislative proposals are now accompanied by 'regulatory impact assessments' which are intended to demonstrate the necessity and proportionality of the proposed measure. From this perspective adopted here, it is possible to conceptualize the application of the public interest as defined, as an interpretative principle in

---

[14] It is referred to as one such in Sunstein, *After the Rights Revolution*, 166. See also Varney, M. R., *Private Property and Competing Values in the Regulation of Digital Media*, Ph.D. thesis (Hull, 2004), forthcoming, for a treatment of this idea in the British and European contexts.

regulation, in terms of a 'democratic impact assessment', or perhaps slightly more precisely, a 'citizenship impact assessment'. By requiring regulatory attention to be given to the potential impact of action or inaction on the ability of all to act effectively as citizens, the public interest may serve the defence of democracy against the ongoing risk of market forces facilitating the group interests of the powerful being translated into and legitimated as 'the general interest'.

It is now necessary to return to the key questions posed in the first two chapters regarding the advisability of abandoning or reinvigorating the concept of public interest. To what extent can the problems traditionally associated with the concept be effectively resolved, and how should the concept's meaning be understood?

If the concept is to be utilized, its value content must be identified, and if this is done in terms which refer to equality of citizenship within a democratic community, the democratic values most obviously under threat in the current era, it has substantial potential to aid the fulfilment of democratic promises and expectations. In emphasizing 'community' it avoids an atomistic vision of citizenship. In emphasizing equality of citizenship, it gives due weight to citizenship values in the face of market forces, offering explicit justification for regulation in democratic, rather than exclusively economic, terms. It looks beyond what might be called a concept of 'public economic interest' which, whether explicitly or implicitly, dominates much of the discourse, and recognizes that the interests associated with a capitalist economy form only one part of the polity. While it was seen that the development of competition-oriented provisions, such as the essential facilities doctrine, represent established modes of regulation of the exercise of private property power 'in the public interest', though they may contingently serve citizenship and other democratic interests, they remain focused on, and essentially justified by reference to, economic factors. Understood in the way suggested here, the concept of public interest justifies the regulation of private property power by reference to clear democratic values and hence legitimates regulation in pursuit of social objectives. Again, understood in this way, the concept avoids the problems of majoritarianism associated with 'common interest' and 'preponderance accounts',[15] and though the 'common goods'[16] it appears to serve may be hard to list authoritatively or exhaustively, it is clear that the fundamental promises of the democratic polity, such as citizenship, can properly be included amongst them.

In serving as an interpretative principle, providing a degree of linkage between high democratic and constitutional values and the 'real world' of law and regulation, it can help to ensure the proper translation of such values into practical reality. In essence, it has the potential to serve to further the legitimate social

[15] See Held, V., *The Public Interest*, and discussion of this typology in Ch. 1.

[16] See Honohan, I., *Civic Republicanism* (London: Routledge, 2002). Also see discussion of common goods in Ch. 6.

responsibility of government, identified by Milne,[17] as that of representing community interests. Used in this way, the concept of public interest will remain contestable, and will be liable to being overridden in specific cases. However, it should serve to impose a heavy burden on regulators to justify actions by specific reference to citizenship values. In practice, therefore, though it will not be conclusive, it might be expected that it should be defeated only on rare occasions, and even in such cases the requirement to take the concept into account should enhance the rationality and democratic legitimacy of regulatory decisions, and help to fulfil the expectation of deliberation informed by a vision of values beyond individual or group interests. 'The public interest', seen in this way, is no longer an empty vessel, or an aspect of the spoils to be claimed by society's dominant groups, nor is it too fluid or too susceptible to change, but instead represents a unitary theory, reflecting the relatively constant value of equality of citizenship within a democratic political community. In the service of the political settlement as a whole, it may fulfil a 'countercultural' function, offering resistance to presently dominant value sub-sets.

Of course, the concept of public interest thus understood does not, and is not intended, to address the larger political question of substantive inequality within society, a matter beyond the scope of this book. However, applying the concept in the way suggested above, does though seek to ensure that within areas of regulation, where objectives valued by the community are being pursued, the basic democratic expectation of equality of citizenship is better served than at present.

Though readers will wish to reach their own conclusions on what practical difference the application of the concept of public interest in this way would make, it is worth highlighting briefly some of the effects application of such a construct could have in key areas of regulatory practice identified in Chapters Three to Five.

In relation to decisions taken by regulators, a requirement to take into account specifically matters of equality of citizenship should serve to structure discretion, ensure more rounded deliberation, and ultimately help to legitimate regulatory action. If regulation is defined as it has been here, by reference to 'objectives valued by a community', it is necessary to be reasonably clear about what such values are if regulation is to be perceived as legitimate. The civic republicanist approach is helpful here, in incorporating such considerations into the debate. However, it is clear that whether from a liberal or civic republicanist perspective, or any hybrid of the two, equality of citizenship must surely rank high amongst such values. In this connection, the application of a concept of public interest, as defined here, may help significantly in legitimating regulation of private property interests in pursuit of social objectives, and in particular may help to re-establish values such as those associated with public service broadcasting without reli-

---

[17] Milne, A. J. M., 'The Public Interest, Political Controversy, and the Judges' in Brownsword, R. (ed.), *Law and the Public Interest* (Proceedings of the 1992 ALSP Conference) (Stuttgart: Franz Steiner, 1993), at 45–6.

ance on technical arguments such as spectrum scarcity or on market-economics driven approaches such as essential facilities. In establishing a prominent place for equality of citizenship within the hierarchy of values which regulators must take into account, a specific set of non-commodity values are incorporated into the process and will be better protected, while any trope from citizen to consumer will be highlighted and might be avoided. In moving beyond the limits of proceduralism, and establishing the linkage between constitutional values and regulatory objectives, it may help to resolve the burden of justification faced by regulatory agencies, and may in particular, by specifying the constitutional values involved, avoid the kind of charges of illegitimacy in the regulatory brief brought against the US FCC by reference to allegations of constitutional vagueness. While it does not resolve the kind of competing narrative, such as that seen in relation to different European and US perspectives on precaution, it does interpose a specific set of democratic values which should inform deliberation. In this sense, in Garrett's terms,[18] it helps to establish a normative baseline against which regulatory outcomes can be judged.

In reality, it is doing no more than to impose on regulators a burden to show that they have taken a 'Hard Look' at all relevant factors,[19] but is specifying and emphasizing a particular set of democratic requirements, which can otherwise too easily be marginalized or ignored, but which must now be demonstrably given the proper degree of attention. By establishing the requirement for the regulatory brief to be interpreted with specific reference to furthering equality of citizenship, the role of courts in reviewing regulatory activity should also be facilitated, by providing a 'hard' legal standard against which to judge actions, perhaps in turn aiding a move away from what may often seem to be an overly deferential attitude to 'expert' bodies. Applying the concept of public interest in this way should in effect serve to assist in ensuring that regulation fulfils its potential as a locus of deliberation within the polity, and should encourage or indeed require the courts to support and enforce that practice of deliberation.

In and of itself, the application of a citizenship-related concept of public interest as an interpretative principle does not resolve perceived problems, referred to in earlier chapters, in relation to legal recognition of group or collective claims. However, it may encourage or force regulators to take full account of such interests, and as a result of establishing a more structured form of regulatory discretion, more susceptible to judicial scrutiny, it may encourage the bringing of, and ease judicial recognition of, representative or group actions where it appears that a regulator may have failed to act in accordance with the principle.

In structuring discretion by the provision of a framework of principle which prioritizes equality of citizenship, the concept of public interest may serve the

[18] See Garrett, E., 'Interest Groups and Public Interested Regulation', *Florida State University Law Review*, 28 (2000), 137.

[19] See Ch. 5. See also, Harden, I. and Lewis, N., *The Noble Lie: The British Constitution and the Rule of Law* (London: Hutchinson, 1986), Ch. 9.

agenda of maximizing the potential benefits of regulatory discretion while avoiding some of the risks. At the same time, its adoption by regulators would serve to liberate them from the shackles of economics, legitimating the overt pursuit of the kind of social objectives they were established to serve. In summary, it may enhance the legitimacy of social regulation by reference to fundamental democratic values, and facilitate the operation of law as a 'surrogate political process'. Whether initially adopted voluntarily by regulators, within their broad statutory briefs, or whether imposed directly by statute, or whether arising from judicial creativity in the courts, it should be expected to become established as a model of best practice in social regulation, just as aspects of consultation and participation have become embedded in British administrative law in relatively recent history.

In serving as an interpretative principle, providing linkage between constitutional values and the semi-autonomous legal and regulatory systems, it contributes to the constitutional discourse identified by Craig,[20] in which it is possible both to recognize property rights and also recognize the legitimacy of their regulation when other constitutional values are at stake. It can serve to help to ensure the recognition of the full set of values inherent in the democratic settlement, serving as a counterbalance against the currently dominant interests of the market. While governments may seek to prioritize macroeconomic policies, a normative vision of the public interest, such as that argued for here, may provide a basis on which to challenge such policies if they serve to diminish equality of citizenship. In Held's words, noted in Chapter One, a policy 'cannot be in the public interest if it conflicts with the elements of the minimal value structures that define the society'.[21]

In terms of the dichotomy raised in Chapter Two, the concept of public interest viewed in this way is neither inherently 'progressive' nor 'conservative'. Rather, it can be seen to serve the potential for social progress through equality of citizenship while contributing to the conservation of the democratic basis of society. The values the concept would serve are not new; they are well embedded in democratic theory but poorly protected by existing constitutional, legal and regulatory practice. Thus, 'the public interest' in regulation need not be viewed either as the unattainable Holy Grail of mythology, or necessarily as an empty vessel, but rather, understood in the sense suggested here, should be seen as a constitutional necessity.

As was noted at the very start of this book, the concept of 'public interest' has a strong intuitive appeal. It is hoped that it has now been demonstrated that it can also be endowed with strong democratic credentials, and that its adoption as an interpretative principle, emphasizing the value of equality of citizenship, within the legal and regulatory systems, is not only advisable, but necessary, in the protection of democratic values.

---

[20] Craig, P. P., 'Constitutions, Property and Regulation', *Public Law*, 1991, Winter, 538.
[21] Held, *The Public Interest and Individual Interests*, 222.

References

Abrams, K., 'Law's Republicanism', *Yale Law Journal*, 97 (1988) 1591.

Adams, J., 'A Richter Scale for Risk?', in Morris, J. (ed.), *Rethinking Risk and the Precautionary Principle* (Oxford: Butterworth-Heinemann, 2000).

Ainsworth, L. and Weston, D., 'Newspapers and UK Media Ownership Controls', *Media Law and Practice*, 16/1 (1995) 2.

Andriof, J. and McIntosh, M. (eds.), *Perspectives on Corporate Citizenship* (Sheffield: Greenleaf, 2001).

Annan Report, *Report of the Committee on the Future of Broadcasting* (London: HMSO, 1977), Cm. 6753.

Anthony, H., 'Food Standards Agency – Three Years On', *Journal of Nutritional and Environmental Medicine*, 11 (2001), 101.

Applegate, J. S., 'Sustainable Development, Agriculture, and the Challenge of Genetically Modified Organisms', *Indiana Journal of Global Legal Studies*, 9 (2001), 207.

Arblaster, A., *Democracy*, 3rd edn. (Buckingham: Open University Press, 2002).

Asimow, M., 'Public Participation in the Adoption of Interpretive Rules and Policy Statements', *Michigan Law Review*, 77 (1975), 520.

—— 'Delegated Legislation: United States and United Kingdom', *Oxford Journal of Legal Studies*, 3/2 (1983), 253.

Attfield, R., 'The Precautionary Principle and Moral Values', in O'Riordan, T. and Cameron, J. (eds.), *Interpreting the Precautionary Principle* (London: Earthscan, 1994).

Bagdikian, B., *The Media Monopoly*, 6th edn. (Boston, Mass.: Beacon Press, 2000).

Bailey, S. K., 'The Public Interest: Some Operational Dilemmas', in Friedrich, C. J. (ed.), *Nomos V: The Public Interest* (New York, N.Y.: Atherton Press, 1962).

Baldwin, R., *Rules and Government* (Oxford: Clarendon, 1995).

—— and Cave, M., *Understanding Regulation: Theory, Strategy and Practice* (Oxford: Oxford University Press, 1999).

—— and McCrudden, C., *Regulation and Public Law* (London: Weidenfeld and Nicolson, 1987).

—— Scott, C. and Hood, C. (eds.), *A Reader on Regulation* (Oxford: Oxford University Press, 1998).

Banfield, E. C., 'Note on Conceptual Schema' in Meyerson, M. and Banfield, E. C., *Politics, Planning and the Public Interest* (New York: Free Press, 1955).

Barbalet, J. M., *Citizenship* (Milton Keynes: Open University Press, 1988).

Barbrook, A., *Protest and Pressure: The Public Interest and Pressure Groups in the USA* (Hull: University of Hull, 1979) Hull Papers in Politics No. 11.

Barendt, E, *Freedom of Speech* (Oxford: Clarendon, 1985).

—— *Broadcasting Law: A Comparative Study* (Oxford: Clarendon, 1993).

Barker, F. and Lucy, W., 'Justifying Property and Justifying Access', *Canadian Journal of Law and Jurisprudence*, VI/2 (1993), 287.

Barling, D. and Lang, T., 'A Reluctant Food Policy? The First Five Years of Food Policy Under Labour', *Political Quarterly*, 74/1 (2003), 8.

Barry, B. M., 'The Use and Abuse of the Public Interest', in Friedrich, C. J. (ed.), *Nomos V: The Public Interest* (New York, N.Y.: Atherton Press, 1962).

Beatson, J. and Tridimas, T. (eds.), *New Directions in European Public Law* (Oxford: Hart, 1998).

Becker, K. M., Flannery, E. J., and Henteleff, T. O., 'Scientific Dispute Resolution: First Use of Provision 404 of the Food and Drug Administration Modernization Act 1997', *Food and Drug Journal*, 58 (2003), 211.

Beckerman, W., 'The Precautionary Principle and our Obligations to Future Generations', in Morris, J. (ed.), *Rethinking Risk and the Precautionary Principle* (Oxford: Butterworth-Heinemann, 2000).

Bell, J., 'Public Interest: Policy or Principle?', in Brownsword, R. (ed.), *Law and the Public Interest* (Proceedings of the 1992 ALSP Conference) (Stuttgart: Franz Steiner, 1993).

Berle, A. and Means, G., *The Modern Corporation and Private Property* (New York, N.Y.: Harcourt, Brace and World, 1932).

Berlin, I., *Four Essays on Liberty* (Oxford: Oxford University Press, 1969).

Birkinshaw, P. J., *Freedom of Information: the Law, the Practice and the Ideal*, 4th edn. (London: Butterworths, 2001).

—— *European Public Law* (London: Butterworths, 2003).

Birkinshaw, P., Harden, I., and Lewis, N., *Government by Moonlight: The Hybrid Parts of the State* (London: Unwin Hyman, 1990).

Bjork, G. C., *Private Enterprise and Public Interest: The Development of American Capitalism* (Eaglewood Cliffs, NJ.: Prentice-Hall, 1969).

Bodansky, D., 'Scientific Uncertainty and the Precautionary Principle', *Environment*, 33/7 (1991), 5.

—— 'The Precautionary Principle in US Environmental Law', in O'Riordan, T. and Cameron, J. (eds.), *Interpreting the Precautionary Principle* (London: Earthscan, 1994).

Bodenheimer, E., 'Prolegomena to a Theory of the Public Interest', in Friedrich, C. J. (ed.), *Nomos V: The Public Interest* (New York, N.Y.: Atherton Press, 1962).

Boeckman, A. M., 'An Exercise in Administrative Creativity: The FDA's Assertion of Jurisdiction Over Tobacco', *Catholic University Law Review*, 45 (1996), 991.

Boehmer-Christiansen, S., 'The Precautionary Principle in Germany – Enabling Government', in O'Riordan, T. and Cameron, J. (eds.), *Interpreting the Precautionary Principle* (London: Earthscan, 1994).

Bollinger, L., 'Freedom of the Press and Public Access', in Lichtenberg, J. (ed.), *Democracy and the Mass Media* (Cambridge: Cambridge University Press, 1990).

Bonner, D. and Graham, C., 'The Human Rights Act 1998: The Story so Far', *European Public Law*, 8/2 (2002), 177.

Boyle, A., 'Freedom of Expression as a Public Interest in English Law', *Public Law*, 1982, Winter, 574.

Bradley, A., 'The Sovereignty of Parliament', in Jowell, J. and Oliver, D. (eds.), *The Changing Constitution*, 4th edn. (Oxford: Oxford University Press, 2000).

Braithwaite, J. and Pettit, P., *Not Just Deserts: A Republican Theory of Criminal Justice* (Oxford: Clarendon, 1990).

Braybrooke, D., 'The Public Interest: The Present and Future of the Concept', in Friedrich, C. J. (ed.), *Nomos V: The Public Interest* (New York, N.Y.: Atherton Press, 1962).

Breger, M. J. and Edles, G. J., 'Established by Practice: The Theory and Operation of Independent Federal Agencies', *Administrative Law Review*, 52/4 (2000), 1111.

Breyer, S., *Regulation and its Reform* (Cambridge, Mass.: Harvard University Press, 1982).

Brownsword, R. (ed.), *Law and the Public Interest* (Proceedings of the 1992 ALSP Conference) (Stuttgart: Franz Steiner, 1993).

—— 'Law and the Public Interest', in Brownsword, R. (ed.), *Law and the Public Interest* (Proceedings of the 1992 ALSP Conference) (Stuttgart: Franz Steiner, 1993).

Cameron, J., 'The Status of the Precautionary Principle in International Law', in O'Riordan, T. and Cameron, J. (eds.), *Interpreting the Precautionary Principle* (London: Earthscan, 1994).

Campbell, D. and Lee, R., 'Carnage by Computer: The Blackboard Economics of the 2001 Foot and Mouth Epidemic', *Social and Legal Studies*, 12/4 (2003), 426.

—— 'The Power to Panic: the Animal Health Act 2002', *Public Law*, 2003, Autumn, 382.

Carroll, A. B., 'The Pyramid of Corporate Social Responsibility: Toward the Moral Management of Organizational Stakeholders', *Business Horizons* (Indiana University Graduate Business School) 34/4 (1991), 39.

—— 'The Moral Leader: Essential for Successful Corporate Citizenship', in Andriof, J. and McIntosh, M. (eds.), *Perspectives on Corporate Citizenship* (Sheffield: Greenleaf, 2001).

Carter, E. J., 'Market Definition in the Broadcasting Sector', *World Competition*, 24/1 (2001), 93.

Cassinelli, C. W., 'The Public Interest in Political Ethics', in Friedrich, C. J. (ed.), *Nomos V: The Public Interest* (New York, N.Y.: Atherton Press, 1962).

Chakrabarti, S., Stephens, J., and Gallagher, C., 'Whose Cost the Public Interest?', *Public Law*, 2003, Winter, 697.

Champlin, D. and Knoedler, J., 'Operating in the Public Interest or in Pursuit of Private Profits? News in the Age of Media Consolidation', *Journal of Economic Issues*, 36/2 (2002), 459.

Christodoulidis, E. A., *Law and Reflexive Politics* (Dordrecht: Kluwer, 1998).

Coase, R. H., 'The Regulated Industries: Discussion', *American Economic Review* (Papers and Proceedings), 54 (1964), 192.

Cohen, J., 'A Lawman's View of the Public Interest' in Friedrich, C. J. (ed.), *Nomos V: The Public Interest* (New York, N.Y.: Atherton Press, 1962).

Collins, R. and Murroni, C., *New Media, New Policies* (Cambridge: Polity Press, 1996).

Colm, G., 'The Public Interest: Essential Key to Public Policy', in Friedrich, C. J. (ed.), *Nomos V: The Public Interest* (New York, N.Y.: Atherton Press, 1962).

Congdon, T., Graham, A., Green, D., and, Robinson, B., *The Cross Media Revolution: Ownership and Control* (London: John Libbey, 1995).

Cooper, J. and Dhavan, R. (eds.), *Public Interest Law* (Oxford: Basil Blackwell, 1986).

Craig, P. P., *Public Law and Democracy in the United Kingdom and the United States of America* (Oxford: Clarendon, 1990).

—— 'Constitutions, Property and Regulation', *Public Law*, 1991, Winter, 538.

—— *Administrative Law*, 5th edn. (London: Sweet and Maxwell, 2003).

—— and Schønberg, S., 'Substantive Legitimate Expectation after *Coughlan*', *Public Law*, 2000, Winter, 684.

Crampton, P. S. and Facey, B. A., 'Revisiting Regulation and Deregulation Through the Lens of Competition Policy', *World Competition*, 25/1 (2002), 25.

Croley, S. P., 'Public Interested Regulation', *Florida State University Law Review*, 28 (2000), 7.

Crouch, C. and Marquand, D., 'Reinventing Collective Action', in Crouch, C. and Marquand, D. (eds.), *Reinventing Collective Action: From the Global to the Local* (Oxford: Blackwell, 1995).

——(eds.), *Reinventing Collective Action: From the Global to the Local* (Oxford: Blackwell, 1995).

Curran, J. and Seaton, J., *Power Without Responsibility: The Press and Broadcasting in Britain*, 5th edn. (London: Routledge, 1997).

——*Power Without Responsibility: The Press, Broadcasting and New Media in Britain*, 6th edn. (London: Routledge, 2003).

Dahlgren, P., *Television and the Public Sphere: Citizenship, Democracy and the Media* (London: Sage, 1995).

Daintith, T. (ed.), *Law as an Instrument of Economic Policy: Comparative and Critical Approaches* (Berlin: Walter de Gruyter, 1988).

——'Law as Policy Instrument: A Comparative Perspective' in Daintith, T. (ed.), *Law as an Instrument of Economic Policy: Comparative and Critical Approaches* (Berlin: Walter de Gruyter, 1988).

——'Legal Measures and their Analysis', in Daintith, T. (ed.), *Law as an Instrument of Economic Policy: Comparative and Critical Approaches* (Berlin: Walter de Gruyter, 1988).

Davies, S., 'The Precautionary Principle and Food Policy', *Consumer Policy Review*, 12/2 (2002), 65.

Davis, K. C., *Discretionary Justice: a Preliminary Inquiry* (Urbana, IL.: University of Illinois Press, 1971).

Dean, M., 'Plans for UK Food Safety Agency go into Reverse', *The Lancet*, 28 November 1998, 1763.

de Burca, G., 'Proportionality and Wednesbury Unreasonableness: The Influence of European Legal Concepts on UK Law', *European Public Law*, 3/4 (1997), 561.

della Cananea, G., 'Beyond the State: The Europeanization and Globalization of Procedural Administrative Law', *European Public Law*, 9/4 (2003), 563.

Department of Culture, Media and Sport, White Paper, *A New Future for Communications* (London: HMSO, 2000), Cm. 5010.

Department of National Heritage, White Paper, *Media Ownership: The Government's Proposals* (London: HMSO, 1995), Cm. 2872.

——White Paper, *Privacy and Media Intrusion* (London: HMSO, 1995), Cm. 2918.

——White Paper, *Digital Terrestrial Television: the Government's Proposals* (London: HMSO, 1995), Cm. 2946.

Department of Trade and Industry, *Business and Society: Corporate Social Responsibility Report* (London: HMSO, 2002).

——White Paper, *Modernising Company Law* (London: HMSO, 2002), Cm. 5553.

Dhavan, R., 'Whose Law? Whose Interest?' in Cooper, J. and Dhavan, R. (eds.), *Public Interest Law* (Oxford: Basil Blackwell, 1986).

Durodié, B., 'Plastic Panics: European Risk Regulation in the Aftermath of BSE', in Morris, J. (ed.), *Rethinking Risk and the Precautionary Principle* (Oxford: Butterworth-Heinemann, 2000).

Dworkin, R., *Taking Rights Seriously* (London: Duckworth, 1977).

——'Is Wealth a Value', *Journal of Legal Studies*, 9 (1980), 191, reproduced in Katz, A. V. (ed.), *Foundations of the Economic Approach to Law* (Oxford: Oxford University Press, 1998).

Echols, M. A., 'Food Safety Regulation in the EU and the US: Different Cultures, Different Laws', *Columbia Journal of European Law*, 4 (1998), 525.

Elliott, M., 'Chasing the Receding Bus: the Broadcasting Act 1980', *Modern Law Review*, 44 (1981), 683.

Elliott, M. C., 'The Human Rights Act 1998 and the Standard of Substantive Review', *Cambridge Law Journal*, 60/2 (2001), 301.

Ely, J. H., *Democracy and Distrust: A Theory of Judicial Review* (Cambridge, Mass.: Harvard University Press, 1980).

Epstein, R., 'Modern Republicanism – Or the Flight From Substance', *Yale Law Journal*, 97 (1988) 1633.

European Communities, Commission, *Promoting a European Framework for Corporate Social Responsibility*, Green Paper, COM (2001) 366 final.

Fainsod, M., 'Some Reflections on the Nature of the Regulatory Process', in Friedrich, C. J. and Mason, E. S. (eds.) *Public Policy: A Yearbook of the Graduate School of Public Administration* (Cambridge, Mass.: Harvard University Press, 1940).

Farina, C., 'Statutory Interpretation and the Balance of Power in the Administrative State', *Columbia Law Review*, 89 (1989), 452; in Schuck, P. H., *Foundations of Administrative Law* (Oxford: Oxford University Press, 1994).

Feintuck, M., *Accountability and Choice in Schooling* (Buckingham: Open University Press, 1994).

—— 'Government Control of Information: Some British Developments', *Government Information Quarterly*, 13/4 (1996), 345.

—— 'The UK Broadcasting Act 1996: A Holding Operation?', *European Public Law*, 3/2 (1997), 201.

—— *Media Regulation, Public Interest and the Law* (Edinburgh: Edinburgh University Press, 1999).

—— 'Walking the High-Wire: The UK's Draft Communications Bill', *European Public Law*, 9/1 (2003), 105.

Fisher, E., 'Drowning by Numbers: Standard Setting in Regulation and the Pursuit of Accountable Public Administration', *Oxford Journal of Legal Studies*, 20/1 (2000), 109.

—— 'Is the Precautionary Principle Justiciable?', *Journal of Environmental Law*, 13/3 (2001), 315.

—— 'The Rise of the Risk Commonwealth and the Challenge for Administrative Law', *Public Law*, 2003, Autumn, 455.

Fowler, M. S. and Brenner, D. L., 'A Marketplace Approach to Broadcast Regulation', *Texas Law Review*, 60 (1982), 207.

Freestone, D. and Hey, E., *The Precautionary Principle and International Law* (The Hague: Kluwer, 1996).

Friedman, M., *Capitalism and Freedom* (Chicago, IL.: University of Chicago Press, 1969).

—— 'The Social Responsibility of Business is to Increase its Profits', *New York Times Magazine*, 13 September 1970, reproduced in Hoffman, W. M. and Frederick, R. E. (eds.), *Business Ethics: Readings and Cases in Corporate Morality*, 3rd edn. (New York, N.Y.: McGraw-Hill, 1995).

Friedman, W., 'The Changing Content of the Public Interest', in Friedrich, C. J. (ed.), *Nomos V: The Public Interest* (New York, N.Y.: Atherton Press, 1962).

Friedrich, C. J. (ed.), *Nomos V: The Public Interest* (New York, N.Y.: Atherton Press, 1962).

—— and Mason, E. S. (eds.) *Public Policy: A Yearbook of the Graduate School of Administration* (Cambridge, Mass.: Harvard University Press, 1940).

Galanter, M., 'Why the "Haves" Come Out Ahead: Speculations on the Limits of Legal Change', *Law and Society Review*, 9/1 (Fall) (1974), 95.

Galligan, D. J., *Discretionary Power: A Legal Study of Official Discretion* (Oxford: Clarendon, 1986).

Gamble, A., *The Free Economy and the Strong State: the Politics of Thatcherism* (Basingstoke: Macmillan, 1994).

—— and Kelly, G., 'The New Politics of Ownership', *New Left Review*, 220 (1996), 62.

—— 'Owners and Citizens', *Political Quarterly*, 69/4 (1998), 344.

Garrett, E., 'Interest Groups and Public Interested Regulation', *Florida State University Law Review*, 28 (2000), 137.

George, V. and Wilding, P., *Ideology and Social Welfare* (London: Routledge and Kegan Paul, 1976).

Gibbons, T., *Regulating the Media*, 2nd edn. (London: Sweet and Maxwell, 1998).

Gilhooley, M., 'The Administrative Conference and the Progress of Food and Drug Reform', *Arizona State Law Journal*, 30 (1998), 129.

—— 'Constitutionalizing Food and Drug Law', *Tulane Law Review*, 75 (2000), 815.

—— 'Constitutionalizing Food and Drug Law: When Avoidance is Right', *Houston Law Review*, 38 (2002), 1383.

Goodie, J. and Wickham, G., 'Calculating "Public Interest": Common Law and the Legal Governance of the Environment', *Social and Legal Studies*, 11/1, 2002, 37.

Goodwin, B., *Using Political Ideas*, 4th edn. (London: John Wiley, 1997).

Graham, C., *Regulating Public Utilities: A Constitutional Approach* (Oxford: Hart Publishing, 2000).

Gray, J., *The Moral Foundations of Market Institutions* (London: Institute of Economic Affairs, 1992).

Green, E., 'Blair Should Listen to the Screamers', *New Statesman*, 11 December 1998, 27.

Griffith, E. S., 'The Ethical Foundations of the Public Interest', in Friedrich, C. J. (ed.), *Nomos V: The Public Interest* (New York, N.Y.: Atherton Press, 1962).

Griffith, J. A. G., 'Judicial Decision Making in Public Law', *Public Law*, 1985, Winter, 564.

Guest, A. (ed.), *Oxford Essays in Jurisprudence* (Oxford: Oxford University Press, 1961).

Guldberg, H., 'Child Protection and the Precautionary Principle', in Morris, J. (ed.), *Rethinking Risk and the Precautionary Principle* (Oxford: Butterworth-Heinemann, 2000).

Gunn, J. A. W., *Politics and the Public Interest in the Seventeenth Century* (London: Routledge and Kegan Paul, 1969).

Haigh, N., 'The Introduction of the Precautionary Principle into the UK', in O'Riordan, T. and Cameron, J. (eds.), *Interpreting the Precautionary Principle* (London: Earthscan, 1994).

Hancher, L. and Moran, M. (eds.), *Capitalism, Culture and Economic Regulation* (Oxford: Clarendon, 1989).

—— 'Organizing Regulatory Space', in Hancher, L. and Moran, M. (eds.), *Capitalism, Culture and Economic Regulation* (Oxford: Clarendon, 1989).

Harden, I. and Lewis, N., *The Noble Lie: The British Constitution and the Rule of Law* (London: Hutchinson, 1986).

Harding, R. and Fisher, L., 'The Precautionary Principle in Australia', in O'Riordan, T. and Cameron, J. (eds.), *Interpreting the Precautionary Principle* (London: Earthscan, 1994).

Harlow, C., 'Public Interest Litigation in England: The State of the Art', in Cooper, J. and Dhavan, R. (eds.), *Public Interest Law* (Oxford: Basil Blackwell, 1986).

—— 'Public Law and Popular Justice', *Modern Law Review*, 65 (2002), 1.

—— and Rawlings, R., Law and Administration, 2nd edn. (London: Butterworths, 1997).

Harremoës, P., Gee, D., MacGarvin, M., Stirling, A., Keys, J., Wynne, B., and, Guedes Vaz, S. (eds.), *The Precautionary Principle in the 20th Century: Late Lessons from Early Warnings* (London: Earthscan, 2002).

Harris, J., 'Is Property a Human Right?', in McLean, J. (ed.), *Property and the Constitution* (Oxford: Hart Publishing, 1999).

Harris, R. A. and Milkis, S. M., *The Politics of Regulatory Change: A Tale of Two Agencies*, 2nd edn. (Oxford: Oxford University Press, 1996).

Harrison, J., 'Interactive Digital Television and the Expansion of the Public Service Tradition', *Communications Law*, 8/6 (2003), 401.

Hart, H. L. A., *The Concept of Law* (Oxford: Clarendon, 1961).

Hawkins, K. (ed.), *The Uses of Discretion* (Oxford: Clarendon, 1992).

Held, D., *Models of Democracy*, 1st edn. (Cambridge: Polity Press, 1987).

Held, V., *The Public Interest and Individual Interests* (New York, N.Y.: Basic Books, 1970).

Hemingway, C., 'An Exploratory Analysis of Corporate Social Responsibility: Definitions, Motives and Values' 2002, *University of Hull Business School Memorandum*, 34.

Henderson, D., *Misguided Virtue: False Notions of Corporate Social Responsibility* (London: Institute of Economic Affairs, 2001).

Herman, E. and McChesney, R., *The Global Media* (London: Cassell, 1997).

Herring, P. E., *Public Administration and the Public Interest* (New York, N.Y.: McGraw-Hill, 1936).

Hertz, N., *The Silent Takeover: Global Capitalism and the Death of Democracy* (London: Arrow Books, 2002).

Hervey, T., *European Social Law and Policy* (Harlow: Addison Wesley Longman, 1998).

Hill, M., *The State, Administration and the Individual* (London: Fontana/Collins, 1976).

Hirst, P., 'Ownership and Democracy', *Political Quarterly*, 69/4 (1998), 354.

Hitchens, L., 'Get Ready, Fire, Take Aim. The Regulation of Cross Media Ownership – An Exercise in Policy-Making', *Public Law*, 1995, Winter, 620.

Hobhouse, L. T., *Liberalism* (London: Williams and Norgate, 1911).

Hoffman, W. M. and Frederick, R. E. (eds.), *Business Ethics: Readings and Cases in Corporate Morality*, 3rd edn. (New York, N.Y.: McGraw-Hill, 1995).

Hoffman-Riem, W., *Regulating Media: The Licensing and Supervision of Broadcasting in Six Countries* (New York, N.Y.: Guilford Press, 1996).

Honohan, I., *Civic Republicanism* (London: Routledge, 2002).

Honoré, A., 'Ownership', in Guest, A. (ed.), *Oxford Essays in Jurisprudence* (Oxford: Oxford University Press, 1961).

—— *Making Law Bind* (Oxford: Clarendon, 1987).

Hood, C., Rothstein, H. and Baldwin, R., *The Government of Risk: Understanding Risk Regulation Regimes* (Oxford: Oxford University Press, 2001).

Hopt, K. J. and Teubner, G. (eds.), *Corporate Governance and Directors' Liabilities: Legal, Economic and Sociological Analyses on Corporate Social Responsibility* (Berlin: Walter de Gruyter, 1985).

Humphreys, P., *Mass Media and Media Policy in Western Europe* (Manchester: Manchester University Press, 1996).

—— 'Power and Control in the New media', paper presented at the ECPR Workshop, *New Media and Political Communication*, Berne, 27 February–4 March 1997.

Hutton Report, *Report of the Inquiry into the Circumstances Surrounding the Death of Dr David Kelly, C. M. G.* (London: The Stationery Office, 2004).

Infante, P. F., 'Benzene: A Historical Perspective on the American and European Occupational Setting', in Harremoës, P., Gee, D., MacGarvin, M., Stirling, A., Keys, J., Wynne, B., and, Guedes Vaz, S. (eds.), *The Precautionary Principle in the 20th Century: Late Lessons from Early Warnings* (London: Earthscan, 2002).

Jacob, J., 'Safeguarding the Public Interest: New Institutions and Procedures', in Cooper, J. and Dhavan, R. (eds.), *Public Interest Law* (Oxford: Basil Blackwell, 1986).

Johnson, N., *Reconstructing the Welfare State: A Decade of Change 1980–1990*, (Hemel Hempstead: Harvester Wheatsheaf, 1990).

Jordan, B., *Freedom and the Welfare State* (London: Routledge and Kegan Paul, 1976).

Joseph, E., 'Promoting Corporate Social Responsibility: Is Market-Based Regulation Sufficient?', *New Economy* (Institute for Public Policy Research), (2002), 96.

Jowell, J., 'The Rule of Law Today', in Jowell, J. and Oliver, D. (eds.), *The Changing Constitution*, 4th edn. (Oxford: Oxford University Press, 2000).

—— and Lester, A., 'Beyond *Wednesbury*: Substantive Principles of Administrative Law', *Public Law*, 1987, Autumn, 368.

—— and Oliver, D. (eds.), *The Changing Constitution*, 4th edn. (Oxford: Oxford University Press, 2000).

Kahn-Freund, O., 'On Uses and Misuses of Comparative Law', *Modern Law Review*, 37/1 (1974), 1.

Kamenka, E. and Neale, R. S., *Feudalism, Capitalism and Beyond* (London: Arnold, 1975).

Kamenka, E. and Tay, A. E. S., 'Beyond Bourgeois Individualism – the Contemporary Crisis in Law and Legal Ideology', in Kamenka, E. and Neale, R. S., *Feudalism, Capitalism and Beyond* (London: Arnold, 1975).

Katz, A. V. (ed.), *Foundations of the Economic Approach to Law* (Oxford: Oxford University Press, 1998).

Keane, J., *The Media and Democracy* (Cambridge: Polity Press, 1991).

Kelman, M., *A Guide to Critical Legal Studies* (Cambridge, Mass.: Harvard University Press, 1987).

Keynes, J. M., *The End of Laissez Faire* (London: Hogarth Press, 1927).

Klingler, R., *The New Information Industry: Regulatory Challenges and the First Amendment* (Washington DC: Brookings Institute Press, 1996).

Klosko, G., *Democratic Procedures and Liberal Consensus* (Oxford: Oxford University Press, 2000).

Krasnow, E. and Goodman, J., 'The Public Interest Standard: the Search for the Holy Grail', *Federal Communications Law Journal*, 50 (1998), 605.

Krause, D., 'Corporate Social Responsibility: Interests and Goals' in Hopt, K. J. and Teubner, G. (eds.), *Corporate Governance and Directors' Liabilities: Legal, Economic and Sociological Analyses on Corporate Social Responsibility* (Berlin: Walter de Gruyter, 1985).

Krotoszynski, R. J., 'The Inevitable Wasteland: Why the Public Trustee Model of Broadcast Regulation Must Fail', *Michigan Law Review*, 95 (1997), 2101.

Kurian, G. (ed.), *The Historical Guide to American Government* (Oxford: Oxford University Press, 1998).

Lang, T. and Rayner, G., 'Food and Health Strategy in the UK: A Policy Impact Analysis', *Political Quarterly*, 74/1 (2003), 66.

Lasswell, H. D., 'The Public Interest: Proposing Principles of Content and Procedure' in Friedrich, C. J. (ed.), *Nomos V: The Public Interest* (New York, N.Y.: Atherton Press, 1962).

Leff, A. A., 'Economic Analysis of Law: Some Realism About Nominalism', *Virginia Law Review*, 60 (1974), 451.

Le Grand, J., 'Quasi Markets and Social Policy', *Economic Journal*, 101 (1991), 1256.

—— *Quasi-Markets and Social Policy* (Basingstoke: Macmillan, 1993).

—— and Estrin, S. (eds.), *Market Socialism* (Oxford: Clarendon, 1989).

Levine, A., 'Saving Socialism and/or Abandoning It', in Wright, E. O. (ed.), *Equal Shares: Making Market Socialism Work* (London: Verso, 1996).

Lewin, L., *Self-Interest and Public Interest in Western Politics* (Oxford: Oxford University Press, 1991).

Lewis, N., 'IBA Programme Contract Awards', *Public Law*, 1975, Winter, 317.

—— 'Markets, Regulation and Citizenship: a Constitutional Analysis', in Brownsword, R. (ed.), *Law and the Public Interest* (Proceedings of the 1992 ALSP Conference) (Stuttgart: Franz Steiner, 1993).

Lewis, N. D., *Law and Governance* (London: Cavendish, 2001).

Leys, C., *Market-Driven Politics: Neoliberal Democracy and the Public Interest* (London: Verso, 2001).

Lichtenberg, J. (ed.), *Democracy and the Mass Media* (Cambridge: Cambridge University Press, 1990).

Little, G., 'BSE and the Regulation of Risk', *Modern Law Review*, 64/5 (2001), 730.

Littlefield, N. and Hadas, N. R., 'A Survey of Developments in Food and Drug Law from July 1998 to November 1999', *Food and Drug Law Journal*, 55 (2000), 35.

Llewellyn, K., 'The Normative, the Legal and the Law-Jobs', 49, *Yale Law Journal* (1940) 1355.

Lobstein, T., 'Crisis in Agriculture: Are We Learning from the Disasters?', *Consumer Policy Review*, 11/3 (2001), 78.

Loughlin, M., 'Tinkering with the Constitution', *Modern Law Review*, 51/4 (1988), 531.

—— *Public Law and Political Theory* (Oxford: Clarendon, 1992).

Loveland, I., *Constitutional Law: A Critical Introduction*, 1st edn. (London: Butterworths, 1996).

Lucy, W. N. R. and Mitchell, C., 'Replacing Private Property: The Case for Stewardship', *Cambridge Law Journal*, 55 (1996), 566.

McAuslan, P., *The Ideologies of Planning Law* (Oxford: Pergamon, 1980).

—— 'Public Law and Public Choice', *Modern Law Review*, 51/6 (1988), 681.

—— and McEldowney, J. F. (eds.), *Law, Legitimacy and the Constitution: Essays Marking the Centenary of Dicey's 'Law of the Constitution* (London: Sweet and Maxwell, 1985).

—— 'Legitimacy and the Constitution: the Dissonance Between Theory and Practice', in McAuslan, P. and McEldowney, J. F. (eds.), *Law, Legitimacy and the Constitution: Essays Marking the Centenary of Dicey's 'Law of the Constitution* (London: Sweet and Maxwell, 1985).

MacCormick, N., 'Beyond the Sovereign State', *Modern Law Review*, 56 (1993), 1.

McFadden, D. B., 'Antitrust and Communications: Changes After the Telecommunications Act of 1996', *Federal Communications Law Journal*, 49 (1997), 457.

McIntosh, M., Thomas, R., Leipziger, D., and Coleman, G., *Living Corporate Citizenship* (London: Pearson Education, 2003).

McLean, J. (ed.), *Property and the Constitution* (Oxford: Hart Publishing, 1999).

McNelis, N., 'EU Communication on the Precautionary Principle', *Journal of International Economic Law*, 3/3 (2000), 545.

Macpherson, C. B., *Democratic Theory: Essays in Retrieval* (Oxford: Oxford University Press, 1973).

McQuail, D., *Media Performance, Mass Communication and the Public Interest* (London: Sage, 1992).

Maitland, F. W., *The Constitutional History of England* (Cambridge: Cambridge University Press, 1908).

Majone, G. (ed.), *Regulating Europe* (London: Routledge, 1996).

—— 'The Rise of the Regulatory State in Europe', *West European Politics*, 17 (1994), 77, reproduced in Baldwin, R., Scott, C., and Hood, C. (eds.), *A Reader on Regulation* (Oxford: Oxford University Press, 1998).

Marsden, C. and Verhulst, S. (eds.), *Convergence in European Digital Television Regulation* (London: Blackstone, 1999).

Marshall, T. H., *Citizenship and Social Class* (Cambridge: Cambridge University Press, 1950).

—— *Sociology at the Crossroads and Other Essays* (London: Heinemann, 1963).

Mashaw, J., 'Prodelegation: Why Administrators Should Make Political Decisions', *Journal of Law, Economics and Organization*, 1 (1985), 81; in Schuck, P. H., *Foundations of Administrative Law* (Oxford: Oxford University Press, 1994).

Matthews, R. A. J., 'Fact Versus Factions: The Use and Abuse of Subjectivity in Scientific Research', in Morris, J. (ed.), *Rethinking Risk and the Precautionary Principle* (Oxford: Butterworth-Heinemann, 2000).

May, R., *A Reform Agenda for the New FCC* (Washington D.C.: Progress and Freedom Foundation, 2001).

—— 'Call Them Off', *Legal Times*, 4 June 2001.

—— 'The Public Interest Standard: Is it too Indeterminate to be Constitutional?', *Federal Communications Law Journal*, 53 (2001), 427.

Meyerson, M. and Banfield, E. C., *Politics, Planning and the Public Interest* (New York, N.Y.: Free Press, 1955).

Michelman, F., 'Law's Republic', *Yale Law Journal*, 97 (1988), 1493.

Miliband, R., *Capitalist Democracy in Britain* (Oxford: Oxford University Press, 1982).

Miller, D., 'Why Markets?', in Le Grand, J. and Estrin, S. (eds.), *Market Socialism* (Oxford: Clarendon, 1989).

Millstone, E. and van Zwanenberg, P., 'The Evolution of Food Safety Policy-Making Institutions in the UK, EU and Codex Alimentarius', *Social Policy and Administration*, 31/6 (2002), 593.

—— '"Mad Cow Disease" 1980s–2000: How Reassurances Undermined Precaution', in Harremoës, P., Gee, D., MacGarvin, M., Stirling, A., Keys, J., Wynne, B., and Guedes Vaz, S. (eds.), *The Precautionary Principle in the 20th Century: Late Lessons from Early Warnings* (London: Earthscan, 2002).

Milne, A. J. M., 'The Public Interest, Political Controversy, and the Judges' in Brownsword, R. (ed.), *Law and the Public Interest* (Proceedings of the 1992 ALSP Conference) (Stuttgart: Franz Steiner, 1993).

Minor, W. S., 'Public Interest and Ultimate Commitment', in Friedrich, C. J. (ed.), *Nomos V: The Public Interest* (New York, N.Y.: Atherton Press, 1962).

Mitnick, B. M., *The Political Economy of Regulation: Creating, Designing and Removing Regulatory Forms* (New York, N.Y.: Columbia University Press, 1980).

Monbiot, G., *Captive State: the Corporate Takeover of Britain* (London: Macmillan, 2000).

Montgomery, J. D., 'Public Interest in the Ideologies of National Development', in Friedrich, C. J. (ed.), *Nomos V: The Public Interest* (New York, N.Y.: Atherton Press, 1962).

Morgan, B., *Social Citizenship in the Shadow of Competition: The Bureaucratic Politics of Regulatory Justification* (Aldershot: Ashgate, 2003).

Morris, J. (ed.), *Rethinking Risk and the Precautionary Principle* (Oxford: Butterworth-Heinemann, 2000).

—— 'Defining the Precautionary Principle', in Morris, J. (ed.), *Rethinking Risk and the Precautionary Principle* (Oxford: Butterworth-Heinemann, 2000).

Mulhall, S. and Swift, A., *Liberals and Communitarians*, 2nd edn. (Oxford: Blackwell, 1996).

Negroponte, N., *Being Digital* (London: Hodder and Stoughton, 1995).

Nehl, H. P., *Principles of Administrative Procedure in EC Law* (Oxford: Hart, 1999).

Niemayer, G., 'Public Interest and Private Utility' in Friedrich, C. J. (ed.), *Nomos V: The Public Interest* (New York, N.Y.: Atherton Press, 1962).

Noah, L., 'What's Wrong With "Constitutionalizing Food and Drug Law"', *Tulane Law Review*, 75 (2000), 137.

—— 'Interpreting Agency Enabling Acts: Misplaced Metaphors in Administrative Law', *William and Mary Law Review*, 41 (2000), 1463.

Noll, R. (ed.), *Regulatory Policy and the Social Sciences* (Berkeley, CA.: University of California Press, 1985).

Ogus, A. I., *Regulation: Legal Form and Economic Theory* (Oxford: Clarendon, 1994).

—— 'Regulatory Law: Some Lessons from the Past', 12/1 *Legal Studies*, (1999), 1.

—— and Veljanovski, C. (eds.), *Readings in the Economics of Law and Regulation*, (Oxford: Clarendon, 1984).

O'Riordan, T. and Cameron, J. (eds.), *Interpreting the Precautionary Principle* (London: Earthscan, 1994).

—— 'The History and Contemporary Significance of the Precautionary Principle', in O'Riordan, T. and Cameron, J. (eds.), *Interpreting the Precautionary Principle* (London: Earthscan, 1994).

O'Rourke, R., 'Food Safety', *New Law Journal*, (1998), 1332.

—— 'Europe Adopts New Approach to Food Safety', *New Law Journal*, (2000), 230.

Osborne, D. and Gaebler, T., *Reinventing Government* (New York, N.Y.: Addison-Wesley, 1992).

Parkinson, J., *Corporate Power and Responsibility: Issues in the Theory of Company Law* (Oxford: Clarendon, 1996).

—— Gamble, A. and Kelly, G. (eds.), *The Political Economy of the Company* (Oxford: Hart, 2000).

Parry, N. D., 'Delivering Fundamental Change in Planning: A Threat to the Environment?', *European Public Law*, 8/3 (2002), 349.

Pennock, J. R., 'The One and the Many: A Note on the Concept', in Friedrich, C. J. (ed.), *Nomos V: The Public Interest* (New York, N.Y.: Atherton Press, 1962).

Pinder, J., 'European Citizenship: A Project in Need of Completion', in Crouch, C. and Marquand, D. (eds.), *Reinventing Collective Action: From the Global to the Local* (Oxford: Blackwell, 1995).

Polyani, K., *The Great Transformation: The Political and Economic Origins of Our Time* (Boston, Mass.: Beacon Press, 1957 [1944]).

Posner, R. A., 'Theories of Economic Regulation', *Bell Journal of Economics*, 5 (1974) 335, reproduced with omissions in Ogus, A. I. and Veljanovski, C. (eds.), *Readings in the Economics of Law and Regulation* (Oxford: Clarendon, 1984).

Powell, J., 'Reviving Republicanism', *Yale Law Journal*, 97 (1988), 1703.

Prosser, T., 'Towards a Critical Public Law', *Journal of Law and Society*, 9/1 (1982), 1.

—— 'Regulation of Privatized Enterprises: Institutions and Procedures', in Hancher, L. and Moran, M. (eds.), *Capitalism, Culture and Economic Regulation* (Oxford: Clarendon, 1989).

—— *Law and the Regulators* (Oxford: Clarendon, 1997).

—— 'Public Service Law: Privatization's Unexpected Offspring', *Law and Contemporary Problems*, 63/4 (2000), 63.

Przeworski, A., *Capitalism and Social Democracy* (Cambridge: Cambridge University Press, 1985).

Puttnam Report, *Report of the Joint Committee on the Draft Communications Bill*, HL Paper 169-I: HC 876-I, 25 July, 2002.

Rabin, R., 'Federal Regulation in Historical Perspective', *Stanford Law Review*, 38 (1986), 1189; in Schuck, P. H., *Foundations of Administrative Law* (Oxford: Oxford University Press, 1994).

—— 'The Administrative State and its Excesses: Reflections on *The New Property*', *University of San Francisco Law Review*, 25 (1990) 273; extracts reproduced in Schuck, P. H., *Foundations of Administrative Law* (Oxford: Oxford University Press, 1994).

Ramberg, B., 'The Supreme Court and Public Interest in Broadcasting', *Communications and the Law*, 8/6 (1986), 11.

Ranson, S., 'From 1944 to 1988: Education, Citizenship and Democracy', *Local Government Studies*, 14 (1988), 1.

Rawls, J., *Political Liberalism* (New York, N.Y.: Columbia University Press, 1993).

Reich, C., 'The New Property', *Yale Law Journal*, 73 (1964), 733.

Reich, R., 'The New Meaning of Corporate Social Responsibility', *California Management Review*, 40/2 (1998), 8.

Reifner, U., 'The Lost Penny – Social Contract Law and Market Economy', in Wilhelmsson, T. and Hurri, S. (eds.), *From Dissonance to Sense: Welfare Expectations, Privatisation and Private Law* (Aldershot: Dartmouth, 1999).

Robertson, M., 'Liberal, Democratic, and Socialist Approaches to the Public Dimensions of Private Property', in McLean, J. (ed.), *Property and the Constitution* (Oxford: Hart Publishing, 1999).

Roemer, J., *A Future for Socialism* (London: Verso, 1994).

Rudenstine, D., *The Day the Presses Stopped: a History of the Pentagon Papers Case* (Berkeley, CA.: University of California Press, 1996).

Russell, M. and Shelton, R. B., 'A Model of Regulatory Agency Behavior', *Public Choice*, 20/Winter (1974), 47.

Salmon, N., 'A European Perspective on the Precautionary Principle, Food Safety and the Free Trade Imperative of the WTO', *European Law Review*, 27 (2002), 138.

Sandalow, T., 'Judicial Protection of Minorities', *Michigan Law Review*, 75 (1977), 1162.

Sauter, W., 'Regulation for Convergence: Arguments for a Constitutional Approach', in Marsden, C. and Verhulst, S. (eds.), *Convergence in European Digital Television Regulation* (London: Blackstone, 1999).

Schelling, T., 'Economic Reasoning and the Ethics of Policy', *The Public Interest*, 63 (1981) 37, reproduced in Katz, A. V. (ed.), *Foundations of the Economic Approach to Law* (Oxford: Oxford University Press, 1998).

Schiller, H., *Information Inequality* (New York, N.Y.: Routledge, 1996).

Schubert, G., 'Is there a Public Interest Theory?', in Friedrich, C. J. (ed.), *Nomos V: The Public Interest* (New York, N.Y.: Atherton Press, 1962).

Schuck, P. H. (ed.), *Foundations of Administrative Law* (Oxford: Oxford University Press, 1994).

Scraton, P., Berrington, E., and Jemphrey, A., 'Intimate Intrusions? Press Freedom, Private Lives and Public Interest', *Communications Law*, 3/5 (1998), 174.

Seidenfeld, M., 'A Civic Republican Justification for the Bureaucratic State', *Harvard Law Review*, 105/7 (1992), 1511, extract in Schuck, P. H., *Foundations of Administrative Law* (Oxford: Oxford University Press, 1994).

Selznick, P., 'Focusing Organizational Research on Regulation', in Noll, R. (ed.), *Regulatory Policy and the Social Sciences* (Berkeley, CA.: University of California Press, 1985).

Seymour-Ure, C., *The British Press and Broadcasting Since 1945*, 2nd edn. (Oxford: Blackwell, 1996).

Shapiro, M., 'Judicial Delegation Doctrines: the US, Britain and France', *West European Politics*, 25/1 (2002), 173.

Six (6), P., 'Ownership and the New Politics of the Public Interest Services', *Political Quarterly*, 69/4 (1998), 404.

Skowronek, S., *Building a New American State: The Expansion of National Administrative Capacities, 1877–1920* (Cambridge: Cambridge University Press, 1982); excerpt in Schuck, P. H., *Foundations of Administrative Law* (Oxford: Oxford University Press, 1994).

Sorauf, F. J., 'The Conceptual Muddle', in Friedrich, C. J. (ed.), *Nomos V: The Public Interest* (New York, N.Y.: Atherton Press, 1962).

Spicker, P., The Welfare State: A General Theory (London: Sage, 2000).

Steele, J., 'Participation and Deliberation in Environmental Law: Exploring a Problem-Solving Approach', *Oxford Journal of Legal Studies*, 21/3 (2001), 415.

Stewart, P. and Gibson, D., 'The Communications Act – a New Era', *Communications Law*, 8/5 (2003), 357.

Stewart, R. B., 'The Reformation of American Administrative Law', *Harvard Law Review*, 88 (1975), 1667.

—— 'Vermont Yankee and the Evolution of Administrative Procedure, *Harvard Law Review*, 91 (1978) 1805.

—— 'Regulation in a Liberal State: The Role of Non-Commodity Values', *Yale Law Journal*, 92 (1983), 1537.

Stewart, R. B. (cont.), 'Environmental Regulatory Decision Making Under Uncertainty', 2002, in Swanson, T. (ed.), 20 *Research in Law and Economics* 71, (2002), 78.

Storey, A., 'Compensation for Banned Handguns: Indemnifying "Old Property" ', *Modern Law Review*, 61 (1998), 188.

Strauss, P. L., *Administrative Justice in the United States*, 2nd edn. (Durham, North Carolina: Carolina Academic Press, 2002).

Sunstein, C. R., 'Beyond the Republican Revival', *Yale Law Journal*, 97 (1988), 1539.

—— *After the Rights Revolution: Reconceiving the Regulatory State* (Cambridge, Mass.: Harvard University Press, 1990).

—— *Free Markets and Social Justice* (Oxford: Oxford University Press, 1997).

—— 'Nondelegation Canons', *University of Chicago Law Review*, 67 (2000), 315.

—— *Designing Democracy: What Constitutions Do* (Oxford: Oxford University Press, 2001).

—— 'Preferences and Rational Choice: New Perspectives and Legal Implications: Beyond the Precautionary Principle', *University of Philadelphia Law Review*, 151 (2003), 1003.

Swann, J. P., *History of the FDA*, http://www.fda.gov/oc/historyoffda/fulltext.html.

Swanson, T. (ed.), 20 *Research in Law and Economics* 71, (2002), 78.

Tawney, R. H., *The Acquisitive Society* (London: Collins, 1961).

Teubner, G., *Juridification of Social Spheres* (Berlin: Walter de Gruyter, 1987), extracts in Baldwin, R., Scott, C., and Hood, C. (eds.), *A Reader on Regulation* (Oxford: Oxford University Press, 1998).

Tomkins, A., *Public Law* (Oxford: Clarendon, 2003).

Turner, B. S. (ed.), *Citizenship and Social Theory* (London: Sage, 1993).

Turpin, C., *British Government and the Constitution: Text, Cases and Material*, 4th edn. (London: Butterworths, 1999).

United Nations, Global Compact Office, *The Global Compact: Corporate Leadership in the World Economy* (New York, N.Y.: United Nations, 2001).

Van Buren III, H., 'Corporate Citizenship and Obligations of Fairness', *Journal of Corporate Citizenship*, 3 (2001), 55.

Van Steenbergen, B. (ed.), *The Condition of Citizenship* (London: Sage, 1993).

Varney, M. R., *Private Property and Competing Values in the Regulation of Digital Media*, Ph.D. thesis (Hull, 2004), forthcoming.

Vick, D., 'The First Amendment Limitations on Broadcasting in the United States After *Turner Broadcasting v FCC*', *Media Law and Practice*, 16/3 (1995), 97.

Votaw, D., 'Genius Becomes Rare', in Votaw, D. and Sethi, S. P. (eds.), *The Corporate Dilemma: Traditional Values and Contemporary Problems* (Eaglewood Cliffs, NJ: Prentice Hall, 1973).

Waddell, S., 'New Institutions for the Practice of Corporate Citizenship: Historical, Intersectoral, and Developmental Perspectives', *Business and Society Review*, 105/1 (2000), 107.

Waddock, S. and Smith, N., 'Relationships: The Real Challenge of Corporate Global Citizenship', *Business and Society Review*, 105/1 (2000), 47.

Wall, P., 'The Food Safety Authority of Ireland', *Consumer Policy Review*, 9/5 (1999), 188.

Warden, J., 'UK Food Standards Agency Aims to Rebuild Trust in Food', *British Medical Journal*, 17 May 1997, 1433.

Wheen, F., *How Mumbo-Jumbo Conquered the World: A Short History of Modern Delusions* (London: Fourth Estate, 2004).

Whitehouse, L., 'Corporate Social Responsibility as Citizenship and Compliance', *Journal of Corporate Citizenship*, 11 (2003) 85.

—— 'Corporate Social Responsibility, Corporate Citizenship and the Global Compact', *Global Social Policy*, 3/3 (2003), 299.

—— 'Railtrack is Dead; Long Live Network Rail. Nationalisation Under the Third Way', *Journal of Law and Society*, 30/2 (2003), 217.

Whyte, G., *Social Inclusion and the Legal System: Public Interest Law in Ireland* (Dublin: Institute of Public Administration, 2002).

Wiener, J. B., 'Whose Precaution After All? A Comment on the Comparison and Evolution of Risk Regulatory Systems', *Duke Journal of Comparative and International Law*, 13 (2003) 207.

Wightman, J., 'Private Law and Public Interests' in Wilhelmsson, T. and Hurri, S. (eds.), *From Dissonance to Sense: Welfare Expectations, Privatisation and Private Law* (Aldershot: Dartmouth, 1999).

Wilhelmsson, T. and Hurri, S. (eds.), *From Dissonance to Sense: Welfare Expectations, Privatisation and Private Law* (Aldershot: Dartmouth, 1999).

Wood, D. J. and Logsdon, J. M., 'Theorising Business Citizenship', in Andriof, J. and McIntosh, M. (eds.), *Perspectives on Corporate Citizenship* (Sheffield: Greenleaf, 2001).

Wright, E. O. (ed.), *Equal Shares: Making Market Socialism Work* (London: Verso, 1996).

Young, I. M., *Inclusion and Democracy* (Oxford: Oxford University Press, 2000).

Zweigert, K. and Kötz, H., *An Introduction to Comparative Law*, 3rd edn. (Oxford: Clarendon, 1998).

Index

Lightning Source UK Ltd.
Milton Keynes UK
UKHW010910100223
416739UK00004B/544

9 780199 269020